The Family Trust

A Financial Consultant's Guide to Trust Funds and Estate Planning

Second Edition

Charles M. Aulino

CCH INCORPORATED
4025 W. Peterson Ave.
Chicago, IL 60646-6085
1 800 TELL CCH

This publication is designed to provide accurate and authoritative information in regard to the subject matter covered. It is sold with the understanding that the publisher is not engaged in rendering legal, accounting, or other professional service and that the author is not offering such advice in this publication. If legal advice or other expert assistance is required, the services of a competent professional person should be sought.

Editorial Staff

Project Editor: Paula Weglarz

Legal Editor: George Cuonzo

ISBN 0-8080-0069-1

Printed in the United States of America

Dedication

This book is dedicated to my father, Charles M. Aulino, Sr., and his Irish bride, my mother, Geraldine. Though they may never leave their children a family trust, they have already given us the boundless wealth of their love and goodness.

Charles M. Aulino

About the Author

Charles M. Aulino is president of Mentor Trust Company, a subsidiary of Wheat First Butcher Singer, Inc., headquartered in Richmond, Virginia. His perspective on trusts, taxation, and estate planning includes previous experience in personal financial planning services for Wheat, as a vice president of investments for a major regional brokerage, a practicing attorney, and a bank trust officer.

Mr. Aulino has written on estate and trust subjects for several publications and was a lecturer in taxation at the Seton Hall University Stillman School of Business for its M.S. in Taxation program.

He holds a Master of Laws degree (in Taxation) from New York University and a J.D. degree (*cum laude*) from Seton Hall University School of Law. He is a member of the International Association for Financial Planning and has served as president of its Northern New Jersey Chapter.

Preface

The Family Trust was originally published a few months before the enactment of the Revenue Reconciliation Act of 1990, which included changes that made an important impact on certain estate planning strategies. In particular, there was a complete overhaul of the federal tax law provisions dealing with retention of temporary and other partial ownership interests in businesses and investments and the lifetime transfer of such interests. This was the last of several attempts to deal with a highly complex topic that, until 1990, seemed to elude the ability of Congress to create a practical, manageable set of rules. The benefit of a few years' experience makes it clear that the rules enacted in 1990 are both practical and manageable. This second edition contains a description of new and modified planning opportunities that now exist.

It always seems that a change in federal tax law is just around the corner, but in the closing weeks of 1995, change appears more than likely to occur soon. Some changes that affect estate planning and the creation of trust funds are included in laws now being proposed. This time, however, the potential changes appear to affect tax calculations more than planning strategies. An increase is proposed, over an initial three-year period, in the value of each decedent's estate that is exempt from federal estate tax, followed by indexing of the exempt amount for inflation in later years. Inflation indexing is also proposed for the value of annual transfers that can be made free of gift tax and for the lifetime value that can be transferred for the benefit of descendants free of the generation-skipping transfer tax. In certain circumstances, part of the value of a family-owned business may be free of estate tax, if current proposals become law.

Some things never change. Clients will always need assistance in developing careful plans for wealth transfer. In some cases, that must include arrangements for ongoing financial and investment management on behalf of beneficiaries who are not equipped to assume those responsibilities for themselves. Even if there is an increase in the amount exempt from tax and indexing for inflation, clients will require a thorough understanding of the tax consequences of their estate plan. That is why maintaining a current, basic reference for financial consultants on this subject is so important.

I am grateful to the project editor, Paula Weglarz, the legal editor, George P. Cuonzo, and others at CCH who made the chore of revision easier and contributed greatly to the quality of the final result.

Charles M. Aulino

October 1995

Summary Table of Contents

Table of Contents

Paragraph

CHAPTER 1—INTRODUCTION

CHAPTER 2—DESIGNING A FAMILY TRUST FUND

CHAPTER 3—FEDERAL INCOME TAXATION OF TRUSTS

Paragraph

CHAPTER 3—continued

CHAPTER 4—THE FEDERAL UNIFIED TRANSFER TAX SYSTEM

Paragraph

CHAPTER 4—continued

CHAPTER 5—USING TRUSTS IN ESTATE PLANNING

Paragraph

CHAPTER 5—continued

CHAPTER 6—LIFE INSURANCE TRUSTS

Paragraph

CHAPTER 6—continued

CHAPTER 7—CHARITABLE TRUSTS

CHAPTER 8—PROFESSIONAL SERVICES FOR TRUSTS AND SETTLEMENT OF ACCOUNTS

Paragraph

CHAPTER 8—continued

CHAPTER 9—TRUST INVESTMENTS

Chapter 1

Introduction

¶ 101 HISTORICAL PERSPECTIVE ON THE USE OF TRUSTS

Circumstances existing in thirteenth-century England made it possible for the modern personal trust to evolve. There was no edict of a king or act of a legislature involved. Instead, the feudal system of property ownership made it desirable to find innovative ways of structuring rights to use, own, and transfer the ownership of property, all of which gradually led to what we know as the trust.

In the feudal England of the thirteenth century, wealth was associated with, and grew out of, the right to occupy land and make it productive. However, every acre of land in England was owned, at least theoretically, by the king who granted its use to feudal overlords. The overlords, in turn, divided the property under their control and granted use of the divided portions to inferior lords. There were numerous further subdivisions and grants of property rights. In this way, a system of tiers of rights to the use of property evolved, all tracing their ultimate source to the king.

The individual who had the right to the use of a particular tract of property did not have the same degree of freedom of ownership that we take for granted in modern times. It was possible, during life, to sell or give away one's rights to real estate, yet there was no legal authority for the transfer of ownership upon death through a will until the year 1540. Until that time, property ownership rights, such as they were, passed at death automatically to certain heirs of the deceased. If there were no surviving heirs, the property reverted to the feudal overlord. This was known as "escheat," the same term used in modern law to describe the transfer of a decedent's property to the state when a decedent has not left a will and there are no surviving heirs. To make matters worse, heirs were not treated equally but were subject to the rule of primogeniture. Under that rule, all of the rights to a decedent's real estate passed at death to the oldest son, subject only to certain lifetime interests reserved for the surviving spouse. There was also a financial burden imposed at death known as the "relief." This was a payment due to the king for the privilege of allowing heirs to succeed to the decedent's property rights. It may be thought of as the feudal equivalent of the modern estate or inheritance tax.

Sometime around the thirteenth century, a practice known as "use" developed. The owner of real estate transferred his or her rights to another individual. From the viewpoint of English common law, this amounted to an absolute, final, and complete transfer of property rights. However, the transferor and the recipient entered into an agreement whereby the recipient was not receiving the valuable property rights for his or her own benefit but rather for the benefit of another or others. In other words, the transferor "trusted" the recipient to hold the property rights for the benefit or for the use of some intended beneficiary. Through this mechanism, it was possible to circumvent the transfer system. The property could be held for the benefit of the original owner for life and, after the original owner's death, it could continue to be held for the benefit of the spouse, for the children in equal shares, or according to the original owner's wishes. This avoided the rule of primogeniture. The original owner technically held no property rights at death; the use would be designed to continue after the death of the original owner. In this way, the problem of the inability to transfer interests in real estate by will, as well as the payment of the feudal relief, was avoided.

The king lost considerable amounts of revenue as a result of the use mechanism. To combat this, Henry VIII managed to persuade Parliament to pass the Statute of Uses in the year 1535. Under this law, the legal ownership rights to any real estate that was held subject to a use was transferred to the person or persons for whose benefit it was held. In effect, the purpose was to eliminate the middle person. Reaction to the Statute of Uses was negative, not only because it increased the payment of feudal reliefs but also because it eliminated the ability to transfer ownership rights to real estate at death. In the year 1540, the Statute of Wills became law in England. This restored the legal power of individuals to convey ownership rights over real estate at death which the Statute of Uses had, in effect, taken away.

By the time these two statutes were enacted, uses had become enormously popular in England. Although this may be attributed to the peculiarities of the legal system of the day, there can be no doubt that the flexibility of dealing with property rights, made possible by the use, had a great deal to do with the widespread use of this device.

Over the centuries, innumerable refinements were made to the laws of England concerning rights with respect to real estate as well as other forms of property. However, the idea of giving to another person the legal ownership of property, not for the benefit of the recipient but for the benefit of others, is the essence of the modern personal trust, and its origins can be traced to the feudal use transaction. Since the laws of England form the basis for most of the legal system of the United States, American trusts share the same heritage.

¶ 102 TRUST TERMS AND DEFINITIONS

The following is a discussion of a few of the basic technical terms used in the field of trusts. Additional terms are introduced later as the concepts to which they relate are explored.

(1) **Grantor.** Every trust begins with a gift, that is, a transfer of ownership of something of value for the benefit of another.

The person who makes a gift in order to establish a trust fund and who sets up the rules for the administration of the trust is known as the "grantor," "settlor," "trustor," "creator," or simply as the "maker" of the trust.

(2) **Trust Fund, Principal, and Income.** The money or property that is placed into the trust may be referred to simply as the "trust fund." However, the property originally placed in trust is distinguished from the interest or other income that it produces. The original trust property is the "principal" or "corpus," while the amount of interest or other investment earnings it produces is known as "income." There are finer distinctions as well. For instance, interest earned on savings deposits and bonds and dividends earned on stocks are generally treated as ordinary income that is paid to a current trust beneficiary. Profits realized on the sale of trust investments, such as stocks,

bonds, and real estate, are usually treated as principal that is not ordinarily distributed to the beneficiary who is entitled to receive ordinary income.

An older term, synonymous with "principal" or "corpus" and still occasionally seen, is "res," a Latin word that means "the thing."

(3) **Trustee.** The "trustee" has the job of managing the trust fund. Where there is more than one trustee, each is referred to as a "co-trustee." It is a good idea to provide for the appointment of a "successor" trustee or trustees in case the original trustee dies, resigns, or is unable to continue managing the trust fund before the purposes of the trust are completed and the trust ends. Just as in the thirteenth century, the trustee is the legal owner of the trust fund. However, that ownership includes the strict duty to use the property exclusively in the beneficiaries' best interests.

(4) **Trust Administration and Settlement.** The work of the trustee in handling a trust fund is generally referred to as the "administration" of the trust. This includes winding up the affairs of the trust and turning over any remaining funds to the beneficiaries—a process known as "trust termination" or "trust settlement." Since this includes the requirement to prepare an accounting of how the trust funds were spent and distributed, it is often called the "final trust accounting."

(5) **Beneficiaries.** Every trust has one or more "beneficiaries" for whose benefit the trust fund is held and administered. Beneficiaries who are entitled to receive distributions from the trust fund currently are distinguished from those who will be entitled to whatever remains in the future. The current beneficiaries may be referred to as "income beneficiaries" or as "lifetime beneficiaries," and those who receive the balance at the end of the trust are known as "remaindermen." Occasionally, there are references to the beneficiary using the ancient term *cestui que trust,* that is, "he or she for whom the trust is held."

(6) **Trust Agreement.** Some written directions must be given to the trustee concerning management of the trust and, specifically, how the trust fund should be distributed to the beneficiaries. When a trust is set up by a gift during the grantor's lifetime, these directions are contained in a "trust agreement."

Ordinarily, the grantor decides how the benefits are to flow from the trust to the beneficiary. The attorney's role, at this point, is to translate these intentions into a legally enforceable document—the trust agreement—which is signed by the grantor as well as by the trustee. In addition to setting forth the plan for distribution of trust benefits, the trust agreement contains a specific description of any powers that the grantor may wish to reserve over the trust fund. Examples of these include the power to change trustees, to change the beneficiaries or modify their interests in the trust, or even to "revoke," that is, to end the trust arrangement and take back the remaining trust funds. Although state laws contain rules governing the trustee's management of the trust fund, the trust agreement often includes special duties imposed on the trustee. There may even be reason to exempt the trustee from duties or restrictions usually imposed by the state's laws. For instance, the laws of a particular state might provide that, where the trust fund includes the ownership of rental real estate, the trustee is not allowed to lease the property for more than five years without a special provision in the trust document permitting longer leases. The trust agreement must specifically provide for any such special exemptions.

(7) **Terms of the Trust and Trust Term.** The provisions contained in a trust agreement are sometimes generally or collectively referred to as the "terms of the trust." This expression is to be distinguished from the "term of the trust," which means the period of time during which the trust administration is to continue.

(8) **Declaration of Trust.** Some trust grantors decide to assume the duty of administering the trust fund themselves. The grantor starts out as the owner of the money or property that is to become the trust fund. After the trust is established, the grantor owns the fund in a trustee capacity; he or she no longer owns it personally but, rather, holds it for the beneficiaries. In this case, there is no trust agreement as such; it would not make sense for the grantor to have an agreement with himself. Nevertheless, it is necessary to have a legal document that specifies the nature of the beneficiaries' interests and the grantor-trustee's duties. This document is a "declaration of trust"—a formal statement that the grantor no longer personally owns the subject fund or property, but instead holds it in the capacity of trustee for the purposes and according to the terms and conditions written in the document.

As discussed later at ¶ 105 of this chapter, assets held in a living trust, including a declaration of trust, may avoid probate. If this is to occur, however, there must be clear evidence that assets are owned under a declaration of trust. Such evidence would be established by changing the title to bank accounts, investments, and real estate to reflect their status as part of the trust fund. If a stock certificate is left in the name of the grantor but is listed on a schedule attached to a declaration of trust, the stock transfer agent may refuse to accept instructions for its transfer from the successor trustee after the grantor's death. This could defeat the grantor's intentions.

(9) **Living Trust.** A trust fund established during the grantor's lifetime, either according to a trust agreement or through a declaration of trust, is usually referred to as a "living trust" because it comes into existence while the grantor, as well as the trustee and beneficiary, is alive. The term "inter vivos trust," incorporating the Latin phrase that means "among the living," is still often used. The typical basic abbreviation for a living trust is "trust u/a," for "trust under agreement."

(10) **Revocable and Irrevocable Trusts.** A basic distinction exists between those living trusts over which the grantor has reserved the power of revocation in the trust document and those over which no such power exists. If the grantor has the right to require the trustee to return part or all of the trust fund, the trust is said to be "revocable." The grantor may hold the power to revoke alone or in conjunction with one or more persons. A living trust that does not contain a power to revoke is designated as an "irrevocable trust."

(11) **Reversion.** A living trust may be designed to benefit a person or persons other than the grantor for a limited period of time, after which the trust fund is to be returned to the grantor. This return of the trust fund is known as a "reversion." A reversion may be certain to occur or it may be contingent on a future event. For instance, if a grantor places funds in trust for the benefit of his child for five years with a reversion at the end of the five-year period, there is no contingency involved. When the five-year period comes to an end, the trust fund reverts to the grantor or, if the grantor has since died, to his estate.

A reversion may be conditional, that is, based on the occurrence of certain future events or circumstances. Suppose, for example, that the grantor places funds in trust for a child for five years with the provision that if the beneficiary-child has any children living at that time, these grandchildren of the grantor are to receive the remainder of the trust. If there are no such grandchildren living, the trust agreement specifies that a reversion of the trust fund to the grantor will occur. This is an example of a reversion that is subject to a contingency.

(12) **Testamentary Trust.** Trust funds are frequently established through the Last Will and Testament of the grantor. A trust established under a will is known as a "testamentary trust," and the grantor in such cases is referred to as the "testator," that is, the maker of the will.

A will is said to be an "ambulatory" document. It "walks forward" in time during the life of the testator with no legal value or effect until the testator's death. A testamentary trust does not come into being until the testator dies. The terms of the trust can be changed at any time during the testator's lifetime simply by changing the will. At the testator's death, however, no further modifications of the terms of a testamentary trust are possible, because only the testator can change the terms of his or her own will and only during his or her lifetime. One might say that the testator's death makes the testamentary trust irrevocable. The typical abbreviation for a testamentary trust is "trust u/w" for "trust under the will."

(13) **Tax Evasion Trust.** In recent years, unscrupulous individuals have promoted the idea that it is possible to establish a trust fund to avoid all federal taxes. Individuals are urged to contribute all of their savings, investments, and other properties and to arrange for the payment of their wages or salaries directly to the trust. The trust income is then either accumulated or distributed among spouses, children, or other relatives and, for reasons invented by the promoters of these schemes, little or no taxes are paid. This arrangement has been referred to as "The American Birthright Trust," "The Family Estate Trust," and "The Constitutional Trust," among other titles.

There is no merit to the theory that a trust can be used in this manner. While there are a great many legitimate purposes for establishing trust funds, some of which may permissibly help to reduce a family's overall tax liability, schemes to evade federal taxes through trusts are fraudulent and will lead to criminal tax prosecution and civil tax penalties. This is one reason why individuals need professional advice before establishing a trust fund. Also, financial consultants must see to it that their clients use the services of an attorney who specializes in trusts, estate matters, and related tax issues to help establish the trust fund.

¶ 103 PHASES OF A TRUST FUND

There are several phases in the life of a trust fund, from inception to termination. These phases are discussed below.

.01 Trust Inception and Administration

The overall objectives in establishing a trust fund are to set aside money, property, or investments for the welfare of the beneficiaries chosen by the grantor and to ensure that the fund is managed by the trustee according to specific rules decided upon by the grantor and incorporated in the trust document. In order to achieve these objectives, certain typical events must commonly occur in the establishment, administration, and ultimate termination of trusts.

The first of these events is the planning that leads to the decision to establish a trust. The idea may be suggested by a professional adviser of the family, such as the attorney, accountant, or financial consultant. The planning phase culminates in the preparation of a trust document. In the trust document, the grantor sets forth all the rules for the operation of the trust, including the appointment of the trustee, the identification of the beneficiaries, the plan for distributing income and principal from the trust fund to the beneficiaries, the term of the trust fund, and the circumstances under which the trust is to end. In the case of a testamentary trust, all of these rules are written in the will; however, they do not take effect until the grantor's death.

The administration of the trust fund actually begins when something of value, such as a sum of money, is transferred into the trust fund. At that point, the trustee's duties commence. The property or funds of the trust must be productively invested. The investment plan might be as simple as depositing the funds in a bank account or it might involve more complex investments, but the trustee must make the fund financially productive as soon as possible.

While pursuing an investment plan, the trustee must follow the directions contained in the trust document concerning distributions to the beneficiaries. Very often the beneficiaries' needs, which are the reason for the trust in the first place, will influence the trustee's investment decisions. For instance, if a trust is established to pay for the immediate costs of nursing home care for an elderly dependent relative, an investment in a savings certificate of deposit that matures in five years would not be appropriate.

Administration of the trust fund frequently falls into several phases, specified in the trust document, in which the rules concerning distributions to beneficiaries change with their changing circumstances. For instance, the first phase of administration of a trust for a minor child might be accumulation of the fund's earnings. This could change to a distribution phase when the child begins higher education or leaves the parent's home and starts to bear his or her own living expenses. In the event of the beneficiary's death, another phase of the trust might begin in which new beneficiaries are specified to receive future trust distributions.

.02 Bringing the Trust to an End

Although a personal trust may last for several decades, at some point it must come to an end. During the termination phase several specific requirements must be met:

(1) The trustee must demonstrate, to the satisfaction of the beneficiaries and sometimes to the satisfaction of a court, that all of the trust funds have been accounted for, have been made productive during the administration of the trust, and have been turned over to the proper recipients at the end of the trust.

(2) If any beneficiary has a serious complaint about the trustee's handling of the administration, that beneficiary must be given the opportunity to have the complaint considered in court. If the court finds fault with the trustee's actions, the court may order the trustee to reimburse the trust fund for losses sustained as a result of trustee misconduct.

(3) The trustee's accounting must be settled and, upon settlement, the trustee is released from all further obligations. In some cases this can be accomplished by an agreement between the trustee and the beneficiaries, while in other cases court supervision of the settlement and discharge of the trustee is necessary.

¶ 104 PROPERTY OWNERSHIP RULES AFFECTING THE CREATION OF TRUSTS

The following sections discuss the five types of property ownership (individual, tenancy in common, community property, joint tenancy, and tenancy by the entirety), the rules involved in each category, and their effect on the creation of trusts.

.01 Forms of Property Ownership

In order to make a gift of property to a trust fund, the grantor's ownership interest must be sufficient to make the transfer of ownership valid. Simply stated, one cannot validly give something away, to a trust or otherwise, unless one owns it. The first step in acquiring a knowledge of trust funds, then, is to learn or review the basics of property ownership.

Property ownership is determined by reference to the legal document governing the item of property. Even a simple savings account has a statement of the rights and privileges of the account holder. Virtually all securities include a registration of ownership that indicates the ownership form, while real estate is held by deed or other written instrument. For certain types of tangible personal property, it is possible that there is no document of ownership. In this case, ownership must be established by proof of either purchase or some other source of acquisition of the item of property involved. The extent of an owner's rights is governed by state law. Even if a legal document is required for property, as is always the case with real estate, where more than one name appears on the deed, it may be necessary to review the appropriate state law in order to determine the exact nature of the owners' respective rights.

.011 Individual ownership

The simplest form of property ownership, individual ownership, implies that only one person possesses all present and future power to use, control, sell, or otherwise dispose of the property. Upon the individual owner's death, ownership is transferred under the term of the owner's will or, if there is no will, according to the laws of descent and distribution (known as intestacy) of the state of domicile. The individual owner has complete power to transfer this form of property during life, which makes individually owned property the most common subject of transfers in trust.

.012 Tenancy in common

In this form of property ownership there are two or more owners, each possessing concurrent property interests. The most remarkable aspects of the rights of tenants in common are:

(1) The percentage or fractional ownership shares of tenants in common need not be equal. For example, it is possible that where there

are two tenants in common, the first holds a 90 percent interest in the property and the second holds a 10 percent interest.

(2) Tenants in common have undivided ownership interests in the whole property. This means that, if two brothers are equal tenants in common of a 200-acre farm, one brother may not claim exclusive use of the northern 100 acres and demand that the other brother be restricted to the southern 100 acres. Instead, the two brothers share all rights over the entire farm.

(3) Upon the death of a tenant in common, ownership of the decedent's interest in the property is controlled by the decedent's will, or by intestacy if there is no will. Ownership does not pass to the surviving tenant or tenants in common, unless the decedent's will so provides.

Because the tenant in common has the power to transfer his proportionate ownership interest, it is possible to place this type of property interest in either a living trust or a testamentary trust. The trust would not own the entire property, but would only succeed to the partial or percentage undivided interest of the transferring tenant.

.013 Community property

Only nine states have community property laws. These states are: Arizona, California, Idaho, Louisiana, Nevada, New Mexico, Texas, Washington, and Wisconsin. The exact nature of the ownership rights and interests in community property varies considerably from state to state; however, some basic common characteristics are:

(1) A community property interest may only be held by husband and wife.

(2) Property acquired during the marriage by either spouse automatically becomes community property, while property owned prior to marriage retains its individual ownership characteristics unless it is converted after marriage into community property.

(3) Aside from the fact that the proportions of ownership of community property are equal between husband and wife, community property is very similar to tenancy in common.

(4) Community property (to the extent of either spouse's interest) may be placed in trust either during life or through the deceased spouse's will.

.014 Joint tenancy

Like tenancy in common and community property, joint tenancy is a form of concurrent property ownership between two or more persons. However, that is as far as the similarity goes.

The principal characteristics of joint tenancy are:

(1) There must be two or more joint tenants, all of whom acquired their interests simultaneously.

(2) The proportionate interests of joint tenants must be equal. If there are two joint tenants, each owns a 50 percent undivided interest; if there are five joint tenants, each owns a 20 percent undivided interest.

(3) Rights of ownership automatically pass to the survivor. Upon the death of a joint tenant, the surviving joint tenant or tenants automatically succeed to the decedent's interest in the property. Any provision in the decedent's will that might attempt to transfer ownership of the decedent's interest in property held in joint tenancy is invalid. For example, if a testator and her sister own an office building as joint tenants and the testator's will leaves her entire estate to her husband, the sister becomes sole owner of the office building upon the tesstator's death.

Under most state laws, in order to establish a joint tenancy it is necessary to include some indication within the ownership title of the property that survivorship is intended, such as: "John Smith and Mary Smith, joint tenants *with rights of survivorship.*" If there is any doubt as to the form of ownership intended, the usual presumption is tenancy in common.

The survivorship aspect of joint tenancy generally makes property held in this ownership form inappropriate for a transfer to a trust by only one of the joint tenants. It would be necessary to terminate the joint tenancy form of ownership first, by conversion into tenancy in common (a process known as "partition"), before a transfer in trust would be practical.

.015 Tenancy by the entirety

Tenancy by the entirety is a form of concurrent property ownership recognized in some states and may be held only by husband and wife. Aside from the fact that there can be only two tenants by the entirety, the characteristics of this ownership form are very similar to those of joint tenancy, including the automatic survivorship feature. Unlike joint tenancy, however, some of the states that recognize tenancy by the entirety restrict its use to the ownership of real estate as opposed to "personal" property interests. Therefore, one may not own a car or stocks and bonds with his or her spouse as tenants by the entirety.

.02 Transfer of Ownership upon Death

Some states have adopted versions of the Uniform Transfers on Death Security Registration Act. This law allows for the registration of marketable securities in a manner that provides for the transfer of ownership upon the death of the original owner to one or more beneficiaries specified in the ownership title. Certificates for stocks, bonds, and other marketable securities may be registered in this manner, or the securities may be deposited with a bank or brokerage firm and held in nominee registration in an account that contains a Transfer on Death (TOD) registration.

This form of registration is allowed for securities owned by an individual or owned as joint tenants, tenants by the entirety, or community property, but it is not available for securities owned by tenants in common.

An example of TOD registration is "John Jones, TOD Andrew Williams."

The effect of this registration is that ownership passes automatically to the named beneficiary or beneficiaries upon the death of the original owner. In the case of joint tenants, ownership passes to the named beneficiary under TOD registration only upon the death of the surviving joint tenant. While the original owner is living, however, he or she retains full and exclusive ownership rights over the security or over the investment account. This includes the right to discontinue the TOD registration or to change the account title in a manner that changes the interest of the beneficiary by adding or removing one or more beneficiaries.

Although the Uniform Transfers on Death Security Registration Act has not been adopted in all states, the Act provides that TOD registration is permitted so long as the Act has been adopted in the state in which the securities issuer or the registering entity is located. That means that an individual living in a state that has not adopted the Act may nevertheless establish a TOD account with a local branch office of a brokerage firm headquartered in a state that has adopted the Act. The registration in TOD form is presumed to be valid as a matter of contract law.

TOD registration has its place in estate planning. Unless the client understands its implications, however, its use may prevent property from passing into a trust fund created by the original owner upon his or her death.

.03 Tabular Summary of Property Ownership Aspects

The following table summarizes the basic aspects of the different forms of property ownership.

	Individual Ownership	*Tenancy in Common*	*Community Property*	*Joint Tenancy*	*Tenancy by Entirety*
Automatic Survivorship upon Death	NO	NO	NO	YES	YES
Two Owners: Husband and Wife Only	NO	NO	YES	NO	YES
Two or More Owners	NO	YES	NO	YES	NO
Equal Proportionate Ownership Interests	NO	NO	YES	YES	YES
Ownership May Be in Unequal Proportions	NO	YES	NO	NO	NO

¶ 105 TRUST FUNDS AND "PROBATE" OR ESTATE SETTLEMENT

The following sections discuss the probate or estate settlement process and its effect on funds held in trust.

.01 The Probate Process

Literally, the term "probate" means "to prove." It refers to the basic requirement that before a decedent's will may be given official recognition, it is necessary to prove the document's authenticity and compliance with the state law governing wills. Over the centuries, however, the term has come to refer to the entire process of settlement of the decedent's affairs. The decedent's assets that are controlled by the will are referred to as the "probate estate." These assets include money, investments, and other property that are:

(1) individually owned by the decedent;

(2) held by the decedent as tenant in common with another or others (to the extent of the decedent's share); or

(3) held as community property by the decedent and his or her surviving spouse (to the extent of the decedent's interest).

Financial resources that permit the designation of a direct beneficiary—such as life insurance, annuity contracts, individual retirement accounts, and qualified pension, profit-sharing, and similar plans—are examples of "nonprobate assets." The payment of benefits to the named beneficiary upon the death of the insured or plan participant is not controlled by the decedent's will. Any provision in the will that might appear to provide for a disposition of such death benefits in a manner inconsistent with the beneficiary designation is simply invalid.

If no beneficiary has been designated for insurance, annuity, or retirement plan death benefits, or if the named beneficiary predeceases the decedent, the amount payable is combined with the deceased insured's or deceased participant's estate. Thus, it becomes controlled by the will and thereby is transformed from nonprobate to probate asset status.

.02 Probate Status of Trust Assets

Are trust assets included in the grantor's probate estate? There are four possibilities:

(1) In the case of a testamentary trust, it might be assumed that the trust assets are always part of the grantor/testator's probate estate because the terms of the trust are provided for in the will and no trust exists prior to the grantor/testator's death. Assets owned by the grantor at death that pass into the trust under the terms of the will are probate assets. However, it is also possible for the grantor/testator to name a testamentary trust as the direct beneficiary of life insurance or other direct death benefits. Nonprobate assets paid directly to a testamentary trust in this manner are not transformed into probate assets.

(2) The terms of a trust established during the grantor's lifetime may provide that it continue after the grantor's death. In this case, the trust fund is not part of the probate estate.

(3) The terms of a living trust could provide, however, that the trust end upon the grantor's death and that the trust funds be added to the grantor's estate. Under this arrangement, known as a "pour-back" trust, the trust assets are included in the probate estate.

(4) The grantor may establish a living trust that, by its terms, continues after the grantor's death and may transfer some, but not all, of his or her assets into the trust fund during his or her lifetime. The grantor's will might name the trust as beneficiary of part or all of the grantor's estate. Under this arrangement, referred to as a "pour-over" trust, assets placed in trust during the grantor's lifetime are nonprobate assets, while assets passing to the trust under the grantor/testator's will are probate assets.

In such a case, avoiding probate through the use of living trusts, particularly those described in situations (2) and (4), above, may have its advantages. In many states, the costs of estate settlement depend on the size of the probate estate. Use of a living trust might lower settlement costs, even after considering the cost of establishing and managing the trust itself. Under some, but not all, circumstances, death taxes may be reduced through living trusts. Finally, there is the advantage of privacy; upon death, a decedent's will becomes a public document available for inspection by any person (whether or not a relative or beneficiary). A living trust document, by contrast, is not generally required to be made public. A trust that keeps assets out of the grantor/testator's probate estate, and particularly one that terminates upon or soon after his or her death, may be referred to as a "will substitute."

Chapter 2

Designing a Family Trust Fund

¶ 201 GRANTOR'S GOALS AND OBJECTIVES

A grantor of a trust must consider many factors in designing a beneficial family trust fund. A grantor should determine goals and objectives for the fund, as discussed below.

.01 Grantor's Prerogative

Since a trust fund contains money, investments, or other property that the grantor gives to the trust, it is the grantor's prerogative to decide the following fundamental aspects of the trust:

(1) Who will receive benefits from the trust fund?

(2) When and how will amounts be given to the beneficiary?

(3) How long will the trust continue?

(4) Upon termination of the trust, who will receive the balance?

(5) Who will act as trustee and thereby have the power to manage the trust fund?

.02 Motives for Establishing Trusts

A financial counselor, attorney, accountant, or other professional adviser may suggest the establishment of a trust to the grantor based on the adviser's review of the overall financial situation of the grantor and family members, taking into consideration stated objectives of the grantor to provide financial benefits for himself or others, either at present or in the future. Some of the objectives of the grantor that might cause the professional adviser to recommend a trust are:

(1) In the case of presently funded living trusts:

(a) To provide professional financial management for the grantor's own benefit. This could be prompted simply by the grantor's distaste for personal financial or investment matters, because the demands of the grantor's profession deprive him of the time necessary for such matters, or by the elderly grantor's fear of becoming unable to manage his own affairs.

(b) To avoid probate and maintain financial privacy.

(c) To provide for the financial needs of others while withholding some or all of the control of the donated resources from the beneficiary (ies).

(2) In the case of testamentary trusts:

(a) To provide financial support to the surviving spouse for life without giving the spouse outright ownership of the inheritance, thus reserving to the testator the power to designate who will receive the balance left upon the death of the surviving spouse.

(b) To establish an alternative to outright inheritance by children so that financial management is placed in the trustee's hands either: (i) throughout the child's lifetime; (ii) for a specified number of years after the parent's death; or (iii) until the child attains a specified age.

(c) To create a fund for the perpetual benefit of charity.

.03 Does a Trust Really Make Sense?

Whenever a trust fund is under consideration, certain specific questions should be posed:

(1) Is there a more simple alternative available, such as a direct gift with or without legally enforceable restrictions placed on the recipient?

(2) Will the cost of administration of the trust outweigh its benefit?

(3) Does the grantor understand the transfer tax and income tax consequences of establishing the trust?

(4) Do the tax consequences result in advantages or disadvantages to the parties?

¶ 202 CHECKLIST APPROACH TO TRUST DESIGN

Another approach a grantor should consider in designing a family trust is the use of a checklist. The following sections discuss the trust design process and the items to be included in the checklist.

.01 Who Should Be Involved in Trust Design?

Once a valid motive for setting up a trust has been identified, all aspects of how the trust will function during the term of its existence must be examined by the grantor with the help of a professional adviser. This process consists of both educating the grantor as to the variety of choices available and eliciting from the grantor specific preferences on each aspect of trust design. All of this may be an entirely appropriate function for a financial counselor other than an attorney, such as an accountant, representative of a bank trust department, investment adviser, or life insurance professional. The actual preparation of legal documents needed to place a trust into existence, however, is the function of an attorney. Furthermore, the attorney will have to be satisfied that use of the trust makes sense, given the facts and circumstances of each individual case, and that the grantor understands how the trust will operate and its tax consequences. For this reason, it is a good idea to involve the attorney early in the planning process.

.02 Items to Include in the Trust Checklist

An item-by-item checklist approach is an ideal procedure that may be used to guide the prospective grantor through the various choices necessary to create an outline of the trust from which the attorney can draft the actual document. The following is an example of the main issues that might be addressed in such a checklist.

.021 Term of the trust

A trust may last for a specific period of time.

Example (1): Trust fund established by parent when child is age 10. Trust continues for 15 years and terminates when child is age 25.

Example (2): Testamentary trust to be held, according to the terms of the parent's will, from the date of the parent's death until the child reaches age 30.

Example (3): Testamentary trust to be held for a period of 10 years after the death of the grantor/testator.

A trust may be created for the lifetime of the beneficiary.

Example (4): Elderly grantor creates trust for his own benefit for life. At grantor's death, trust terminates.

Example (5): Married grantor/testator establishes testamentary trust for the life of surviving spouse. At death of surviving spouse, trust terminates.

The term of a trust may be measured by multiple lives.

Example (6): Grantor establishes living trust for his own benefit. At grantor's death, trust continues for benefit of surviving spouse. After death of spouse, trust continues until the death of the last survivor of the grantor's children.

The trust term may be for the beneficiary's lifetime plus an additional specified time period.

Example (7): Testamentary trust to be held for the life of the grantor's child and for 21 years after the child's death, for the benefit of the grantor's grandchildren.

.022 Beneficial interests—Successive or concurrent

Single current beneficiary. If the trust is intended to end during the current beneficiary's lifetime, the same beneficiary may also be designated to receive the distribution of the remainder. If the trust is to continue throughout the beneficiary's lifetime, a successive beneficiary or beneficiaries must be named.

Multiple current beneficiaries. A trust may have multiple current beneficiaries, each with a separate share of the trust fund.

Example (1): A trust fund is divided into separate shares for the children of the grantor. Each child receives income from her share during the time the trust is held. As each child attains age 25, her share is distributed to her. The division of the trust may be made in equal shares for the children or in other than equal shares, according to the grantor's wishes.

Another possibility for a trust with multiple current beneficiaries is the single-share trust fund. Compare the following trust with the trust in Example (1).

Example (2): A single trust fund is established for the grantor's children. Income is distributed to the beneficiaries during the time the trust is held. At the occurrence of a future event, the trust terminates and the fund is divided among the children.

Events that the grantor might choose to trigger termination of a trust with multiple current beneficiaries include: (1) the youngest child's attainment of a specific age; (2) the expiration of a specific period of time after the death of the grantor or his spouse; or (3) the death of the last survivor of the grantor's children. Compare Examples (1) and (2) with the following trust fund, which starts as a single trust fund and then, at a specified point in the future, is divided into separate shares.

> **Example (3):** A single testamentary trust fund is created for the benefit of grantor's spouse and children. After the death of grantor's spouse, the trust continues as a single trust fund for the grantor's children until the youngest child finishes his or her college education. At that point, the trust is divided into separate shares for the children. Note that the trust distributions among the beneficiaries could be unequal according to their respective needs as determined annually by the trustee. After the division of the trust into separate shares, each beneficiary could be given the exclusive benefits flowing from his individual share.

.023 Distribution or accumulation of trust income

Trust income may be distributed to the beneficiaries or accumulated within the trust to be distributed at a later date or upon termination of the trust. The trust income may be distributed or accumulated as follows:

(1) All income is distributed currently. Some trusts specify the time intervals at which income distributions are to be made, such as annually, quarterly, monthly, or even weekly.

(2) All income is accumulated within the trust fund for future distribution either to the current beneficiary (ies) or to one or more successive beneficiaries.

(3) Income is accumulated for a specified period, and thereafter the income is distributed.

> **Example:** Until the beneficiary reaches age 21, the income is accumulated and combined with the principal of the trust fund. Beginning at age 21, the income is distributed to the beneficiary as it is earned by the trust.

(4) Part of the income is distributed currently and part is accumulated. The amount distributed might be a pre-set proportion of the income earned, or the determination of whether to accumulate and how much to accumulate could be made annually at the discretion of the trustee.

.024 Distribution of the principal of the trust fund

The principal of the trust fund may be distributed as follows:

(1) No principal is distributed until termination of the trust.

(2) Specific amounts of principal are distributed at set time intervals or upon attainment by the beneficiary of designated ages.

> **Example:** A testamentary trust consists of separate trust shares for the testator's children. As each child reaches age 25, one-half of the principal of his share is distributed to him.

(3) The trustee may have the discretion to distribute the principal before the termination of the trust. This discretion may be limited to specific purposes, such as for higher educational expenses, medical expenses, a down payment on the purchase of a home, or the start-up costs of a business.

Instead, the grantor may wish to direct that the trustee's discretion in this regard is absolute, so that principal distributions can be made for any purpose the trustee considers worthwhile.

However, if discretionary distributions of principal are allowed, limitations nevertheless can be placed on the amount or percentage of the principal that can be distributed in any year. Some instruments name a cumulative total in terms of amount or percentage of the original value of the trust that may be distributed by the trustee prior to the trust's termination.

(4) A beneficiary may be given the right to make withdrawals from the principal of the trust prior to its termination. As in the case of a trustee's discretionary power to distribute principal, the grantor may wish to place limitations on the beneficiary's right to make such withdrawals based on (a) an annual or cumulative amount or percentage or (b) the purposes for which any principal amounts withdrawn may be used.

¶ 203 TRUST DESIGN CHECKLIST IN OUTLINE FORM

The following is an example of a trust design checklist in an outline form. This will aid the financial planner or practitioner in designing the proper trust for his clients' specific needs.

SAMPLE TRUST DESIGN CHECKLIST

A. Term of Trust.

1. Specific time period.
2. One lifetime.
3. Multiple lifetimes.
4. One or more lifetimes plus additional time period.

B. Beneficial Interests.

1. Single current beneficiary (B1).

a. If trust ends during B1's life, remainder to B1.

b. If trust continues after B1's death, successive beneficiary (ies).

2. Multiple current beneficiaries, separate shares.

a. Each share distributed at beneficiary's specified age.

b. Each share distributed after specified number of years.

c. Each share distributed when youngest beneficiary attains specified age.

3. Multiple current beneficiaries of single-share trust.

a. Terminates at specific age of youngest beneficiary.

b. Terminates after specified number of years.

c. Each beneficiary receives a distribution of a share of principal upon reaching a specified age and thereafter is no longer a beneficiary of the trust.

4. Initially, multiple current beneficiaries of single-share trust with subsequent division into separate shares (see B.2.a. through B.2.c.).

C. Distribution or Accumulation of Income.

1. All income distributed currently (annually, quarterly, monthly, etc.).

2. Accumulate all income.

3. Accumulate initially and later distribute.

a. Begin to distribute after specified number of years.

b. Begin to distribute after beneficiary attains a specified age.

4. Part of income distributed and part accumulated.

a. Pre-set percentages.

b. Discretion of trustee.

D. Distribution of Trust Principal.

1. No principal distributions until trust terminates.

2. Specific principal distributions at identified time intervals.

a. Distribution of 1/3 of principal at age X, 1/2 balance at age Y, and remaining balance at age Z.

b. Distribution of 1/2 of principal five years after trust established and balance 10 years after trust established.

3. Trustee's discretion to distribute principal.

a. Limited by "standards" such as education, medical expenses, or general support.

b. Unlimited distribution of principal permitted in absolute discretion of trustee.

c. An overriding limitation on cumulative principal distributions prior to trust termination.

4. Beneficiary's right of principal withdrawal.

¶ 204 SPECIAL CONSIDERATIONS FOR "SPRINKLE" TRUSTS

A single trust fund with a "sprinkle" provision that allows the trustee to make distributions of principal and income other than in equal shares may be a desirable trust design. The following sections discuss the use of sprinkle trust provisions.

.01 Added Advantages

A single trust fund with more than one current beneficiary can provide increased flexibility in the management of financial resources, particularly where the size of the trust fund is not large enough to ensure that all of the needs and wants of each beneficiary will be provided for through the trust. If a single fund is used, one of the designs available is to grant the trustee discretion to make distributions of income and principal other than in equal shares, according to the relative needs of the beneficiaries.

For some people, however, equal treatment of each beneficiary is a high priority, even if this means that some beneficiaries are fully provided for while other beneficiaries are left in need. If this attitude is encountered, an alternative to the single trust fund should probably be considered.

Some particular motivations exist for selecting a single trust with multiple beneficiaries. One, typically, is the recognition by the grantor that he might not live long enough to see how things turn out. In fact, in the case of a testamentary trust, the testator can be absolutely certain of this. Next there is the recognition that, even if the grantor were to live forever and could make all future financial decisions for his descendants, he might not insist on treating them equally for a variety of reasons. One grantor might base the proportions of his largesse on the differing needs of the objects of his bounty, while another grantor might wish to reward greater effort or achievement in life with a larger ultimate inheritance. Finally, there is the grantor's willingness to give the trustee the responsibility of distributing the grantor's wealth according to the circumstances that affect the beneficiaries as their lives develop. The trustee attempts to make the necessary choices among the beneficiaries' needs based on the trustee's perception of what the grantor might have decided in each circumstance.

The single trust fund for multiple beneficiaries derives added flexibility from a provision in the trust instrument that directs the trustee to make distributions other than in equal shares. The decision concerning proportions of shares among the beneficiaries may be made each year and need not be the same from year to year. The trust document might contain a direction, for instance, requiring the trustee to take into consideration the relative needs of each beneficiary and the overall best interests of the beneficiaries as a group. On the other hand, the grantor may prefer to place absolute and unrestricted discretion as to distributions in the trustee's hands. A single trust fund that permits or directs distributions of unequal proportions among a group of beneficiaries is referred to as a sprinkle trust or "spray" trust.

.02 Variations of the Sprinkle Trust

Since the sprinkle provision of a trust may relate to either income or principal, or to both, there is a wide range of possibilities as to the exact design of the trust from which the grantor may choose. The following list is a sample of some sprinkle trust designs.

(1) Trustee is directed to pay income in equal shares. Principal distributions are permitted during any year of the trust on a sprinkle basis.

(2) Trustee is not required to distribute any income but is given discretion to sprinkle income among beneficiaries. Income not distributed is accumulated and added to principal.

(3) Trustee has discretion to distribute both income and principal on a sprinkle basis.

(4) During trust administration, trustee may sprinkle income and/or principal. At trust termination, the remainder is distributed in equal shares.

(5) Upon termination of the sprinkle trust, the trustee must make a division of the remainder, taking into account any unequal distributions during the administration. This is a difficult design to handle in actual practice due to changes in investment values and rates of return as well as "time value of money" considerations.

(6) Trustee has sprinkle power over income and/or principal. As each beneficiary reaches a specified age, that beneficiary receives a percentage of whatever principal then remains, such that the distribution of the youngest child's share represents the final distribution of the principal.

Example: A trust is created under the will of A for his children, B, C, and D. The trustee makes distributions of income and principal in each year of the trust on a sprinkle basis. When B, the oldest child, reaches age 25, he receives 1/3 of whatever principal then remains, and B is thereafter no longer a beneficiary of the trust. When C, the middle child, reaches age 25, he receives 1/2 of whatever the principal then remains, and C's benefits from the trust end. After that, the trust continues for the exclusive benefit of D, who receives the entire remaining balance upon reaching age 25.

It might be noted that this carving out of proportionate parts of a trust for individual beneficiaries at different times is also possible in the case of a single trust fund in which there is no sprinkle power but only equal beneficiary interests. A single trust fund that mixes beneficiary interests with an intention of making the ultimate distributions equal is referred to as a "hotchpot." The necessity of providing for contingencies, such as the death of a beneficiary prior to receiving his share, makes this trust design somewhat more difficult to handle than the description in the preceding example suggests.

¶ 205 INCREASED FLEXIBILITY THROUGH POWERS OF APPOINTMENT

A power of appointment is often used by a grantor to permit necessary changes to a trust. The following sections discuss how the power of appointment functions and the components that make up a power of appointment.

.01 How the Power of Appointment Functions

The very nature of a trust requires to some extent a guess on the part of the grantor as to the future needs of the beneficiary. The terms of an irrevocable living trust or testamentary trust, once in existence, cannot be modified by the grantor. If the beneficiary's needs change or if unforeseeable needs arise, the grantor is either legally powerless to help or deceased.

In view of this, consideration may be given to designating a third party who will have the power to make special distributions from the trust before its termination or to decide on when, how, and to whom the final distribution of the remainder will be made. This arrangement, known as a power of appointment, must be contrasted with a trustee's discretionary power to make principal distributions during the trust's existence. The power of appointment is held by a third party; typically, it is not held by the trustee. In fact, one motivation for including a power of appointment in the trust might be concern on the part of the grantor that the trustee may not exercise discretionary powers over the trust or may do so in too restrictive or too generous a manner.

.02 Technical Terms Relating to the Power of Appointment

Following is a list of special terms associated with the power of appointment, including further discussion and explanation of the design and operation of these powers.

(1) **Donor of the Power.** This is the person who has created the power. Since the grantor of a living trust or, in the case of a testamentary trust, the testator, dictates the trust's terms and conditions, the grantor or testator is the donor of the power.

(2) **Donee of the Power (also called the holder of the power).** This individual can "exercise" the power, thereby causing a distribution from the trust. Although the word "donee" suggests receiving something, it must be understood that the donee of a power of appointment does not necessarily receive a financial benefit. What this donee receives is a power to control part or all of the trust rather than a beneficial interest in the trust. The donee of the power may be thought of as an agent, delegated by the donor to make changes in the plan of distribution of the trust as conditions warrant. The power of appointment may be exercisable after the donor's death—in some cases several decades after the donor's death. By creating the power, the donor can make it possible for the power holder to change the outcome of the trust in ways the donor might have wanted if the donor could have foreseen future events.

(3) **Object or Objects of the Power.** The person or persons for whose benefit the power is permitted to be exercised under the terms of the controlling document, the will, or the trust agreement is the "object" of the power.

(4) **Testamentary Power of Appointment.** The exercise of a testamentary power of appointment is made through a provision contained in the Last Will and Testament of the donee of the power. Consequently, the donee does not have the right to exercise the power during the donee's own lifetime.

> **Example:** Testator's will establishes a trust fund to pay income to the surviving spouse for life, with the remainder to be distributed among the testator's children. The proportions of the final distribution among the children, however, are to be designated in the will of the surviving spouse.

In the foregoing example, the testator may have had a will prepared while his children were very young. The rationale for giving the surviving spouse a testamentary power of appointment over the remainder may have been reliance on the surviving spouse to judge how the children "turn out," as well as to review their relative financial situations later in their lives, and to make a division of the final balance of the trust taking these factors into consideration. Alternatively, the testator may feel that if the children realize that the surviving spouse can increase or decrease the overall proportions of their inheritance, even from the estate of the first deceased parent, the children may be more likely to take better care of, and be more attentive to, the surviving spouse. This latter motivation can prove to be a significant factor where the trust fund subject to the power is extensive in value.

(5) **Power of Appointment Presently Exercisable (also known as a power of appointment by deed).** This term describes a power of appointment that may be exercised while the donee of the power is living. This is in contrast to the testamentary power. It is possible to create a power that can be exercised either during lifetime or through the will of the donee of the power.

(6) **Joint Power.** The donor of the power may wish, in effect, to set up a "committee" to make decisions on trust distributions through the power of appointment. A joint power is one that requires the consent of two or more persons to exercise the power.

(7) **General Power of Appointment.** This is a power that may be exercised for the benefit of any one of the following objects:

(1) the donee of the power;

(2) the donee's estate;

(3) the donee's creditors; and

(4) the creditors of the donee's estate.

The right of an individual to make withdrawals from the trust principal for his own use or benefit is an example of a general power of appointment because it is the equivalent of a power of appointment exercisable in favor of the donee of the power. The distinction between a general power of appointment and a non-general or limited power is significant for its federal estate and gift tax consequences, which are examined in Chapter 4.

(8) **Limited Power of Appointment (also called a non-general, or special, power of appointment).** Any power of appointment that does not meet the definition of a general power is a limited or non-general power of appointment. In the most expansive case, there is the power of appointment that is exercisable for the benefit of any person except the holder of the power, the holder's estate, or the creditors of either. However, it is possible to design a non-general power to be much more restrictive according to the preference of the donor. An example of a limited power of appointment is a power of appointment exercisable in favor of any lineal descendant of the donor.

¶ 206 THE DISCLAIMER—INTENDED BENEFICIARY'S VETO POWER

No one can be forced to accept a gift or inheritance, although some might wonder why anyone would want to turn down a gratuitous transfer. One motive might be the avoidance of gift and estate tax. The recipient of a gift or beneficiary of an estate must realize that if he, in turn, gives away what he has received or if he dies owning it, a transfer tax may be involved. From that perspective, if the recipient does not intend to use or spend the gift or inheritance for his own benefit, it might be better never to have obtained it in the first place.

A disclaimer is a formal decision to turn down a gift or inheritance in part or in whole. If certain specific requirements are met, as explained at ¶ 401.071, the transfer is treated as passing from the original donor to whomever actually receives the subject property as a result of the disclaimer. While the "disclaimant," as the intended recipient is called, may not control who will ultimately receive the disclaimed transfer, the disclaimant can certainly ascertain who will benefit from the disclaimer and make the decision whether to accept the transfer or to disclaim based on that fact.

While the law concerning the effects of a disclaimer varies somewhat from state to state, the general rule is that the disclaimer results in the transfer of the property to whomever would have received it if the disclaimant had been deceased.

> **Example (1):** A's Last Will and Testament gives $50,000 to B, who is A's son, and specifies that if B predeceases A, the bequest passes to B's daughter, C. B survives A but disclaims the bequest. The $50,000 is then transferred to C. It is treated as if C had inherited this amount from A, and not as a gift from B to C.

If the will makes no provision for the contingency of the beneficiary predeceasing the testator, it may take some additional research to determine who would benefit from the disclaimer. Depending on such factors as the laws of the testator's state of domicile, the terms of the bequest contained in the will, and the degree of family relationship between the testator and the intended beneficiary, a disclaimed transfer might pass to the disclaimant's descendants or to the remaining beneficiaries named in the will or trust agreement.

There is growing interest in advance planning for the use of disclaimers, that is, designing provisions in wills and trust agreements with the express intention of creating an alternative disposition in case a disclaimer occurs. This tends to alert the initial named beneficiary to the planning potential and gives that intended beneficiary certainty of the consequences of making a disclaimer.

> **Example (2):** A's will leaves her entire estate to her daughter, B, with the provision that if and to the extent B disclaims, the inheritance will be distributed among B's children.

In this example, at the death of A, B is given the opportunity to judge whether her own financial condition is sufficiently secure to permit her to give up part or all of the inheritance and, if so, to determine the needs of her children and whether the children's level of maturity is adequate to enable them to handle the responsibility of receiving an inheritance at that point in their lives.

If those who would receive a disclaimed transfer are minor children at the time the planning is undertaken, consideration might be given to using a type of contingent trust, sometimes referred to as a "disclaimer trust," which only comes into existence in the event a disclaimer is made.

> **Example (3):** D's will leaves his estate to his son, E, who is now age 38 and who has two children of his own, F and G, who are ages 8 and 5. D's will provides that if E predeceases D or disclaims, the estate is held in separate trust shares for F and G. Each of the grandchildren receives his share upon reaching age 30, with the trustee having discretion to make distributions for their needs in the meantime.

¶ 207 TERMINATING BENEFITS THROUGH RENUNCIATION

After a trust fund is in existence, either providing income or principal or accumulating income, the beneficiary may have some reason to give up his rights to all current and future trust benefits. The formal notification by the beneficiary to the trustee of this giving up of benefits is known as renunciation. When this occurs, the trustee's responsibility is to determine what action is to be taken according to the terms and conditions of the trust document.

Ordinarily, the trustee is required to treat the situation as if the renouncing beneficiary had died. Depending on the design of the trust, it might be necessary to continue to administer the trust fund for the benefit of one or more successive beneficiaries or to terminate the trust fund and distribute the balance to the remaindermen. Renunciation is said to cause an "acceleration" of the trust, that is, an advancement to the next stage of the trust administration that would not otherwise have occurred until the end of the renouncing beneficiary's interest.

Through renunciation, it is possible for a current beneficiary or beneficiaries to modify the term of the trust. This can provide a benefit to the entire family, particularly where circumstances that may not have been foreseeable by the grantor make it more desirable for the trust to terminate or for the current beneficiary's interest to end before the planned termination, as specified in the trust document.

> **Example:** B is the income beneficiary of a testamentary trust established under his mother's will. Upon B's death, the remainder is to be distributed to B's children, who are now entering college. Although B can afford to do without the income that the trust is producing, he does not have the financial resources outside of the trust to pay for his children's education. Upon B's renunciation, the trust terminates and the children receive their shares of the principal, which they can then use to pay for their own educational costs.

The basic distinction between the renunciation and the disclaimer is timing. While a disclaimer, by definition, takes place before the disclaimant has received any benefits from the trust, a renunciation may occur at any time after the renouncing beneficiary has become entitled to receive benefits from the trust. This distinction has significance for federal gift tax purposes. A disclaimer that meets specific gift tax requirements is not treated as a gift by the disclaimant for federal gift tax purposes, while a renunciation is treated as a taxable gift made by the renouncing beneficiary.

¶ 208 DIVISION OF REMAINDER INTERESTS AMONG CLASSES OF BENEFICIARIES

It is possible, even likely, that the grantor of a trust may not know to whom the remainder will ultimately be distributed.

> **Example (1):** A's will establishes a testamentary trust for the benefit of A's spouse, B. Upon B's death, the remainder is to be distributed among the surviving descendants of A and B. One or more of the children of A and B may bear children (grandchildren of A and B) after A's death. The share of the trust remainder intended for a child of A who predeceases B will then be distributed to a grandchild of A whom A had never met.

This example can help to explain why it is not usually practical to specify all successive beneficiaries of a trust fund by name. Instead, particularly in the case of future trust interests, groups of beneficiaries may be specified by reference to a described class of persons. The use of classes has two important advantages: (1) it makes practical the inclusion of beneficiaries who may be born after the trust is established; and (2) it simplifies the disposition of any future trust benefit that was intended to pass to someone who did not live long enough to receive it.

A simple description of class beneficiaries is contained in the term "descendants," which is defined as all succeeding generations, from the ancestor to the most remote degree, with no limitation as to the number of intervening family generations. Under state laws, adopted children and their descendants are generally included. If this term is used, however, uncertainty may arise in the event that, at the termination of the trust, the living descendants of the grantor represent different degrees of family relationship to the grantor.

> **Example (2):** H's will established a trust fund to provide income to W, his wife, for life. At W's death, the remainder is to be distributed to the descendants of H and W then living. H and W had three children, A, B, and C, each of whom had three children, and C predeceases W. At the trust termination, the family tree may be illustrated as follows:

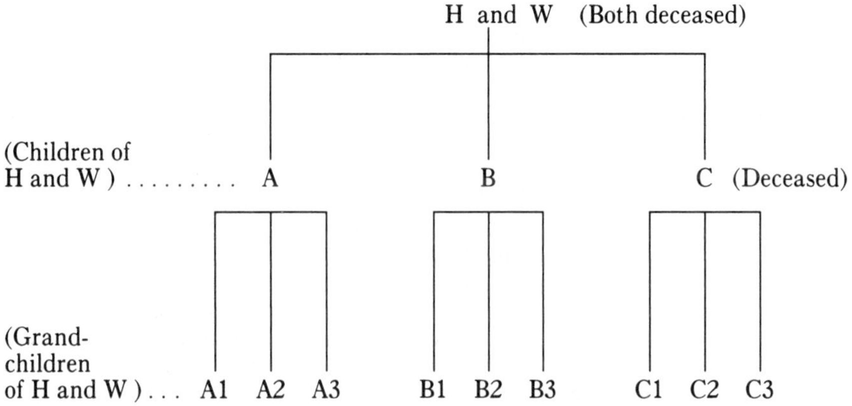

As a general rule, the surviving descendants of the grantor who are more nearly related to the grantor receive shares of the remainder, to the exclusion of their own descendants. In other words, in the preceding example, A and B each receive a share of the remainder, but their children do not receive any shares. On the other hand, since C is deceased when the remainder becomes distributable, C's children also receive shares of the remainder.

There are two primary methods of calculating the division of the shares of a remainder among descendants. In the first method, each surviving descendant who is entitled to a share of the remainder receives an equal share regardless of the remoteness of the family relationship. This is the "per capita" method of division, which may be specified by a provision in the trust document requiring a division "among the descendants of the grantor in equal shares per capita" or by the use of the phrase "among the descendants of the grantor, share and share alike."

In the preceding example, a per capita distribution would result in the distribution of one-fifth of the remainder to each of the following: A, B, C1, C2, and C3.

The antithesis of the per capita method is a division of the remainder into shares that are equal at that generation level nearest to the grantor in which there are surviving descendants, with a further division of shares among those of the more remote descendants who are entitled to shares of the remainder. This is the "per stirpes" method of dividing the remainder. In the preceding example, it would result in the distribution of one-third of the remainder each to A and to B. The last one-third of the remainder, which would have been distributed to C if living, is redivided among C's three children so that each of them (C1, C2, and C3) receives one-third of this last share, or one-ninth of the total remainder. This method of calculating the remainder shares may be specified by the use of the phrase "among the descendants of the grantor in equal shares per stirpes." However, some document drafters prefer to use what they may consider to be more descriptive language, such as "among the surviving children of the grantor in equal shares, provided that the share of any child of the grantor who predeceases him shall be distributed among such deceased child's descendants in equal shares per stirpes."

Although the laws of the various states cannot require the grantor to choose a per stirpes method of distribution over a per capita method, state law may specify which method is to be used in the event that there is ambiguity in the wording of the trust document.

¶ 209 THE RULE AGAINST PERPETUITIES

State law makes it impermissible to establish a trust that will never come to an end. There are only limited exceptions to this rule, such as legally permissible perpetual trusts for the maintenance of cemetery properties and trusts in perpetuity for charitable purposes.

While the exact restrictions of the rule vary from state to state, a typical rule against perpetuities provides that a trust is invalid unless, by the terms of its creating document, it must come to an end within 21 years after the death of an identifiable, living person or within 21 years after the death of the survivor of a group or class of persons. If the trust document uses the surviving member of a class of persons as the "measuring life," the class must be reasonable in size so that it is not overly difficult to keep track of its members. Furthermore, every person who is a member of the class of measuring lives must have been born at the time the trust becomes irrevocable, although an unborn infant whose mother is pregnant at that time is a permissible measuring life, provided that the child is later born alive.

A few examples may help to illustrate the basic principles of the rule against perpetuities.

> **Example (1):** Testamentary trust to terminate 21 years after the death of the last surviving child of the grantor.

This does not violate the rule because all of the grantor's children, who are the measuring lives, naturally must have been born before the grantor's death. If the grantor is a man, he may have a child born up to approximately nine months after his death; however, that child would be a permissible measuring life, as already explained.

> **Example (2):** Trust fund established for the descendants of D to continue until the death of the last survivor of all inhabitants of the continent of North America who are alive on the date the trust is created.

In Example (2), although the measuring lives must all be people who were living at the inception of the trust, the trust violates the rule because of the impossibility of determining who the last survivor of the class might be.

Example (3): Testamentary trust to continue until 21 years after the death of the last survivor of all descendants of the grantor (no matter how remote) *who are living at the date of the grantor's death.*

There is no restriction against identifying remote descendants as measuring lives so long as they are all persons living on the date of the trust's inception. Therefore, in Example (3) the rule is not violated.

Example (4): Testamentary trust to continue until 21 years after the death of the last of the grantor's grandchildren.

The problem in Example (4) is that, while the grantor may have had in mind those of his grandchildren who were living when the will or trust agreement was written, the document does not limit the class to those grandchildren. It is entirely possible for additional grandchildren to be born after the trust becomes irrevocable. Even if it can be proven that, at the inception of the trust, all of the grantor's children are sterile because they are past childbearing age or for any other reason, so that it would have been impossible for any additional grandchildren to have been born (or adopted) after the trust began, the trust may violate the rule.

The result in Example (4) illustrates an adjunct to the rule against perpetuities still recognized in some states, although peculiar by modern standards, known as the "fertile octogenarian" rule. By virtue of this precept, in order to avoid the necessity of looking into the childbearing ability of persons who are measuring lives, all living persons are presumed capable of bearing children for the purpose of applying the rule against perpetuities.

Originally, any trust determined to violate the rule was *void ab initio,* that is, invalid from its inception. The modern trend, however, is to allow a trust that appears to violate the rule to continue according to its own terms but to permit a court action to be brought for the purpose of terminating the trust if and when it turns out to violate the rule as the facts and circumstances unfold. This approach, which might permit a trust to continue for decades, is referred to as the "wait and see" doctrine.

Chapter 3

Federal Income Taxation of Trusts

¶ 301 RELATED INCOME TAX PRINCIPLES

The subject of federal income taxation of trusts and estates is a specialized field. Relatively few accountants and attorneys are routinely involved in the area, and the majority of professional financial advisers have virtually no exposure to its intricacies. The subject itself deals with the separate-entity status of estates and certain trusts for income tax purposes. These separate entities are required to file their own income tax returns apart from the tax returns filed by their beneficiaries. Some of the issues encountered in the preparation of fiduciary returns are:

(1) When does the tax year for the separate entity begin and end?

(2) If an estate or trust receives taxable income and distributes it to a beneficiary, which taxpayer is subject to income tax—the estate or trust, the beneficiary, or both?

(3) What is the character of amounts received by a beneficiary from an estate or trust for income tax purposes?

Besides these issues, which are examined in this chapter, there are certain related income tax rules that the financial consultant must understand in order to appreciate the full impact of the fiduciary income tax laws.

.01 Cost Basis Adjustments for Estates, Trusts, and Beneficiaries

There are many cost basis adjustments that are required to be made by an estate, a trust, or a beneficiary. The following sections analyze the cost basis rules in detail.

.011 Review of ordinary cost basis rules affecting gain or loss upon asset sales

Upon the sale of any asset, the difference between the sales proceeds and the seller's adjusted cost basis is either a taxable gain or a loss that may be deductible for income tax purposes.[1] If the asset sold is a capital asset, as defined in the Internal Revenue Code, the gain or loss is accounted for separately from other types of income.[2]

The determination of a taxpayer's adjusted cost basis begins with the amount originally paid for the assets by the taxpayer.[3] Examples of adjustments made to this cost include additions to the cost basis for any amounts expended by the taxpayers for capital improvements and reductions in the cost basis for deductions attributable to depreciation.[4]

---

[1] Code Secs. 165(f), 1211, and 1212.

[2] Code Secs. 1221 and 1222.

[3] Code Sec. 1012.

[4] Code Sec. 1016.

.012 Basis step-up—Effect of death on the cost basis

After death, the decedent's estate, as well as any beneficiary who succeeds to assets included in the taxable estate of the decedent, is required to disregard the adjusted cost basis as it had been in the decedent's hands and to use a new cost basis equal to the value of the asset as of the date of the decedent's death[5] or the value on the date six months after the date of death if the latter value is used for federal estate tax purposes.[6] This new "stepped-up" cost basis, as it is called, is used to determine gain or loss upon a future sale and, in the case of depreciable assets, future amounts to be claimed as depreciation deductions.

The basis step-up rule is often regarded as a windfall to the taxpayer that eliminates what would have been substantial taxable gain on assets received from a decedent where the date of death value is much greater than the original cost. It is important to realize, however, that the basis step-up rule is mandatory rather than elective, so that it may represent a disadvantage instead of an advantage. Consider, for instance, the situation in which investments have a value at the decedent's death that is less than their original cost. The decedent, if living, could have sold the asset, recognized the loss for tax purposes, and possibly obtained some income tax advantage. The intervention of death, however, eliminates any potential loss deduction in the same manner as any potential gains would be eliminated by the basis adjustment.

In view of this, on occasions where the financial consultant is called on to review a family's financial situation because death is imminent, it is useful to obtain cost basis information. It is also advantageous, where practical, to advise selling assets where the result will be a deductible loss and holding other assets that are subject to potential taxable gain, in order to take maximum advantage of the results of the basis step-up rule.

.013 Basis adjustments affecting the principal assets of trust funds

The principal assets of a trust fund may also be subject to the basis step-up rule at the death of either the grantor or a beneficiary. The key is inclusion of the trust assets in the decedent's taxable estate. If the principal assets are subject to federal estate tax, basis step-up occurs.[7] If the principal assets are not included in the decedent's taxable estate, there is no basis adjustment as a result of death. In situations involving living trusts, the principal assets are included in the taxable estate of the grantor if any of the estate tax "string section"[8] rules, which are discussed at ¶ 402.04 of Chapter 4, apply. It is the estate tax consequences that determine this; the fact that a trust may be subject to the income tax "substantial ownership"[9] rules, which are explained at ¶ 302 of this chapter, does not cause a basis adjustment. For testamentary trusts as well as living trusts, a basis adjustment may also occur upon the death of a beneficiary. Once again, this depends on whether or not the principal assets of the trust are included in the beneficiary's taxable estate, another subject considered at ¶ 402 of Chapter 4.

Living trusts are somewhat more complex in situations where the principal assets transferred to the trust fund by the grantor do not consist entirely of cash. Assets transferred to a living trust, where the fair market value on the

[5] Code Sec. 1014.
[6] Code Sec. 2032.
[7] Code Sec. 1014(b).
[8] See Code Secs. 2036-2038, inclusive.
[9] See Code Secs. 671-678, inclusive.

date of transfer is not equal to the grantor's adjusted cost basis, are subject to separate gift basis rules[10] and to a special two-year rule concerning gain on the sale or exchange of this property by the trust within two years after it is transferred to the trust.[11]

Gift basis rules. Property transferred by gift, as in the case of the transfer of assets to a living trust, may have two different cost bases, one for the purpose of determining gain and another for the purpose of determining loss. In the unlikely event that the value of the property on the date of the transfer is equal to the donor's adjusted cost basis, no special problems exist and the trust's cost basis or other recipient's cost basis is equal to the donor's. Otherwise, gain is computed by the trust with reference to the donor's adjusted cost, while loss is computed by referring to the lower of the fair market value on the date of the transfer or the donor's adjusted cost.[12] Where the size of the gift is large enough to require the payment of gift tax by the donor, there may also be a cost adjustment based on the gift tax paid that is attributable to the transferred property.[13]

Two-year rule for transfers of appreciated property. If property is transferred to a trust in circumstances where (1) the fair market value on the date of transfer is greater than the donor's adjusted cost basis; and (2) this appreciated property is sold by the trust within two years after the transfer, a special additional income tax may be payable on the gain. This additional tax is equal to the excess, if any, of (1) the amount of income tax that would have been paid if the transferor had personally sold the asset during the year in which the trust in fact sold it, over (2) the amount of income tax payable by the trust as a result of the sale.[14] For an extra amount of tax to be payable under this rule, it is necessary for the transferor's marginal income tax rate to be higher than the marginal income tax rate imposed on the trust. The likelihood of this is now reduced because trusts reach the highest marginal income tax bracket sooner (i.e., at a lower amount of taxable income) than do individuals.[15] The chances of an addition to a trust's income tax based on the Code Sec. 644 two-year rule in years after 1987 are remote.

.014 Restriction on the use of the basis adjustment rule for tax avoidance

Although it may seem macabre on first impression, some taxpayers are inclined to transfer appreciated assets to a spouse or other family member who is near death for the express purpose of obtaining a stepped-up basis. This could result in an income tax advantage if it is predictable that no adverse gift or estate tax consequences will result and if it is known that the donor, as beneficiary of the recipient's estate, will reacquire the transferred asset with a brand new cost basis. While there is no absolute restriction on attempting this, it is important to note that the basis adjustment rules do not apply to any asset received by the decedent by gift within one year before the date of death.[16]

---

[10] Code Sec. 1015.

[11] Code Sec. 644.

[12] Code Sec. 1015.

[13] Code Sec. 1015(d).

[14] Code Sec. 644(a).

[15] Code Sec. 1.

[16] Code Sec. 1014(e).

.015 Basis step-up and income in respect of a decedent

Any item of property that represents income in respect of a decedent (see below) is not affected by the basis step-up rule.

.02 Income in Respect of a Decedent

As a general rule, principal amounts received by a beneficiary from a decedent's estate or from the principal of a trust are in the nature of a gift or inheritance that is specifically excluded from taxable income under the Internal Revenue Code.[17] Only the income generated by estate assets after the decedent's death and the income produced during the period of administration of a trust are potentially taxable to the beneficiary. Income in respect of a decedent, called "IRD" or "section 691 income" by practitioners, is an important exception to the general rule under Code Sec. 102. IRD is income that was earned but not collected by a decedent prior to death that is received by the executor of the estate or a beneficiary.[18] This income may be in the nature of earnings from the decedent's employment, but it may also be interest or other investment income or capital gains. Some examples of typical IRD items are:

(1) A paycheck for hours worked by the decedent before death but received by the estate after the date of death.

(2) Bonus payments and sales commissions paid to the estate after the date of death, based on the decedent's work performance or sales made by the decedent before death.

(3) Interest on mortgages, notes, bonds, or savings held by the decedent that has accrued from the date of the last interest payment to the date of death.

(4) Cash dividends paid on stocks owned by the decedent, but only if the record date for the dividend falls before the date of death and the payment date occurs after the date of death.

(5) Distributions from any form of qualified retirement plan paid to the decedent's estate or to a named beneficiary after the date of death. This includes pension, profit-sharing, section 401(k), and employee stock ownership plans, as well as individual retirement accounts.

The only portion of these payments that is not IRD is any balance contributed to the plan by the decedent which constitutes an "already taxed" amount. For instance, some qualified retirement plans either require or permit participants to make contributions to the plan on an after-tax basis. Also, since 1987, it has been permissible for some taxpayers who receive earned income to make contributions to individual retirement accounts that are not deductible for current income tax purposes.[19] These nondeductible contributions would eventually have become distributable to the participant as a nontaxable return of contributions from the plan. If death intervenes, these amounts are nontaxable and are not IRD to the estate or to the named beneficiary who receives them.

This is a very significant aspect of IRD because of (a) the growing number of Americans who are participants in some form of qualified

---

[17] Code Sec. 102.

[18] Code Sec. 691(a).

[19] Code Sec. 219(g).

retirement plan; (b) the growing amounts held in such plans; and (c) the flexibility of the payout schedules that are permitted. It is fair to say that many or most plan participants will die leaving some potentially taxable plan balance subject to IRD treatment at death. For many estates, the IRA or other qualified plan balance may prove to be the largest asset.

(6) Death benefits of fixed or variable investment annuities to the extent of the difference between the investment in contract and the total paid.

(7) Capital gain upon the liquidation of a closely held corporation of which the decedent was a shareholder.

Not all corporate liquidation payments received after the date of death are IRD, however. As a prerequisite to IRD status, the steps necessary to complete the corporate liquidation, other than the liquidating payments to shareholders, must have been substantially completed before the date of death. Exactly which liquidation steps must have been completed and the degree of required completion is not precisely specified in the income tax regulations and, as a result, this issue has been the subject of a fair amount of controversy between taxpayers and the government.

> **Example:** Decedent D owned 70 percent of the common stock of XYZ corporation, which was in the process of liquidation on the date of D's death. D's cost basis for the stock was $7,000, and his shares had a liquidation value at his death of $700,000. The value of D's XYZ shares is included in D's taxable estate for federal estate tax purposes regardless of the income tax consequences. If it is determined that the procedures for liquidating XYZ were not sufficiently completed, D's estate receives a basis step-up for the XYZ shares so that the estate recognizes no gain and there is no IRD when the liquidating distribution is received. On the other hand, if it is determined that all steps in the liquidation were substantially completed before D's death, the difference between D's pre-death cost basis for the shares and the amount of the liquidating distribution, or $693,000, represents capital gain and is taxable income in respect of a decedent. Clearly, the stakes are high in liquidation cases.

(8) Capital gain resulting from the sale of marketable securities could have resulted in IRD at one time. Under present income tax timing rules, however, capital gains are always included in taxable income on the trade date. As a result, there are two possible results if the sale of marketable securities at a gain takes place near the date of death:

> (a) If the trade date occurs on or before the date of death, the capital gain is properly reportable on the final income tax return of the decedent, not on the estate's fiduciary income tax return. Such gain is not an IRD item.
>
> (b) If the trade date occurs after the date of death, the estate receives a basis step-up. This has the effect of either eliminating any capital gain or reducing the amount of gain or loss to an insignificant amount in most cases. Any gain or loss, however, is reported on the fiduciary income tax return of the estate and is not IRD.

The IRD rules result in double taxation since the same amounts are subjected to both federal income tax and federal estate tax. Since the highest current income tax rate is 33 percent and the highest current estate tax rate is 55 percent, were it not for some form of relief, the combined taxes might be considered confiscatory. Relief, however, is provided through an income tax deduction allowable for the portion of the federal estate tax attributable to the IRD items included in taxable income.[20] The amount of this deduction is determined as follows:

Step 1: Compute the federal estate tax in the ordinary way (as explained at ¶ 402.02), including the appropriate amount of IRD items.

Step 2: Recalculate what the federal estate tax would have been if the net IRD items had been excluded. For this purpose, the net IRD items are all items of income in respect of a decedent, less certain deductible expenses, accrued before death but paid after death.

Step 3: The excess of the result of Step 1 over the result of Step 2 is the total allowable deduction for the estate tax paid on income in respect of a decedent.

The deduction may have to be apportioned to several income tax returns in cases involving several different IRD items paid, and therefore taxable, to different taxpayers in different taxable years. In the case of individual taxpayers, this is treated as a miscellaneous itemized deduction but is not subject to the two percent of adjusted gross income floor under Code Sec. 67.

¶ 302 THE SUBSTANTIAL OWNERSHIP RULES

A trust may not be treated as a separate taxpayer for income tax purposes if the grantor is considered the substantial owner of the trust. This section discusses the substantial ownership rules.

.01 Is the Trust a Separate Taxpayer?

A trust may be treated as a separate taxpayer for federal income tax purposes, thus requiring the trustee to file a federal income tax return on behalf of the trust. Under specific rules contained in the Internal Revenue Code,[21] however, any time the grantor or a beneficiary has such extensive control over the trust fund that the grantor or beneficiary is in a position equivalent to direct ownership of the trust property, the trust is not treated as a separate taxpayer. In such cases, the items of income, as well as any tax deductions or credits that are attributable to the trust, must be reported directly on the personal income tax return of the grantor or beneficiary who is considered to be the "substantial owner."[22] Trusts that fall into this category, called "grantor trusts," may be regarded as fundamentally simple. In some cases, no separate income tax return is required of the trust. This chapter examines the grantor trusts before discussing trusts that are treated as separate taxable entities.

The substantial ownership rules are applied on a year-by-year basis; it is possible that one or more of the substantial ownership tests might be met in some years but not in others. For instance, if the grantor is treated as the substantial owner due to powers over the trust reserved to the grantor for life under the terms of the trust document, in years after the grantor's death, the trust will begin to be treated as a separate taxpayer.

---

[20] Code Sec. 691(c).

[21] See Code Secs. 671-678, inclusive.

[22] Code Sec. 671.

It is possible for a trust to fall within the substantial ownership rules only with respect to principal transactions or income. In this case, the trust is a separate taxpayer only for those transactions that are not governed by these rules.[23]

.02 Survey of the Substantial Ownership Rules

The following is a summary and brief discussion of some of the highlights of the substantial ownership rules. It is not intended to be an exhaustive review of this very complex subject.

.021 Reversionary interests

The grantor is treated as the substantial owner of any living trust under the terms of which there may be either a reversion of the trust fund to the grantor or a distribution of the remainder to the grantor's spouse at any time in the future if the remainder or reversion has an actuarial value of more than five percent as of the date on which the trust becomes irrevocable.[24] As explained at ¶ 401.01, the present value of the reversionary interest is calculated by reference to actuarial tables prescribed by Code Sec. 7520. The tables take into account prevailing rates of interest when the value is to be determined. This is called the "applicable federal rate." A review of these tables indicates that a trust for the lifetime of an individual beneficiary (other than the grantor or spouse) has a remainder or reversion value not exceeding five percent if the applicable federal rate is eight percent and the lifetime beneficiary is under age 27 at the inception of the trust. Also, at the same applicable federal rate, a trust for a specific term of at least 39 years has a remainder/reversion value not exceeding five percent. In view of this, it is clear that the opportunities for trust design where there is to be a reversion to the grantor and which avoids the substantial ownership rules are very limited. There is, however, an exception to this rule.

The exception provides that the grantor is not treated as the substantial owner if all present beneficial interests in the trust are held by a minor lineal descendant of the grantor and the reversion to the grantor would occur only at the death of such descendant before reaching age 21.[25]

> **Example:** A establishes a trust fund for the benefit of C, his child, to be held until C reaches age 30, at which time the remainder is distributed to C. If C dies before reaching age 21, the principal of the trust reverts to A.

.022 Control over trust benefits

The grantor is treated as the substantial owner of a trust if the grantor can control the distribution of trust benefits.[26] This rule applies to powers reserved personally to the grantor under the terms of the trust document as well as to general powers held by the trustee if the grantor happens to be the trustee or one of the trustees.

> **Example:** A establishes a trust for the benefit of his adult children in which A names himself as trustee. All income must be distributed to the children in equal shares until the youngest child reaches age 45,

---

[23] Code Sec. 671.

[24] Code Sec. 673(a).

[25] Code Sec. 673(b).

[26] Code Sec. 674(a).

> at which time the trust ends and the remainder is distributed among A's descendants per stirpes. Although A is trustee, he has reserved no power to control the trust benefits, which must be distributed equally. The substantial ownership rules, therefore, do not apply.

There are a variety of exceptions to imposition of the substantial ownership rules relating to powers to control trust benefits. Some of the more noteworthy exceptions are:

> (1) A power held by the grantor to distribute trust principal among a class of beneficiaries does not cause substantial ownership status if the power is limited by a reasonably definite standard detailed in the trust document.[27]
>
> (2) If the grantor can make principal distributions to one of several current income beneficiaries, or cause the trustee to do so, substantial ownership status does not exist so long as the principal distributed is required by the trust document to be charged against the share of principal held for the income beneficiary who received the principal distribution as if that share were a separate trust fund.[28]
>
> (3) A power held by the grantor to withhold income temporarily from distribution to the current beneficiary does not cause substantial ownership status if the trust document contains certain specific provisions directing how the accumulated income is to be distributed in the future.[29] These rules are designed to give possession or control over the accumulated income to the beneficiary from whom the income distribution was withheld, or at least to require that the trust document specify how the accumulations are handled at the final trust termination without any future control exercisable by the grantor.

.023 Administrative powers

There are three categories of administrative powers that the grantor might possess, any one of which would cause substantial ownership treatment:

Dealing with trust property for less than adequate monetary consideration. Any power, such as a power permitting the grantor to purchase property from the trust at a price less than its objective value, will result in substantial ownership treatment.[30]

Borrowing. A right to borrow funds from the trust without posting adequate security or without paying a fair rate of interest causes substantial ownership treatment, whether or not the grantor actually takes any loan from the trust. Even where adequate security and interest are required for loans to the grantor, substantial ownership status exists in any year in which the loan balance plus interest is not repaid by the beginning of the trust's income tax year, unless the trustee is someone other than the grantor and other than certain relatives or business associates of the grantor.[31]

General administrative powers. These powers, which result in substantial ownership treatment, include powers the grantor might possess over closely held business interests that are assets of the trust as well as any power

---

27 Code Sec. 674(b)(5)(A).
28 Code Sec. 674(b)(5)(B).
29 Code Sec. 674(b)(6).
30 Code Sec. 675(1).
31 Code Sec. 675(2) and (3).

held by the grantor to take property from the trust fund in exchange for other property of equal value.[32]

.024 Power to revoke

The grantor is treated as the substantial owner of the trust if he has the right to reacquire assets from the trust. If this power to revoke exists with respect to only a portion of the trust fund, the grantor is treated as the substantial owner of that portion.[33]

.025 Income for grantor's benefit

Substantial ownership status exists if the trust income may be disposed of in any of the following ways. In most cases, it does not matter whether the income is actually so used.

(1) The trust income is distributed to the grantor or to the grantor's spouse.[34]

(2) The trust income is held for future distribution to the grantor or to the grantor's spouse.[35]

(3) The trust income is used to pay premiums on policies of life insurance where the grantor or the grantor's spouse is the insured, unless a charity is the irrevocable beneficiary of the life insurance policy.[36]

(4) The trust income is used to pay for the expenses of support of any person, other than the grantor or spouse, whom the grantor is legally obligated to support, such as the grantor's children. However, in cases involving support, substantial ownership treatment is imposed only to the extent that the income is actually used for such support purposes unless the grantor possesses the power to use trust income in this manner in a non-trustee capacity.[37]

Example: A establishes a living trust for the benefit of his dependent child, C. T, the trustee, has the discretion either to pay out the income to C (or for C's benefit) or to accumulate the income for future distribution to C. During the current year, T pays out of the trust income $5,000 to purchase new clothing for C and $10,000 for C's international travel. A must report $5,000 of income from the trust because of the payment for clothing, which constitutes a support obligation of A. Assuming that the payment for C's travel is not a support obligation, the $10,000 payment is not treated as income to A under the substantial ownership rules.

.026 Spousal attribution

For purposes of applying the grantor trust rules, any beneficial interest in the trust possessed by the grantor's spouse and any power over the trust held by the spouse are treated as possessed or held by the grantor.[38] For example, income payable to the grantor's spouse causes grantor trust status to be imposed on the grantor. Also, a trust in which the spouse is the remainderman is treated as if there were a reversionary interest held by the grantor.

[32] Code Sec. 675(4).
[33] Code Sec. 676.
[34] Code Sec. 677(a)(1).
[35] Code Sec. 677(a)(2).
[36] Code Sec. 677(a)(3).
[37] Code Sec. 677(b).
[38] Code Sec. 672(e).

Similarly, any power of withdrawal held by the spouse is treated as a power of revocation possessed by the grantor.

.027 Substantial owner other than grantor

Under some circumstances, a person other than the grantor can be treated as the substantial owner of part or all of the trust.

Withdrawal rights. A beneficiary who has the right to withdraw income or principal is treated as the substantial owner.[39]

> **Example (1):** A's will creates a testamentary trust for the benefit of B, who is A's spouse. B has the right to withdraw up to five percent of the principal in any year of the trust. B is treated as the substantial owner of five percent of the principal and must include five percent of all capital gains and losses on her personal income tax return even if B never exercises her right of withdrawal.

Partial release or modification. A beneficiary who possessed any withdrawal right but who partially released or modified that right is treated as if he were the grantor for purposes of applying all of the other substantial ownership tests.[40]

> **Example (2):** A's will establishes a testamentary trust for the benefit of his daughter, D, and her children with income to be "sprinkled" among all beneficiaries in the trustees' discretion. D has the right to make withdrawals from the trust. D and a bank are co-trustees. D renounces all rights to receive trust distributions and withdrawals. D is the substantial owner of the trust income, despite the renunciation, because her power to sprinkle income among the other beneficiaries, held as a co-trustee, is a power to control trust benefits.

Overriding substantial ownership status of grantor. Given the complexity of the substantial ownership rules, it is possible for both the grantor and a beneficiary to meet the substantial ownership tests at the same time. If that happens, the grantor is treated as the substantial owner and the beneficiary is not.[41]

¶ 303 TRUSTS THAT ARE SEPARATE TAXABLE ENTITIES

The following sections describe the tax ramifications with respect to a trust that is determined to be a separate taxable entity.

.01 Trust Taxable Income and Tax Year

As mentioned earlier, any trust that does not fall within the substantial ownership rules is treated as a separate taxpayer. It is the purpose of the federal income tax system to impose a tax on the income of these trusts either at the trust level or at the beneficiary level. The system is not intended to tax income twice. To avoid this double taxation, the Internal Revenue Code permits the trust to take an income tax deduction for amounts properly

---

39 Code Sec. 678(a)(1).

40 Code Sec. 678(a)(2).

41 Code Sec. 678(b).

distributed to beneficiaries.[42] The beneficiary is required to include in personal taxable income the same amount that the trust is allowed to deduct.[43]

Decedents' estates are always treated as separate taxpayers because they are not subject to the substantial ownership rules. An estate may be placed on an income tax reporting year beginning with the decedent's date of death and ending at the end of any calendar month, provided that the tax year does not exceed 12 months.[44]

Example: Decedent D dies on March 4 of year 1. The administration of the estate takes a little more than two years and is completed on May 19 of year 3.

The executor of estate D may choose a tax year-end corresponding with the last day of March of year 1 or corresponding with any other month-end up to the month of February of year 2. Once the executor chooses a tax year-end, however, the estate must continue using the same year-end until the estate administration is completed. If the executor, in this case, happens to choose a year ending January 31, there will be three fiduciary income tax returns required as follows:

(1) March 4 of year 1 through January 31 of year 2.

(2) February 1 of year 2 through January 31 of year 3.

(3) February 1 of year 3 through May 19 of year 3.

A trust fund that qualifies as a separate taxpayer does not have the same freedom to choose its fiscal year-end. Trusts are required to file their income tax returns on a calendar-year basis.[45] The first income tax year of any trust fund begins on the date on which the trust receives assets and starts to generate income and ends on December 31 of the same year. The last tax reporting year of a trust begins on January 1 of the year in which the trust distributes the final balance to the remaindermen and ends on the date of the final distribution.[46]

.02 Trust Calculation of Taxable Income

The trust calculates its taxable income in a manner very similar to the calculation of taxable income by an individual, as follows: [47]

(1) All items of taxable income are added to the taxable income base.

(2) Most deductions to which an individual is entitled are also allowed for trusts, except that the trust is not entitled to a standard deduction.

(3) Where the trust document requires all income to be distributed in the year in which it is earned by the trust, the trust deducts a specific exemption, which roughly corresponds to the individual taxpayer's personal exemption, except that it is limited to $300.[48] Trusts that distribute all income currently are referred to as "simple" trusts for income tax purposes.

---

[42] Code Secs. 651 and 661.

[43] Code Secs. 652 and 662.

[44] Code Sec. 441.

[45] Code Sec. 645.

[46] Code Sec. 443(a)(2).

[47] Code Sec. 641(b).

[48] Code Sec. 642(b).

(4) Trusts that may accumulate some or all of the current income deduct a specific exemption of $100 and are known as "complex" trusts for income tax purposes.[49]

(5) The trust is specifically entitled to deduct expenses of administration, including trustee's commissions and attorney fees. Even where these expenses are required to be paid from the principal of the trust fund, and therefore do not reduce the amount payable to the current income beneficiary, they are deductible for income tax purposes. In that event, the amount distributable to the current income beneficiary, known as "accounting net income" (ANI), exceeds the taxable income of the trust. The policy reason behind this is simply to avoid wasting the deductions. However, if any of the trust income consists of tax-exempt municipal bond interest, the trust's deduction for administration expenses is limited to a proportion of the total administration expenses in the same ratio as the taxable income bears to the total of taxable and tax-exempt income. Also, the trust is subject to the two percent floor that is imposed on miscellaneous itemized deductions of individuals under Code Sec. 67. As with individuals, the two percent floor does not apply to (1) expenses of a trade or business owned by the trust, (2) expenses in connection with property held for production of rents or royalties, or (3) losses from sales or exchanges of property.

.03 Tax-Free Quality of Trust Principal Distributions

The principal of the trust fund is ultimately distributed to the beneficiaries, at the latest upon termination of the trust. Trust principal represents either a gift or an inheritance received by the beneficiary from the grantor. Gifts and inheritances are neither taxable income to the recipient nor deductible from taxable income by the donor.[50] Even though the outright receipt of this gift or inheritance may be delayed for many years during the trust's administration, the income-tax-free quality of the principal distribution is retained. Since some amounts may be distributed from principal before the trust termination, it is necessary for the trust to be able to distinguish taxable distributions from tax-free distributions. Federal income tax law avoids the use of "tracing" the source of distributions between trust income or trust principal to accomplish this purpose. Instead, the Internal Revenue Code creates a special computation[51] referred to as "distributable net income" (DNI) as well as special rules concerning taxability of distributions. Basically, the approach is to compute all taxable income regardless of whether it arose from a principal transaction of the trust or from an income transaction. All distributions, whether made in cash or by direct, in-kind transfer of trust principal assets to the beneficiary, are treated as distributions of DNI.

.04 Special Rules Concerning Distributable Net Income and Distributions

There are two primary functions of distributable net income: (1) to set the maximum amount that the trust is entitled to take as an income tax deduction for distributions to beneficiaries; and (2) to set the maximum amount that the beneficiaries are required to include in their income. Due to

---

[49] Code Sec. 642(b).

[50] Code Sec. 102.

[51] Code Sec. 643(a).

the nature of trust income and the interrelationship between income transactions and principal transactions, some special adjustments are necessary.

.041 Exemption adjustment

The specific exemption that the trust is permitted to deduct from its taxable income is not allowed in calculating DNI so that this does not reduce the amount potentially taxable to the beneficiary.[52] For trusts that are required to distribute all income currently and that have no recognized capital gains or losses, this always results in trust taxable income of negative $300.

.042 Interest adjustment

Interest derived from tax-exempt municipal bonds is included in distributable net income. However, the trust must account for the portion of its DNI consisting of tax-exempt interest separately.[53] Although the trust theoretically "deducts" the full amount of its DNI, it deducts the portion consisting of tax-exempt interest specifically from that source and, as a result, does not reduce the amount of the trust taxable income by the part of the distribution deduction that consists of tax-exempt interest. Correspondingly, the beneficiary includes the full amount of DNI attributable to trust distributions that the beneficiary has received in income, including any tax-exempt interest income included in DNI. However, amounts distributed from the trust retain the same quality in the hands of the receiving beneficiary as those amounts had in the hands of the trust.[54] As a result, the municipal bond interest received by a beneficiary from a trust remains tax exempt.

.043 Capital gain and loss adjustment

Capital gains and losses resulting from the sale of principal assets of the trust, which are usually considered part of trust principal, present a special issue. The income tax regulations specify that capital gains are "ordinarily" excluded from the DNI of the trust. The regulations give instances where capital gains are included in DNI, however, and these include situations in which the amount of the capital gains is (1) required to be included in trust income under the terms of the trust document or under the particular state's law; and (2) utilized on a regular basis by the trustee to decide how much to distribute to the beneficiary in circumstances where the trustee has the discretion to make distributions from principal to the current beneficiary.[55] If capital gains are excluded from DNI, the trust reports the capital gains on the trust's separate income tax return and pays the income tax from trust principal. The income tax regulations direct the exclusion of capital losses from DNI except where the amount of the loss is taken into account in determining the amount to be distributed to any beneficiary during the tax year of the trust.[56]

For simple trusts that are required to distribute all ordinary income in each year and that contain no provision for principal distributions until the trust terminates, the only category of income that ends up on the taxable income line of the fiduciary income tax return is net capital gain or loss. There is a particular disadvantage to using these trusts if a net capital loss exists.

---

[52] Code Sec. 643(a)(2).

[53] Code Sec. 643(a)(5).

[54] Code Secs. 652(b) and 662(b).

[55] Reg. § 1.643(a)-3.

[56] Reg. § 1.643(b).

Capital loss may be used to reduce capital gain without limitation. A net capital loss in excess of any capital gain can be used to offset other taxable income only up to a maximum of $3,000 per year.[57] Any loss not used up in this manner may be carried forward to future tax years of the trust.[58] The loss is treated as if it were a capital loss recognized in the future year, and the same limitations and carryforward rules continue to apply. Only capital losses that are not used in the calculation of the current year's taxable income qualify for the carryforward privilege, however. If the amount of capital loss exceeds that year's capital gain, the net capital loss, up to a maximum of $3,000, must be taken into account in computing that year's taxable income, whether or not there is any other taxable income against which to apply the loss.[59] This means that a trust with a net capital loss must "use up" up to $3,000 of the loss each year, making the used-up portion unavailable for carryforward, even if this produces a trust taxable income figure of negative $3,000. In simple trusts, which distribute all ordinary income currently, if a capital loss occurs, it will be available to offset capital gain only. If no capital gain is recognized, there will never be any ordinary trust income available to offset the loss. Consequently, the loss carryforward will be reduced by $3,000 per year, and if the term of the trust is long enough, even a very substantial capital loss may gradually be wasted.

> **Example (1):** Testamentary trust T is required to distribute all of its ordinary income to beneficiary B each year for the next 10 years, until B attains age 30, at which time trust T ends and the principal is distributed to B. In the current year, trust T produces $20,000 of ordinary income and recognizes a capital loss of $15,000.

The capital loss is excluded from DNI and consequently the full $20,000 of ordinary income is taxable to B. However, $3,000 of the capital loss must be included in the trust's taxable income, which would have been negative $300 without the inclusion of the loss. Only $12,000 of the loss may be carried forward. Unless capital gains are recognized by the trust in future years, the loss will be consumed in five taxable years of the trust without producing any income tax saving for any taxpayer.

In the tax year during which a decedent's estate or trust terminates, capital gains, as well as capital losses, are specifically required to be included in DNI,[60] which causes the ultimate result of passing on these gains or losses to the personal income tax return of the remaindermen who succeed to the estate's or trust's assets.

The following example is intended as a comprehensive overview of these principles. In order to avoid undue complexity, however, the Code Sec. 67 adjustment for expenses exceeding two percent of adjusted gross income, is ignored.

> **Example (2):** A trust fund under H's will is for the benefit of W for life, with the remainder to H and W's children. W has been receiving all income each year, under the trust terms, for the past five years. The trustee has the discretion to make any principal distributions

[57] Code Sec. 1211(b).

[58] Code Sec. 1212(b).

[59] Code Sec. 1211(b)(2)(B).

[60] Code Sec. 642(h).

needed for W's support, and this year the trustee distributes $5,000 in excess of the trust's income in view of W's needs. Although the trust has realized capital gains in prior years, no principal distributions have been made before this year.

Nontax summary of the trust account:

	Income Transactions	*Principal Transactions*
Receipts		
Income Dividends	$15,000	
Tax-Exempt Municipal Bond Interest	5,000	
Net Capital Gains		$10,000
Total Receipts	$20,000	$10,000
Expenditures		
Trustee Income Commission	−1,200	
Trustee Principal Commission		−600
Accounting Net Income	$18,800	
Net Credit to Principal		$ 9,400

In Example (2) above, before DNI can be calculated, it is necessary to determine (1) how much of the administration expenses (trustee commission) can be deducted; and (2) whether or not the capital gain is included in DNI.

The calculation of the amount of expense that is deductible is as follows:

Income Item		*Totals for Allocation*	*Allocated Share of Expense*
Dividends	$15,000		
Capital Gains	10,000		
Total Taxable		$25,000	$ 1,500
Tax-Exempt Interest		5,000	300
Totals		$30,000	$ 1,800

Assuming that the state law does not require the capital gain to be allocated to income and in view of the fact that the trustee has not adopted a regular practice of distributing the amount of capital gains to the current beneficiary, it is fair to assume that the gain is excluded from DNI. As a result, DNI is calculated as follows:

Items Taken into Account for DNI	
Dividends	$ 15,000
Tax-Exempt Interest	5,000
Admin. Expense	−1,800
DNI	$ 18,200
Adjustments to Trust's Distribution Deduction	
Tax-Exempt Interest	($ −5,000)
Admin. Expense	+300
Distribution Deduction	$ 13,500

The beneficiary, in turn, will include the following in her taxable income:

Item	*Taxable Amount*	*Tax-Exempt Amount*
Dividends	$15,000	$5,000
Less Allocable Part of Admin. Expense	−1,800	−300
Includible	$13,200	$4,700

.05 Tiers of Beneficiary's Interests

Where multiple current trust beneficiaries are entitled to trust distributions in different amounts, and where the total amount distributed among the beneficiaries exceeds DNI, the portion of each beneficiary's distribution that is treated as consisting of DNI (as opposed to tax-free distribution of principal) is not in proportion to the amount received. Instead, any beneficiary who is required to receive an amount from current income is considered to have received DNI to the full extent of the current income distribution.[61] This is known as the "first tier." After the trustee has allocated DNI to first-tier distributions, if there is any DNI remaining, the balance is allocated among those beneficiaries who have received other permissible distributions from the trust in the proportion that each of these "second-tier" beneficiaries' receipts bears to the total of all second-tier distributions.[62]

Example: H's will establishes a testamentary trust for the benefit of W, who is H's wife, and for H's children, A, B, and C. Z, the trustee, is required to distribute ½ of all current income to W each year. In addition, Z is given the discretion to make other distributions from either income or principal of the trust among W, A, B, and C, in any amounts decided on by Z, in order to enable each beneficiary to maintain his accustomed standard of living. This year, the trust's net income is $30,000. No principal expenses have been paid and DNI is also equal to $30,000. Z distributes to W the mandatory sum of $15,000 plus an additional sum of $5,000 based on Z's judgment of W's needs. Z also distributes $10,000 to A and $5,000 to B. Z makes no distribution to C. In this example, the only first-tier distribution is the payment of ½ of the current income to W. Accordingly, Z calculates the shares of DNI to be reported to the beneficiaries as follows:

Beneficiary	*Amounts Received* 1st Tier	*Amounts Received* 2nd Tier	*Share of DNI Allocated*	*Amt. Distributed as Tax-Free Principal*
W	$15,000		$15,000	$ -0-
W		$ 5,000	3,750	1,250
A	-0-	10,000	7,500	2,500
B	-0-	5,000	3,750	1,250
C	-0-	-0-	-0-	-0-
Totals	$15,000	$20,000	$30,000	$ 5,000

In this example, over 93 percent of the total amount distributed to W is considered to be DNI while only 75 percent of the amounts distributed to each of the other beneficiaries is DNI due to application of the tier system.

[61] Code Sec. 662(a)(1).

[62] Code Sec. 662(a)(2).

.06 Special Principal Transactions Affecting DNI and Current Income

Not all amounts received by a trust that are subject to federal income tax constitute current income that is distributable to the income beneficiary. For example, the grantor may name a trust as recipient of death benefits payable under a pension, profit-sharing, or other qualified retirement plan sponsored by the grantor's employer or as beneficiary of the grantor's individual retirement account. Any amounts the trust might receive from these sources upon the grantor's death constitute an addition to the principal of the trust fund and are not ordinarily distributable to the current income beneficiary. Nevertheless, most or all of these death benefits constitute taxable income to the trust in the nature of income in respect of a decedent.

> **Example:** Some years ago, A established a living trust for his son, S, for life. All current income is distributed to S each year, with the remainder to S's descendants per stirpes. During the current year, the trust receives interest on its principal investments in the amount of $20,000 plus $150,000 as a lump-sum distribution of death benefits under a pension plan in which A had been a participant. Although DNI is $170,000, S is only entitled to receive the current income, for which the trust receives a distribution deduction. The trust pays income tax on the balance.

Taxable income received by a trust attributable to items which, by their nature, are properly allocated to the trust principal and are not distributable to the current income beneficiary have been referred to as "principal income" or as "corpus income," which presents an amusing oxymoron.

.07 Related Issues—Estate Distributions to Testamentary Trusts

If the decedent's will directs that part or all of the estate is to be held in trust, there are two separate administrative processes. First, there is the estate settlement, which consists of gathering and making an inventory of assets, paying and settling expenses and claims against the estate, and filing the necessary income, estate, and inheritance tax returns. The executor then distributes the assets; if there is a testamentary trust, that means turning the assets over from the estate to the trustee. The second administration begins in the trustee's hands only after the estate distributes to the trust. Depending on such factors as the extent and complexity of the estate, whether there are legal claims against the estate, and the executor's work load, estate administration may require from several months to several years. The income generated by the estate assets during estate administration, before the principal is turned over to the trust, raises the following questions: (1) Who is entitled to this income? (2) Do the income tax consequences remain with the estate or pass through to the trust? (3) If tax consequences pass through to the trust, do they stop there or do they continue into the hands of the trust income beneficiary? There are various possibilities.

.071 Entitlement to estate income

Whether a beneficiary of a testamentary trust has a right to the income from assets held in an estate before distribution from the estate to the trust depends upon the governing state law and the terms of the decedent's will. As a general rule, the estate is not required to account to the trust beneficiaries for the income generated on estate assets after the date of death and before the trust is established. This is a practical rule that gives the executor greater freedom to use estate income, as well as principal estate assets, for the needs of estate settlement. There are significant exceptions to this rule, as described below.

Specific requirements of the will. The will may contain a provision that the income from the trust share be distributed to the trust beneficiary beginning with the date of death. While it might not be possible or practical for the executor to make a principal distribution to the trust immediately, the executor can be required to calculate the amount of income that would have been produced by the trust, if a trust had been set aside, and to pay that income to the trust beneficiary directly from the estate. In some cases, the starting date for these mandatory distributions is within a very short period of time after the date of death.

Executor discretion. Where the assets of the estate are clearly sufficient to pay all claims and taxes, the payment of income from the estate to the trust beneficiary will not cause cash flow problems or otherwise hinder estate settlement. Because failure to pay the income may cause financial difficulty to the beneficiary, the executor may make payments directly to the trust beneficiary, even in the absence of a specific direction in the will.

State law protection of surviving spouse and other family members. The laws of some states provide for required distributions to the surviving spouse and other surviving dependent family members. These distributions, usually described as a percentage of the value of the principal assets, must be made in each year before the trust fund is established, beginning with the year of death. These laws are known as "widow's allowance" and "family allowance" payment laws.

Qualification for federal estate tax marital deduction. Testamentary trusts that are intended to qualify for the federal estate tax marital deduction are required to contain a provision that causes the income rights of the surviving spouse to arise as of the date of death of the first spouse. The general rules governing marital deduction trusts and their use in estate planning are discussed in detail at ¶ 504 of Chapter 5.

.072 Pass-through of income tax characteristics

In line with the general purpose of the fiduciary income tax system to avoid tracing as much as possible, all amounts distributed from estates are treated as distributions of DNI to the extent that the estate has DNI in the tax year during which the distribution occurs.[63] Since estate distributions are not ordinarily required to be made in the year the income is received by the estate, the majority of estate distributions are second-tier amounts. If the executor makes distributions directly to the income beneficiary of a testamentary trust, it is proper for the executor to report the DNI directly to the trust beneficiary as if there were no trust involved.

When estate principal distributions occur as partial or full funding of a testamenary trust, all income tax characteristics are passed along from the estate to the trust; the estate must take an income tax deduction for distributions to beneficiaries to the extent of the amount of the distribution or the amount of the estate's DNI, whichever is less. The principal of the trust must

[63] Code Secs. 661 and 662.

report a corresponding amount in the nature of "principal income." This is another example of an instance in which the trust receives an amount that is treated as taxable income for income tax purposes but that is part of the principal assets of the trust, not distributable to the current trust income beneficiary. This is known as a "trapping distribution" because the income tax consequences passing from the estate are trapped at the trust level and are not permitted to be passed along to the trust income beneficiary. In order to assist the trustee with the trust's income tax reporting in providing the income tax information to the trust, the executor may identify such distributions as "a share of DNI due to corpus distributions" or similarly, so that the trustee will be reminded not to include any of this income in the part of the trust DNI used to determine the amount that the trust income beneficiary receives.

While the income tax characteristics passing from an estate to a testamentary trust due to a corpus distribution do not affect the amount to which the trust's current income beneficiary is entitled, a trapping distribution may affect the character of the amount received by the beneficiary.

Example: The estate of D and the testamentary trust TT are both on calendar-year income tax reporting. On December 31 of year 1, estate D makes a partial principal distribution to trust TT in the amount of $164,060, consisting entirely of taxable DNI. The trustee pays federal income tax from the trust principal in the amount of $64,060 and immediately invests the balance of $100,000 in tax-exempt municipal bonds yielding seven percent. On December 31 of year 2, estate D makes an additional corpus distribution to trust TT in the amount of $28,000, also consisting of fully taxable DNI. During year 2, trust TT receives $7,000 of tax-exempt municipal bond interest based on the investment made on December 31 of year 1 and the trustee distributes $7,000 to B, the income beneficiary of trust TT.

DNI of trust TT for year 2 is computed as follows:

(1) Share of DNI from estate D—due solely to corpus distribution	$28,000
(2) Municipal Bond Interest earned by Trust TT on its own investments	7,000
Total DNI	$35,000

Of the total DNI, the only taxable amount represents "principal income" caused by the trapping distribution from estate D. B is not entitled to this amount. It may be tempting to conclude that the trustee may allocate the municipal bond interest of $7,000 to B, since that is the only amount of current income that B receives, and report this to B as trust DNI consisting exclusively of tax-exempt municipal bond interest. However, the allocation rules[64] require that the components of DNI, including any "principal income" distributions from another fiduciary, must be included in determining the character of the trust DNI distributed to B, even though B has no claim to the amount of the trapping distribution that is principal in nature. As a result, a proportionate allocation must be made by the trustee of trust TT as follows:

---

[64] Reg. § 1.662(b)-1.

	Total DNI of Trust TT	Amount of DNI Reported to B
Taxable DNI passed through from Estate D	$28,000	$5,600
Municipal Bond Interest	7,000	1,400
Total	$35,000	$7,000

.08 In-Kind Principal Distributions

In some cases, it is appropriate for the trustee to make trust principal distributions "in kind," that is, by transferring ownership of a principal asset of the trust to a beneficiary. When this occurs, three income tax issues present themselves:

(1) To what extent, if any, does an in-kind distribution result in DNI passing from the trust to the beneficiary?

(2) If the value of the principal asset, distributed in kind, exceeds the trust's cost basis, does the trust recognize a capital gain?

(3) What is the beneficiary's cost basis for determining future gain or loss when the beneficiary later sells the asset?

To some extent, the Internal Revenue Code specifies the income tax consequences and, to some extent, the trustee is permitted to make elections that determine the results.

.081 Effect on DNI

In the case of an in-kind distribution from a trust, the trust is entitled to a distribution deduction and the beneficiary is treated as receiving an appropriate amount of DNI. However, in most cases, in-kind distributions are second-tier. Therefore, if the total of first-tier distributions equals or exceeds the amount of DNI, there is no income tax consequence to the beneficiary as a result of receiving the transfer of the trust principal asset.

> **Example:** A testamentary trust is required to distribute all current income to beneficiary A, and the trustee, T, has the discretion to make principal distributions to beneficiary A or beneficiary B. In the current year the trust's DNI is $15,000. The trustee distributes $15,000 to A and also distributes 100 shares of XYZ stock to B as a permissible distribution of principal. The first-tier distribution to A carries with it all of the DNI, and the in-kind distribution to B is a tax-free distribution.

.082 Election to recognize gain or loss at the trust level

When an in-kind distribution occurs, if the cost basis of the principal asset in the trustee's hands is either more or less than the current fair market value of the asset (which is almost always the case), gain or loss is ordinarily not reportable by the trust for income tax purposes. However, the trustee has the option of electing to treat the distribution as if it were a sale of the asset, in which case taxable gain or loss is reportable by the trust.[65] If the trustee does not make this election, the maximum amount of DNI that is reportable to

[65] Code Sec. 643(e)(3).

the recipient is equal to the cost basis of the distributed asset in the trustee's hands.[66] Conversely, if the trustee makes the election, the maximum amount of DNI that may be reportable to the recipient is the fair market value of the asset as of the date on which it is distributed. Note, however, that since in-kind distributions are second tier, the amount of DNI to be allocated is often zero.

.083 Tax cost basis in the hands of the recipient

In-kind distributions of trust principal assets ordinarily result in a carryover cost basis; that is, the cost basis for purposes of determining gain upon the future sale of the asset in the recipient's hands is the same as if the basis had been in the hands of the trustee immediately before the distribution.[67] However, if the trustee makes the special election to treat the distribution as if it were a sale and to recognize gain or loss, then the cost basis in the recipient's hands is the fair market value on the date of distribution.[68]

.084 Satisfaction of specific obligations of the trust

If the trust's distribution of an asset in kind is in satisfaction of a specific dollar obligation owed by the trust, the trustee has no election, and gain or loss is recognized for income tax purposes.[69]

> **Example:** The terms of a trust established under A's will provide that income is payable to A's child, B, until B reaches age 30, at which time the balance of the trust must be distributed to B. The will further provides that the trustee is required to distribute $50,000 from the principal of the trust fund if and when B becomes married before reaching age 30. B is married at the age of 26, whereupon the trustee distributes 500 shares of XYZ stock, with a tax cost to the trust of $10,000 and a fair market value of $50,000. The trust must include a capital gain of $40,000 on its federal income tax return. B's tax cost basis for the stock is $50,000.

¶ 304 TRUST ACCUMULATION DISTRIBUTIONS

The following sections discuss the rules and income tax consequences of trust accumulation distributions.

.01 Purpose of Special Rules

The Internal Revenue Code provides special rules for trusts that permit income to be accumulated for future distribution to a current beneficiary or to the remaindermen, that is, to anyone other than the grantor or spouse. These rules were originally intended to avoid potential income tax advantages that taxpayers might otherwise obtain through the use of trusts owing to potential differences in income tax brackets. If the trust document gives the trustee sufficient discretion regarding income accumulations and distributions, the trustee might accumulate income in years during which the beneficiary's other taxable income is high and distribute the accumulations when the beneficiary has little taxable income from sources outside the trust. In prior years, there was greater potential to use trust accumulation distributions in this manner.

---

[66] Code Sec. 643(e)(2).
[67] Code Sec. 643(e)(1).
[68] Code Sec. 643(e)(1)(B).
[69] Code Sec. 1001(c).

Under the current income tax rate structure, however, this potential is greatly reduced. For 1995, the lowest income tax rate of 15 percent is imposed only on the first $1,550 of trust taxable income and a trust reaches the highest income tax rate of 39.6 percent on taxable income in excess of $7,650. Married people who file separate returns are subject to the least favorable income tax rate structure of all individual taxpayers. For them, the 15 percent bracket extends to the first $19,500 of taxable income and they do not reach the 39.6 percent top bracket until taxable income exceeds $128,250. Since the trust income tax rate structure is much more severe than that imposed on even the most highly taxed individual taxpayer, the use of trust income accumulation strategies to lower the overall income tax burden is very unlikely. Nevertheless, these rules still exist.

Under the trust accumulation rules, it is necessary for the trustee of any trust that is permitted to accumulate income according to the trust terms to maintain records concerning accumulations as long as the trust exists, even if it spans several decades. In any year during which the total of trust distributions exceeds the current year's income, the trustee must determine whether the excess constitutes a distribution of previously accumulated income.

.02 Calculating Separate Income Tax on Accumulation Distributions

The following is a simplified, thumbnail sketch of how the trustee and the beneficiary calculate the income tax on a trust accumulation distribution.[70]

(1) The trustee determines the number of years (N − 1) preceding the excess distribution year during which the trust has made accumulations of income. However, any preceding year during which the amount of the accumulation is less than 25 percent of the average accumulation amount made during all accumulation years is disregarded.

(2) The beneficiary who is the recipient of the accumulation distribution selects three out of five tax years immediately preceding the year in which the excess distribution occurs as a calculation base period. In making the selection, the beneficiary must exclude the year in which personal taxable income was the highest and the year in which taxable income was the lowest during the five-year period.

(3) The amount of the excess distribution is divided by N − 1 to arrive at an average accumulation amount.

(4) The average accumulation amount is added to the beneficiary's actual taxable income for each of the three base period years, and the beneficiary's personal income tax for each base period year is re-calculated in order to determine what the theoretical income tax for each of the base period years would have been if the average accumulation amount had been included in the beneficiary's income for each year.

(5) The beneficiary's actual income tax for each base period year is subtracted from the theoretical income tax for each base period year, and the sum of the three excess tax amounts is divided by three in order to arrive at the average increase in tax.

(6) Next, the average increase is multiplied by N − 1 to determine the beneficiary's gross separate tax on the accumulation distribution.

[70] Code Secs. 665-668, inclusive.

(7) Finally, the amount of the income tax paid by the trust during the accumulation years allocable to the excess distribution (which is computed by another special formula) is subtracted from the gross separate tax, and the result is the amount of income tax that the beneficiary must actually pay as a result of receiving the accumulation distribution. It is just about that simple!

.03 Avoiding Accumulation Distributions

Obviously, the computations relating to accumulation distributions are extremely complex. The trustee, as well as the beneficiary, may wish to avoid these special calculations. There is an important exception to the accumulation rules, as well as a permissible method, which the trustees of certain trusts may use to prevent accumulations from occurring.

.031 Exception to accumulation rules

Amounts accumulated during any year of the trust before the birth of the beneficiary who will ultimately become the actual recipient of the excess distribution, or before such beneficiary has attained age 21, are completely disregarded for purposes of the accumulation distribution rules.[71] However, that does not mean that the trustee can dispense with the recordkeeping requirements for such years. If a beneficiary, who is presumed to be the ultimate recipient and who is under age 21 when the accumulation occurs, should die before receiving the excess distribution, it is possible that the remainder may become distributable to a person who was over age 21 when the accumulation was made.

.032 Avoidance of accumulation rules

The trustee of a trust that is not required but permitted to accumulate income may properly make a policy decision that accumulations are to be avoided except in the case of compelling nontax considerations. The process of accounting for all of the trust income and making sure that all net income is distributed before the end of the year could create a serious logjam for the trustee during the last week in December. For this reason, the trustee is given a 65-day time period after the end of the trust's tax year in which to make elective distributions.[72] If the trustee makes the special election on the trust's income tax return, distributions during this time period are treated as if made during the preceding tax year of the trust.

---

[71] Code Sec. 665(b).

[72] Code Sec. 663(b).

Chapter 4

The Federal Unified Transfer Tax System

¶ 401 LIFETIME TRANSFERS—THE GIFT TAX

The Federal Unified Transfer Tax System contains two major components: the gift tax and the estate tax. This section discusses the federal gift tax rules, the exclusions to these rules, and the exemptions from this system.

.01 General Application of the Federal Gift Tax Rules

The Internal Revenue Code imposes a gift tax on gratuitous transfers, which are transfers of money, property, or investments made under circumstances in which the recipient either pays nothing in return or pays something in return that has a value less than that received.[1] There is no requirement that the transferor intended to cause a benefit to the recipient; the transferor's motive is not relevant.[2] There is an exception, however, for transfers of unequal value and payments of insufficient value made in the ordinary course of business so that no taxable gift occurs in case of a "bad bargain."[3]

Before any gift tax is imposed, it must be clear that the gift is "complete" in the sense that the transferor has given up substantially all control over the gift property.[4] In case of a gift to a revocable trust, or to a trust over which the grantor has retained the right to remove the original beneficiaries and to substitute new beneficiaries in their place, a completed gift has not occurred. The importance of this distinction is twofold:

(1) If a completed gift has taken place at the time of the transfer to the trust, any and all gift tax liability is calculated and paid immediately. Thereafter, distributions made by the trustee to the beneficiary are not counted as taxable gifts made by the original grantor.

(2) On the other hand, if the transfer to the trust is an incomplete gift, no gift tax event takes place upon the initial transfer to the trust; however, each trust distribution to any person other than the grantor is counted as a taxable gift made by the grantor.

The transfer of money or property to a trust fund is not a gift to the trust as an entity. The gift tax law requires further analysis of all transfers to corporations, partnerships, and trusts in order to determine the natural person or persons who benefit from the transfer.[5] In the case of multiple current trust beneficiaries, the fact that each individual beneficiary might be considered to receive a percentage of the value transferred presents no particular problem because the gift tax calculations focus on the total value transferred rather than on the amount each beneficiary receives. However, where the interests of different trust beneficiaries do not arise simultaneously, the transfer to the trust is treated as a series of two or more separate gifts. The gift to those who receive the immediate benefits from the trust is a percentage value, based on

[1] Code Sec. 2501(a)(1).
[2] Reg. § 25.2511-1(g)(1).
[3] Reg. § 25.2512-8.
[4] Reg. § 25.2511-2.
[5] Reg. § 25.2511-1.

the duration of the initial beneficiary's interest. The portion of the value of a gift made to a trust beneficiary whose interest will arise in the future, such as a remainderman, is the discounted present value of the beneficiary's future interest. For transfers that take place after April 30, 1989, the calculation of these values is made under section 7520 of the Internal Revenue Code, which takes into account not only the value transferred and the time period of the interest but also the prevailing rate of interest. The regulations[6] refer to IRS Publication No. 1457, "Actuarial Tables Alpha Volume," which provides tables and explanations for the calculation of actuarial factors in more complex fact situations, and state[7] that the Internal Revenue Service will provide factors in response to a ruling request in extremely complicated cases.

Even though the remainderman's interest may not come into existence for many years, perhaps only after the death of one or more current beneficiaries, any gift tax imposed with respect to the remainder interest is payable at the time of the initial transfer so long as the transfer to the trust meets the "completed gift" test.

> **Example:** In February 1995, A transfers $100,000 to an irrevocable living trust, which provides for income to A's spouse, B, for life, with the remainder distributable to the children of A and B in equal shares. B is age 56 at the time of the transfer. If the current interest rate for purposes of this calculation is eight percent, the value of B's life interest is $76,315 and the children's remainder interest is valued at $23,685.

.02 Gift Tax Exclusions and Exemptions

A taxpayer is entitled to an exemption or an exclusion for present transfers of property. The following sections describe these rules.

.021 Annual exclusion and present interest rule

In order to reduce the administrative burden of gift tax reporting and to permit transfers of a moderate amount of wealth free of all transfer tax, the Internal Revenue Code provides for an annual gift exclusion of $10,000 per recipient.[8] There is no limit to the number of recipients; therefore, the potential donor with the following specific attributes can make large tax-free transfers of wealth in any year or in every year:

(1) significant wealth beyond his personal needs;

(2) a large number of family members or other objects of his bounty; and

(3) the desire to transfer wealth during his lifetime.

Owing to the high gift and estate tax rates, the wealthy are often well advised to make annual transfers in order to utilize as many annual exclusions as possible in each year. This is particularly important because:

(1) a gift that qualifies for the annual exclusion can escape estate tax and generation-skipping transfer tax as well as gift tax; and

(2) the exclusion is not allowed to be stored for future use. It is lost for any year in which the donor makes no qualifying transfer.

---

[6] Reg. § 25.2512-5(d).

[7] Reg. § 25.2512-5(d)(4).

[8] Code Sec. 2503(b).

While gifts that take advantage of the annual exclusion are appealing from a pure tax-planning perspective, the potential donor may hesitate for fear that the recipient would not handle the responsibility of wealth in a mature manner. A living trust can provide the solution to this dilemma in some circumstances.

In order to qualify for the annual exclusion, the value transferred must be in the nature of a present interest; with respect to any gift or any part of a gift that constitutes a future interest, the annual exclusion is not available.[9] In the example at .01, above, the value transferred from A to B is a present interest that can qualify for the annual exclusion, while the remainder interest, transferred to the children of A and B, is a future interest for which no annual exclusion is allowed.

The "present interest" requirement is strictly applied in the sense that even a brief delay in the right of the recipient to use or to receive the income or other benefits of the transferred property results in loss of the annual exclusion.

> **Example:** A transfers $50,000 to an irrevocable living trust for the benefit of his five children. The trustee is directed to distribute the income among the beneficiaries each year on a sprinkle basis according to their relative needs, with no requirement of equality of treatment among them as to income shares. After 10 years, the trust terminates and the balance is distributed in equal shares to the children.

In this example, although the income benefit will flow from the trust to the children immediately, it is impossible to predict how much of the income any particular child will receive. For this reason, no annual exclusion is permitted,[10] and the full value of the transfer is a taxable gift. By contrast, if the terms of the trust had required the income to be distributed in equal shares, five annual exclusions would have been available, each one equal to the actuarial value of one-fifth of the income interest.

Since the actuarial value of an income interest for 10 years (using an eight percent interest rate for purposes of the Code Sec. 7520 valuation) is .53681, each annual exclusion would be:

$$1/5 \times .53681 \times \$50{,}000 \text{ or } \$5{,}368.10.$$

The actuarial factor for the remainder interest is .46319 so that the part of the gift attributable to the remainder is:

$$\$50{,}000 \times .46319 \text{ or } \$23{,}159.50.$$

No part of the remainder qualifies for the annual exclusion.

.022 Crummey *withdrawal power and hanging power*

Establishing a trust with immediate income rights given to children or other beneficiaries may not be in accord with the financial plan of the prospective donor. In fact, an important goal may be to withhold or accumulate funds for the beneficiary's future needs or until the beneficiary is older and, presumably, wiser. There are a few trust designs that can accommodate this objective without sacrificing the annual exclusion. One alternative is the

---

[9] Code Sec. 2503(b).

[10] Reg. § 25.2503-3(c), Ex. (3).

Code Sec. 2503(c) trust, described at ¶ 503.052. It is also possible to obtain the annual exclusion for a transfer to an irrevocable living trust if the beneficiary has the right to make a withdrawal from the trust. This aspect of trust design, whereby a beneficiary has the right to make a withdrawal each time a transfer is made to the trust, with the idea of making annual gifts to the trust in order to use the annual gift tax exclusion efficiently, is called the "*Crummey* power," named for a tax case in which the validity of the technique was first recognized.[11] There may be several beneficiaries who each hold *Crummey* powers, resulting in multiple gift tax annual exclusions. It is permissible for the donor to make it known to these beneficiaries that the withdrawal power has been placed in the trust for the purpose of obtaining the gift tax annual exclusion and that the grantor does not want the beneficiaries actually to exercise their withdrawal rights. Even a verbal agreement not to withdraw is allowable. However, any legal restriction on the beneficiary's right to withdraw, such as a written agreement signed by the beneficiary, results in loss of the annual exclusion.

In order to qualify for a *Crummey* power, the beneficiary must have:

(1) an unrestricted right to withdraw;

(2) a reasonable period of time in which to exercise that right; and

(3) reasonable notification of the existence of the right.

Where the right arises each time a transfer to the trust is made, the third requirement includes notification to the beneficiary each time a transfer to the trust occurs. Within the confines of these requirements, considerable restrictions may be placed on the *Crummey* power. Although the right must be unrestricted, it may be limited to a maximum yearly amount and made noncumulative so that if no withdrawal is made in one year it does not increase the maximum withdrawal allowed in any subsequent year. Conferring a *Crummey* power on a beneficiary who is a minor, and therefore legally incapable of making the withdrawal, nevertheless results in an annual exclusion so long as a guardian could exercise the withdrawal right on the minor's behalf and no legal impediment to the appointment of a guardian exists.

Some trusts have been designed to include a significant number of holders of *Crummey* powers—often every relative who can reasonably be relied upon *not* to exercise his right to withdraw! In this way, the number of annual exclusions allowable, and therefore the total value that may be transferred into the trust each year, can become very significant. Over a number of years, considerable wealth might escape all transfer tax. The IRS has taken a generally favorable view of the *Crummey* power. In recent years, however, it has advanced the position that the *Crummey* power held by an individual who has no other significant beneficial interest in the trust does not result in the transferor's receiving an annual gift tax exclusion. This suggests moderation in planning for the number of separate *Crummey* powers to be incorporated in tax-planning-oriented trusts.

A potential obstacle to maximum use of the *Crummey* power is the gift tax event that occurs when the holder of the withdrawal right (intentionally) fails to take any withdrawal. The result is sometimes called a "reverse gift"; that is, the holder of the power may be treated as making a gift back to the trust through failure to take what was available under the right of withdrawal.

---

[11] *Crummey v. Comm'r*, 397 F2d 82 (9th Cir. 1968).

The result, then, is two potential gift tax events that arise when periodic gifts are made to a trust that contains *Crummey* powers:

(1) the gift made by the grantor of the trust, which gives rise to the beneficiary's right to withdraw; and

(2) the gift made by the power holder by failure to take the withdrawal.

Since a *Crummey* withdrawal power is treated as a general power of appointment for gift tax purposes, its exercise *or release* is treated as a gift by the person holding the power.[12] In the typical case, the power holder does not formally release the power in any year, but the failure to exercise the power is treated as a lapse. The lapse of a general power of appointment is, in turn, treated as a release to the extent that the value controlled by the power, lapsed in any year, exceeds the greater of $5,000 or five percent of the value of the trust fund.[13] Some trust funds contain little principal value initially but are used as receptacles for annual gifts. In that case, the lapse rule can cause the power holder to be treated as making a gift each year to the extent that the amount given to the trust, and covered by the *Crummey* power, exceeds $5,000.

One solution to this dilemma is to construct the *Crummey* withdrawal right so that it does not exceed $5,000 per year. In case of this design, the lapse of the power does not cause a gift tax event because of the so-called "five-and-five" aspect of the lapse rule.

Another solution is a kind of hybrid *Crummey* power known as a "hanging" power. The trust document specifies that, at the end of each year, any unused portions of *Crummey* withdrawal powers lapse only to the extent that the lapse does not result in the power holder's being treated as making a gift. The excess value subject to the withdrawal right continues or "hangs around" until the first future year during which its lapse will not result in a reverse gift.

> **Example:** B creates a living trust to which he intends to make periodic gifts. The trust provides for *Crummey* powers to be held by C, D, and E, who are B's children. Each child has the right to withdraw up to $10,000 per year from the trust fund. The document further provides that the lapse of these withdrawal rights occurs only to the extent that the C, D, and E are not thereby treated as making a taxable gift. B transfers $30,000 in cash to the trust fund in the first year and nothing in the second year. None of the children make any withdrawals from the trust fund.

Because of the *Crummey* powers contained in the trust, the transfer by B in the first year is treated as if it were a transfer of a present interest in property of $10,000 to each of his children. Assuming no other gifts are made by B that year, the transfer is fully covered by B's gift tax annual exclusions.

By failing to make any withdrawals during the first year, C, D, and E might each be treated as making a reverse gift of $5,000, the extent to which the total subject to their withdrawal rights exceeds the amount permitted to lapse under the five-and-five part of the lapse rule. Because the withdrawal rights are designed in the trust document as hanging powers, however, only $5,000 of each power holder's withdrawal right lapses in the first year, and the

---

[12] Code Sec. 2514(b).

[13] Code Sec. 2514(e).

balance of each withdrawal right lapses in the second year. Consequently, no reportable gift transactions occur.

.023 Political, educational, and medical exemptions

All gifts to political parties and political campaign funds are exempt from the gift tax.[14] The payment of educational and medical expenses is also exempt, subject, however, to the peculiar requirement that the benefactor make all payments directly to the provider of the services.[15] This means that if you wish to send your favorite nephew to Harvard, you have to make the check payable to the bursar. If you give the payment to your nephew, even if it can be proved that he used the funds for tuition, you have made a taxable gift. There is neither an annual limitation nor a lifetime maximum placed on the amounts that can qualify for these special gift tax exemptions.

.03 Interspousal Transfers—The Unlimited Gift Tax Marital Deduction

Direct transfers between husband and wife, which would qualify as taxable gifts, are subject to an unlimited deduction of 100 percent of the value of all such interspousal transfers.[16] The marital deduction is not allowed, however, for gifts of certain types of terminable interests.[17] A terminable interest is a property ownership right that will come to an end after a period of time or upon the occurrence of some specified event in the future. There is also an unlimited marital deduction for federal estate tax purposes.[18] The concept of terminable interests and the application of the tax rules is similar both for gift tax purposes and for estate tax purposes. For this reason, a more detailed discussion of this concept is presented at ¶ 402.053, which deals with the estate tax marital deduction.

There is one special restriction on the marital deduction, however, that must be mentioned here. If the transferor's spouse is not a U.S. citizen, the marital deduction does not apply.[19] The annual exclusion remains available for lifetime transfers to a non-U.S.-citizen spouse, and the amount of the annual exclusion is expanded in case of such transfers from $10,000 per year to $100,000 per year.[20]

.04 Tax Rates and the Unified Credit Against Gift Tax

Once a donor's total gifts in any year exceed the annual exclusion, a gift tax is imposed at tax rates ranging from 18 percent to 55 percent. The rate is based on a graduated table,[21] depending on the total value transferred. Furthermore, the rates are cumulative over the donor's lifetime. This cumulative effect is obtained through a three-step calculation system,[22] as follows:

Step 1: A first tentative tax is computed from the graduated table based on the sum of the donor's present-year taxable gifts (in excess of any and all annual exclusions) plus the cumulative total of all prior years' taxable gifts.

---

[14] Code Sec. 2501(a)(5).

[15] Code Sec. 2503(e).

[16] Code Sec. 2523(a).

[17] Code Sec. 2523(b).

[18] Code Sec. 2056(a).

[19] Code Sec. 2523(i)(1).

[20] Code Sec. 2523(i)(2).

[21] Code Sec. 2001(c). See ¶ 1002.02.

[22] Code Sec. 2502(a).

Step 2: A second tentative tax is computed from the table based only on the cumulative total of prior years' taxable gifts.

Step 3: The result of Step 2 is subtracted from the result of Step 1 in order to arrive at the current year's gift tax.

There is an automatic unified credit against the gift tax, to which every taxpayer is entitled, in the amount of $192,800.[23] This credit has the effect of eliminating the gift tax payable on $600,000 in value of all cumulative lifetime taxable gifts. Any gift tax credit not used is carried forward to future years. The cumulative amount of $600,000 in value of gift transfers that is shielded from tax by the gift tax credit is sometimes referred to as the "exemption equivalent" or the "credit-shelter equivalent."

.05 Gift Splitting by Married Donors

A married donor may be entitled to treat all gifts made to persons other than his spouse as if one-half of the gift were made by the non-donor spouse to the recipient if the non-donor spouse consents in writing to this so-called gift-splitting election.[24] This has the effect of doubling both the annual exclusion, for gifts of present interests, and the $600,000 credit-shelter equivalent. Consent of the non-donor spouse is required because of the potential disadvantage to the non-donor spouse resulting from "using up" the non-donor spouse's available exclusions and, more specifically, the non-donor spouse's gift tax credit. The financial consultant must exercise care in advising the non-donor spouse on the advisability of consenting to gift splitting, particularly in the case of second marriages where each spouse has children by a first marriage.

.06 Special Gift Tax Treatment of Powers of Appointment

The transfer of property pursuant to a power of appointment may not be a taxable gift by the power holder.[25] The underlying theory is that the power holder is acting as an agent of the original donor rather than making a gift in his own right. If the rights of the person who possesses a power of appointment are so extensive as to rise to the equivalent of outright ownership of the property subject to the power, then the exercise, release, or lapse of the power is a taxable gift. Under the Internal Revenue Code definition, a power of appointment is equivalent to outright ownership of the subject property if it may be exercised in favor of any one or more of the following:

(1) the holder of the power or the holder's spouse;

(2) the creditors of the holder of the power;

(3) the estate of the holder of the power; or

(4) the creditors of the power holder's estate.

Powers exercisable in this manner are categorized as "general powers of appointment."[26] Powers that restrict the holder so that they may not be exercised in favor of any of the four specified categories of recipients are referred to as "limited," "non-general," or "special" powers of appointment. The exercise, release, or lapse of a non-general power is not a taxable gift.

A power of withdrawal over a trust fund is treated as a general power of appointment for gift tax purposes (that is, a power exercisable in favor of the

[23] Code Sec. 2505. See ¶ 1002.01.

[24] Code Sec. 2513.

[25] Code Sec. 2514(b).

[26] Code Sec. 2514(c).

power holder). Any actual withdrawal is not a taxable gift because that would amount to a gift by the power holder to himself. The release or lapse of a power of withdrawal may result in a taxable gift if the consequence is to increase the amount that some beneficiary other than the power holder will receive from the trust.

> **Example (1):** A's will establishes a testamentary trust that provides income to A's child, B (presently age 45), for life, with the remainder to B's children in equal shares. B is also given the right to withdraw up to 20 percent of the principal value of the trust in any year on a noncumulative basis. The trust has a value of $200,000 in the current year. B receives the income but makes no withdrawals from principal.

In this case, B makes a taxable gift by the lapse of his general power of appointment. B's children will benefit because the remainder would have been diminished if B had made a withdrawal. The amount of the gift is not 20 percent of $200,000, however, since B continues to receive the income. Once again, B cannot be considered to make a taxable gift to himself. The amount of B's gift is the present value of the remainder interest in the $40,000 of principal that B could have withdrawn from the principal of the trust. The actuarial factor for a remainder interest, where the life beneficiary is age 45 and the applicable federal rate is eight percent, is .13590, resulting in a gift by B to the remaindermen of:

$$.13590 \times \$40{,}000 \text{ or } \$5{,}436.00.$$

There is some relief from the harsh effects of the gift tax rules affecting lapsed powers of withdrawal from trusts.

(1) If the withdrawal power is restricted to amounts needed for the health, education, support, or maintenance of the power holder, it is not a general power of appointment and its lapse is not a taxable gift.[27] This is known as the "ascertainable standard" rule. Examples of phrases that create ascertainable standard withdrawal powers are: support; support in reasonable comfort; maintenance in health and reasonable comfort; support in (the power holder's) accustomed manner of living; education, including college and professional education; health; medical, dental, hospital and nursing expenses; and expenses of invalidism. Use of the words comfort, happiness, and welfare with no further limitations do not create ascertainable standard withdrawal powers.[28]

(2) If the withdrawal power is subject to an annual maximum of no more than the greater of $5,000 or five percent of the value of the trust principal, and the power is noncumulative from year to year, its lapse does not result in a taxable gift. This is the five-and-five power.[29]

(3) If the withdrawal power is noncumulative and based on an annual amount or percentage greater than the limit of the five-and-five power rule, only the value subject to the power of withdrawal in excess of the five-and-five limit is a potential taxable gift in the event of lapse. In Example (1), this means that, in the actual gift tax calculation, the actuarial factor of .13590 would be multiplied by $30,000, that is, the value subject to the withdrawal power in excess of five percent of the

---

[27] Code Sec. 2514(c)(1).

[28] Reg. § 25.2514-1(c)(2).

[29] Code Sec. 2514(e).

total value of the trust ($40,000 minus $10,000). The result is a taxable gift of only $4,077.00.

(4) If the terms of the trust agreement give to a beneficiary a combination of an ascertainable standard withdrawal power, a five-and-five withdrawal power, and non-general powers of appointment, each power is judged separately for gift tax purposes. In the event of the lapse of one or more such powers, no taxable gift by the power holder is deemed to have occurred. This makes it possible for the grantor, through careful design of the trust document, to give a great deal of flexibility to the trust beneficiary without causing him to be treated as making taxable gifts as a result of the lapse of these powers.

Example (2): A's will creates a testamentary trust for the benefit of A's child, C, for life, with the remainder to C's children. C receives all trust income annually. In addition, C has the right to make withdrawals from the principal of the trust to the extent necessary to pay for any actual educational or medical expenses incurred by C, as well as any additional amounts needed by C to maintain his accustomed standard of living. In addition, C has the unrestricted right, in each year of the trust, to withdraw up to the greater of $5,000 or five percent of the total principal value of the trust, calculated as of the date of the withdrawal, on a noncumulative basis. Finally, C has the right to direct the trustee to make distributions of any amounts from the principal of the trust fund to anyone other than to C himself, to C's creditors, to C's estate, or to the creditor's of his estate. In the current year, C neither makes any principal withdrawals nor directs the trustee to make any principal distributions to others.

The lapse of all of these powers of appointment by C does not result in any taxable gifts. The ascertainable standard withdrawal power and the five-and-five withdrawal power are each considered separately, and each qualify for exceptions to the general rule that the lapse of a power of withdrawal or other general power of appointment is a taxable gift. The power of appointment through which C could have directed principal distributions to others is also considered separately from C's withdrawal rights. This power of appointment is clearly designed to permit C to make principal distributions to almost anyone. Since the power contains restrictions that prevent its exercise in favor of the four specific categories of possible recipients that would cause general power of appointment status, however, this is a non-general or limited power, the exercise, release, or lapse of which is not a taxable gift.

.07 Disclaimers

A disclaimer is the formal decision not to accept a gift or inheritance made by the intended recipient, who is referred to as the "disclaimant." While some might wonder why anyone would choose not to accept a gratuitous transfer, the answer lies in the gift and estate tax consequences of the transfer. A disclaimer can provide certain advantages if all of the following underlying conditions exist:

(1) The disclaimant does not need the money or property that is the subject of the intended transfer.

(2) The disclaimant wants his child or some other individual (referred to here as "the preferred recipient") to receive the subject money or property.

(3) The preferred recipient will receive the subject money or property if the disclaimer is made, either due to the terms and conditions of the original gift or bequest or by operation of the governing state law.

The advantage to the disclaimant is that a qualified disclaimer is treated as a modification of the original gift or bequest rather than as a gift by the disclaimant to the preferred recipient.[30]

Example: Grandfather GF's will provides for a bequest of $100,000 to his child, C, with the provision that if C predeceases GF, the bequest is to be distributed to GF's grandchild, GC (C's child). GF's will goes on to provide that the balance of GF's estate is to be distributed to his spouse, GM.

If C, having accepted the inheritance, transfers the funds to GC, naturally C is treated as making a taxable gift. If C disclaims the inheritance instead, under the laws of most states, C is treated as having predeceased GF so that the bequest becomes distributable to GC because of the provision of GF's will to that effect. Consequently, the ultimate economic effect of the disclaimer is the same as the intermediary gift by C to GC. The transfer tax consequences of the disclaimer, however, are different. If C disclaims, he is not treated as making a taxable gift. It is important to note, however, that from the viewpoint of the estate of GF, the transfer is treated as passing directly to GC, which may subject GF's estate to the additional transfer tax imposed on generation-skipping transfers, as explained at ¶ 403.

In order to make an intelligent decision concerning a potential disclaimer, the disclaimant must be sure of the consequences in advance. Learning, after a disclaimer has been made, that the preferred recipient will not receive the disclaimed assets is a disastrous result. This means that the financial consultant must know or must find out what the result of a prospective disclaimer will be in any particular case before discussing the technique with a client. The answer is not always found in the terms of the original document of transfer. For instance, in the above example, suppose that GF's will made no provision for the disposition of the bequest if C predeceased GF. There are two possible results of C's disclaimer under these circumstances depending on the provisions of the governing state law:

(1) The bequest to C might lapse and therefore become distributable as part of the residuary estate of GF, in which case GM receives an additional $100,000.

(2) The bequest to C might become distributable to C's descendants, the result of which is distribution to GC assuming he is C's only child.

There are provisions of laws in many states that prevent or lapse if a named beneficiary predeceases the testator or disclaims and that direct the bequest to be divided among the predeceased or disclaiming beneficiary's descendants. Such laws, known as anti-lapse statutes, would cause the result described in (2), above. Furthermore, anti-lapse statutes may apply only if the predeceased or disclaiming beneficiary is within a certain specified class of family relationship to the original transferor or testator. These complex inter-

[30] Code Sec. 2518.

relationships between the federal gift tax rules and state laws involved in disclaimer issues make the guidance of an attorney absolutely necessary in this area.

.071 Formal requirements of the qualified disclaimer

The federal gift tax law provides very specific conditions[31] that must be met in order for a disclaimer to escape treatment as a taxable gift by the disclaimant to the preferred recipient. These are:

(1) The disclaimer must be in writing and must be delivered to the original transferor or, in the case of an inheritance, to the executor or other representative of the estate.

(2) The disclaimant must not have accepted the subject property or any use or other benefit from it before making the disclaimer.

(3) The disclaimer must be made within nine months after the effective date of the transfer. In the case of an inheritance, that is nine months after the date of the testator's death rather than after the date of the will. In the case of a beneficial interest in a trust, however, the nine-month time period begins with the date on which the trust is created or, if the transfer in trust does not initially meet the completed gift test, the date on which the transfer in trust first meets that test.

It is possible that one who receives a beneficial interest in a trust might not become aware of that interest until more than nine months after the pertinent date. The federal law, however, does not currently provide any specific rule in such a case so that the more conservative assumption is that the beneficiary who finds out about the existence of a beneficial interest too late is unable to make a qualified disclaimer.

If the prospective disclaimant is under age 21 on the pertinent date, however, the nine-month period does not begin until that person reaches age 21.

(4) As a result of the disclaimer, the subject property must be distributed either under the provisions of the original document of transfer or according to the applicable state law. The disclaimant must not direct how the transfer is to be made.

(5) Generally, the disclaimed property must pass to someone other than the disclaimant, although there is something of an exception to this rule in cases where the disclaimant is the spouse of the original transferor. The usefulness of this exception in estate planning is considerable and is explored in greater detail at ¶ 505.

¶ 402 TRANSFERS TAKING PLACE AT DEATH—THE ESTATE TAX

.01 Scope of the Tax

The federal estate tax is an excise tax imposed on all property in which the decedent owns any interest at the time of death.[32] The amount subject to this tax is that part of the date-of-death fair market value of each separate

---

[31] Code Sec. 2518(b).

[32] Code Sec. 2001.

property attributable to the decedent's share of ownership.[33] For such assets as bank accounts and marketable securities, the fair market value is readily ascertainable. For other types of property, such as jewelry, art works, real estate, and closely held business interests, precise valuation is not possible.[34] The executor of the estate is required to report the value at which such property would change hands between a willing buyer and a willing seller if each had fair knowledge of the property's circumstances and if neither was compelled to buy or sell.[35] This theoretical fair market value is most frequently reported based on expert appraisals.

Certain specific property types and forms of property ownership are affected by special rules.

.011 Concurrent property interests

Any form of concurrent property interest logically suggests that the decedent's ownership was less than complete and, therefore, that less than the full value of the property may be subject to estate tax. In fact, the extent to which property interests are included in the taxable estate depends on the form of concurrent ownership involved.

Tenancy in common. A proportionate part or percentage of the value of the property owned by the decedent is included in the taxable estate.[36] By the nature of tenancy in common interests, this part may be equal to, larger, or smaller than the interests owned by the other surviving tenant or tenants in common.

Joint tenancy. During life, joint tenants hold equal interests. For estate tax purposes, however, upon the death of any one joint tenant, the full value of the property is included in the taxable estate except to the extent that the surviving tenant or tenants can prove that they supplied part or all of the funds originally used to purchase the property and that they had not received those funds by way of gift from the decedent.[37] If "contribution" to the original acquisition cost by the surviving tenant(s) is proved, a ratable share of the fair market value of the property at the date of death is excluded from the taxable estate, calculated as follows:

$$\text{Percentage of the date-of-death fair market value excluded from estate of deceased joint tenant} = \frac{\text{Part of acquisition cost furnished by surviving tenants}}{\text{Total acquisition cost}} \times \text{Total fair market value at date of death}$$

For this purpose, the amount of any borrowing used to acquire the property is included as part of the original cost, and each individual joint tenant is treated as having contributed an equal share of the borrowed amount if the joint tenants share equal liability for repayment of the borrowing.

There is a significant exception to the general rule of inclusion of joint tenancy interests that applies to married couples. If the husband and wife are the only two joint tenants, then, at the death of either spouse, only one-half of the value of the property is included in the deceased spouse's estate, regardless of the source of funds for the original acquisition.[38] Property interests of

---

[33] Code Sec. 2031(a).
[34] Reg. § 20.2031-6(b).
[35] Reg. § 20.2031-1(b).
[36] Code Sec. 2031.
[37] Code Sec. 2040(a).
[38] Code Sec. 2040(b).

husband and wife held in tenancy by the entirety receive the same estate tax treatment as joint tenancy interests. Tenancy by the entirety is a form of property ownership that is valid only in certain states and only between husband and wife.

Community property. In those states that have community property systems, the general rule is that property acquired during the marriage is automatically owned one-half by each spouse, regardless of who "earned" it. There may be exceptions for property received by a spouse through gift or inheritance. The federal estate tax rules require inclusion of only one-half of the value of community property.

.012 Life insurance

The net proceeds of the death benefit payable under all life insurance policies are included in the estate of the deceased insured for federal estate tax purposes if either one of two conditions exist:[39]

(1) If the estate is the beneficiary of the insurance policy or if, given the manner of designating the beneficiary, the executor of the deceased insured's estate has access to the insurance proceeds for use in the payment of estate expenses, debts, or taxes.

(2) If the decedent was the owner of any one or more of the incidents of ownership of the life insurance policy or if the decedent made a gift of the ownership within three years prior to the date of death. Examples of incidents of ownership of a life insurance policy include the right to change the beneficiary, the right to borrow from the accumulated policy cash value, the right to cancel the policy, etc.

.013 Annuities

For annuities payable under qualified retirement plans, as well as for commercial annuities owned by the decedent, two conditions must exist as of the date of death of the annuitant (that is, the owner of the benefit) in order to cause inclusion of the balance of the annuity's value in the owner's taxable estate:[40]

(1) Prior to death, the decedent either must have been receiving payments under the plan or must have been entitled to receive payments.

(2) After the death, some beneficiary other than the decedent must be entitled to a death benefit, whether as continuing payments or as a lump sum. In the case of a "straight life annuity," with respect to which all payments end at the death of the annuitant, this means that there is nothing left to tax. All death benefits payable under all forms of qualified retirement plans are included in the decedent's taxable estate regardless of the form of payment to the beneficiary.

.014 Beneficial interests in estates and trusts

It is possible for the beneficiary of an estate to die after the death of his benefactor but before the inheritance is received. If this occurs, the inheritance from the first estate is included as a taxable asset in the second estate. Beneficial interests in trusts, however, require more complex analysis. It is

---

[39] Code Sec. 2042.

[40] Code Sec. 2039.

only the portion of the trust subject to personal control, withdrawal rights, or other general powers of appointment that is included in the taxable estate of the trust beneficiary. For instance, if the trust beneficiary were entitled to receive all of the trust income produced by the trust during his lifetime and nothing more, then, at the death of the beneficiary, his estate would include only the amount of any income that the trust had earned during the beneficiary's life but had not yet distributed before the beneficiary's death. No part of the principal of the trust fund would be included in the trust beneficiary's taxable estate. An area of major concentration in estate planning is the design of trusts that provide lifetime benefits for the beneficiary while avoiding estate tax at his death.

.015 Powers of appointment

For federal estate tax purposes, the estate of a decedent who holds a general power of appointment at death includes the date-of-death value of the fund or property that is subject to the power.[41] As is the case for gift tax purposes, the classification of powers of appointment depends upon the identity of the person or persons for whose benefit the power of appointment may be exercised. A general power of appointment is one that may be exercised in favor of any of the following:[42]

(1) the holder of the power;

(2) the creditors of the holder of the power;

(3) the estate of the holder of the power; or

(4) the creditors of the power holder's estate.

Under current estate tax rules, the mere possession of the general power of appointment at death is enough to cause inclusion of the subject fund or property in the power holder's taxable estate. If the power of appointment provides for a disposition of the property in default of appointment, the result may be the imposition of estate tax on assets that are not directly available to help pay the tax imposed.

> **Example:** A's will establishes a trust to pay income to B for life. B also has the unrestricted right to designate who is to receive the remainder through a provision in B's will. If B does not exercise this power of appointment, A's will specifies that the remainder is to be distributed to A's nieces and nephews in equal shares.

Whether B exercises the power of appointment or fails to do so, the trust fund is included in B's estate for federal estate tax purposes. Note that if the power is not exercised by B, the remainder must be distributed to the nieces and nephews of A and is not, therefore, available to help pay B's estate tax liability.

If the provisions governing a power of appointment would have required the deceased power holder to give notice before exercising the power so that (in the absence of such notice) the power could not have been exercised at the date of death, the subject property is nevertheless included in the taxable estate of the power holder. This rule exists in order to prevent the construction of a power of appointment that escapes taxation because of skillful design rather than the true economic loss of the power.

---

[41] Code Sec. 2041.

[42] Code Sec. 2041(b)(1).

Powers of withdrawal fall into the category of general powers of appointment for purposes of the estate tax just as for purposes of the gift tax rules. The same two favorable limitations on taxation of powers of withdrawal contained in the gift tax rules are included in the estate tax provisions. These are the ascertainable standard rule and the five-and-five limitation. If the decedent's right to withdraw is limited to amounts needed to provide for his support, health, maintenance, or education, the property subject to such power that remains unexercised at death is not included in the power holder's taxable estate.[43] Under the estate tax five-and-five power rule, if there is an annual limitation placed on the power of withdrawal permitting withdrawals of up to the greater of $5,000 or five percent of the value of the subject property and if the power is noncumulative from year to year, no part of the value of the subject property is included in the taxable estate.[44] If the power of withdrawal controls a larger part of the value of the subject property, then only the part of the value of the property that could have been withdrawn in excess of the five-and-five rule limit is included.

.02 Estate Tax Calculation System

A major revision of the federal estate and gift tax system in 1976 introduced the concept of imposing a cumulative tax, under a graduated rate table (the same table used for gift tax purposes), on the combined total of lifetime taxable gifts and transfers of wealth at death.[45] This was accomplished by the design of a three-step process for calculation of the federal estate tax, as follows:

Step 1: Calculate a tentative tax based on the sum of the decedent's taxable estate plus the cumulative total of all taxable gifts made after 1976.

Step 2: Calculate a tentative tax based only on the the post-1976 taxable gifts.

Step 3: Subtract the result of Step 2 from the result of Step 1.

By combining lifetime gifts made after the effective date of the new tax system with the total taxable estate, it was possible to accomplish the goal of one graduated tax system on all gratuitous transfers made. This reduces the possible tax saving that might result from making lifetime taxable gifts in order to reduce the taxable base at death. Double taxation is avoided, however, by giving an effective credit for the gift tax through the mechanism of requiring the subtraction of the result of Step 2 from the result of Step 1.

For the purpose of this system, the total of post-1976 taxable gifts is net after allowing for any annual exclusions. Also, if a taxable gift is made after 1976, but the property that was the subject of the gift is nevertheless required to be included in the taxable estate, it is not counted twice. These items are included in the taxable estate but deducted from the total of post-1976 taxable gifts.[46]

.03 Credits Against the Estate Tax

There are several credits against the federal estate tax that must be taken into account. These credits are discussed individually below.

---

[43] Code Sec. 2041(b)(1)(A).

[44] Code Sec. 2041(b)(2).

[45] Code Sec. 2001.

[46] Code Sec. 2001(b), last sentence.

.031 Unified credit

This is a dollar-for-dollar credit that is available to each estate in the amount of $192,800.[47] Since the rates of tax are the same for both gift tax and estate tax, this credit also has the effect of eliminating all estate tax payable on each taxable estate valued at $600,000 or less. Even though the unified credit is taken for estate tax purposes whether or not the decedent has utilized any gift tax unified credit on lifetime transfers, the effective result is only one unified credit for each individual. This result is brought about through the design of the three-step estate tax calculation system described above. In Step 2, the calculation of the tentative tax on all post-1976 taxable gifts requires that the gift tax unified credit be subtracted, lowering the result of the Step 2 calculation by up to $192,800. Since the result of Step 2 is subtracted from the tentative tax calculated under Step 1, by lowering the result of Step 2 the tax payable is increased. In a roundabout way, then, this three-step estate tax calculation process "gives back" any unified credit that the decedent had used for gift tax purposes within the calculation of the estate tax itself. Therefore, allowing the unified credit to be claimed by each estate does not result in a doubling of the credit.

.032 State death tax credit

There is also a dollar-for-dollar credit against the federal estate tax available in case any inheritance or estate tax is required to be paid to any state.[48] This credit is subject to a ceiling based on a federal rate schedule. The credit allowed is the lesser of the amount of state death tax paid or the amount computed by reference to this separate federal schedule.

.033 Gift tax credit

As previously discussed, one of the results of the three-step estate tax calculation process is to allow a credit for gift taxes paid (by subtracting the result of Step 2 from the result of Step 1). If property transferred during life, which had been subject to the gift tax, is included in the taxable estate, then, it loses its status as a post-1976 taxable gift and is therefore removed from the computation base for purposes of Step 2 of the process and, consequently, the effective credit for gift tax paid, which is incorporated within the estate tax calculation process is lost, even though gift tax may have actually been paid by the decedent prior to death with respect to the subject property.

To prevent this result, there is a separate credit for gift tax that applies only in cases where the transfer of property during life caused the payment of a gift tax, and the same property is included in the transferor's taxable estate at death.[49]

.034 Prior estate tax credit

This credit is allowed in order to avoid imposition of two or more estate taxes on the same assets within a short period of time, which might otherwise occur, for instance, as a result of serial deaths within a family. The credit is available any time the decedent's estate includes property that had been received from another decedent's estate (and therefore subjected to a prior

---

[47] Code Sec. 2010.

[48] Code Sec. 2011. See ¶ 1002.03.

[49] Code Sec. 2012.

estate tax) within 10 years preceding the date of the second death.[50] The credit is equal to the first estate tax paid that is attributable to the property also taxed in the second estate. The amount of the credit is reduced by 20 percent, however, for each two-year period of time that elapsed between the first death and the second death, resulting in a phaseout of the credit if the second death occurs more than 10 years after the first.

.035 Foreign tax credit

The federal estate tax is imposed on all property owned by the decedent, regardless of whether it is located within the United States. In case of property located in a foreign country, there is a credit against the federal estate tax for any tax imposed on that property by the foreign country.[51] This credit is subject to two restrictions: (1) to limit the amount of the credit to the part of the foreign tax that is proportionate to the ratio of the value of the foreign assets to the total taxable estate; and (2) to restrict the credit to no more than the amount of federal estate tax that would be attributable to the foreign asset (disregarding, for this purpose, the existence of the foreign tax credit).

.04 "String Sections"

The "string sections," as they are commonly called, are the Internal Revenue Code sections that affect lifetime property transfers subject to rights retained by the transferor.

.041 General purpose of the rules

When a person transfers property during life, through a living trust or otherwise, but retains certain forms of benefits or control over the transferred property, the federal estate tax requires that the transferred property be included in the taxable estate of the decedent for federal estate tax purposes. These provisions of the Internal Revenue Code are referred to as the string sections.

This may seem peculiar on first impression because, through unification of the estate and gift tax systems, all post-1976 lifetime gifts are taken into account in the calculation of the federal estate tax payable. However, in the three-step estate tax calculation system, post-1976 gifts are included based on the value as of the date of gift. Any appreciation that may occur after the transfer is free of tax. The result of these special provisions of the tax law is to cause property given away "with strings attached" to be included in the estate tax calculation system based on the date-of-death value of the subject property so that any post-transfer appreciation is captured for tax purposes. It is important to realize that the string sections do not cause any property to be included in the estate tax calculation system that would not have otherwise been included. These provisions of the law affect only the valuation date of the subject property. In case of assets transferred during a person's lifetime that have potential for appreciation in value, the difference in estate tax resulting from date-of-death valuation as opposed to date-of-gift valuation may be very dramatic.

---

[50] Code Sec. 2013.

[51] Code Sec. 2014.

.042 Types of retained interests covered

Only specific types of retained lifetime control result in application of the string section rules:

(1) The grantor makes a transfer and retains the right to the personal use, occupancy, enjoyment, or income of the property.[52] One example of this is a gift by a parent to a child of the deed to the family home with a restriction in the deed by which the parent retains the right to continue living in the home for the rest of the parent's life. Another example is a living trust in which the grantor receives the income for life, with the remainder to others.

(2) The grantor makes a transfer in which no personal benefits are retained, but the grantor retains the power (alone or in conjunction with others) to control who receives the benefits of the property.[53]

> **Example (1):** A establishes an irrevocable living trust for the benefit of his children, B, C, and D. Income is to be distributed on a sprinkle basis and A is one of three co-trustees.
>
> In this case, A has retained the power to determine how benefits are distributed among the beneficiaries. Although this power is held by A in his capacity as trustee, and although A's power is not absolute because A is only one of three trustees, the string section rule applies. The full value of the trust fund, valued as of A's date of death, is included in A's taxable estate.

(3) The transfer of stock ownership interests in a closely held corporation, in which the transferring shareholder retains the voting rights[54] over the stock, is subject to the string section rules if certain specific requirements are met:

(a) Twenty percent of the total voting power of the corporation is owned either by the transferor individually or by the transferor and certain family members or by partnerships, estates, trusts, or other corporations in which the transferor holds substantial interests.

(b) This required amount of voting control continues to be held by the transferor after the ownership of the stock is transferred.

(c) The voting control is retained by the transferor until death or, if relinquished by the transferor while still living, if death occurs within three years after the voting control is given up.

(4) The transfer contains a reversionary interest. If the principal purpose of the trust fund is to provide benefits for someone who is older than the grantor, such as a dependent parent, it may make sense to include a provision in the trust requiring the return of the trust fund to the grantor after the death of the beneficiary. Even if the grantor does not plan on ever receiving a return of the trust fund, if all named beneficiaries and remaindermen of a living trust who are identified in the trust document should predecease the grantor and there is no person or organization specified in the agreement to receive the balance, the trust fund reverts to the grantor under state law.

---

[52] Code Sec. 2036(a)(1).

[53] Code Sec. 2036(a)(2).

[54] Code Sec. 2036(b).

Where there is the possibility of a reversion to the grantor under the terms and conditions of a trust and where, as of the grantor's death, both of the following conditions exist, the date-of-death value of the trust fund is included in the grantor's taxable estate.[55]

(a) No person could have obtained the principal of the trust fund without having survived the grantor.

(b) The actuarial value of the possibility of the reversion to the grantor is greater than five percent. This valuation is made as of the date of the grantor's death by ignoring the actual fact of the grantor's death.

Example (2): A establishes a trust fund for his child, C, for a period of 10 years. At the end of the trust term, the remainder is distributed outright to C. There is no provision in the trust agreement to address the possibility that C might die before the end of the 10-year time period and, under the applicable state law, the trust fund would then revert to A at C's death. Two years before the end of the trust term, A dies.

The reversionary interest rule does not apply in this case, and the date-of-death value of the trust fund is not added to A's taxable estate. The first requirement of this rule is not met because C could obtain the entire balance of the trust fund at the end of the 10-year period, and the distribution of the remainder to him was not conditioned on C's having survived A. It is not even necessary to calculate the actuarial value of the possibility of reversion to A (the second requirement of this rule).

(5) The transfer is revocable. If there is any condition attached to a property transfer through which the transferor could alter, amend, revoke, or terminate the transfer, the date-of-death value of the property is included in the transferor's taxable estate.[56] It makes no difference, for purposes of this rule, whether the retained power was held by the transferor alone or in conjunction with one or more others, and powers held by the transferor in a fiduciary capacity are treated just as those that are personally held.

Example (3): A established a trust fund for the benefit of his children, C, D, and E to be held for their benefit until the youngest child reaches age 25, at which time the remainder is to be distributed to the children in equal shares. A and his brother, B, who are the co-trustees, have the power to bring the trust to an end before the youngest child reaches age 25; however, they must then distribute the remainder among the children in equal shares.

The transferor's retained power to terminate the trust, although held in a fiduciary capacity and only exercisable in conjunction with the other co-trustee, is sufficient to cause applicability of the string section rule. If A dies before the trust comes to an end, the fair market value as of the date of his death is included in his taxable estate.

---

[55] Code Sec. 2037.

[56] Code Sec. 2038.

(6) The transfer results in the application of the three-year rule. In a separate provision of the Internal Revenue Code, there is a special rule for any situation that qualifies, as follows:

(a) There has been a transfer made in the past that would have been subject to any one of the string section rules if the transferor had held the requisite interest or power over the subject property as of the date of the transferor's death.

(b) The transferor takes the additional step of terminating the retained interest or power within the three-year period prior to death.[57]

This separate provision applies whether or not the individual string section rule, applicable in any particular case, contains a three-year limit of its own.

The same three-year provision is the authority for imposing estate tax on the proceeds of transferred life insurance policies. If the deceased insured transfers any one or more of the incidents of ownership of a life insurance policy within three years of death, the policy proceeds are included in the transferor's taxable estate.

.043 Exception to the string section rules for consideration paid

There is an exception to the application of most of the string section rules[58] if the recipient of the transfer actually pays to the transferor the fair market value of the transferred property interest. Planning strategies involving the purchase of remainders or temporal interests in trusts have been severely restricted under the Revenue Reconciliation Act of 1990 (RRA '90) (P.L. 101-508). Some planning opportunities that remain in spite of the string sections and RRA '90 are discussed beginning at ¶ 503.06.

.05 Estate Tax Deductions

An estate may claim several deductions to reduce its tax. Some of these deductions are analyzed below.

.051 Debts and expenses

Bona-fide debts of the decedent reduce the amount of the taxable estate in one of two ways:[59] (1) the amount of the debt is an estate tax deduction; or (2) where property is held subject to a mortgage, the value of the property to be included in the taxable estate is the net value after taking into account the debt outstanding. The balance of income tax due (calculated up to the date of death) on the decedent's final personal income tax return is an example of a deductible debt.

Funeral and funeral-related expenses are allowable estate tax deductions. Other expenses in connection with the estate administration and settlement, however, are permitted to be deducted for estate tax purposes only if the same items of expense are not claimed as deductions for income tax purposes. Examples of these administration expenses are executor commissions and attorney fees. A similar rule applies to any medical expenses of the decedent

[57] Code Sec. 2035(d)(2).

[58] Code Secs. 2036, 2037, and 2038.

[59] Code Sec. 2053.

paid after death. If these final medical expenses are paid within one year after death, a deduction is permitted on the decedent's final personal income tax return. These medical expenses are allowed for estate tax purposes only if they are not claimed on the decedent's last income tax return.

There is a certain amount of strategy involved in making the election as to whether these deductions should be claimed on the personal income tax return or the estate tax return. For estates valued at not more than $600,000, the federal estate tax is eliminated by the unified credit, as explained at .031, above. For estates of this size, it therefore makes no sense to "waste" administration expenses by claiming them as estate tax deductions. On the other hand, if the value subject to estate tax exceeds $600,000, the estate tax rate is at least 37 percent. To determine the most efficient means of claiming administration expense, it is necessary to compare the effective estate tax rate with the marginal income tax bracket to be affected if the expense is claimed for income tax purposes. For expenses incurred in years before termination of the estate, the marginal income tax bracket of the estate is affected. However, it is not uncommon to pay a substantial amount of administration expenses in the year of termination of the estate. In that case, the expenses may exceed the estate income. When that occurs in the year of termination, the excess deduction is available to the residuary beneficiaries of the estate.[60] It is important, then, to analyze which marginal income tax bracket to compare with the estate tax bracket for planning purposes.

.052 Charitable deduction

As a general rule, amounts donated to charity through the decedent's will and other charitable transfers that take place at death are deductible from the taxable estate.[61] Where the decedent establishes a trust fund for charitable purposes or partly for family purposes and partly for charity, more restrictive rules apply. These are considered in depth in Chapter 7.

.053 Estate tax marital deduction

Basic requirements. The taxable estate of a married individual is entitled to deduct the full value of all assets included in the taxable estate of the first deceased spouse to the extent that ownership of these assets passes to the surviving spouse, whether under the will of the deceased spouse or otherwise.[62] The specific requirements for the marital deduction may be summarized as follows:

(1) The decedent must have been validly married at the time of death.

(2) The decedent's spouse must have survived the decedent.

(3) Each asset for which the marital deduction is claimed must have been included in the taxable estate of the deceased spouse.

(4) The ownership of each asset for which the marital deduction is claimed must have passed from the decedent to the surviving spouse.

(5) The surviving spouse must be a U.S. citizen.

---

[60] Code Sec. 642(h).

[61] Code Sec. 2055.

[62] Code Sec. 2056.

Validity of the marriage. Issues as to the validity of the marriage should arise only infrequently in most parts of the country since virtually no states recognize the validity of common law marriages based on some time period of cohabitation. This is one instance where a rule of federal law (the marital deduction) requires interpretation of a state law (validity of the marriage). Some state courts have recognized a divorce law palimony concept, which may support a financial claim by an unmarried individual against his or her close companion at the termination of their relationship. Since the federal estate tax system is based on statute and court interpretation is quite limited, there seems to be no possibility of obtaining a marital deduction upon the transfer of money or property to anyone but one's valid spouse. Those who choose to share life "without benefit of ceremony" must therefore realize that they do so at the expense of losing the marital deduction.

Survivorship requirement and simultaneous death. The requirement of survivorship by a spouse can become complicated in case of the death of both husband and wife in close time proximity, such as in the case of multiple deaths as a result of a common accident. If, under the factual circumstances, the order of death cannot be determined, the estate laws of most states treat each spouse as having predeceased the other. The non-tax purpose of this rule is to avoid requiring that the property of one decedent's estate be distributed to another decedent's estate. For estate tax purposes, however, this may result in loss of the marital deduction for both estates. The estate tax rules make it permissible to prevent this result by placing a provision in the wills of the married couple that specifies the order of death to be assumed in the event of simultaneous death. Under estate tax regulations, the Internal Revenue Service will honor the designation of an assumed order of death specified in the will unless the physical evidence proves otherwise.

Some advisers recommend a will provision requiring a brief period of survivorship before any beneficiary can receive an inheritance in order to avoid multiple estate administrations in the event two or more members of a family should die in close time proximity. If the will of a married person contains a requirement that the surviving spouse must live for a specified period of time (not in excess of six months) in order to receive an inheritance, loss of the marital deduction does not result unless the surviving spouse actually dies within the time period of the survivorship requirement.[63]

Below is a summary of some combinations of circumstances involving the issue of the order of death and its effect on the marital deduction, based on the commonly encountered situation where the will of Spouse 1 leaves his entire estate to Spouse 2. The question presented is whether the estate of Spouse 1 will be entitled to the marital deduction under various factual situations.

Factual Variation	*Marital Deduction Permitted?*
(1) Spouse 1 and Spouse 2 die in close time proximity so that the order of death cannot be determined with certainty, and:	
(a) The will of Spouse 1 contains no special directions as to the presumed order of death.	No Marital Deduction.

[63] Code Sec. 2056(b)(3).

(b) The will of Spouse 1 specifies that, if the order of death is uncertain, Spouse 2 is presumed to have survived.	Marital Deduction Permitted.
(2) The will of Spouse 1 provides that Spouse 2 must survive Spouse 1 by a time period not exceeding six months in order to inherit, and:	
(a) Spouse 2 actually survives Spouse 1 by more than the specified time period.	Marital Deduction Permitted.
(b) Spouse 2, having survived Spouse 1, dies before the end of the specified time period.	No Marital Deduction.
(3) The will of Spouse 1 provides that Spouse 2 is presumed to have survived under all possible circumstances, and:	
(a) The physical evidence proves that Spouse 2 actually survived Spouse 1.	Marital Deduction Permitted.
(b) The physical evidence fails to determine the order of death.	Marital Deduction Permitted.
(c) The physical evidence proves that Spouse 2 actually predeceased Spouse 1.	No Marital Deduction.

Standard will clauses used by some attorneys make reference to death resulting from a common accident or disaster instead of the more precise reference to simultaneous death or death in close time proximity. However, if the objective is to obtain the marital deduction for the estate of a married person, it is the order of death rather than the cause of death that is significant. A married couple may die as a result of a common accident in circumstances where Spouse 2 dies instantly while Spouse 1 lingers for several days or weeks. Even if the will of Spouse 1 directs that Spouse 2 be treated as the survivor if both die due to a common accident, the marital deduction is not permitted to the estate of Spouse 1 because Spouse 2 in fact died first. In view of this, the so-called "common disaster" clause should be regarded as bad form in the wills of married couples where the intention is to obtain the marital deduction for one of them.

Inclusion of assets in the taxable estate of the first deceased spouse. If the estate of the first deceased spouse is to be allowed a marital deduction for amounts of money or property interests, each such asset must be included in the taxable estate of the first spouse. While this rule may seem simple and obvious, it is occasionally the source of mistakes in estate planning. Perhaps this results from the fact that, if all of the other basic requirements for the marital deduction are met, the financial consultant may overlook the fact that an asset passing to the surviving spouse at the death of the first spouse is not included in the first taxable estate.

> **Example (1):** The surviving spouse is the owner of all incidents of ownership of a life insurance policy on which the first deceased spouse is the insured. The surviving spouse is also the beneficiary of the policy and, as such, receives the policy proceeds at the death of the first spouse.

In this example, the requirements of validity of the marriage, survivorship by a spouse and the passing of the asset to the surviving spouse are all met. The marital deduction is not allowed with respect to the insurance proceeds, however, because no part of the proceeds are required to be included in the taxable estate of the first spouse under the circumstances of the example.

This principle also applies to powers of appointment. If a general power is exercised by the first deceased spouse in favor of the surviving spouse, the marital deduction is allowed for the value of the property subject to the power. On the other hand, if the power exercised is a non-general or limited power, no marital deduction is allowed.

The marital deduction is allowed for only part of the value of property if the full ownership passes to the surviving spouse, but only part of the value is included in the first spouse's taxable estate. This occurs in all cases of property owned by husband and wife as joint tenants and tenants by the entirety because these forms of property ownership result in inclusion of only 50 percent of the value in the taxable estate of the first deceased spouse and, by operation of the rights of survivorship under state property law, the surviving spouse automatically becomes the owner when the first spouse dies. Similarly, a partial marital deduction occurs in cases of community property. Since community property does not carry automatic survivorship, the partial marital deduction is only allowed where the first deceased spouse leaves his share of the community property to the surviving spouse.

Passing of assets to the surviving spouse. This basic requirement of the marital deduction may be satisfied by almost any means of ownership transfer or succession. This includes direct bequests under the will of the first deceased spouse and automatic survivorship as in the case of the joint tenancy form of ownership. The required passing of ownership may also be accomplished by the designation of the surviving spouse as beneficiary under life insurance, annuity contracts, pensions, and other employee benefit plans. Exceptions to the "passing" requirement are payments and property transfers to the surviving spouse that are not gratuitous in nature. An illustration of this exception is the repayment, by the deceased spouse's estate to the surviving spouse, of a legally enforceable debt owed to the survivor by the first deceased spouse assuming the debt is bona fide and based on something of true value previously furnished by the survivor to the decedent. Also, a debt deduction might well be available for estate tax purposes under these circumstances, but the marital deduction is not.

Transfers of partial interests in property from the decedent to the surviving spouse may result in a marital deduction for a proportionate part of the value.

> **Example (2):** Under the terms of his will, Spouse 1 transfers ownership of property A to Spouse 2 and B (the child of Spouse 1 and Spouse 2) as tenants in common with equal ownership interests.

The result in this example is a marital deduction of 50 percent of the value of property A for the estate of Spouse 1. However, if property were given to B and Spouse 2 as joint tenants, the result might be different, depending upon the nature of the respective rights of B and Spouse 2 under state law. If any one of them has the right to terminate the automatic survivorship associated with joint tenancy, the transfer is treated as passing equally to the joint tenants. If consent of both joint tenants is required to terminate the automatic survivorship, however, the proportionate share of the value treated as passing to Spouse 2 is something other than an equal 50 percent share depending on the relative ages of Spouse 2 and B. Furthermore, state law may permit termination of automatic survivorship with respect to certain types of property by any individual joint owner while requiring the consent of all joint owners in order to terminate survivorship with respect to other types of property. For instance, joint bank accounts and joint tenancy in real estate can usually be terminated by any one of the owners, while discontinuing joint tenancy of securities requires the consent of all owners.

Citizenship of surviving spouse. The marital deduction is generally not available if the surviving spouse is not a U.S. citizen.[64] Exceptions exist in the following circumstances:

(1) The surviving spouse becomes a U.S. citizen by the due date for filing the estate tax return of the first spouse, provided that the survivor was a U.S. resident, before becoming a citizen, during the time after the first spouse's death.[65] There is no flexibility in the rules for anyone who has applied for citizenship but whose application has not yet been approved on the estate tax return due date.

(2) The interest passes to the surviving spouse in a trust fund, designated as a "qualified domestic trust" (QDOT),[66] subject to rules[67] designed to make certain that estate tax is imposed when the corpus of the trust is distributed to the noncitizen surviving spouse or at the death of such spouse, whichever occurs first. The QDOT is explained at ¶ 504.043.

(3) Certain assets that cannot be held in a QDOT may nevertheless be treated as a QDOT if specific requirements are met. These include annuities, interests in qualified retirement plans, and Individual Retirement Accounts (IRAs). Under proposed regulations, the marital deduction is allowed if either one of two methods is used to ensure payment of tax:

(a) Distributions are made directly to the noncitizen surviving spouse from the annuity, qualified plan, or IRA and the spouse agrees in writing to make annual payments of deferred estate tax on the portion of distributions that constitutes "corpus." A detailed information statement must be filed with the estate tax return on which a QDOT election is made.[68]

(b) The noncitizen surviving spouse contributes the corpus portion of each distribution to a QDOT within 60 days after receiving each distribution. This procedure must be made pursuant to a written agreement signed by the spouse and filed with the estate tax return on which the QDOT election is made. A detailed information statement is also required.[69]

The corpus amount of each annuity or similar payment is determined by a formula that takes into account the present value of the annuity as of the date of death of the first deceased spouse and the mortality and interest rates prescribed by Code Sec. 7520.[70]

---

[64] Code Sec. 2056(d).
[65] Code Sec. 2056(d)(4).
[66] Code Sec. 2056(d)(2).
[67] Code Sec. 2056A.
[68] Prop. Reg. § 20.2056A-4(c)(2).
[69] Prop. Reg. § 20.2056A-4(c)(3).
[70] Prop. Reg. § 20.2056A-4(c)(4).

Terminable interest rule. It is possible to create partial property interests that are successive in time rather than concurrent. One example of this is the temporary ownership of real estate, such as lifetime use and occupancy of the property where the remainder passes to someone other than the life tenant or his estate. Through the use of trusts, a married individual can provide lifetime or other temporary benefits for his spouse in any type of property he chooses to place in the trust fund. The federal estate tax rules refer to temporary ownership interests passing to a surviving spouse as "terminable interests." A terminable interest cannot qualify for the marital deduction if each of the following characteristics is present:[71]

(1) An interest in property passes from the decedent to the surviving spouse.

(2) The surviving spouse's ownership rights will end either after a period of time or upon the occurrence of a future event.

(3) An interest in the same property also passes from the decedent to someone other than the surviving spouse.

(4) The interest passing to this other person will arise after the termination of the property interest of the surviving spouse.

It should be clear from a review of these specific requirements that some terminable interests can, in fact, qualify for the marital deduction.

Example (3): Deceased Spouse A received annuity payments under his former employer's pension plan up to the date of his death. Under the terms of the plan, surviving Spouse B receives the payments after A's death for the balance of B's lifetime.

The annuity is a taxable asset in A's estate. Its estate tax valuation depends on B's life expectancy. The benefit passing to B at A's death is an example of a terminable interest because the payments to B will end upon the occurrence of a future event (B's death). However, since no interest in the same property passed from A to anyone other than B, A's estate is entitled to the marital deduction with respect to the annuity.[72]

Given the inherent flexibility of trust design, it is not difficult to produce instances of trust benefits given to the surviving spouse that fall into the category of terminable interests.

Example (4): The will of deceased Spouse A directs that the residuary estate is to be held in trust for the benefit of surviving Spouse B for life with the remainder payable to the children of A and B. If B should remarry after A's death, however, the trust benefits for B end, the trust terminates, and there is an accelerated distribution of the remainder to the children.

In Example (4), the termination of B's benefits in the trust will definitely occur; the only question is which of the two specified future events will trigger the termination. B might never remarry after A's death, but the fact that B's benefits from the trust will end in the event of remarriage is enough to satisfy the second of the four terminable interest requirements. The children of A and B receive the remainder of the trust after B's interest ends. Although the children's interest is a future interest, it is an interest in property transferred by the deceased spouse to someone other than the surviving spouse. Therefore,

---

[71] Code Sec. 2056(b)(1).

[72] Reg. § 20.2056(b)-1(g), Ex. (3).

the third and fourth requirements are also met. Under these circumstances, B's benefits in the trust constitute a nondeductible terminable interest.

In order to allow for reasonable estate planning relating to the marital deduction, the Internal Revenue Code provides for two specific types of trusts that provide terminable interest benefits for the surviving spouse but still qualify for the marital deduction. These special marital deduction trusts are explained at ¶ 504.04.

Taxation of marital deduction assets in the estate of the surviving spouse. The marital deduction offers the opportunity for married couples to avoid all federal estate tax when the first spouse dies. In effect, the couple is regarded as a single economic unit for purposes of the imposition of this tax. If a significant amount of tax had to be paid at the death of the first spouse, financial hardship could result in some cases. The availability of the marital deduction eliminates the potential for harsh results. Assets that pass from the first deceased spouse to the surviving spouse and qualify for the marital deduction in the first estate are always subject to estate tax upon the death of the surviving spouse. There are only two exceptions to this rule:

(1) If the surviving spouse expends the value of the assets on true consumables such as food and travel, there is no value remaining that can be subjected to tax at the survivor's death. Some regard this as a good reason to spend it all!

(2) If the surviving spouse remarries and if at the death of the surviving spouse qualifying transfers are made to the new spouse, the marital deduction is permitted, in effect, the second time around. This is difficult to plan for, however, and in any event it is not a popular form of planning, particularly from the viewpoint of the original first-deceased spouse.

There are no qualifying marital deduction trusts that permit temporary or terminable interests to be created for the benefit of the surviving spouse under circumstances where the remainder is free of estate tax at the subsequent death of the surviving spouse.

¶ 403 GENERATION-SKIPPING TRANSFER TAX

The rule against perpetuities, an aspect of state law, makes it impermissible to establish a trust that continues from generation to generation without ever terminating and distributing its principal. It is legally possible, however, for a trust to last for several generations.

Example (1): A's will provides for a trust fund to last until 21 years after the death of the last survivor of A's descendants who is living on the date of A's death. A dies at age 80, leaving the following surviving descendants:

(1) Child B, who is age 55.

(2) Grandchild C, who is age 30.

(3) Great-grandchild D, who is age 5.

None of the surviving descendants hold any power of appointment over the trust fund. Each of them is entitled to the trust income, successively, for life. At the trust termination, the remainder is to be distributed among A's then-living descendants per stirpes.

The trust fund under A's will may continue until 21 years after the death of D without violating the rule against perpetuities. If D survives to normal life expectancy, this trust will last for about one hundred years and may provide trust income benefits to three generations of A's descendants and make its final distribution to a fourth successive generation. The federal estate tax is imposed on all property in which the decedent owns any interest at the date of death. As discussed at ¶ 402.014, the estate of a trust beneficiary who does not hold a general power of appointment over the assets held in trust does not generally include the value of those trust assets. In Example (1), this means that the assets of the trust, having been included in A's taxable estate, are not subject to estate tax again in the estates of B, C, or D. Only after the trust terminates and distributes the principal, and then only upon the subsequent death of the remainderman who shall have received the principal, will a second estate tax be payable. Compared to a non-trust estate plan, in which A may have left an outright inheritance to B who would then leave an outright inheritance to C and so on, the estate tax is imposed only once over three generations instead of three times.

The purpose of the generation-skipping transfer tax (referred to throughout this section as GST) is to prevent large amounts of wealth from passing along over several generations, providing benefits to the members of each generation in the meantime, all without being subjected to any gift or estate tax. The GST is separate and distinct from the unified estate and gift tax system and may be thought of as a backstop to the system. It is established and governed by a separate chapter of the Internal Revenue Code.[73]

The objective of the GST is achieved by imposing a flat rate of tax on any property transferred under the following circumstances:

(1) The property is available to provide economic benefits to an initial beneficiary who is within a generation younger than that of the transferor.

(2) This initial beneficiary holds neither direct ownership nor a general power of appointment over the property; therefore, upon subsequent disposition of the property, the initial beneficiary is not subject to gift or estate tax.

(3) The property is ultimately transferred to a subsequent beneficiary who is more than one generation younger than the original transferor. Such a beneficiary is designated as a "skip person."[74] This term can also be used to refer to a trust if the only trust beneficiaries are skip persons, and no future distributions can be made from the trust to any beneficiary who is not a skip person. Conversely, any individual whose generation assignment, compared to that of the transferor, is older, the same, or just one level younger, or any trust from which distributions can never be made to a skip person, may be referred to as a "non-skip person."

Example (2) (generation-skipping transfer): A establishes a trust fund for the benefit of his child, C, with the remainder to his grandchild, GC.

---

[73] See Internal Revenue Code Chapter 13, generally.

[74] See Code Sec. 2613(a). See also, Technical and Miscellaneous Revenue Act of 1988 (TAMRA) (P.L. 100-647), § 1014(g)(5).

Since C is in a younger generation than A, a generation-skipping transfer occurs, not upon the transfer to C, but upon the transfer to GC, who is more than one generation younger than A.

> **Example (3) (transfer not subject to generation-skipping rules):** H establishes a trust fund for his spouse, W, with the remainder to their child, C.

In Example (3), the initial beneficiary is in the same generation as the transferor, and the subsequent beneficiary is not more than one generation younger than the transferor. Either one of these factors would be sufficient to exclude this transaction from the reach of the GST rules.

In order to provide an effective deterrent to tax avoidance through generation skipping, the flat rate of the GST is equal to the highest percentage rate of estate tax in effect at the date of the event causing the GST to be imposed.[75] Currently, this is a flat rate of tax of 55 percent. Since these taxes are separate, it is possible that a transfer might be subject to both gift or estate tax and GST at the same time. If a sufficiently large amount is transferred in this manner, the highest bracket amount transferred could be subjected to a combined total rate of 110 percent of the value transferred.

There are specific rules covering the assignment of generations among transferor and beneficiary and the kinds of transactions and events that trigger imposition of the tax. There are also exclusions and exemptions available.

.01 Generation Assignments

Where the question of assigning generations involves natural family lines, the family tree, relating back to the transferor's grandparents, is used for purposes of generation assignment.[76] In this manner, for instance, the transferor's nieces and nephews, as well as the transferor's children, are considered one generation younger than the transferor. In all cases other than natural descendants of the transferor's grandparents, special rules are provided. These rules include the following:

(1) The transferor's spouse is always placed in the same generation as the transferor, even in the event of a substantial difference in their ages.[77] This generation assignment is not changed in the event of divorce.

(2) The descendants of the transferor's spouse are treated as if they were natural descendants of the transferor. In second marriage situations where each spouse has children of his or her respective first marriages, the result could easily be a stepchild of the older spouse who is 60 years younger or more but who is treated as only one generation younger than the stepparent.

(3) Adopted children and their descendants are treated in the same manner as natural children, and relationships by half blood are treated the same as relationships by full blood for purposes of these rules.

(4) If a family relationship does not exist between the transferor and the beneficiary or between the transferor's spouse and the beneficiary,

---

[75] Code Sec. 2641.

[76] Code Sec. 2651(b).

[77] Code Sec. 2651(c)(1).

then the assignment of generations is based on the respective ages of the transferor and the beneficiary, as follows:[78]

(a) Any beneficiary who is not more than 12½ years younger than the transferor is treated as being within the same generation as the transferor.

(b) A beneficiary is counted as one generation younger than the transferor if the beneficiary is more than 12½ years younger but not more than 37½ years younger.

(c) If the beneficiary is more than 37½ years younger than the transferor, he is treated as being two generations younger than the transferor. Thereafter, additional generations are counted at subsequent 25-year intervals. More than 62½ years younger is considered three generations, more than 87½ years younger is four generations, etc.

.02 Generation-Skipping Taxable Events

This separate tax might not be imposed when the transfer first takes place. There are three possible taxable events, any one of which can cause imposition of the GST. These are designed generally to parallel the gift and estate tax system.

.021 Taxable termination

When property is transferred to a beneficiary who is at least two generations younger than the transferor, after having been held for the benefit of one whose generation assignment is younger than the original transferor but older than the ultimate recipient, a taxable termination occurs.[79]

Example: A's will establishes a living trust for the benefit of his daughter, D, for life. At D's death, the balance of the trust fund is distributed to D's descendants in equal shares per stirpes.

At D's death, a taxable termination occurs.

.022 Taxable distribution

A taxable distribution may occur at any time before the final transfer of the property or final distribution of a trust fund. There must be an amount distributed to a beneficiary who is at least two generations younger than the transferor, and there must also be some other beneficiary of the property or trust fund who is in a generation older than the recipient but younger than the transferor.[80]

In view of the inherent potential for flexibility of trust design, it is possible for a partial distribution to be subject to GST as a taxable distribution even in circumstances where the final distribution of the trust fund would not constitute a taxable termination for purposes of this separate tax.

Example: By the terms of a testamentary trust under the will of his deceased spouse, A receives all of the income for life. At A's death the remainder is to be distributed among A's children in equal shares. The

---

[78] Code Sec. 2651(d).

[79] Code Sec. 2612(a).

[80] Code Sec. 2612(b).

trustee is permitted to make distributions of principal to A, or to any of A's descendants who are living, from time to time during the term of the trust, to provide for their support, maintenance, or education.

If no principal distributions are made during the term of this trust, then at its termination, no GST will be imposed because the ultimate recipients are not more than one generation younger than the original transferor. If interim principal distributions are made to A or to A's children, there is no generation-skipping distribution for the same reason. However, if the trustee makes interim distributions to a grandchild of A, GST is imposed.

Taxable distributions are not limited to principal amounts. Where, for instance, a sprinkle trust permits income to be distributed among a class of beneficiaries that includes one or more non-skip persons and one or more skip persons, even an income distribution may be treated as a taxable distribution for purposes of GST.

.023 Direct skip

Prior to 1987, it was possible to avoid the effects of GST through so-called "layering" transfers, whereby the transferor would provide some benefits, through a trust or outright, to those who were one generation younger and also some benefits directly to those more than one generation removed. However, in the case of the trusts or other benefits for the more remote descendants, the transfer would be structured to avoid any interim benefits for children or other non-skip persons. In this manner, the transaction did not fall into the category of either a taxable termination or a taxable distribution. The Tax Reform Act of 1986 (TRA '86) (P.L. 99-514) established a new taxable event, "the direct skip," subject to GST in order to remove the advantage of layering.

A direct skip is any transfer, in trust or otherwise, to a recipient who is more than one generation younger than the transferor.[81] There is a limited amount of relief from this rule in case of the death of a child of the transferor or of the transferor's spouse. If any such child is deceased at a time when transfers are made to their descendants, each generation of descendants of the deceased child is treated as "moving up one rung" of generation assignment for purposes of this tax. The children of a deceased child, who are actually grandchildren of the transferor, are treated as if they were the children of the transferor, and so on. As a result, after the death of a child, the transferor would have to make a transfer to a great grandchild or some more remote descendant before a direct skip would be considered to have occurred. There are significant restrictions placed on this relief provision:

(1) Reshuffling of generations only occurs in the case of the death of a child of the transferor or of the transferor's spouse. It does not take place in the event of death of any other individual whose generation assignment is one younger than the transferor. No reshuffling occurs, for instance, in the event of death of a niece or nephew.

(2) This relief provision may result in avoidance of GST on direct skips only. The generations are not reshuffled in the event of a taxable termination or of a taxable distribution.

---

[81] Code Sec. 2612(c).

The direct skip is the only one of the generation-skipping transfers that can be subject to the separate tax immediately upon the event of the initial transfer itself. Both the taxable termination and the taxable distribution presuppose some interim time period (however brief it may be) after the initial transfer of the property when it is held for the potential benefit of one or more interim-generation beneficiaries. By contrast, in a direct skip, as the name implies, the ownership of the subject money or property is either transferred directly to a skip person or placed in a trust, the initial beneficiary of which is a skip person. In either case, the GST is payable immediately.

Due to the complexity of these rules, it is possible for a particular transaction to meet the definition of either taxable distribution and direct skip or taxable termination and direct skip. If so, each such transaction is treated as a direct skip.[82]

.03 Responsibility for Payment of GST

The source of payment of the GST depends on the type of generation-skipping transfer involved.

.031 *Payment of GST in case of a taxable distribution*

The transferee is primarily liable for payment of the tax.[83] If the tax is actually paid from the trust, this is treated as if it were an additional generation-skipping taxable distribution. A taxable distribution that consists exclusively of trust distributable net income (DNI) other than tax-exempt interest must be included in the recipient's taxable income, including any amount paid from the trust as a direct payment of the GST.

Example (1): Trust T is a sprinkle trust, as to both income and principal, held for the benefit of the grantor's children and grandchildren. No generation-skipping exemptions apply to Trust T. During Year 1, the accounting net income (ANI) and DNI of Trust T is $50,000, which consists of taxable income. The trustee makes a distribution of $50,000 to a grandchild of the grantor. The trust also pays the full amount of the GST from trust principal.

The GST paid is approximately $61,111 on this taxable distribution. This is much more than 55 percent of the amount distributed because the tax itself, to the extent paid by the trust, is counted as an additional taxable distribution. In order to calculate the GST in this case, it is therefore necessary to "gross up" the amount distributed. This is simply a matter of dividing the net amount distributed by the reciprocal of the GST rate, which is 45 percent. In this example, the tax computation is as follows:

Net Amount Distributed	$50,000	=	$111,111	× 55%	=	$61,111
Reciprocal of Tax Rate	45%		Gross Amount Treated as Distributed	GST Rate		GST Payable

The recipient includes the amount of trust DNI in his personal income according to the regular fiduciary income tax rules and is entitled to an income

[82] *Id.*

[83] Code Sec. 2603(a)(1).

tax deduction for the GST paid to the extent that this deduction does not exceed the DNI included in the recipient's taxable income. In Example (1), $50,000 is included in the recipient's taxable income, and a like amount is deducted by the recipient since the GST paid exceeds DNI.

The recipient of a taxable distribution for GST purposes is not entitled to this offsetting income tax deduction if the amount received from the trust constitutes an accumulation distribution.

In the event that the amount distributed to the beneficiary is less than DNI but the trust pays the GST, for income tax purposes an additional amount is deemed to be distributed from the trust equal to the lesser of the following:

(1) the excess of DNI over the net amount distributed to the beneficiary; or

(2) the amount of GST paid by the trust.

Example (2): Assuming the same terms and conditions as in Example (1), Trust T's ANI and DNI for Year 2 is equal to $45,000. The trustee makes a distribution in the amount of $30,000 to a grandchild of the grantor and pays GST, in the amount of $36,667, from the balance of Trust T's income and, to the extent needed, from principal.

Although the recipient actually receives $30,000, for income tax purposes as well as for GST purposes, additional amounts are treated as if distributed.

Since the recipient is primarily liable for the payment of GST in case of a taxable distribution, the payment of GST by the trust must be reconstructed as if the trust had paid an additional amount to the recipient and the recipient then paid the GST. For fiduciary income tax purposes, this is only significant to the extent that DNI exceeds the amount actually distributed to the recipient while for GST purposes, the full amount of GST paid is deemed to be an additional distribution.

The result of reconstruction in Example (2) is that the beneficiary, who actually received only $30,000, is required to include $45,000 in personal taxable income. The income tax deduction available to the beneficiary is the full GST paid or $36,667, which happens to be more than the actual distribution but less than $45,000, the amount of DNI that is included in the beneficiary's taxable income in this case. The following summary, based on Example (2), illustrates the fact that it is possible that the actual amount distributed, the amount treated as distributed for purposes of computing GST, the amount included in the beneficiary's taxable income, and the amount that the beneficiary is entitled to deduct on account of the GST paid may all be different amounts:

(a) Actual amount distributed	$30,000
(b) Amount treated as distributed for purpose of computing GST	$66,667
(c) Amount included in beneficiary's personal taxable income	$45,000
(d) Beneficiary's income tax deduction for GST paid by trust	$36,667

.032 *Payment of GST in case of a taxable termination*

The trustee is primarily liable for the payment of GST in case of a taxable termination.[84] Since the full value of the subject property is taxable, rather than just the amount of a particular distribution, there is no need for a gross-up calculation.

The income tax deduction available to the remaindermen as a result of the payment of GST in case of a taxable termination is limited to those items of income included in the taxable income of the trust after the effective date of the taxable termination.

.033 *Payment of GST in case of a direct skip*

The transferor is personally liable for the payment of GST incurred because of a direct skip.[85] Furthermore, for direct skip transactions that take place during the lifetime of the transferor and which are, therefore, subject to gift tax, the amount of the taxable gift is increased by the amount of GST imposed.

> **Example:** During the time that A's son, C, is living, and after having used all available GST exemptions, A makes a gift in the amount of $110,000 to C's child, GC.

Assuming this qualifies as a present interest gift, the annual exclusion is available for GST purposes as well as for gift tax purposes. As a result, A is required to pay GST in the amount of 55 percent of $100,000, or $55,000. For gift tax purposes, the amount of the taxable gift is treated as the sum of the value of the actual gift plus the amount of GST paid by A, or $165,000.

In this kind of non-trust, direct skip transfer situation, there is no income tax deduction for the GST paid available to any of the parties. However, where the direct skip is made through a trust under circumstances in which the GST becomes payable upon the death of the transferor, the recipient is entitled to an income tax deduction for the amounts of income includible by the trust after the date of the event that causes the GST to be imposed.

.04 Exclusions and Exemptions

Some of the exclusions and exemptions allowed with respect to GST closely parallel those provided for the gift tax and apply simultaneously to both tax systems. This section discusses the overlapping provisions as well as the application of separate GST exclusions and exemptions.

.041 *Exclusion where tax is imposed on interim generation beneficiary*

Any taxable termination or taxable distribution in which gift tax or estate tax is imposed on a person who is one generation younger than the original transferor is not subject to the GST.[86] This may occur, for instance, as a result of the existence of a general power of appointment over the subject property in the hands of the interim generation beneficiary.

---

[84] Code Sec. 2603(a)(2).

[85] Code Sec. 2603(a)(3).

[86] Code Sec. 2611(b)(1).

Example: A establishes Trust T to pay the income to child B for life, with the remainder to grandchild G. B has the right to direct the trustee to make distributions of up to the greater of $5,000 or five percent of the value of the trust fund in any year of the trust to any person including C himself, or his creditors. This power of appointment is noncumulative. During the current year, C directs the trustee to distribute $25,000, which does not exceed five percent of the principal value of Trust T, to G.

The right, held by C, to direct distribution of principal is clearly a general power of appointment. Had C failed to exercise this power, the lapse would not have been a gift tax event because of the five-and-five exception. However, since C actually exercised the power, C is treated as having made a taxable gift to G in the amount of $25,000. For GST purposes, C is one generation younger than A, the original transferor. Consequently, the payment from the trust to G, which would otherwise have been a taxable distribution, is not subject to GST. If C never exercised the power of appointment during his lifetime, under the estate tax five-and-five rule, the lapse of the power for years prior to the year of C's death does not result in the inclusion of any part of the trust fund in C's taxable estate. At C's death, only the part of the trust value subject to the power that C could have exercised during the year of his death is included in C's taxable estate. Assuming that five percent of the trust fund's value is greater than $5,000 on C's date of death, the final result is that five percent of the value of the trust fund is included in C's taxable estate, and 95 percent of the value is subject to GST as a taxable termination.

In appropriate circumstances, the exclusion from GST because of inclusion of a trust fund in the taxable estate of an interim beneficiary may be desirable. Considering the fact that the first $600,000 in estate value is shielded from estate tax by the estate tax unified credit and the fact that the effective rates of federal estate tax above the $600,000 level range from 37 percent to 55 percent, there is room for some legitimate planning. Since the rate of the GST is a flat 55 percent, causing a trust to be included in an interim beneficiary's taxable estate may result in a smaller tax payable, but it can never result in a higher rate of tax being imposed. It is important to remember that double taxation is prevented only if the gift tax or estate tax is imposed on an interim beneficiary who is generally one generation younger than the original transferor. Double taxation caused by the original transfer, such as gift tax imposed on the original transferor plus GST because of a direct skip, is not prevented. In fact, this is a specific objective of the GST.

.042 Annual exclusion

The taxable amount of any generation-skipping transfer, subject to both the federal gift tax and to the GST, is reduced by the annual exclusion of $10,000 per year, per recipient.[87] If the annual exclusion is to be available for this purpose, the transfer must qualify as a present interest in property. The exclusion is not limited to outright direct skip transfers. Any amount transferred to a trust fund that qualifies for the annual exclusion remains free of the GST upon future trust distributions provided that both of the following requirements[88] are met:

---

[87] Code Secs. 2503 and 2652(a)(1)(B).

[88] Code Sec. 2642(c)(2).

(1) During the lifetime of the trust beneficiary (a skip person), no income or corpus distributions may be made to any other person.

(2) At the beneficiary's death, the trust must be designed such that the trust assets must be included in the beneficiary's taxable estate, unless the trust terminates before the beneficiary's death.

Keeping future trust distributions free of GST is accomplished by the method of computing GST itself. The tax is computed by a fraction that is multiplied by the GST rate and then multiplied by the amount of all trust distributions in order to determine the GST payable. The fraction (and therefore the amount of GST as well) remains at zero to the extent that all money or property transferred to the trust qualifies for the annual exclusion.

The actual computation of this fraction, designated as the "inclusion ratio," is discussed further at .045, below.

If subsequent transfers that qualify for the gift tax annual exclusion are made to the trust, the inclusion ratio is recomputed.

.043 Medical and educational exclusion

Any transfer that qualifies for the exclusion from taxable gifts for payments made directly to the providers of medical care or educational services, if made in the circumstances of a generation-skipping transfer, is free of the GST.[89] As in the case of the corresponding gift tax exemption, there are no dollar amount limitations of the medical and educational exclusion and no restrictions as to family relationship between the transferor and the recipient of the services.

It is possible to establish a trust fund to make payments to the providers of medical care and educational services. The part of the value transferred to the trust that is devoted to these purposes enters into the calculation of the inclusion ratio used in the calculation of the GST upon future taxable distributions or upon a future taxable termination.

.044 Lifetime exemption for generation-skipping transfers

The most significant of the exclusions and exemptions for purposes of the GST is the lifetime exemption. This permits the transfer, free of the GST, either through trusts or outright, of up to $1,000,000 in value through what would otherwise be a taxable distribution, taxable termination, direct skip, or any combination of the three.[90] If any generation-skipping transfer is made, the transferor has the right to elect either to use up part or all of the lifetime exemption or to save the exemption and allocate it to future transfers.

The exemption applies to the value of money or property transferred at the date of the original transfer. A taxable distribution or taxable termination of a trust may occur years after the original transfer. Any appreciation of the part of the value covered by the lifetime exemption, as well as that covered by the other exclusions, that occurs after the original transfer and before the generation-skipping taxable event is free of the GST.

Example: A establishes a living trust fund to pay the income to his child, C, for life, with the remainder to his grandchildren in equal shares. C is age 50. A elects to allocate the maximum exemption

[89] Code Sec. 2611(b)(2).

[90] Code Sec. 2631(a).

available for GST purposes to this trust. A transfers cash and investments with a value of $1,160,000 to the trust. C dies 15 years later, when the trust has a value of $2,780,000.

In addition to the gift tax, which will be payable by A for the year in which the transfer to this trust occurs, there will be GST payable upon the distribution of the remainder to A's grandchildren at the death of C. This trust's final distribution constitutes a taxable termination. The value of the trust fund at the time will be multiplied by the product of the GST rate and the applicable fraction in order to determine the amount of GST payable.

.045 Calculation of the inclusion ratio

The inclusion ratio is calculated as follows:

Compute the "applicable fraction." The numerator is the amount of the GST lifetime exemption allocated to the subject transfer.[91] The denominator is the value of the cash and any other assets transferred, adjusted by subtracting the following amounts:

(1) any available gift tax annual exclusion;

(2) any available medical or educational exclusions;

(3) any part of the value transferred for which a charitable deduction would be allowed under the gift or estate tax rules; and

(4) any federal estate tax or state death tax actually paid from the transferred property.

Subtract the applicable fraction from the number 1.

In the example at .044, above, the first step in this process is to determine whether any gift tax exclusion is available. Since C, the life income beneficiary, is age 50 at the trust's inception and is using an applicable federal rate of eight percent, the actuarial factor to determine the part of the transfer attributable to the life estate is .82303. The product of this factor, multiplied by the amount transferred to the trust, is the value of C's life estate:

.82303	×	$1,160,000	=	$954,715
Life Estate Factor		Amount of Transfer		Value of Life Estate

Since the value of the life estate far exceeds the maximum gift tax annual exclusion, $10,000 must be subtracted from the denominator of the applicable fraction. The full $1,000,000 GST exemption is available, so that the applicable fraction is as follows:

$$\frac{\text{GST Exemption}}{\text{Value of Subject Transfer as Adjusted}} \quad \frac{\$1{,}000{,}000}{1{,}150{,}000} = .86957 \text{ Applicable Fraction}$$

When the applicable fraction is subtracted from the number 1, the result is .13043.

In the example at .044, above, on the date of C's death, a taxable termination takes place. The product of the GST rate and the inclusion ratio

[91] Code Sec. 2642(a)(2), as amended by TAMRA § 1014(g)(4)(B).

multiplied by the value of the trust fund on the date of this taxable termination is the GST payable.

$2,780,000	× (55%	× .13043)	= $199,427
Value of Fund at Date of Taxable Termination	GST Rate	Inclusion Ratio	GST Payable

The result is a GST that amounts to just under 7.2 percent of the final distribution. Consider the following: The maximum GST exemption is $1,000,000, there is only one annual exclusion of $10,000 available, the amount of the final distribution is $2,780,000, and the GST rate is 55 percent. In view of this, how can the amount of tax be so small? The answer lies in the nature of the inclusion ratio. It is computed when the property is first transferred. It is unaffected by any appreciation of the subject property between the transfer date and the date of the GST taxable event. Naturally, then, the smaller the inclusion ratio, the smaller the portion of taxable assets consumed by the GST. In other words, if the total value at the date of the original transfer does not exceed the sum of the GST exemption plus any available exclusions, the inclusion ratio is zero and there is no GST payable upon any future taxable distribution, taxable termination, or direct skip, no matter how much appreciation may occur in the meantime.

.046 GST planning hints

The principles described above provide some rules of thumb for GST planning purposes.

Where possible, a trust that will be subject to GST at any time in the future should receive transfers of property shielded, to the maximum extent possible, by the GST exemption and annual exclusions.

Also, in choosing property to transfer to a trust with an inclusion ratio of zero or a small percent, preference should be given to assets with the potential for appreciation in value.

Finally, if assets with little or no appreciation potential are to be transferred in a transaction subject to GST other than a direct skip where the tax is imposed immediately, there may be advantages in electing not to allocate the GST exemption to such transfer.

.05 Multiple Skips

Where a trust specifies several beneficiaries, it is common to provide for the shifting of benefits in the event of the death of a beneficiary prior to a specified date or event. Such a shifting of benefits may constitute a GST taxable event. The imposition of the GST is effectively limited, however, to one tax payable for each generation.[92] A test is made as of the shifting of benefits to determine the identity of the recipient(s) of future trust benefits. Imposition of the GST depends on the relative generation levels of the previous beneficiary and the succeeding beneficiary and whether or not GST was paid with respect to the subject property in the past, according to the following rules:

---

92 Code Sec. 2653(a).

(1) If the succeeding beneficiary is in the same generation or an older generation compared to the previous beneficiary, and if GST was imposed when the previous beneficiary's interest in the trust began, no GST is payable.

(2) If the succeeding beneficiary is in a younger generation than the previous beneficiary and the transfer meets the other requirements of a taxable termination or taxable distribution, GST is payable, regardless of whether GST had ever before been imposed on the subject property.

Example: A had three children and three grandchildren, all living at the date of A's death. A's will establishes a trust fund to pay all of the income to his children, in equal shares. After the death of any child, the deceased child's share of the income becomes payable to the grandchildren in equal shares. After the death of any grandchild, the deceased grandchild's share of the income is redistributed among the surviving grandchildren. At the death of the last surviving grandchild of A, the remainder of the trust is distributable among A's descendants per stirpes.

Below are the possibilities for multiple skip transactions that result in imposition of GST as well as for multiple skips that are free of the GST.

(a) At the death of any child, future income distributions to the grandchildren are taxable distributions. This is not an example of a multiple skip because no previous GST event had taken place.

(b) At the death of the last surviving child, a taxable termination is deemed to occur because this is the equivalent of a transfer to the generation that is two levels younger than the original transferor after having been held for the benefit of those who were one generation younger. However, there has not yet been a multiple skip.

(c) Thereafter, at the death of any of the grandchildren, the decedent's interest in the trust shifts to others who are in the same generation as the deceased grandchild. The multiple skip rule prevents the imposition of the GST at this point.

(d) At the death of the last surviving grandchild, another taxable termination occurs. This time, however, the multiple skip rule does not prevent GST from being imposed because the beneficial interest is shifted to those in the next younger generation or below.

.06 Pour-Over Trusts and Basis Adjustment

The following sections discuss pour-over trusts and their relationship to the GST and the basis adjustment to the cost basis upon imposition of the GST.

.061 Pour-over trusts and GST

The term "pour-over" has been used for decades in the field of estate planning to describe a situation in which a distribution is made from one fiduciary entity to another. The most common example of the pour-over is the inter vivos trust, which continues after the death of the grantor and which the grantor names as beneficiary of his estate. In this situation, the trust may contain assets while the grantor is still alive. It receives additions to principal from the grantor's estate. The distribution from the estate to the trust is a type of pour-over. Examples of pour-overs from one trust to another are also frequently encountered in estate planning. Some of the general planning aspects of the pour-over are discussed in greater detail at ¶ 503.

In the context of the GST, a pour-over from one trust to another may cause an adjustment of the inclusion ratio. This is accomplished in the following manner:

(1) A nontax portion of the distribution into the pour-over trust is computed by multiplying the applicable fraction of the distributing trust by the amount of the pour-over distribution.

(2) In computing the applicable fraction of the resulting pour-over trust, the nontax portion of the pour-over distribution is treated as if it were a GST exemption amount.

Example: Grandparent G's will established two generation-skipping transfer trusts. Trust 1 pays the income to G's spouse for life and, after the spouse's death, the income pours over into Trust 2. Trust 2 pays the income to G's child, C, for life and at C's death, distributes the remainder to G's grandchildren. At G's death, each trust had a value of $600,000. The executor of G's estate allocated the GST exemption as follows:

(a) $400,000 to Trust 1.

(b) $600,000 to Trust 2.

At the death of G's spouse, the balance of Trust 1, in the amount of $1,200,000, is combined with Trust 2, which also has a value of $1,200,000.

Assuming for the purpose of this example that there were no federal or state death taxes payable at the death of G and that no charitable deduction was allowed in connection with either trust, the applicable fraction for Trust 1 would have been two-thirds, calculated as follows:

$$\frac{\text{GST exemption allocated to Trust 1}}{\text{Value of assets transferred to Trust 1}} = \frac{\$400{,}000}{\$600{,}000} = 2/3$$

Making the same assumptions, the applicable fraction for Trust 2 would have been one, calculated as follows:

$$\frac{\text{GST exemption allocated to Trust 2}}{\text{Value of assets transferred to Trust 2}} = \frac{\$600{,}000}{\$600{,}000} = 1$$

At the time of the pour-over, it is necessary to adjust the inclusion ratio of the pour-over trust as follows:

(1) Combine the value of both trusts that would not be subject to GST if the total value of both trusts were distributed in a transaction subject to GST. For each separate trust, the value at the time of the pour-over, multiplied by each trust's applicable fraction, is the value that would not be subject to GST.

(2) Divide this combined value by the total combined value of both trusts at the time of the pour-over transfer. The result is the new applicable fraction.

(3) Subtract the applicable fraction from the number 1 in order to determine the new inclusion ratio for the pour-over trust.

In the preceding example, the applicable fraction for Trust 1 is 2/3. Therefore, the value not potentially subject to GST is calculated as follows:

2/3 Applicable Fraction	×	$1,200,000 Value at Date of Pour-Over	=	$800,000 Value Not Subject to GST

The applicable fraction for Trust 2 is one, resulting in an inclusion ratio for Trust 2 of zero. Therefore, no part of the value of Trust 2 is potentially subject to GST. As a result, 2/3 of the value of Trust 1, or $800,000, plus the total value of Trust 2, or $1,200,000, is not potentially subject to GST. Based on this, the applicable fraction and the inclusion ratio for the resulting combined pour-over trust are:

Applicable Fraction:

$$\frac{\text{Combined value of Trust 1 and Trust 2 not potentially subject to GST}}{\text{Total combined value of Trust 1 and Trust 2}} = \frac{\$2{,}000{,}000}{\$2{,}400{,}000} = .83333$$

Inclusion Ratio:

$$\begin{array}{rl} 1.00000 & \\ -\ .8333 & \text{(Applicable Fraction)} \\ \hline .16667 & \end{array}$$

As a result, in order to calculate the GST at the time of a taxable distribution or taxable termination of the pour-over trust, the value distributed will be multiplied by the product of the GST rate and .16667.[93]

.062 Adjustment to cost basis upon imposition of GST

The recipient of any property (other than cash) subject to GST is allowed to increase the cost basis of the property by a proportionate part of the amount of GST paid.[94] The proportionate part of the GST is the ratio of the excess of the fair market value of the property over its adjusted cost basis before the GST adjustment. If the GST is imposed upon the death of any person, the cost basis is determined in the same manner as if the subject property had been included in that person's taxable estate. Generally, this has the effect of increasing the cost basis to the fair market value of the subject property as of the date of the GST event. However, if the inclusion ratio is less

[93] Prop. Reg. § 26.2642-4(a)(2).

[94] Code Sec. 2654(a).

than 100 percent, the potential increase in basis is multiplied by the inclusion ratio and the result is the allowable increase in the cost basis.

As the result of any GST event, the cost basis of any asset may not be increased in excess of the asset's fair market value.

.07 Planning to Minimize the Impact of GST

A taxpayer can use planning as a technique to minimize GST. The following sections discuss how to determine the need for GST planning, general strategies, possible trust investments and life insurance considerations, among other matters.

.071 Determining the need for GST planning

Not all estate plans require making special provision to minimize the impact of GST. In any family, the parents have the right to make the basic planning decisions. A great many parents choose planning strategies that control the management and distribution of resources for the benefit of the surviving spouse and for children only until they reach a predetermined age. In these cases, the parents prefer an outright distribution at some point during the lifetime of their children rather than a trust that continues throughout the children's lives, as well as into or beyond their second younger generation of descendants. Multiple generation estate plans are definitely beyond the level of sophistication preferred by the majority of families without regard to tax savings potential. Even if the impact of GST is likely to be significant, the decision makers in the family may be disinclined to establish trust funds that continue beyond the lifetimes of their children. Trusts that complete their term and make distribution of the balance to the generation that is only one level younger than the original transferor are never subject to GST.

Another consideration is the total value of the combined resources of the family, which may consist of the combined assets of husband and wife or the assets of a surviving spouse. The mere fact that the total value is near to the level of the GST exemption, or moderately in excess of the exemption, should not be the exclusive criterion for deciding whether or not to consider strategies to control GST. Even if the value is below the GST exemption amount, if the planning couple or individual is relatively young and if it appears that their general financial pattern is likely to result in accumulation of wealth in excess of the GST exempt amount, discussion of GST avoidance may be indicated. On the other hand, planning oriented toward control of GST may be unnecessary when the following circumstances or combinations of circumstances are encountered:

(1) The total value of the resources is below the GST exemption.

(2) Aspects of the overall financial situation, such as spending needs in order to maintain the accustomed standard of living, make significant additions to wealth unlikely.

(3) There is aversion to the prospect of establishing trusts that last beyond the children's generation.

.072 General strategies

Where both the level of wealth and client motivation support the more complex and sophisticated planning needed to reduce the impact of the GST, there are several steps that the financial consultant may consider with the client. These include certain choices in trust selection and design, creation of several trusts whereas previously one might have been adequate to the non-GST plan, one investment approach for those resources that are likely to be subject to GST and another approach for assets that can be predicted to be exempt, and the use of life insurance, where appropriate.

Trust selection and design. The complexity of the calculations relating to the inclusion ratio makes it desirable to plan for one or more trusts from which all future distributions will be fully sheltered from GST (GST exempt trust) and, if necessary, another trust or trusts from which distribution will be subject to GST (GST taxable trust). This can be accomplished by including in the will or trust agreement a direction to set aside, in a separate trust fund, the maximum amount that can be placed in a trust resulting in an inclusion ratio of zero.

Sprinkle trusts, which may provide benefits to children as well as to more remote descendants, can "waste" some of the GST exemption because the inclusion ratio is based on the total value placed in the trust. Any distributions to children of the transferor are not actually subject to GST. To the extent that the GST exemption has been allocated to a sprinkle trust, the exemption can have the effect of shielding distributions to children that would never have been subject to the GST in the first place.

If it is in keeping with the transferor's objectives to permit or direct a trust to accumulate income, which is not currently needed, for ultimate distribution to a skip person, there may be a double benefit in allocating the GST exemption to the trust. To the extent that the trust is shielded from GST by the exemption, any accumulated income, as well as any appreciation of the trust assets, are free of the GST upon any future GST taxable event.

With these principles in mind, it may be appropriate in some cases to establish one trust for the assets that will eventually pass to the transferor's first younger generation, a second trust for assets that will eventually pass to one or more skip persons, and a third trust for assets that may be distributed on a sprinkle basis, partly to skip persons and partly to non-skip persons.

Trust investments in general. Every trust fund should have formal written investment objectives that should be reviewed periodically in order to determine whether factors such as changed circumstances of the beneficiaries and the drawing near of the termination date require adjustments in the investment plan. Where both GST exempt trusts and GST taxable trusts are used in the same estate plan, the investment objectives may be influenced by the potential tax considerations.

The certainty that GST will eventually consume 55 percent of current principal, income accumulations, and appreciation of a GST taxable trust to the extent that distributions are made to skip persons may seem to create a disincentive to invest for growth, particularly since the potential for investment growth generally varies directly with the risk of investment loss. This certainty almost turns the investment performance of a GST taxable trust into a "no win" situation. If losses are incurred, the fact that the potential GST is reduced is small consolation. If the investment program is successful, more than half of the profits will be consumed by the tax. However, there are some points in favor of growth investments in GST taxable trusts:

(1) Why not risk the government's money? Although an investment loss can never really be regarded as an advantage, more than half of the risk is borne by the tax collector.

(2) Especially where the GST taxable event will be a taxable termination not likely to occur for 10 or 20 years, growth potential up to the date of the taxable event may be regarded as one of the best methods of offsetting the effects of the tax.

(3) Investments that provide moderate income and moderate growth of both income and principal value, given a sufficient term of years, have the potential to provide the following:

(a) Income which, although smaller than fixed investments in the early years of the program, may grow to a level that is much higher in the later years of the trust. Cumulative income may eventually exceed that produced by fixed investments.

(b) Enough growth of principal so that, even after GST is imposed, the remainder is greater than the result if fixed investments had been used.

.073 Trust investments for an estate plan with both GST taxable and GST exempt trusts

A great many trust investment plans use a balanced approach between fixed, income-oriented investments and equity investments, which usually produce less income but which may offer the potential for a growing level of income as well as growth of principal value. Theoretically, if the estate plan calls for both a GST exempt trust and a GST taxable trust, the trustee should try to place the fixed investments in the GST taxable trust and the equity investments in the GST exempt trust. That is a sensible rule of thumb. However, taking that theory one step further, to the conclusion that no growth should be sought in the GST taxable trust, may prove to be a mistake.

> **Example:** A, who is widowed, establishes two testamentary trust funds. A's will directs the trustee to place an amount equal to the GST exemption in Trust 1, which is to be a GST exempt trust, and the balance of A's estate in Trust 2, which is a GST taxable trust. Trust 2 is a sprinkle trust for the benefit of A's children and grandchildren. Trust 1 is directed to pay all income to A's children in equal shares. The remainder of each trust is to be distributed among A's descendants upon the death of the last survivor of A's children. A's estate, after payment of expenses, but before payment of taxes, is $4,000,000.

For the sake of making a comparison of the consequences of investment strategies, assume that the trustee can reasonably expect a return on higher income-oriented investments of eight percent per year with little potential for growth. If the trustee invests for moderate income and growth, an income of three percent per year plus average annual appreciation of five percent can be expected. While the rate of income does not increase, the amount of income will increase for the moderate growth investments because it is assumed to be a constant three percent of a gradually increasing principal sum. The following illustrations compare the results of (1) investing the GST taxable trust for higher income and the GST exempt trust for moderate income and growth with (2) using the investment goal of moderate income and growth for both trusts.

ILLUSTRATION 1

Investment Strategy:

GST Exempt Trust: Moderate income & growth.
GST Taxable Trust: Higher income.

Total Estate:	$ 4,000,000
Federal Estate Tax after unified credit:	– 1,648,000
Net Estate:	$ 2,352,000

GST EXEMPT TRUST Initial Value $1,000,000		GST TAXABLE TRUST Initial Value $1,352,000
$ 992,000	Income Distributions over 20 years	$2,163,000
$2,653,000	Principal Value in 20 years	$1,352,000
– 463,000	Less Potential Income Tax on Appreciation	– 0 –
– 0 –	Less GST Payable on Termination	– 744,000
$2,190,000	Net Remainder	$ 608,000

Combined Remainder of Trust Funds:	$ 2,798,000
Plus	
Cumulative Income Distributions:	+3,155,000
Less	
Income Tax @28%	– 833,000
Total Economic Benefit:	$5,070,000

ILLUSTRATION 2

Investment Strategy:

GST Exempt Trust: Moderate income & growth.
GST Taxable Trust: Moderate income & growth.

Total Estate:	$ 4,000,000
Federal Estate Tax after unified credit:	– 1,648,000
Net Estate:	$ 2,352,000

GST EXEMPT TRUST Initial Value $1,000,000		GST TAXABLE TRUST Initial Value $1,352,000
$ 992,000	Income Distributions over 20 years	$1,341,000
$2,653,000	Principal Value in 20 years	$3,587,000
– 463,000	Less Potential Income Tax on Appreciation	– 0 –
– 0 –	Less GST Payable on Termination	– 1,973,000
$2,190,000	Net Remainder	$1,614,000

Combined Remainder of Trust Funds:	$ 3,804,000
Plus	
Cumulative Income Distributions:	+2,333,000
Less	
Income Tax @28%	– 653,000
Total Economic Benefit:	$5,484,000

No comparison of anticipated results is perfect, and a comparison based on rates of income return and growth that are not actually predictable and can fluctuate cannot be used as proof of the wisdom of any particular investment program. There are also some technical aspects of the comparisons that should be pointed out:

(1) All amounts were rounded off to the nearest $1,000.

(2) In both illustrations, for simplicity, capital gains tax is shown as being paid for the GST exempt trust at the end of the term of the trust. However, in reality, individual investments would be sold at various intervals and this would affect the cumulative income from the GST exempt trust as well as the amount of capital gains tax.

(3) In both illustrations, the assumption of capital gains tax on the GST taxable trust is zero. In Illustration 1, this results from the fact that no growth of principal is assumed. In Illustration 2, where there is considerable growth, the trust fund is entitled to a GST cost basis adjustment that has the effect of giving the investments a stepped-up basis. However, in reality, the trustee would more likely make sales and reinvestments during the term of the trust, resulting in the payment of capital gains tax prior to the GST taxable termination.

(4) In each case, the assumed capital gains tax rate is 28 percent.

Despite the example's limitations, it points out the fallacy of making a blanket decision to seek no growth in a GST taxable trust. In this case, although the GST payable in Illustration 2 was more than double the amount of GST in Illustration 1, the overall after-tax economic consequences were considerably improved as a result of using an investment balance of moderate income and growth for each trust.

.074 Using life insurance in connection with GST planning

There are estate planning uses of life insurance other than the traditional use of replacing economic loss resulting from the death of the family member who had provided the family's basic financial support through earnings from employment. Specifically, life insurance has been used to replace the portion of an estate or trust fund that has been consumed by estate and inheritance taxes. There is equal if not increased justification for the use of life insurance in this manner to recoup amounts taken through GST. The high GST rate and the fact that this tax is based on a flat rate rather than on a graduated rate provides serious motivation to consider "paying the tax with discounted dollars," the function of insurance in this context. Life insurance does not make sense in every GST plan. Factors such as the health and age of the proposed insured must be taken into account. If the GST taxable event takes place other than upon the death of a non-skip person, as in the case of a non-trust direct skip, there may not be any opportunity to use life insurance at all. However, there are certain commonly encountered circumstances which lend themselves well to the inclusion of life insurance in a GST-oriented estate plan:

(1) The design of the plan is such that the GST taxable event will be a taxable termination taking place upon the death of a non-skip person or upon the death of the last survivor of a group of non-skip persons, such as the children of the transferor.

(2) At least one of the non-skip persons is reasonably young and in sufficiently good health to obtain life insurance coverage without a prohibitive cost.

(3) The life insurance death benefit can be kept free of both estate tax and GST at the death of the insured non-skip person. While this requires careful planning, it is not difficult to accomplish. For instance, the life insurance proceeds are completely free of tax if the policy is purchased within a GST exempt trust because the insured non-skip person holds none of the incidents of ownership of the policy. This assumes that the policy proceeds are not receivable by the executor of the insured's estate.

If the principal value of both the GST taxable trust and the GST exempt trust remains constant, the replenishment function of the life insurance is easy to see. In reality, however, maintaining a constant trust principal value would not generally be considered adequate. If the principal value of the trusts increases before the GST is paid so that the GST is partly or fully covered in this manner, the value of life insurance in the overall plan may be overshadowed.

Example: C, age 50, is the life income beneficiary of two testamentary trusts established under his parent's will, one of which is a GST exempt trust with an initial value of $1,000,000, and one of which is a GST taxable trust with an initial value of $500,000. C does not possess a general power of appointment over either trust fund. The trustee of the GST exempt trust considers the purchase of a life insurance policy on C's life with a death benefit of $500,000 in order to help offset the erosion of the principal through GST at C's death. C dies 20 years after the trust is established.

At C's death, neither trust fund is included in his taxable estate for federal estate tax purposes, and the GST exempt trust is free of GST as well. However, the distribution of the remainder of the GST taxable trust to GC is a GST taxable termination.

The purpose of the following illustrations is to help the trustee determine whether or not it is economically worthwhile to use part of the income of the GST exempt trust to purchase life insurance that will help to replenish the part of the GST taxable trust consumed by the tax. The investment assumption is yearly income of four percent. While the income rate remains constant, the amount of income increases each year based on the additional assumption of principal growth at the rate of four percent per year.

ILLUSTRATION 1

No Life Insurance

GST EXEMPT TRUST		GST TAXABLE TRUST
Initial Value $1,000,000		Initial Value $ 500,000
$1,191,000	Income Distributions over 20 years	$ 596,000
$2,191,000	Principal Value in 20 years	$1,096,000
– 333,000	Less Potential Income Tax on Appreciation	–0–
–0–	Less GST Payable on Termination	– 603,000
$1,858,000	Net Remainder	$ 493,000

Combined Remainder of Trust Funds:	$2,351,000
Plus	
Cumulative Income Distributions:	+1,787,000
Less	
Income Tax @28%	– 500,000
Total Economic Benefit:	$3,638,000

ILLUSTRATION 2
Using Life Insurance

GST EXEMPT TRUST Initial Value $1,000,000		GST TAXABLE TRUST Initial Value $ 500,000
$1,191,000	Income Distributions over 20 years	$ 596,000
– 150,000	Less Income Spent on Life Insurance Premiums	– 0 –
$2,191,000	Principal Value in 20 years	$1,096,000
– 333,000	Less Potential Income Tax on Appreciation	– 0 –
– 0 –	Less GST Payable on Termination	– 603,000
+ 500,000	Plus Life Insurance Death Benefit	– 0 –
$2,358,000	Net Remainder	$ 493,000

Combined Remainder of Trust Funds:	$ 2,851,000
Plus	
Cumulative Income Distributions:	+1,787,000
Less	
Income Tax @28%	– 500,000
Less	
Income Spent on Insurance Premiums:	– 150,000
Total Economic Benefit:	$3,988,000

Merely comparing the increase in the total economic benefit between Illustrations 1 and 2 does not tell the whole story. The net increase, which is $350,000 or 9.6 percent, does take into account the premiums paid out as well as the death benefit, but it does not account for the time value of the money. The internal rate of return in this case, based on 20 years of premium payments at the rate of $7,500 per year followed by receipt of a death benefit in the amount of $500,000, is about 10.4 percent, which compares favorably with the investment assumptions.

All aspects of the comparison must be viewed in light of the limitations discussed in relation to the preceding example. Because of the growth of principal of the trusts, the life insurance, even though equal in face value to 100 percent of the beginning principal of the GST taxable trust, did not fully pay the GST at the taxable termination of the trust. Furthermore, as a result of the growth of principal, the combined remainder value of the trusts, exclusive of life insurance proceeds, was over 125 percent of the beginning principal value, even after payment of the GST.

Nevertheless, the insurance may be viewed by the client as a positive element in the overall plan if the annual cost does not reduce the amount of income available for distribution to the interim beneficiary to an unacceptable level. Arguments in favor of using life insurance in this manner are:

(1) Since investment growth is not certain to occur, the insurance proceeds provide absolute assurance of the preservation of some part of the basic value that would otherwise have been consumed by the tax.

(2) The insurance death benefit provides very significant protection in the early years of the trust. In later years, if this benefit is overshadowed by investment growth, this growth should be viewed as creating an improvement in the overall result rather than as disproving the value of the insurance.

(3) Since it is the child of the transferor rather than the transferor on whose life the insurance is purchased, the cost may be more acceptable.

.075 Intentional inclusion of trust principal in the estate of non-skip person

In a situation in which a taxable termination might otherwise have occurred, if the value of the trust fund is included in the taxable estate of a non-skip person, no GST is payable. The federal estate tax payable in this manner may be lower than the GST would have been; however, that result is not likely to be predictable many years in advance of the taxable termination. If the non-skip person, upon whose death a taxable termination occurs, holds a general power of appointment, part or all of the value of the trust principal is included in this person's taxable estate. Solely from a tax point of view, this cannot result in a higher effective rate of tax on the subject property. However, if inclusion in the estate results in exposure of the assets to the claims of estate creditors, a potential disadvantage exists. It would be preferable to use a trust design that gives the family the flexibility of either choosing inclusion for federal estate tax purposes or avoiding inclusion so that the GST applies, depending on the circumstances that exist at the death of the non-skip person when the taxable termination occurs.

The provisions of a GST taxable trust may include a discretionary power, held by an independent trustee, to distribute part or all of the principal of the trust to the estate of the non-skip person. In this manner, the trustee has the ability to distribute the principal and cause it to be included in the taxable estate of the non-skip person if the estate tax triggered by the distribution is less than the amount of the GST that would have resulted.

In order to obtain this advantage, some coordination between the estate plan of the original transferor and that of the non-skip person is necessary. The remaindermen of the GST taxable trust designated to receive the trust balance if the trustee fails to make the distribution should be the beneficiaries of the estate of the non-skip person's estate. If this is not the case, the trustee's power to distribute determines who receives the trust remainder value as well as the tax consequences of the distribution. The family may not wish to place this form of control in the trustee's hands.

Example: D, the life income beneficiary of a GST taxable trust, is a non-skip person upon whose death a taxable termination occurs. D's taxable estate is $1,500,000. The value of the trust at D's death is $750,000.

If the trustee makes a discretionary distribution of the balance of the trust fund to D's estate, the increased estate tax is less than the GST would have been, as shown in the following illustration.

Reduction of Overall Tax Payable
Through Intentional Inclusion of GST Taxable Trust
in the Taxable Estate of a Non-skip Person

(1) Potential GST:			
$1,000,000 Value of Trust at Taxable Termination	×	55% GST Rate	= $550,000 GST Payable
(2) Increase in federal estate tax:			
Federal estate tax imposed if trust included in D's estate:		$475,500	
Less Federal estate tax imposed on D's estate excluding trust:		– 55,500	
Federal estate tax allocable to trust:			– 420,000
(3) Overall reduction in tax through discretionary distribution of trust to D's estate:			$130,000

It is clear that any power given to the trustee, or interest possessed by a beneficiary, that is intended to cause inclusion in the beneficiary's taxable estate must have substantial economic consequences. An interest that is established for the purpose of avoiding imposition of GST will be disregarded.[95]

[95] Code Sec. 2652(c)(2).

¶ 404 REVIEWING CLIENTS' EXISTING WILLS AND TRUST DOCUMENTS

There were important modifications made to the federal estate and gift tax systems in 1976, 1978, and 1981, as well as in 1986 and 1988. The GST system, which was first introduced in 1976, was completely overhauled on a retroactive basis under the Tax Reform Act of 1986 (TRA '86) (P.L. 99-514) and less significantly altered by the Technical and Miscellaneous Revenue Act of 1988 (TAMRA) (P.L. 100-647).

These changes in the law have forced attorneys to recommend various modifications to their clients' existing wills and revocable trust agreements. In certain cases, disadvantages result from failure to make updates.

Perhaps the most serious change is that caused by modification of the marital deduction limit. Many wills and trust documents written and signed since 1976 are affected by this change. If the financial consultant is called upon to "look over" wills and trust documents of his clients, it is especially important to observe the date. If questions present themselves, the client's attorney must be alerted.

Until the end of 1976, the marital deduction allowed for gift and estate tax purposes was limited to the total value passing from the first deceased spouse to the surviving spouse not to exceed 50 percent of the first spouse's taxable estate. That limitation had been in effect since 1948, and wills and trusts in existence for many years prior to 1976 had never required any change in order to carry out their tax-planning purposes. From 1977 through 1981, the maximum deduction for interspousal transfers was limited to the greater of $250,000 or 50 percent of the value transferred. The present rule, permitting an unlimited marital deduction, became effective for transfers made on or after January 1, 1982.

Prior to 1977, it was therefore customary to prepare a will and trust agreement that set aside a marital deduction share based on 50 percent of the value that was available for transfer between husband and wife. Between 1977 and 1981, reference was commonly made to the "maximum marital deduction," which was interpreted to mean the greater of 50 percent of the value available or $250,000.

When the unlimited marital deduction was introduced under the Economic Recovery Tax Act of 1981 (ERTA) (P.L. 97-34) for transfers occurring on or after January 1, 1982, a question of interpretation of existing documents was presented: Does the phrase "maximum marital deduction," in a document prepared before 1982, mean (1) the full amount of the transferor's estate, (2) the greater of $250,000 or 50 percent of the decedent's estate, or (3) the entire estate? Interpreting this phrase to refer to the entire estate eliminates the estate tax in the estate of the first deceased spouse, but this interpretation does not necessarily accord with the testator's intentions and may result in a greater estate tax liability when the surviving spouse later dies.

The interpretation of the phrase "maximum marital deduction," in wills executed prior to 1982, is a matter of state law and is not uniform. In view of this, whenever the financial consultant reviews the will of a married person that provides for trusts or other trust document dated prior to 1982, special attention is necessary.

Prior to the retroactive changes to the generation-skipping transfer tax provisions made by TRA '86, it was common practice to make transfers either outright or in trust for grandchildren or other skip persons. Estates of substantial value could be subject to a combined estate tax and GST tax of up to 100 percent of the amount transferred. This necessitates a special review of pre-1986 wills and trusts with an eye toward GST tax issues. In reviewing these documents, the so-called tax apportionment clause is of particular importance. A popular clause in wills requires the payment of "all taxes imposed as a result of my death" from the decedent's residuary estate. Because of the current GST tax rules, this type of clause might cause a substantial amount of tax, which would otherwise be payable directly from a GST trust at the time of a GST taxable termination, to be paid instead from the estate of the intermediary beneficiary whose will contained this "standard" clause. There is the potential for a similar problem in the will of a surviving spouse who is the beneficiary of a QTIP trust. The surviving spouse-beneficiary's will does not ordinarily control the final disposition of the QTIP trust, but the value of the trust is taxable at the survivor's death. For this reason, the "standard" tax apportionment clause can cause estate tax attributable to the value of the QTIP trust to be paid from the estate of the surviving spouse instead of from the trust itself.

Chapter 5

Using Trusts in Estate Planning

¶ 501 OVERVIEW

The financial consultant should always take an expansive view of estate planning. Rather than merely a system for putting the client's financial affairs in order in contemplation of death, estate planning must be regarded as including:

(1) all aspects of the acquisition of wealth;

(2) the arrangement of ownership of resources to provide financial management assistance in the event of incapacity;

(3) financial protection in the event of the untimely death of the family members who provide financial support to dependents;

(4) the lifelong process of planning for and carrying out the gradual transfer of family wealth to the natural objects of one's bounty;

(5) recognition of the fact that the steps in this process may be accomplished partly during lifetime and partly at death;

(6) to the extent appropriate, withholding direct ownership of wealth from the recipients until they are sufficiently mature to handle the responsibility; and

(7) the selection of forms of ownership, methods, and timing of wealth transfer that result in the smallest possible tax cost.

Tax saving is not the central goal of estate planning. In fact, where the estate planning process begins and ends with the objective of saving taxes, it is possible to lose sight of the ultimate aim and responsibility facing each of us, namely, to ensure that, following our death, whatever we have managed to accumulate provides the maximum benefit for those who are dear to us.

In the area of estate planning, more so than in many other fields, a small amount of knowledge can be dangerous. Attorneys and financial consultants are often confronted by clients who have learned a little about the subject of estate and gift tax. Frequently, the level of understanding is just enough to enable the client to jump to the wrong conclusion about the most appropriate planning course. For this reason, it may be useful to begin the estate planning process with a particular question intended to avoid half-understood tax concepts and to get to the heart of the issue. For example, clients may be taken off guard by the question, "What would you want to have happen to your property after your death if taxes were not a consideration?" In fact, in answering this question, clients often include a precautionary statement that they are willing to change their plans and goals if taxes can be saved. The role of the financial consultant is not to suggest alternatives to what the client really wants to do with wealth just to save taxes, but rather to find ways of accomplishing the client's true non-tax objectives with the smallest reasonable tax cost.

This chapter focuses on specific types of trusts used in estate planning. Some of these trust plans have no impact on gift tax, estate tax, or generation-skipping transfer tax (referred to throughout this chapter as GST) at all. That is, in some cases, the use of trusts results in payment of the same amount of tax as if the grantor had kept ownership of the trust assets in his own name until death. The reason for examining the use of these trusts is that they offer estate planning advantages other than tax saving. In other cases, tax saving clearly does play a role. Some explanation of the income tax consequences, as well as transfer tax consequences, is included in the discussion of each trust plan.

¶ 502 THE BYPASS PRINCIPLE

A trust fund that provides lifetime benefits to a surviving spouse is designated as a "bypass" if the trust design is such that the trust escapes estate tax at the survivor's death. If property ownership between husband and wife is divided in an advantageous manner, significant tax savings for the combined estates can be achieved.

.01 A Common Objective in Estate Planning for Married Couples

For married couples, one of the most common objectives of the estate plan is to make sure that maximum use is made of each spouse's available transfer tax exemptions and exclusions. Because of the unlimited marital deduction for lifetime transfers of wealth, as well as transfers at death, there is some tendency to focus only on the advantages of passing wealth between husband and wife free of gift and estate tax. This tendency leads to the failure to take into account the ultimate consequences on the combined estates of husband and wife if the surviving spouse has outright ownership of all the family wealth after the death of the first spouse. The following illustration helps to redirect attention on planning for the estates of husband and wife while both are still alive.

ILLUSTRATION 1

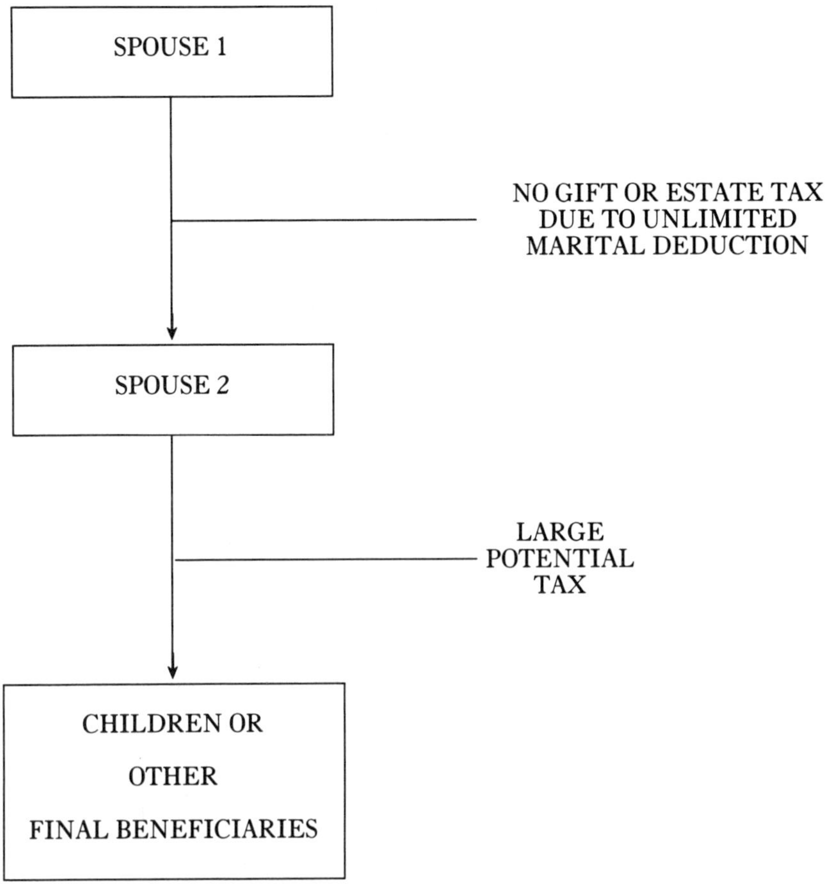

This diagram emphasizes the point that it is no great accomplishment to avoid transfer taxes when ownership of property passes between husband and wife. Whether the transfer occurs during lifetime or at death, the unlimited marital deduction is available. As a result, the most simple estate plan might seem to be the best. "If I die first, I will leave everything to my spouse. I know I can trust my spouse to look after the children and, after we are both gone, the children will be able to divide whatever is left among them." The "I love you" estate plan, as this has been called, may result in a significant tax at the death of the second spouse. In analyzing the situation, what becomes clear is:

(1) In the case of the first estate, it is not necessary to be concerned with annual exclusions and unified credits. It is easier to rely on the marital deduction in order to avoid tax on interspousal transfers.

(2) As a result, the first spouse may make no transfers that require the annual exclusion or unified credit to eliminate the tax payable.

(3) At the death of the second spouse, all of the family wealth has been "bunched" in the second taxable estate. At this point, there is only one unified credit available to offset the estate tax payable.

(4) In the end, after it is too late, the realization may occur that a considerable dollar amount of assets could have passed from the first spouse to beneficiaries other than the recipient spouse free of tax because of the availability of the unified credit. In other words, the first spouse's unified credit has been wasted.

One of the most simple and efficient strategies used to avoid this problem is to have the first spouse create a trust fund for the benefit of the second spouse. The second spouse can have remarkably free access to the benefits of the trust fund, but as long as the second spouse does not possess any right or combination of rights that amounts to a general power of appointment, the value of the trust fund at the death of the second spouse will not be included in the survivor's estate.

ILLUSTRATION 2

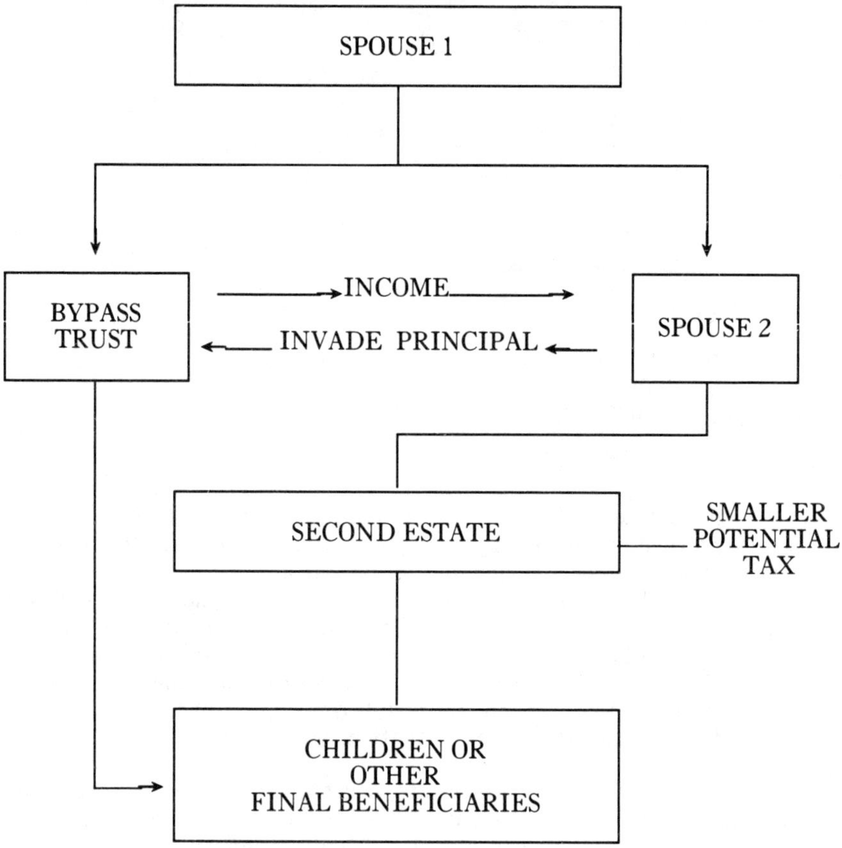

The full amount that can pass through the taxable estate of the first spouse, shielded from gift and estate tax by the unified credit, is transferred to the bypass trust. This exact sum, described as the "credit shelter equivalent" may be set aside through the use of specific references, in the will or trust agreement, to the provisions of the Internal Revenue Code pertaining to the unified credit.[1] Because these references make it necessary for the executor or trustee to follow a multiple step calculation process, they are frequently referred to as "formula clauses." There are several types of formulas, which are described at ¶ 504.08.

The transferor spouse, within certain limits, may place as many or as few restrictions on the beneficiary spouse's access to this trust fund as the transferor wishes. There is also a separate section of this chapter to explain the nature of the rights that may be given to the beneficiary spouse.

Ideally, the ownership of the family wealth between husband and wife should be arranged so that money, investments, and other forms of property owned separately by each spouse are sufficient to enable each spouse's estate to utilize fully the unified credit against gift and estate tax that is available to each estate. The form of ownership is important. If all property is held by husband and wife as joint tenants, for instance, at the death of the first spouse, ownership passes to the surviving spouse automatically. The will of the first deceased spouse cannot override the survivorship feature. Therefore, if the will provides for a bypass trust, there is no property in the probate estate of the first deceased spouse that can be transferred to this trust and no trust comes into existence.

.02 Considering the Form of Property Ownership

No matter how carefully the estate plan has been designed, if the financial consultant fails to consider the form of ownership of property, the result may be a failure to achieve either the tax-saving goals or the non-tax goals. Losing sight of the form of property ownership may be the most common and the most basic failure of the estate planning process. This mistake can lead the client to believe that there is a sound, well-considered, and taxwise estate plan in existence only to have surviving family members discover, when it is too late to correct, that the automatic survivorship feature of certain forms of property ownership takes precedence over the provisions of the will. To prevent this, any professional adviser involved with estate planning must make it a disciplined practice to include in the information-gathering process a complete listing of the items and values of each asset owned by the client and to detail the form of property ownership. The values of assets are then grouped according to:

(1) those items owned individually by each spouse that constitute probate assets and are, therefore, controlled by the owner's will at death;

(2) those property items owned by husband and wife as joint tenants or tenants by the entirety and that, therefore, pass automatically to the surviving spouse by operation of law;

(3) any community property, if applicable;

---

[1] Code Sec. 2010.

(4) benefits payable at death under any contractual arrangement, such as life insurance and retirement plans (including individual retirement accounts); and

(5) assets that are completely outside of the control of the client but are, nevertheless, included in his or her taxable estate, such as QTIP trusts or other family trust funds over which the client holds a general power of appointment.

After arranging the information in this manner and adding the totals in each category, it is possible to determine the portion of the total value that is available to be placed in the bypass trust at the death of the first spouse. At the same time, it is useful to make calculations and comparisons of the potential estate tax liability under two or more separate assumptions. By first calculating the estate tax that will be incurred if no trust is used in the estate plan and comparing this amount with the tax that will result if a bypass trust is used, the potential estate tax saving available through the use of the trust can be demonstrated.

One of the easiest methods of presenting the concept of the bypass trust and its advantages to a client is through the use of comparative illustrations that include hypothetical calculations and comparisons based on the client's personal situation.

.03 Illustration of the Bypass Trust Concept

The following extensive example illustrates the basics of arrangement and presentation of the bypass trust concept. It is based on a married couple, referred to as H and W, who have no significant liabilities and own the following assets:

Estate Plan of H and W
Value and Ownership of Assets

Description	*Ownership:* *H*	*W*	*Joint*	*Contractual*
Home			$250,000	
Savings, C.D.s	$ 25,000	$50,000	10,000	
Bonds		25,000	100,000	
Stocks	240,000			
Life Insurance Death Benefit (on H's life)				$300,000
H's Retirement Plan Benefits				200,000
Totals	$265,000	$75,000	$360,000	$500,000

.031 Arrangement of information

Continuing the example, assume that W is the designated beneficiary of both the life insurance and the retirement plan death benefits. Also assume that the value shown for H's life insurance is actually the face value or benefit payable upon his death and that H holds all incidents of ownership of this policy.

After gathering the basic information and arranging it according to ownership as in the preceding summary, the next step in the process is to calculate the value that would be included in the taxable estate if either spouse were to die.

Estate Plan of H and W
Values Potentially Subject to Federal Estate Tax

	H's Estate	*W's Estate*
Separately Owned Assets	$265,000	$ 75,000
1/2 Each of Jointly Owned Assets	180,000	180,000
Contractual Assets	500,000	– 0 –
Totals	$945,000	$255,000

This information makes it possible to create illustrations for H and W that help to explain:

(1) the potential consequences of a non-trust estate plan;

(2) the tax advantages of the bypass trust;

(3) how the arrangement of asset ownership may interfere with the optimal result; and

(4) what steps H and W may take to improve their estate planning picture.

Estate Plan of H and W
Potential Consequences of a Non-trust Estate Plan

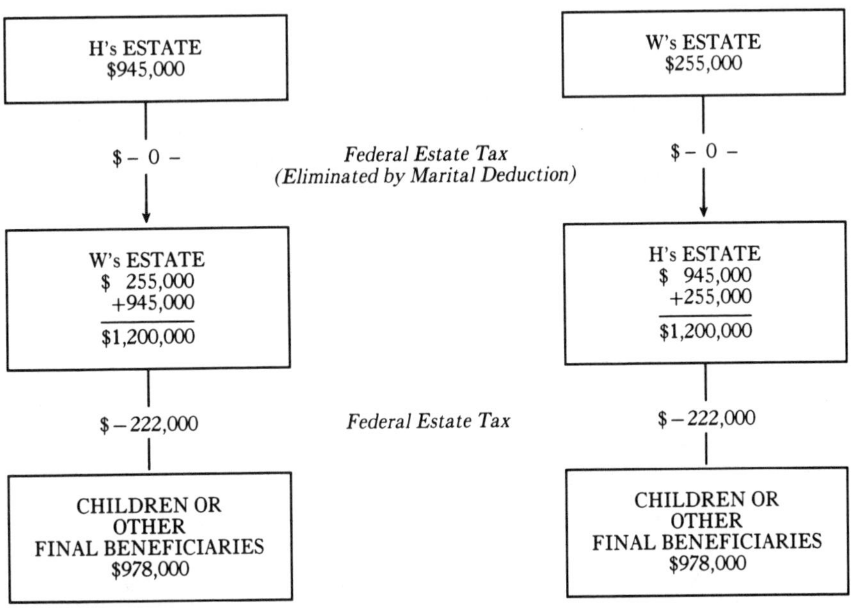

The preceding illustration shows that, regardless of the order of death of H and W, there is a significant potential federal estate tax liability upon the death of the survivor. The next step in the presentation may be an illustration of the savings available through the use of the bypass trust. In some cases, however, financial consultants present idealized illustrations, based on the best possible result but ignoring the realities of property ownership. This should be avoided by presenting alternative bypass trust illustrations showing the consequences, first, based on the current division of property ownership and second, based on possible redistribution of assets between spouses. The comparative illustration method, based on the H and W example, follows.

In this case, the hypothetical calculations are made based on either of the possible orders of death. Some financial consultants prefer to present only the example based on the death of the husband survived by the wife. This tendency is based on prior years' statistics which suggest that, at least in the past, wives have outlived their husbands in the vast majority of marriages. The advantages of the abbreviated presentation are that (1) it is less work to prepare, and (2) it is less likely to seem overwhelming to the client whose attention span may be limited with respect to what is probably an unfamiliar subject. The disadvantages are that (1) mortality statistics based on prior years may not provide a reliable prediction of the future, especially in view of the increase in the number of working couples, and (2) failure to present examples based on both possible orders of death may conceal the fact that, if the wife predeceases the husband, it may not be possible to achieve the same favorable tax result because of the consequences of the distribution of property ownership.

Estate Plan of H and W
Use of Bypass Trust
Assuming W Survives H
Based on Current Distribution of Property Ownership

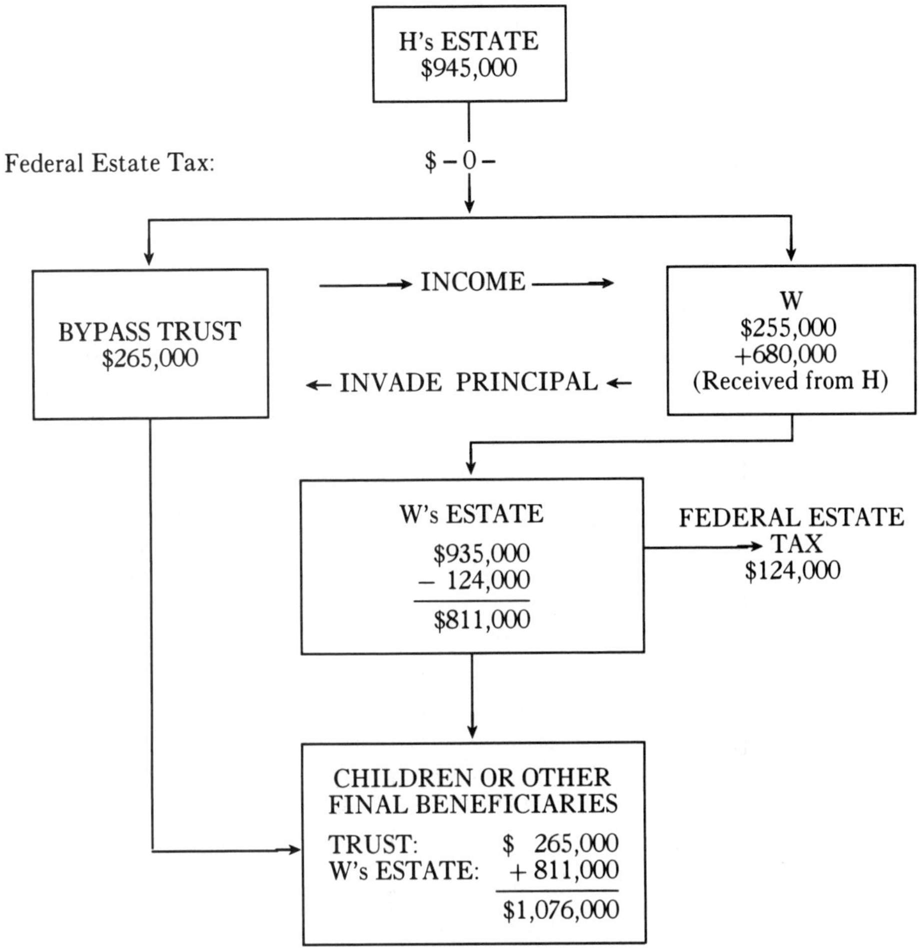

Estate Plan of H and W
Use of Bypass Trust
Assuming H Survives W
Based on Current Distribution of Property Ownership

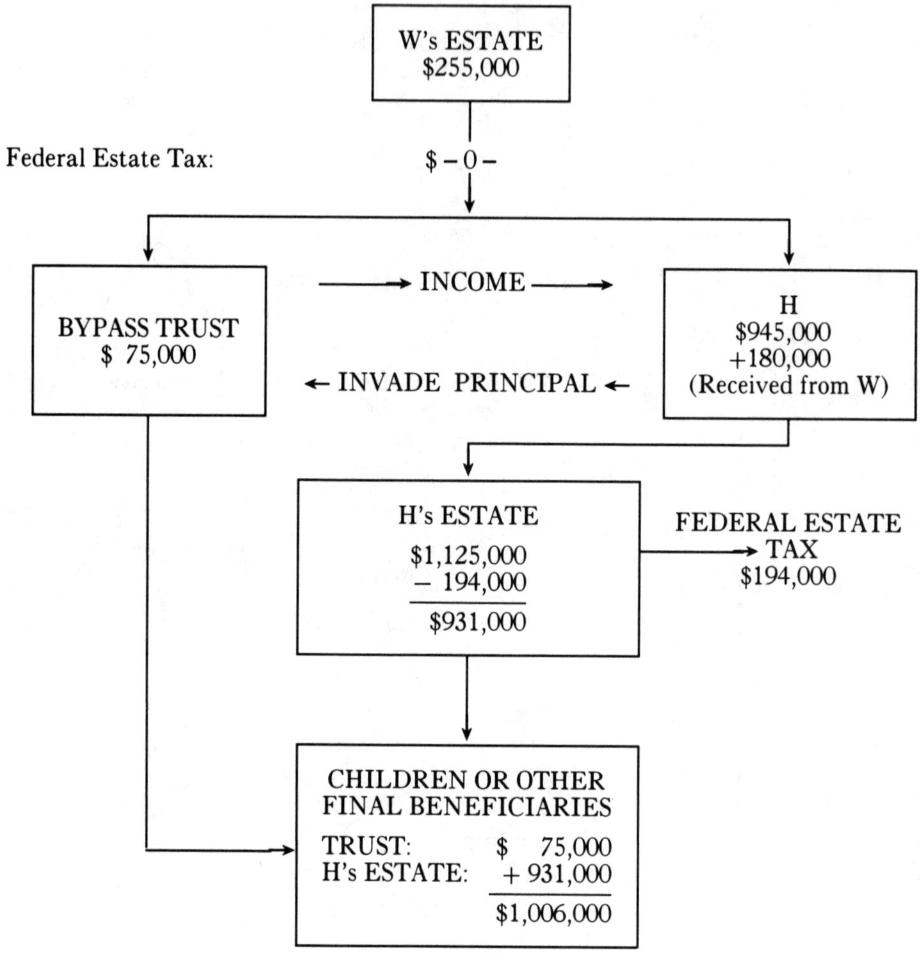

.032 *Limitations within example*

There are some limitations in the information presented by the bypass trust illustrations that represent a trade-off. The format of these illustrations is comparatively simple. For example, there is very little detail as to the sources of assets passing from the first deceased spouse to the trust and to the surviving spouse. Also, there is no explanation of how the potential estate tax was calculated. The financial consultant must provide supplemental explanations, either written or oral, in order to give the client a complete understanding. Some of the additional points, in the case of the illustration based on W surviving H, are:

(1) H's estate, shown as $945,000, consists of $265,000 of probate assets, $500,000 of contractual assets, and the balance, or $180,000, which actually represents 50 percent of the value of the assets that are held jointly with W.

(2) Only the individually held assets, which total $265,000, are controlled by H's will; therefore, only this amount can pass from H's estate to the bypass trust.

(3) The total sum of $680,000 is shown as passing from H's estate to W. However, no part of that value passes to W from H's probate estate, since $500,000 of this amount represents death benefits from H's life insurance and retirement plan, and the balance of $180,000 is 50 percent of the jointly owned property.

(4) The potential federal estate tax on H's estate is zero because the $680,000 that passes to W qualifies for the marital deduction and the federal estate tax on the $265,000 passing to the bypass trust is eliminated by the available unified credit.

(5) It is assumed that neither H nor W had made any taxable gifts.

(6) The federal estate tax payable by W's estate is the net tax, after allowing for the unified credit available to W's estate.

A comparison of the bypass trust illustrations with those based on the non-trust estate plan reveals some potential savings of estate tax, but very little. The maximum value that might have been placed in the bypass trust is $600,000 because that is the largest sum that can be shielded from tax by the unified credit. However, it is not possible for either spouse to transfer the maximum amount to the bypass trust because of the existing division of property ownership and the existing beneficiary designations.

.033 *Changes that can enhance the final result*

The next step in the presentation should be an explanation of the potential changes that H and W can make in order to improve the tax results. The financial consultant's analysis begins with the totals shown on H and W's list of assets and then proceeds to an item-by-item review. The following points should be covered:

(1) The large proportion of this couple's assets held jointly with right of survivorship is part of the problem. On the other hand, the most valuable of these assets is the home, which many couples prefer to own jointly. Also, because the home is not an income-producing investment, it is not the most likely choice to be placed in trust.

(2) Comparing the total value of assets individually owned by H and by W, it is obvious that H's total is much higher. This suggests transfers of some jointly owned assets to W's individual ownership.

(3) H's contractual assets may provide a source of funds for the bypass trust if W survives H. It is a simple matter to have H designate the bypass trust under his will as the life insurance beneficiary. There are some additional considerations, however, regarding the death benefit under H's retirement plan:

(a) Under the Retirement Equity Act of 1984 (P.L. 98-397), H must designate W as beneficiary unless W agrees in writing to some other designation. Also, if the reason for the bypass trust is simply to save tax and if W is the lifetime beneficiary of the trust, there is a good reason for W to give the necessary consent.

(b) Death benefits paid from any qualified retirement plan constitute income in respect of a decedent, taxable to the recipient except to the extent of any after-tax contributions made by the deceased participant in the plan. The surviving spouse, as beneficiary, is permitted to transfer these taxable death benefits into a rollover IRA with no current income tax liability. No other beneficiary, including a bypass trust, has such a rollover privilege. The fully taxable balance must be distributed to a beneficiary that is a trust fund over a period of time not exceeding five years. While there may be some small income tax relief available through the special five- or 10-year income averaging allowable in the case of lump-sum retirement plan distributions, the prompt payment of a substantial amount of income tax on a large retirement plan death benefit is a disadvantage.

Where the bypass trust is the beneficiary of a taxable distribution from a retirement plan, the distribution constitutes "principal income" under the fiduciary income tax rules so that the income tax must be paid from trust principal. As a result, the bypass trust advantage of keeping the maximum principal amount free of estate tax at the death of the surviving spouse is diminished. By contrast, if the surviving spouse receives the taxable distribution and pays the income tax, the second taxable estate is thereby diminished.

Considering these points, H and W might be encouraged to rearrange the ownership of their assets and designate the bypass trust as the beneficiary of H's life insurance policy.

Estate Plan of H and W
Revised Value and Ownership of Assets
Based on Planning Recommendations

Description	*Ownership:* *H*	*W*	*Joint*	*Contractual*
Home			$250,000	
Savings, C.D.'s	$ 25,000	$ 50,000	−10,000	
		+10,000	←	
Bonds		25,000	−100,000	
		+100,000	←	
Stocks	240,000			
Life Insurance Death Benefit (on H's life)				$300,000
H's Retirement Plan Benefits				200,000
Totals	$265,000	$ 185,000	$250,000	$500,000

The results of the property transfers and the change in beneficiary designation of H's life insurance affect the potential amounts of each spouse's taxable estate as well as the results of the bypass trust. The impact of these changes is demonstrated in the following revised illustrations.

Estate Plan of H and W
Values Potentially Subject to Federal Estate Tax
Revised—Based on Planning Recommendations

	H's Estate	*W's Estate*
Separately Owned Assets	$265,000	$185,000
½ Each of Jointly Owned Assets	125,000	125,000
Contractual Assets	500,000	– 0 –
Totals	$890,000	$310,000

Estate Plan of H and W
Use of Bypass Trust
Assuming W Survives H
Based on Changed Property Ownership

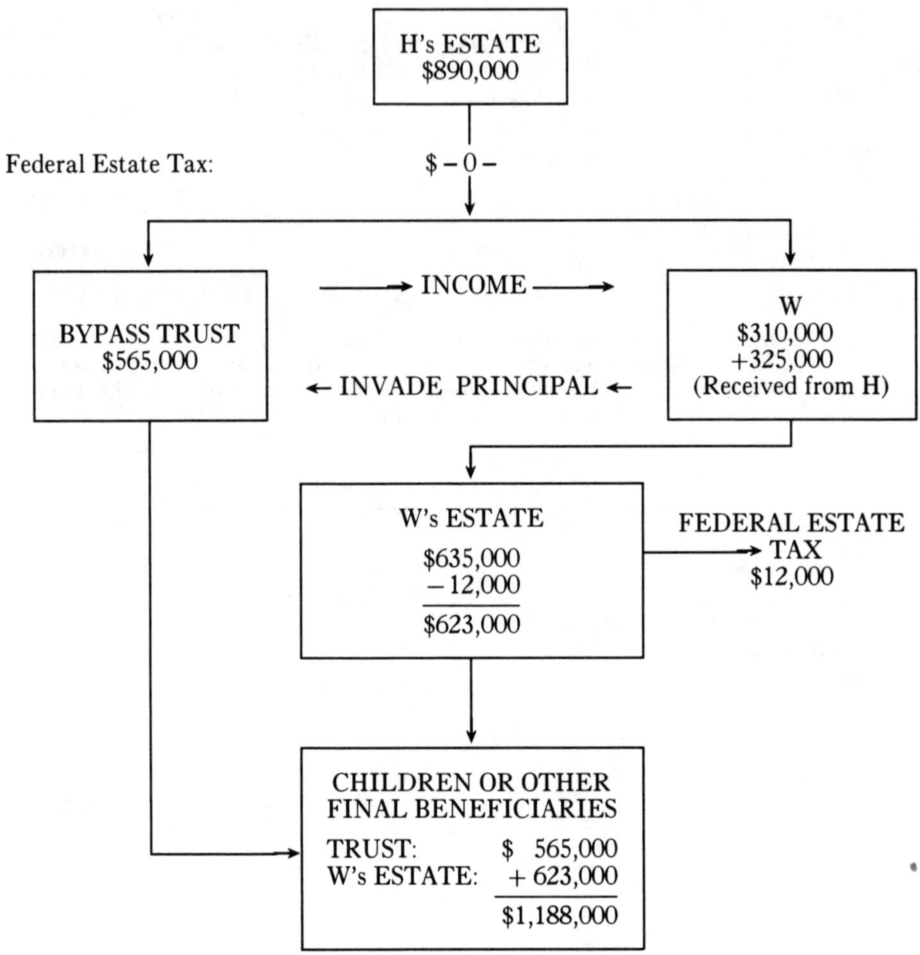

Estate Plan of H and W
Use of Bypass Trust
Assuming H Survives W
Based on Changed Property Ownership

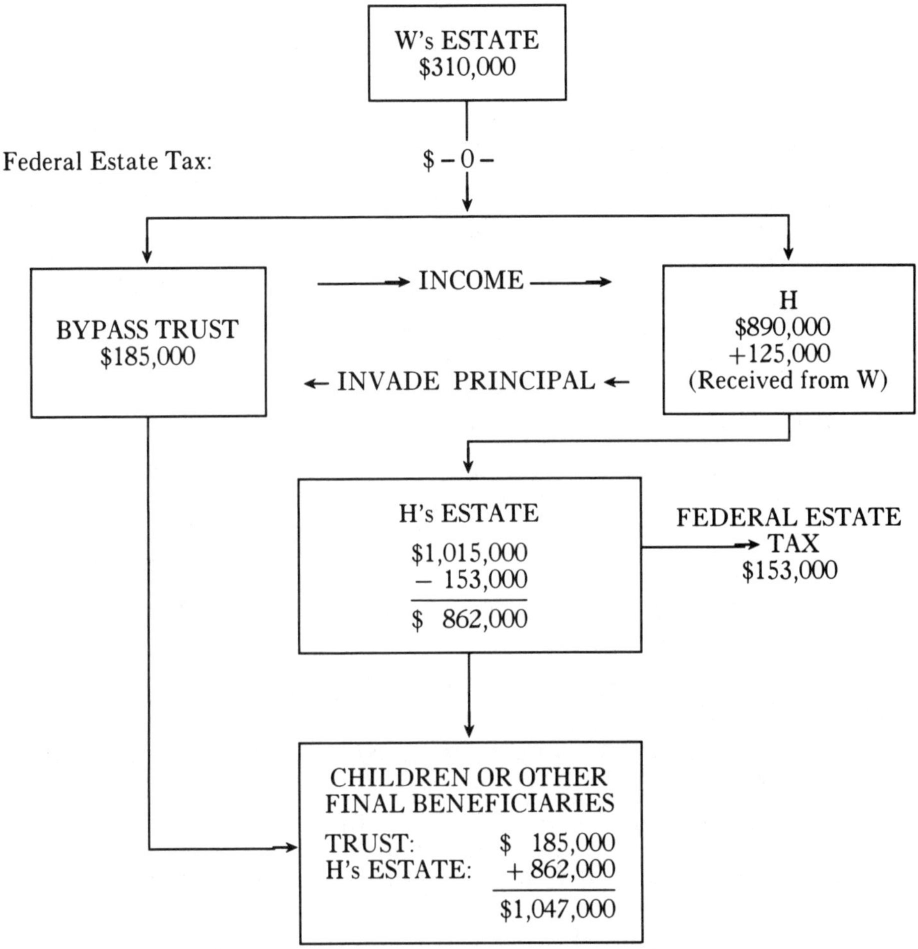

The rearrangement of assets substantially reduces the potential estate tax payable in the event that H predeceases W, but the potential reduction if H survives is not as dramatic, as reflected in the following table:

	Potential Federal Estate Tax Payable			
	Non-trust Plan	*Bypass Trust Plan*	*Amount Saved by Trust*	*% of Tax Saved*
H predeceases W	$124,000	$ 12,000	$112,000	90%
W predeceases H	194,000	153,000	41,000	21%

The reason for the comparatively small potential improvement in the event that W predeceases H is the fact that, even after the reduction of jointly held property and redesignation of the life insurance beneficiary, the amount of assets that can be controlled by W's will and thereby placed in a bypass trust if H survives is far less than $600,000, the maximum amount shielded from tax by the unified credit. If H and W wish to make further improvements in the potential tax cost to their estates, it will be necessary to consider transferring ownership of some additional assets to W as an individual. However, few family financial situations offer the opportunity to make simple changes that permit elimination or substantial reduction of the potential tax.

.034 Conflicting planning considerations

There are some conflicts presented in the case of H and W. First, transfer of the stocks owned by H to W may appear to be a good method of increasing the value that W could place in a bypass trust and thereby reducing the potential estate tax if W dies first. However, upon closer inspection, it becomes obvious that, while this transfer increases the value of W's assets, it also decreases the value that H can place in the bypass trust if W survives. The final outcome of this change is:

(1) a decrease in the potential estate tax on H's estate if W dies first; and

(2) an increase in the potential estate tax on W's estate if H dies first.

It may be possible to correct H's estate picture, if some or all of the stocks are transferred from H to W, by designating the bypass trust as beneficiary of H's retirement plan death benefit, although this results in less than optimum income tax consequences, as previously discussed.

In this case, only the final step of transferring ownership of the home to W's individual ownership enables the bypass trust plan to produce the lowest possible tax for the estate of the surviving spouse regardless of the order of death. The attorney who prepares W's will may wish to make special provisions because of the fact that a home is not an example of a typical trust investment. Directions in the will that require the trustee to retain ownership of the home for the use of H, despite the fact that the home is not an income-producing asset, may be used. In the alternative, W's will may include a life estate in the home for H's benefit. This is a way of making the use and occupancy of the home available to H for life without giving H the degree of ownership rights that would require inclusion of the home's value in his estate at death. In effect, it is an alternative to the bypass trust that can be used for the ownership of real estate.

Beginning with the original asset list of H and W, all of the changes necessary to carry out more effective reduction in potential estate tax are as follows:

Estate Plan of H and W
Revised Value and Ownership of Assets—
Based on Planning Recommendations

Description	*Ownership: H*	*W*	*Joint*	*Contractual*
Home			$ – 250,000	
		$250,000	←	
Savings, C.D.s	$25,000	50,000	– 10,000	
		+10,000	←	
Bonds		25,000	– 100,000	
		+100,000	←	
Stocks	240,000			
	– 165,000			
	→	+165,000		
Life Insurance Death Benefit (on H's life)				$300,000
H's Retirement Plan Benefits				200,000
Totals	$100,000	$600,000	$ – 0 –	$500,000

Estate Plan of H and W
Values Potentially Subject to Federal Estate Tax
Second Revision—Based on Planning Recommendations

	H's Estate	*W's Estate*
Separately Owned Assets	$100,000	$600,000
½ Each of Jointly Owned Assets	– 0 –	– 0 –
Contractual Assets	500,000	– 0 –
Totals	$600,000	$600,000

Estate Plan of H and W
Use of Bypass Trust
Based on Second Revised Changes to Property Ownership

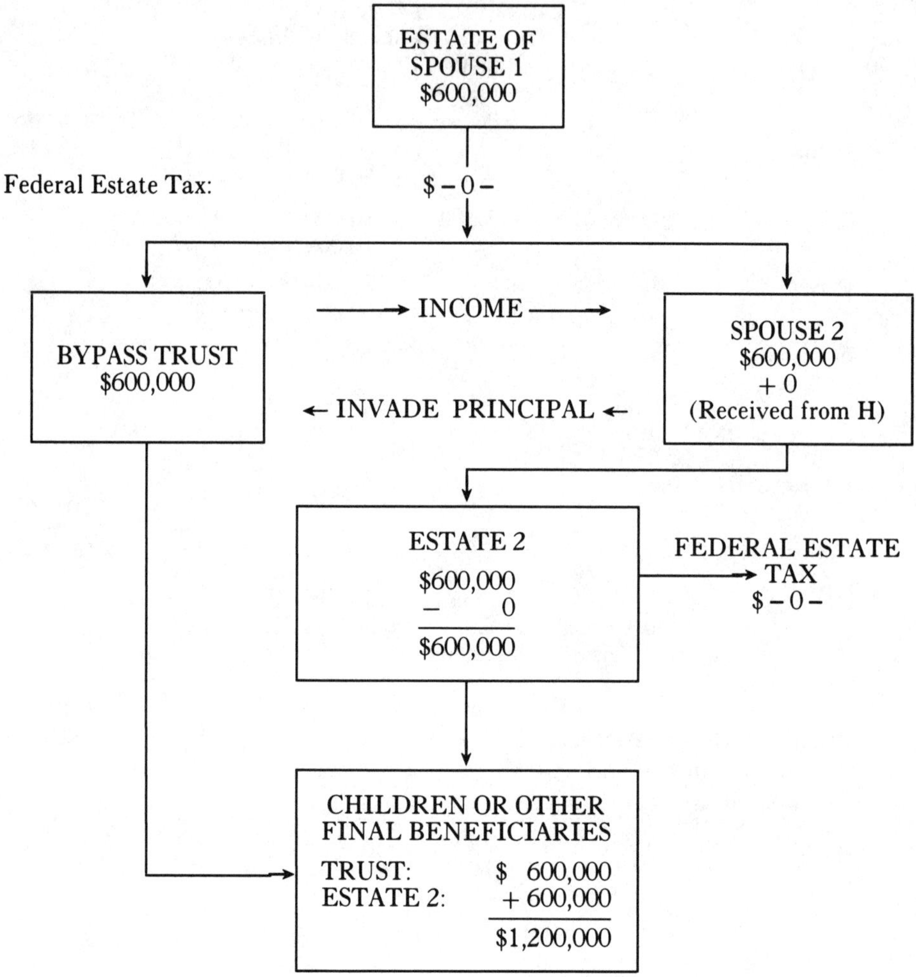

.035 General conclusions

In the last example, since the estates were equalized in value and since the value of each estate is exactly the amount shielded from estate tax by the unified credit, the potential estate tax is eliminated regardless of the order of death. While this exact situation is not encountered often in practice, there are certain conclusions to be drawn from it:

(1) Care should be taken to divide ownership of property equally between husband and wife, or as nearly equally as practical, so that a bypass trust may be established by the first deceased spouse, regardless of the order of death.

(2) If equalization is accomplished, all federal estate tax may be avoided in the estates of both husband and wife where the combined value of their estates does not exceed $1,200,000.

(3) The benefit of equalization, availability of the unified credit to each estate, and bypass trust planning gradually diminishes as the total combined value of the estates increases.

The last of these conclusions may be demonstrated by comparing the potential estate tax savings resulting from bypass trust planning in cases of estates of differing sizes.

The most typical arrangement, after the death of the first spouse, is to place the maximum amount into the bypass trust and to pass the balance to the surviving spouse. This results in no estate tax at the death of the first spouse. Where the combined value of both estates exceeds $600,000 but does not exceed $1,200,000, provided that adequate estate equalization has been accomplished, the result will always be a 100 percent reduction in the amount of estate tax that would have been imposed on an "I love you" estate plan. If the second estate, including any amount that the surviving spouse received from the first deceased spouse, exceeds $600,000 in value, there is federal estate tax payable. As the taxable amount of the second estate increases, the relative effect of estate tax reduction caused by use of the bypass trust diminishes. The following table demonstrates this principle.

Combined Value of Estates of Husband & Wife	*Estate Tax Payable upon Second Death:*		*Estate Tax Saved Through Bypass:*	
	(1) No Trust	*(2) Using Bypass*	*Amount*	*Percent*
$1,200,000	$ 235,000	$ 0	$235,000	100
1,500,000	363,000	114,000	249,000	69
2,000,000	588,000	320,000	268,000	46
2,500,000	833,000	543,000	290,000	35
3,000,000	1,098,000	784,000	314,000	29
3,600,000	1,428,000	1,098,000	330,000	23
5,000,000	2,198,000	1,868,000	330,000	15

¶ 503 TRUSTS USED IN LIFETIME PLANNING

Trust funds may be established during a grantor's lifetime for his own benefit or for the benefit of others. There may be virtually no income, gift, estate, or generation-skipping transfer tax (referred to throughout this section as GST) consequences resulting from the creation of the trust, or the tax consequences may be considerable. See the grantor trust rules at ¶ 302.

The following is an examination of some of the more commonly used lifetime trusts, including a discussion of whether there is tax planning motivation and, if so, an explanation of any tax advantages.

.01 Use of the Revocable Living Trust

The grantor may place some or all of his financial resources in a trust fund for his own benefit for a variety of reasons:

(1) A demanding career may make it difficult to attend to financial matters. By establishing a trust for his own benefit, the grantor can rely on the trustee to take care of investment of the funds as well as payments of personal and family expenses and financial recordkeeping. Some people

who are retired or who do not have very busy lives use living trusts simply because they have an aversion to financial management.

(2) If there is concern about the possibility of becoming mentally disabled, a revocable living trust may provide peace of mind to the grantor. The trust must be established while the grantor is competent; however, it can continue in existence if the grantor later becomes incapable of handling his own affairs.

(3) A trust fund designed to provide initial benefits to the grantor during life, and either to continue after the grantor's death or to distribute the remainder at the death of the grantor, is known as a "will substitute." Whatever funds are held in the trust are immediately available after the grantor's death and are not subject to the delays associated with estate settlement. In addition, while a will must be made available for public inspection, the terms and conditions of living trusts are not generally disclosed.

Frequently, revocable living trusts serve several purposes. Because of their inherent flexibility, they can be modified, based on changing circumstances, in order to meet the ongoing needs of the grantor and family members.

.02 Revocable Living Trust Tax Consequences

The tax consequences associated with a revocable living trust are very simple:

(1) The grantor cannot be treated as making a taxable gift to himself. If the grantor is the initial beneficiary, no taxable gift takes place.

(2) If there are beneficiaries other than the grantor, the revocable feature of the trust results in an incomplete gift. No taxable gift takes place unless and until there is an actual distribution to someone other than the grantor. In the case of any such actual distribution, the annual gift tax exclusion of $10,000 is likely to be available. Distributions made to the grantor's spouse are subject to the unlimited gift tax marital deduction.

(3) The incomplete gift aspect of the revocable living trust also prevents imposition of any GST at the time the trust fund is created. An actual distribution made to a skip person, however, may be treated as a direct skip.

(4) At the death of the grantor, the full value of the trust fund as of the date of the grantor's death is includible in the grantor's taxable estate. Inclusion may result either from the fact that the grantor retained the right to trust income for life or from the fact that the trust could be revoked, altered, or amended by the grantor.

(5) For income tax purposes, the grantor is treated as the substantial owner of a revocable trust. All items of income, as well as any allowable deductions and credits, are reported on the grantor's personal income tax return.

The revocable living trust essentially does not exist from a tax standpoint. Clearly, the nontax planning advantages serve as the motivation to use revocable living trusts.

Example: H transfers all of his assets to a revocable living trust in which the trustee is directed to use all income to pay the living expenses of H and of his spouse, W, for life. The trust agreement specifies that, after H's death, the trust fund is to be divided into two parts:

(1) The maximum amount that can pass free of estate tax continues in trust, initially for W's benefit for life and then for the benefit of H and W's children for their lives. After the death of the survivor of the children, this part of the trust is distributed to the grandchildren of H and W.

(2) The balance of the trust fund is distributed to W.

While there are virtually no tax consequences to the establishment of this trust fund during H's lifetime, after H dies, this trust transforms into a sophisticated estate planning device. The part of the trust that continues is free of estate tax at H's death because of the availability of the unified credit. Assuming that W has no right over the trust fund that amounts to a general power of appointment, the entire balance is excluded from the taxable estate of W. Because of the continuation of the trust beyond the lifetimes of the next younger generation of H's descendants, this trust is potentially subject to GST. However, if the proper election is made, the full value of the trust may be covered by H's GST exemption so that no GST taxable termination occurs at the final distribution of the remainder.

The design of H's living trust may be depicted in graphic fashion as follows:

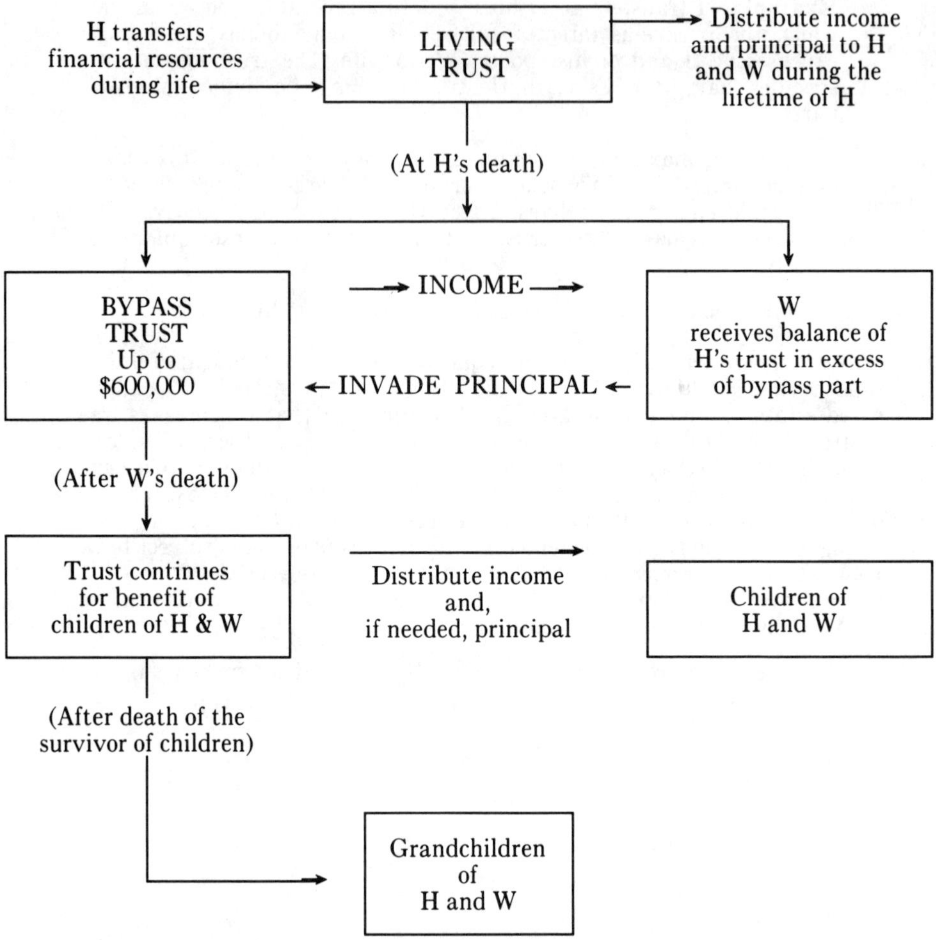
H transfers financial resources during life
LIVING TRUST
Distribute income and principal to H and W during the lifetime of H
(At H's death)
BYPASS TRUST Up to $600,000
INCOME
W receives balance of H's trust in excess of bypass part
INVADE PRINCIPAL
(After W's death)
Trust continues for benefit of children of H & W
Distribute income and, if needed, principal
Children of H and W
(After death of the survivor of children)
Grandchildren of H and W

.03 Where the More Sophisticated Variation Is Indicated

Because the GST exemption is $1 million, and the unified credit shields only $600,000 from the estate tax, the bypass trust cannot take maximum advantage of both estate tax and GST avoidance. For this reason, a slightly more complex plan may be appropriate if the following criteria are met:

(1) The total value of the estate is much in excess of $1 million.

(2) The original transferor and spouse wish to maximize multiple generation estate planning.

(3) The family finds it agreeable to place a sum initially in excess of the $600,000 unified credit exemption equivalent in a trust fund that will last during the lifetimes of the children of the original transferor.

The plan may be modified to take full advantage of the GST exemption by incorporating an additional trust after the death of the original transferor (H, in the preceding example). This additional trust is designed to be equal to the excess of the GST exemption over the $600,000 estate tax unified credit equivalent. For practical purposes, then, it should have an initial funding value of $400,000. Since the estate tax unified credit equivalent exemption will have been "used up" by the bypass trust, it is necessary to find a way to avoid the imposition of estate tax on the value of this separate GST exempt trust at the death of the first spouse. This may be accomplished by qualifying the value passing to this trust for the marital deduction, which is explained in greater detail at ¶ 504.04.

The scheme of the estate plan as modified in this manner appears as follows:

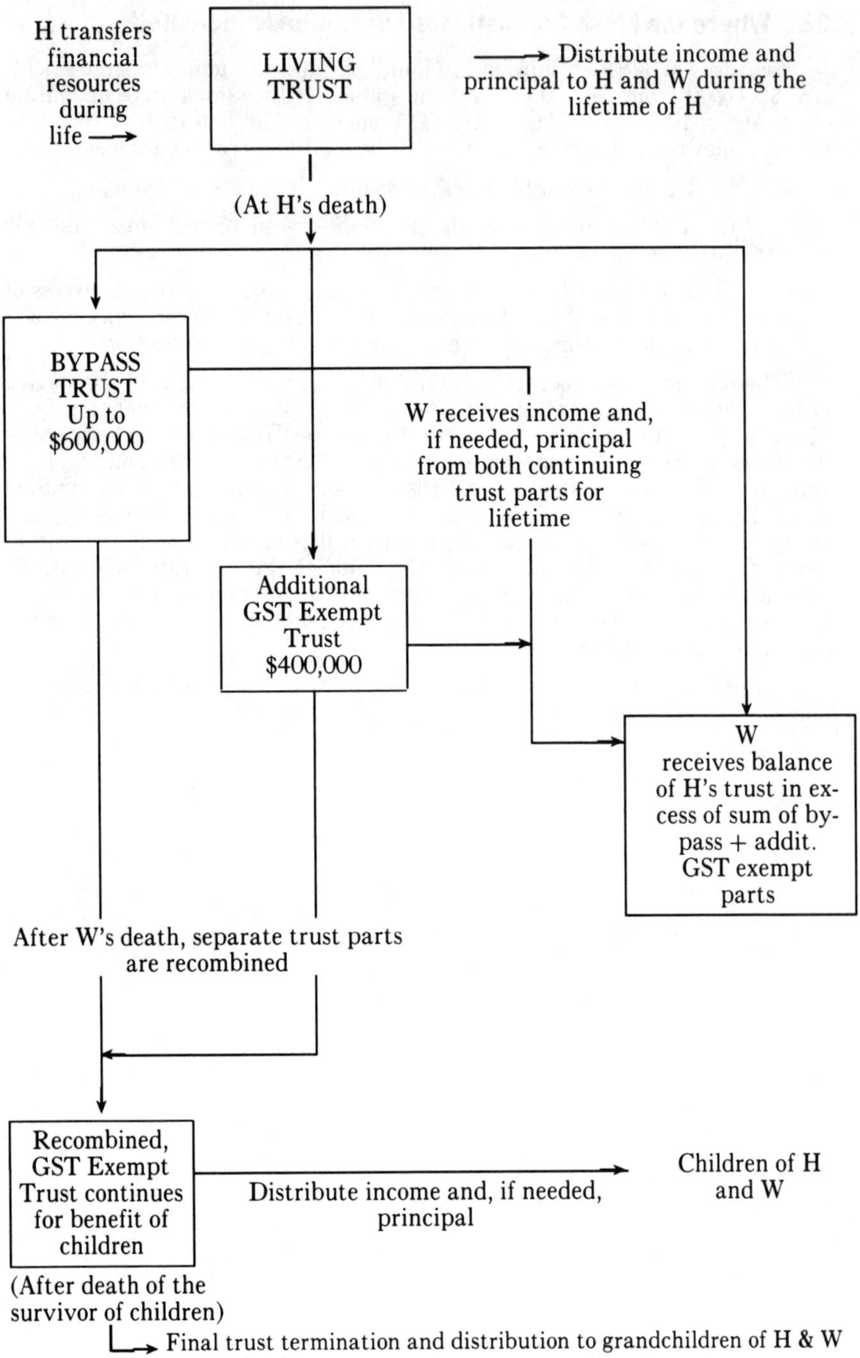
H transfers financial resources during life
LIVING TRUST
Distribute income and principal to H and W during the lifetime of H
(At H's death)
BYPASS TRUST Up to $600,000
W receives income and, if needed, principal from both continuing trust parts for lifetime
Additional GST Exempt Trust $400,000
W receives balance of H's trust in excess of sum of bypass + addit. GST exempt parts
After W's death, separate trust parts are recombined
Recombined, GST Exempt Trust continues for benefit of children
Distribute income and, if needed, principal
Children of H and W
(After death of the survivor of children)
Final trust termination and distribution to grandchildren of H & W

.04 Declaration of Trust, Self-Administered Living Trust, and Standby Arrangements

Freedom from financial management and recordkeeping, avoidance of most of the problems resulting from incompetency, and avoidance of probate are primary motivations for the establishment of the living trust. However, some potential grantors might have reservations about turning over all control to a trustee, and some prefer to turn over the "paperwork" while retaining control over investment decisions. To accommodate these cases, there are variations on living trust design. In considering the potential use of these, the financial consultant must bear in mind that the transferor cannot act as the sole trustee of a trust for his exclusive personal benefit. Under the trust law doctrine of "merger," no trust is considered to exist because there is no difference between direct personal ownership of the trust assets and a trust fund set up and administered by the same person who is both grantor and beneficiary. Merger may be avoided, however, simply by adding a cotrustee or by including additional beneficiaries.

.041 Declaration of trust

This trust document is a formal, written statement to the effect that the grantor no longer owns certain money, investments, or other property in his own right, but holds the subject assets in trust according to the terms and conditions set forth in the declaration. The transferor may or may not also be one of the initial beneficiaries, but the transferor may not be the sole beneficiary. If one of the goals in establishing the trust is avoidance of probate, it is necessary to designate a successor trustee to assume control after the transferor's death.

This arrangement enables the grantor to retain maximum control, but it may not provide much protection in the event of incompetency of the transferor unless some additional measures are taken, such as the standby arrangement, discussed at .043, below.

Perhaps the most serious practical problem associated with the declaration of trust is identification and segregation of the trust assets. This is particularly important if the trust is designed to continue after the grantor's death. It is possible to sign a valid declaration of trust, which specifies certain assets to be included in the trust fund, without taking the additional step of transferring ownership of the subject property. For instance, the grantor may execute a declaration of trust which indicates that a particular savings account is the trust fund, but may make no change on the bank book or other bank document that names the account owner. In fact, some trust documents go so far as to authorize the grantor to maintain trust property in the grantor's individual name. After the grantor's death, it may turn out to be impossible for the successor trustee to transfer the trust property to the remaindermen based on the authority of the declaration of trust. Instead, the trust assets may be treated as if they continued to be the individual property of the grantor, subject to the terms of the grantor's will. This does not mean that the declaration of trust or the authorization to hold trust assets in the grantor's name is legally impermissible. It simply means that the legal entity which is liable in case of the unauthorized transfer of ownership may be unwilling to assume the responsibility of permitting the transfer from the deceased grantor's name where the only evidence of trust ownership is the trust document itself. Examples of legal entities that might balk at such ownership transfers are banks (in the case of savings accounts and C.D.s), corporate trust companies (acting as transfer agents for stocks and bonds), and county clerks or other recording officers (in the case of real estate). Under these circumstances, it is preferable to change the ownership records of all assets held subject to a declaration of trust or any other living trust.

The declaration of trust may be revocable or irrevocable. If it is revocable, the income, gift, estate, and generation-skipping transfer tax consequences are identical to those of the revocable living trust. The tax consequences differ somewhat if the declaration of trust is irrevocable, depending on such factors as whether or not the grantor is also the lifetime beneficiary.

.042 Self-administered living trust (SALT)

This is a variation on the revocable living trust in which either the grantor is the sole trustee or the trust document reserves certain powers and authorities over trust administration to the grantor. A common use of the self-administering living trust (SALT) is the delegation of all administrative functions to a trustee with reservation to the grantor of the investment-making decisions over the trust fund. A cotrustee or a successor trustee should be designated to take over the trust responsibilities in the event of incapacity of the grantor.

As in the case of the declaration of trust, a SALT may be designed to continue on after the death of the grantor as a will substitute and may achieve the same complex tax planning advantages as the revocable living trust previously described.

The income, gift, estate, and generation-skipping transfer tax consequences are the same as those associated with the revocable living trust where the SALT is revocable.

.043 Standby arrangements

If the only appeal of a living trust to the potential grantor is the protection afforded in case of incompetency, the trust may prove to be too much trouble to the grantor while he is in good physical and mental health. Thus, as an alternative to establishing a trust immediately, consideration might be given to some form of standby arrangement. While there is a fair variety of specific types of standbys, a major distinction should be recognized between those that are likely to result in a court-supervised incompetency proceeding and those that are intended to avoid such a proceeding, along with its expense and emotional discomfort. Each of these arrangements depends on the preparation and execution of a living trust agreement, including the appointment of a trustee under the agreement.

A valid trust does not exist unless it owns something of value. Thus, the usual standby arrangement involves minimum funding, such as the transfer to the trust of $10, with the direction that the trustee is under no duty to invest the fund unless and until additional sums are added to it. The mechanism chosen to make it possible to transfer additional amounts of the grantor's money, investments, or other property to the trust may determine whether an incompetency proceeding might be needed. Also, the grantor can always voluntarily place additional assets into the trust fund if he is capable of doing so.

The main purpose of a standby trust is to provide for the contingency of incompetence, however, and it is not likely that the grantor will make additional transfers just before incapacity sets in. For this reason, there must be an additional element in the standby arrangement, which is ordinarily a power of attorney. The power of attorney is a document that permits a designated agent, the attorney-in-fact, to sign documents and to take other legally binding actions on behalf of the person who executes the power, referred to as the "principal." The grantor of the standby trust executes a power of attorney in addition to the trust agreement. The attorney-in-fact, who may or may not also be the trustee, assumes the responsibility of signing any documents necessary to transfer most or all of the grantor's separately owned assets into the trust if the grantor/principal becomes incompetent.

A power of attorney may be revoked at any time and, until recent times, it became invalid automatically upon the death or incompetency of the principal. Most state laws, however, now authorize the creation of so-called "durable" powers of attorney which remain valid, unless revoked, until the death of the principal. The particular type of durable power of attorney used in connection with the standby arrangement determines whether a court-supervised incompetency proceeding can be avoided.

Durable power of attorney. Certain durable powers of attorney become valid only upon the incompetence of the principal. This may be regarded as a true standby power. The intention is to avoid turning over any control to the attorney-in-fact unless it becomes absolutely necessary. The problem with this method is that no one may be willing to recognize the validity of the power of attorney without some additional proof that the principal is actually incompetent. Since the only convincing proof of this would be a court judgment, the incompetency proceeding is not avoided. Some grantors feel that the possible need for a court-supervised incompetency is preferable to placing wide power over property in the hands of another. Moreover, in cases of incompetency, it is typically the close relatives, rather than the incompetent himself, who become emotionally upset. The incompetent may be in a peaceful state, not upset by what is taking place around him. In any event, while some potential standby trust grantors view the incompetency as a disadvantage, others do not.

The second type of durable power of attorney becomes valid as soon as it is signed by the principal and remains effective, unless revoked, until the death of the principal, without being affected one way or another if the principal becomes incompetent. In this arrangement, the principal relies on the attorney-in-fact not to use the power of attorney unless it becomes necessary. If the principal has sufficient confidence in the attorney-in-fact, this type of durable power of attorney may be a way to avoid the court-supervised incompetency proceeding.

.05 Trusts for Minors

The following sections discuss the gift and state tax ramifications to parents and grandparents in creating and administering trusts for minors.

.051 Transfers to custodians for minors

Grandparents, as well as parents, often try to help their descendants build up a fund for higher education or just try to provide them with a "start in life." The legal fact that a minor cannot sign binding documents, combined with a personal fear that the funds might be squandered if available to the child before maturity, make some form of control over a minor's funds desirable. State laws provide one mechanism suitable for this purpose—in some cases through the state's Uniform Transfers to Minors Act (UTMA). These statutes allow for the transfer of ownership of savings, investments, and other property to a "custodian" who is responsible for holding the assets until the minor becomes an adult. Depending on the particular state's law, the special arrangement may terminate when the child reaches age 18 or 21. Money or assets transferred in this manner are the property of the child, and transfers to minors under the authority of these laws are irrevocable. This means that transfers to minors are completed gifts for federal gift tax purposes. However, until released to the child, the assets are under the control of the custodian who has the authority to spend the funds for the child's needs.

The person making a transfer for a minor in this manner may designate himself as custodian. However, if the transferor dies before the assets are released to the child, this is considered to be a transfer with the retained right to control the benefits of the subject property so that the subject assets, valued as of the date of death, are includible in the transferor's taxable estate under the string section rules.

Any taxable income generated by funds or assets held for a minor must be included on the child's individual income tax return. Under the current federal income tax system, this is subject to what have come to be known as the "kiddie tax" rules.[2] A minor child's taxable income, other than earnings and other than the first $1,300 per year (for 1995) of unearned income, is subject to income tax at the same rate as if taxable to the minor child's parent. In the year the minor attains age 14 and in subsequent years, the kiddie tax rules no longer apply. The purpose of this is to discourage the transfer of large amounts of savings and investments to children in order to cause the income generated to be taxed at a lower rate.

Transfers to minors under state custodianship laws are a limited planning tool because of two disadvantages:

(1) Flexibility is limited because of the fact that the transferred property must be released to the child at age 18 or 21. Grandparents and parents are not always confident in the child's ability to handle the responsibility of a significant amount of wealth at either of those ages.

(2) The kiddie tax rules may result in a higher rate of tax on the income of the transferred property than that which would otherwise be imposed.

Where the family economic resources make it economically possible to set aside a considerable amount for children, some form of trust may offer greater advantages than custodianship under a state transfers to minors law. An irrevocable living trust established for the exclusive benefit of a child is treated as a separate taxpayer for federal income tax purposes so long as none of the grantor trust substantial ownership rules apply. Under the fiduciary income tax system, if the trust makes distributions to the minor beneficiary from DNI, the beneficiary must include the taxable income portion of the distribution on his individual income tax return. Consequently, the income may be subject to the kiddie tax. For trusts treated as separate entities, the

---

[2] Code Sec. 1(g).

lowest federal income tax rate of 15 percent is imposed only on the first $1,550 of taxable income per year for 1995. Income accumulated during years of the trust in which the distributee has not yet reached age 21 is not subject to the accumulation distribution rules. These factors make it possible to create trust funds for minor beneficiaries that can continue until age 25, age 30, or even longer. Income accumulations may be used, up to a point, to avoid the kiddie tax rules without subjecting the trust to future accumulation distribution problems. However, because the trust reaches higher income tax brackets with a comparatively small amount of taxable income, the opportunity to accumulate income within the trust itself is limited.

Nevertheless, trusts designed to accept relatively moderate annual contributions can be used to accumulate income, particularly if the terms of the trust include a trustee's discretionary power to make distributions to an account established under the Uniform Transfers to Minors Act (UTMA account). The strategy depends on careful annual monitoring of the amount of taxable income of the trust and of the minor beneficiary, as follows:

(1) The trust may accumulate income up to the point at which the trust would reach an income tax bracket greater than 15 percent.

(2) In any year before the beneficiary reaches age 14, income earned by the trust that would be subject to a higher income tax rate is distributed to a UTMA account and, thus, treated as a distribution to the minor beneficiary. This makes two 15 percent brackets available—the trust's lowest bracket for amounts accumulated and the minor beneficiary's lowest bracket for amounts distributed to the UTMA account.

(3) Beginning with the year the beneficiary reaches age 14, since the kiddie tax rules no longer apply, larger distributions to the UTMA account can be made without encountering higher income tax rates.

Of course, the more income the trust generates, the more that must be distributed to the UTMA account in order to avoid the higher income tax rates. As already explained, the very motive for this type of trust is to avoid the necessity of accumulation within a UTMA account. The choice of investments for the minor's trust may offer a good solution to this dilemma. If investments are selected that produce little current income but offer the potential for growth in value, greater amounts can be accumulated within the trust without smaller, if any, distributions to the UTMA account.

The transfer of anything of value to an irrevocable trust for a minor is a completed gift and may well constitute a future interest. However, there are specific provisions of the gift tax law that make the gift tax annual exclusion available for gifts in trust for minors. Two types of trusts for minors, designed to take advantage of the favorable gift tax treatment, have been named after the sections of the Internal Revenue Code that permit use of the annual exclusion.

.052 Code Sec. 2503(c) trust

A transfer in trust for a minor is treated as a present interest in property for gift tax purposes, regardless of how many years the beneficiary will have to wait until the trust is terminated, if the trust meets the following requirements:

(1) The trust must be irrevocable, established for the exclusive benefit of the minor child.

(2) The trustee must have the authority to distribute the income and also the principal of the trust fund to the beneficiary or to spend income and principal for the beneficiary's needs at any time after the trust is established. This requirement, however, only makes it necessary for the trustee to have the authority to make distributions. If the trustee never elects to make discretionary distributions before the termination of the trust, qualification for the gift tax annual exclusion is not lost.

(3) The trust must terminate and distribute the balance of the principal, along with any accumulated or undistributed income, to the beneficiary at age 21 or sooner. In recent years, the courts, as well as the IRS, have interpreted this requirement in a somewhat expansive manner, to the effect that the requirement is met if, under the trust's terms, the beneficiary has the right to receive the entire balance of the trust at age 21. It is permissible for the trust terms to provide that, upon the beneficiary's failure to exercise this right, the trust continues for a longer period of time.

The maximum age of the beneficiary before termination of the Code Sec. 2503(c) trust may not be higher than the age for termination of state transfers to minors act custodian arrangements. Therefore, the principal advantage of the trust is avoidance of the kiddie tax rules for income tax purposes rather than increased postponement of the child's ability to control or spend the funds.

Example: P is considering using a Code Sec. 2503(c) trust in order to accumulate the maximum amount possible for the benefit of his child, D, who is a newborn infant. P would like to avoid exposure of the taxable earnings within the trust to tax rates above 15 percent and also to avoid kiddie tax entanglements. Based on recent investment experience, as well as P's preference for fairly conservative savings and investment programs, P anticipates an average total taxable investment return of eight percent.

If P transfers $2,000 each year to the trust until D reaches age 21, the trust will grow to $21,755 by the end of the eighth year. This assumes that the trust earns eight percent per year, with accumulation of the earnings and compounding, and that the trust pays income tax at the rate of 15 percent. During the ninth year, the trust will earn $1,900. It will be subject to income tax rates in excess of 15 percent that year on the amount exceeding $1,750 at that time, assuming that the 15 percent income tax bracket for trusts increases with inflation by about two percent per year.

In the ninth year, and each successive year thereafter, the trust income in excess of the amount that would be taxed at a rate in excess of 15 percent may be distributed to a UTMA account for D. Even considering the kiddie tax rules in years before D reaches age 14, there will be little, if any, income tax payable by D because of the small amount of income earned within the UTMA account during those years. After D reaches age 14, little or no income tax will be payable by the beneficiary, although the UTMA account produces greater amounts of income in those years because the kiddie tax rules no longer apply. Making income distributions to a UTMA account for D prevents the child from having access to these income distributions, as well as their earning accumulations, until age 21.

In the preceding example, the projected amount of total after-tax accumulation is $99,345, of which $68,623 is accumulated within the trust and

$30,722 within the UTMA account. One disadvantage of this arrangement is that almost one-third of the total accumulation within the UTMA account is available for withdrawal by D at age 21. If this is objectionable to the client, the use of investments, such as growth stocks or growth stock mutual funds, may be used so that little or none of the income need be distributed to the UTMA account.

.053 Code Sec. 2503(b) trust

Actually, Internal Revenue Code Sec. 2503(b) does not set forth requirements for a specific type of trust fund for minors. Code Sec. 2503(b) is the provision of the tax law that grants the gift tax annual exclusion for transfers of present interests in property. In practice, however, the label has been used to describe a trust for minors that is not limited by the age 21 termination requirement. The Code Sec. 2503(b) trust must require that the income be distributed to the minor in the year in which it is earned by the trust. In years during which the beneficiary is under age 14, the income may be subjected to the kiddie tax rules. There are planning steps that may be taken, however, to minimize this potential disadvantage.

(1) Since the first $1,300 per year (for 1995) of the minor child's income is effectively free of the kiddie tax, the amount of principal transferred to the trust may be kept at a level that produces no more than this amount of income.

(2) The trustee may choose investments that offer greater growth potential and produce a smaller rate of income during the trust years in which the beneficiary is under age 14.

Because of the current income distribution requirement, a percentage of the value transferred to the trust is considered to be the actuarial present value of the income interest. This constitutes a present interest in property. The longer the trust lasts, the higher the proportion allocated to the present interest, under the valuation principles of Code Sec. 7520.

> **Example:** Grandfather A transfers $20,000 to a trust fund for the benefit of his grandchild, B, who is 10 years old when the trust is established. The trust requires that all income be distributed to B during the year in which it is earned by the trust. When B attains age 30, the trust terminates and the principal balance is distributed to B.

Assuming that gift splitting is not available and that the applicable federal rate is eight percent, A's gift consists of two elements: (1) a present interest gift of the actuarial value of the income interest; and (2) future interest gift of the remainder. B is treated as the recipient of both gift elements. The allocation of the value transferred is as follows:

		Actuarial Factor				
Total Value of Gift		*20-Year Term Certain*		*Remainder*		*Value Allocation*
$20,000	×	.785452	=			$15,709
$20,000			×	.214548	=	$ 4,291

The annual gift tax exclusion, in the maximum amount of $10,000, may be used to reduce the value allocated to the 20-year term certain, which is $15,709. As a result, only $5,709 of the term certain value plus $4,291, the entire value allocated to the remainder, is a taxable gift by A to B.

.054 *Relative advantages of minors' trusts*

Comparing the Code Sec. 2503(b) trust with the Code Sec. 2503(c) trust, the relative advantages and disadvantages are as follows:

Advantage or Disadvantage:	*Code Sec. 2503(c) Trust*	*Code Sec. 2503(b) Trust*
(1) The full amount transferred to the trust, up to $10,000 in each year per transferor, is subject to the gift tax annual exclusion.	YES	NO
(2) The part of the value transferred to the trust allocated to the present interest, under IRS actuarial tables, is subject to the gift tax annual exclusion; however, some part of each transfer is subject to gift tax.	NO	YES
(3) The income of the trust must be required to be distributed to the beneficiary in each year of the trust.	NO	YES
(4) The trustee must have the discretion to distribute income as well as principal to or for the beneficiary in any year of the trust.	YES	NO
(5) The trust must be distributed to the estate of the beneficiary if the beneficiary dies before the trust terminates.	YES	NO
(6) The trust must terminate, or the beneficiary must have the right to receive the entire balance of the trust by age 21.	YES	NO

.06 Tax Planning Advantages of Other Living Trusts

A variety of other types of living trusts may offer tax planning advantages in particular situations. These include trusts in which the grantor receives income-like payments for a period of time—the grantor retained annuity trust (GRAT) and the grantor retained unitrust (GRUT). Also included is the grantor retained income trust (GRIT), which is a trust used to hold tangible property and residential property. Residential property may be held in a personal residence trust (PRT) or in a qualified personal residence trust (QPRT). This section covers the intentional grantor trust and the lifetime bypass trust as well.

.061 *Retention by the grantor of temporary interests in trust*

As explained at ¶ 402.042, the date-of-death value of a trust is included in the grantor's taxable estate if the grantor retains an interest, such as an income interest, for life. However, if the grantor's retained interest is designed to last for a period of time that ends before the grantor's death, the pertinent string section[3] does not apply. So long as the grantor actually lives beyond the

---

[3] Code Sec. 2036(a)(1).

expiration of the retained interest, the value of the trust is not included in the grantor's taxable estate. Of course, part or all of the value transferred to the trust is a taxable gift. However, the gift value is fixed at the time of transfer.

> **Example:** X establishes an irrevocable trust that provides for annual distributions to X of five percent of the value of the trust each year for 10 years. Thereafter, the balance remaining in the trust is to be distributed to X's child, Y.

Part of the value of the assets transferred to the trust, representing the discounted present value of the remainder, is a gift from X to Y. The balance represents the present value of X's temporary interest, which is not a gift. There are two potential tax-saving advantages to be gained in this situation:

(1) The difference between the value of the remainder interest and the total value transferred to the trust is not a taxable gift. Unless the transaction is later included in X's taxable estate under the string section rules, it escapes the unified transfer tax system.

(2) Any post-transfer appreciation of the trust fund escapes gift and estate tax as well, again, subject to successful avoidance of the string section rules.

These principles are depicted graphically as follows:

A	B

A represents the value of the interest retained by the grantor, which is not a taxable gift. B represents the value of the remainder, treated as a taxable gift of a future interest at the time the trust is funded. The relative proportions of A and B vary from case to case, depending upon the length of the term of the grantor's retained interest and the amount paid to the grantor during the term.

At the grantor's death, assuming that there has been considerable appreciation of the principal of the trust fund, the proportions of value may be viewed as follows:

A	B	C

A represents the value treated as the grantor's retained interest, which is neither subject to gift tax at the date of the original transfer nor includible in the grantor's taxable estate. B is the discounted present value of the remainder, as of the inception of the trust, and constitutes a taxable gift of a future interest that is taken into account for estate tax purposes at the grantor's death as an adjusted taxable gift. C depicts the portion of the date-of-death value of the trust consisting of appreciation that occurs during the term of the grantor's retained interest. Like A, C is free of gift and estate taxes.

Without specific rules for accurate valuation of A's temporary interest, opportunities would exist to reduce or avoid gift and estate tax through temporary retained interests in trusts. This has been the subject of continuing rule changes in recent years. Section 2036(c) of the Internal Revenue Code, created under the Technical and Miscellaneous Revenue Act of 1988 (TAMRA) (P.L. 100-647), sought to treat so-called "estate freeze" transfers, in circumstances similar to the preceding example, as an absolute gift from X to Y. The law did carve out an exception for a "qualified trust income interest" that lasted for no more than 10 years and was based on retention by the grantor of the actual income of the trust. There was a serious flaw in this creature of statute that could be used to the taxpayer's advantage. Simply by investing the trust for very low income, the potential to cause growth of the remainder value (and thereby shift more wealth away from the grantor) could be enhanced. Since the "income" interest retained was not tied to any definite standard, this advantage was not quantifiable. For a variety of reasons, Section 2036(c) was retroactively repealed under the Revenue Reconciliation Act of 1990 (RRA '90) (P.L. 101-508). To take its place, Code Secs. 2701 through 2704 were created, effective for transfers made after October 8, 1990. The current rules create a more precise framework for the valuation of temporary retained interests in trust than that which existed under prior law. Provided the trust meets certain design requirements, valuation of the retained interest takes into account not only the amount and term period of payments made to the grantor but also the rate of interest prevailing at the time the transfer is completed. If the trust design requirements are not met, the value of the grantor's retained interest is placed at zero.[4]

.062 Grantor retained annuity trust (GRAT) and grantor retained unitrust (GRUT)

There are two alternative designs for the grantor's temporary retained interest that constitute "qualified interests"[5] and offer tax-saving potential. These are the grantor retained annuity trust (GRAT) and the grantor retained unitrust (GRUT). If an interest retained by the grantor does not meet the specific statutory requirements, it is valued at zero for gift tax purposes.[6] In that case, the grantor is treated as having made a present taxable gift of a future interest valued at 100 percent of the value of the assets transferred to the trust.

A non-contingent remainder interest retained by the grantor is another example of a qualified interest under the statute, but that arrangement is not included in this discussion because it does not offer the same opportunity as the GRAT and GRUT to deliver asset value to beneficiaries, in excess of the amount subject to transfer tax.

GRATs and GRUTs may provide that qualified interests be retained by the grantor or held by certain other family members.[7] Reference here is made only to retention of qualified interests by the grantor for convenience, and because it is likely that most planning opportunities will involve retention of qualified interests.

The GRAT is designed to make annual or more frequent payments to the grantor of a specific amount for a specific period of time. As an alternative, it is permissible to direct that the payments continue for the grantor's lifetime. Since that could cause inclusion of the date-of-death value of the trust in the grantor's taxable estate,[8] however, the lifetime payment does not offer transfer tax planning advantages.

The annuity payment may be expressed as a stated dollar amount or as a fixed fraction or percentage of the fair market value of assets initially transferred to the trust. An alternative design allows for increasing or decreasing annual payments, provided that the grantor's payment amount for any given year does not exceed the amount paid to the grantor for the preceding year by more than 120 percent.[9] A right to withdraw possessed by the grantor, rather than a mandatory payment to the grantor, does not qualify. The annuity payment amount does not change. Any additions to the GRAT after

---

[4] Code Sec. 2702(a)(2)(A).
[5] Code Sec. 2702(b).
[6] Code Sec. 2702(a)(2)(A).
[7] Code Sec. 270(e)(2).
[8] Code Sec. 2036(a)(1).
[9] Reg. § 25.2702-3(b)(1)(i).

its inception would, therefore, undermine the gift tax valuation, and such additions are prohibited.[10]

At the end of the GRAT's term, the remainder is distributed to family members[11] or held in continuing trust for their benefit.

Rules are provided for modified annuity amounts to be paid in case of short taxable years and in the last taxable year of the term.[12]

> **Example (1):** G, age 50, transfers $480,000 in securities to trust to pay G $1,400 at the end of each month (that is, 3.5 percent per year of the original value placed in trust) for 15 years, after which the remainder is to be distributed to G's children.

Because G's annuity is a "qualified interest," the value of the remainder (which is a taxable gift), as well as the value of G's retained annuity interest, is determined under Code Sec. 7520.[13] If the applicable federal rate is eight percent for the month during which the transfer is made, these values are:

Total Value Transferred: $480,000

A G's Retained Annuity Interest	B Remainder (Taxable Gift)
$141,480	$338,520[14]

The design of a GRUT differs mainly in that the payment made to the grantor must be described as a fixed fraction or percentage of the value of the trust fund, recomputed annually. The trust document may direct that the fraction or percentage changes from year to year, provided that the fraction or percentage for any given year does not exceed that for the preceding year by more than 120 percent.[15] The unitrust payments to the grantor must be mandatory; a right held by the grantor to withdraw the amount does not satisfy the requirement. Modification of the amount to be paid, in case of short taxable years and in the last taxable year of the term, is required for GRUTs as it is for GRATs.[16]

> **Example (2):** T, also age 50, transfers $480,000 in securities to trust to pay T eight percent of the value of the trust fund as determined on the first day of each year of the trust. Payments are to be made at the end of each month for a period of 15 years, after which the trust continues for the benefit of T's descendants. As a result, T receives $3,200 at the end of each month for the first year.

The main differences between the GRAT and GRUT described in Examples (1) and (2) are:

(1) The amount of the GRAT payments to G in Example (1) remains constant; the GRUT payments to T in Example (2) increase at the beginning of any year if the value of the trust has increased or they decrease at the beginning of any year if the value of the trust has decreased.

(2) Because of the lower payout rate, the value of the remainder of the trust in Example (1) is more likely to increase.

---

[10] Reg. § 25.2703-3(b)(4).

[11] The special valuation rules of Code Sec. 2702 do not apply if the remaindermen are not applicable family members as defined in Code Sec. 2704(c)(2).

[12] Reg. § 25.2702-3(b)(3).

[13] Code Sec. 2702(a)(2)(B).

[14] Computation of the remainder (taxable gift) component is based on Reg. § 25.2702-3(e), Ex. 5.

[15] Reg. § 25.2702-3(c)(1)(ii).

[16] Reg. § 25.2702-3(c)(3).

(3) Even if the value of the GRUT in Example (2) increases, the resulting higher payment to T in subsequent years tends to prevent appreciation of the remainder.

Given the higher rate of payments made to the grantor in Example (2), the value of the remainder, subject to gift tax, is lower. The valuation results for this example are as follows:

Total Value Transferred: $480,000

A G's Retained Annuity Interest	B Remainder (Taxable Gift)
$318,338	$161,662

If the GRAT in Example (1) is designed to pay G eight percent each year, so that the amount paid to G is the same as the amount paid to T in Example (2) (at least for the first year), the taxable gift of the remainder in case of the GRAT is somewhat lower. The pertinent valuations for an eight percent GRAT, with the same facts (other than the payment percent) as in Example (1), are as follows:

Total Value Transferred: $480,000

A G's Retained Annuity Interest	B Remainder (Taxable Gift)
$323,382	$156,618

It is even possible to design a GRAT so that the value of the remainder, which is treated as a taxable gift, is zero or nearly zero. This is accomplished with an annuity payment amount that represents a high percentage of the value transferred to the trust. Increasing the term during which the annuity is paid to the grantor also helps to reduce the remainder value. For instance, in Example (1), if the annuity amount is increased to $4,760 per month, the gift value is zero. That annuity amount represents 11.9 percent of the initial value transferred to the trust. Alternatively, if the term of the annuity in Example (1) is increased to 25 years and the annuity amount is set at $3,980 per month (9.95 percent of the trust's initial value), the amount treated as a gift is zero.

A "zero-gift GRAT" might appeal to clients who believe that the trust can acquire investments with the potential to maintain or increase value even after paying the required annuity to the grantor. Given historic investment rates of return for traditional financial investments, however, the more likely outcome is that the zero-gift GRAT will deplete its principal during the term of payments to the grantor.

The GRUT payments to the grantor are adjusted each year to take into account the updated value of the trust. Reduction in the principal value of the trust causes reduced payments to the grantor in future years. For this reason, total depletion of the principal of the GRUT during the payout term cannot occur in the same manner as it can for the GRAT. Although a high percentage GRUT payment may very substantially diminish the remainder, under the Code Sec. 7520 computation process, GRUTs do not create zero-gift situations in the same manner as GRATs. For instance, if the payment to the grantor in Example (2) is increased to 11.9 percent with the other facts of the example unchanged, there could still be a taxable gift of $95,286.

Certain common requirements are prescribed for GRATs and GRUTs:[17]

(1) A right to receive the lesser of a fixed amount or the stated annuity or unitrust amount does not qualify, but a right to receive the greater of the two values does.

(2) The annuity or unitrust payments must be required from the inception of the trust.

(3) The term of the grantor's retained payments must last for the life of the grantor, for a specified term of years, or for the shorter (but not the longer) of the two periods.

(4) The trust document must prohibit paying off the balance of grantor's interest by computing and paying to the grantor the discounted present value of the remainder of the payments at any time prior to the stated end of the term. This is called "commutation."

Estate planning strategies using GRATs or GRUTs vary depending on the results the client wishes to achieve, the client's own need (or lack of it) for the retained payments, and investment risk tolerance.

Example (1), above, demonstrates a strategy used to retain a moderate stream of payments for most of the grantor's remaining lifetime and to enhance the value to be distributed to the remaindermen. The low rate of payments to the grantor, by comparison with Example (2) and with the applicable federal rate (AFR), provides the potential to accumulate principal. It also helps to secure the annuity payments. Since the annuity payout percent is at or near the dividend rate on equity securities, it is possible to structure an investment program for maximum growth, retaining all increases in value within the trust for future distribution to the remaindermen. This strategy is appropriate for clients who fit into the following profile:

(1) The client does not require maximum income from his or her savings and investments. This attribute may exist because of a large amount of personal wealth or a moderate lifestyle or because the client retains substantial resources outside of the trust fund that supplement present and future spending needs.

(2) Growth of the remainder is a dominant motivation, and the client is willing to accept the trade-off of a comparatively high taxable gift element in return for enhanced potential growth of the remainder.

(3) The client is not adverse to fluctuation of investment value.

A more conservative strategy is portrayed in Example (2), above. The initial unitrust payment rate is set at the same rate as the AFR. This makes it possible for the trustee to purchase good quality fixed-income investments that pay periodic interest at the rate needed to meet the unitrust payment obligation to the grantor. If the principal value of the trust declines, future-year payments to the grantor may be reduced, but that also helps to preserve the value of the trust and to provide security of some level of continuing payments.

The relative advantages and disadvantages of the two different strategies in Examples (1) and (2), above, can only be evaluated based on the final outcome that occurs when each trust comes to an end. To illustrate the future results, Example (3) shows the gift and retained interest components based on the facts of Example (1), together with the projected appreciation that would occur and the total value transferred free of the unified transfer tax system. Example (4) relates, in the same manner, to Example (2). However, the total

---

[17] Reg. § 25.2702-3(d).

investment rate of return assumed for Example (2) is equal to the GRUT payments to the grantor. As a result, there is no projected appreciation in the remainder value in Example (4). The result in Example (3) is a significant increase in the value of wealth transferred to the remaindermen, but G receives a much smaller annual payment from the trust. Also, G makes a much greater initial gift, thereby causing G either to use more of his unified credit or, if G has made substantial previous gifts, to pay a larger gift tax. In Example (4), T makes a smaller gift and retains a more substantial stream of annual payments from the trust, but there is no potential for appreciation of the remainder. In each example, the annual total investment rate of return is assumed to be eight percent.

Example (3): 15-year GRAT with 3.5 percent annuity payment to grantor.

$941,546
Total Value of Remainder

Value of Original Transfer		Appreciation During Term of Trust
Taxable Gift $338,520	Grantor's Retained Interest $141,480	Appreciation $461,546
	Portion Transferred Free of Tax $603,026	

Example (4): 15-year GRUT with 8 percent unitrust payment to grantor.

$480,000
Total Value of Remainder

Value of Original Transfer		Appreciation During Term of Trust -0-
Taxable Gift $161,662	Grantor's Retained Interest $318,338	
	Portion Transferred Free of Tax $318,338	

The preceding comparisons are based on a constant total investment rate of return of eight percent, equal to the assumed AFR. In reality, however, the client in Example (3) has greater stated risk tolerance, and the annuity payout amount has been structured to facilitate investments primarily in equity securities. If the total rate of return actually obtained exceeds eight percent, the remainder value is increased dramatically, both in absolute terms and in terms of the excess over the value subject to gift tax. For instance, if the total annual rate of return achieved in Example (3) is 10 percent, the projected remainder value is $1,234,483. The result is a final distribution to the remaindermen that exceeds the amount subject to gift tax by $935,695.

If the grantor dies before the expiration of the retained annuity interest or retained unitrust interest, the anticipated tax consequences change. The most likely results, based on a strict reading of the statute are:

(1) The total date-of-death value of the trust fund is included in the grantor's taxable estate. The operative statutory phrases are retention by the grantor, for a period of time "which does not in fact end before (the grantor's) death" of the "possession or enjoyment of, or the right to the income from, the property (previously transferred to the GRAT or GRUT)."[18] Although rights retained by the grantor in either a GRAT or GRUT are not exactly pure income interests, these rights may well constitute retention of possession or enjoyment.

(2) The value that was treated as a taxable gift when the trust was established is also not taken into account as an adjusted taxable gift for purposes of computation of the grantor's estate tax liability.[19] That is because a taxable gift reported as such during life loses its status as an adjusted taxable gift for purposes of the estate tax calculation if, by operation of the string section rules, the property transferred is included in the grantor's taxable estate. The ultimate effect of this rule, though convoluted, is to prevent double taxation of the value transferred.

If these tax results occur, the advantage of avoiding transfer tax on part of the original value placed in trust plus all of the post-transfer appreciation, is lost. It is fair to say, however, that the tax result is no worse than if the grantor had simply retained ownership of the assets placed in trust.

Also, the grantor's death before the end of the retained interest term of a GRAT or GRUT might not cause total inclusion of the date-of-death value of the trust fund in the grantor's taxable estate. The provision of Code Sec. 2036(a) that appears to be the most applicable authority for GRAT and GRUT retained interests addresses the retention of income interests. Since neither GRAT nor GRUT payments are based strictly on the income of the trust, it may be appropriate to use a different measure of taxable value. This is the conclusion presented in two published IRS rulings that examine the results of the grantor's death during the term of a charitable remainder annuity trust (CRAT) or a charitable remainder unitrust (CRUT).[20] Charitable remainder trusts are discussed at ¶ 702. Logically, the same rules should exist for GRATs and GRUTs as those for CRATs and CRUTs because the nature of the retained interests are virtually identical. From the government's viewpoint of revenue collection, however, the consequences are quite different. The inclusion of part or all of the value of a CRAT or CRUT in the grantor's taxable estate is partially or fully offset by the charitable deduction available to the estate because the remainder ultimately passes to charity. In case of a GRAT or GRUT, there is no charitable deduction, the full amount included in the grantor's estate is potentially subject to estate tax and, therefore, the tax-collection stakes are higher. It is noteworthy that CRATs and CRUTs have existed in their present form since 1969, while GRATs and GRUTs were created much more recently, under the 1990 legislation,[21] and that the published rulings specifying the estate tax treatments for CRATs and CRUTs pre-date the creation of GRATs and GRUTs.

---

[18] Code Sec. 2036(a)(1), parentheticals added for emphasis.

[19] Code Sec. 2001(b).

[20] Rev. Ruls. 82-105, 1982-1 CB 133, and 76-273, 1976-2 CB 268.

[21] Act Sec. 11062(a) of the Revenue Reconciliation Act of 1990 (P.L. 101-508).

Because the grantor's death occurs before the end of the retained interest term, under the ruling applicable to CRATs,[22] a portion of the value of the trust is included in the grantor's taxable estate. The amount to be included is calculated by dividing the grantor's annual annuity amount by the Code Sec. 7520 applicable rate. In Example (3), above, the result is:

Annual Retained Annuity Amount	÷	Code Sec. 7520 Rate	=	Amount Included in Grantor's Estate
$16,800		8%		$210,000

A somewhat different formula is used to calculate the taxable portion of a CRUT (and, arguably, a GRUT) where the grantor dies during the term of the retained interest.[23] Applied to the facts of Example (4), above, the result is:

Code Sec. 7520 Rate	÷	Unitrust Payout Rate	×	Date of Death Trust Value	=	Amount Included in Grantor's Estate
8%		8%		$480,000		$480,000

The result is much more favorable in the first of the two examples because the rate of the annuity in Example (3) is much lower than the AFR, while the unitrust payout rate in Example (4) is exactly equal to the AFR. Also, the investment result assumptions in Example (3) allow for growth of trust principal, enhancing the value delivered to the remaindermen free of tax.

A GRAT or GRUT can be part of a generation-skipping estate plan, determined by the terms of the trust after the grantor's retained interest terminates. This might take the form of an on-going trust for the benefit of the grantor's children, with the remainder distributed to grandchildren or other skip persons. Instead, the trust could be designed to distribute the remainder to the grandchildren immediately after the grantor's death.

For generation-skipping transfer tax planning purposes, there is little advantage in designing the GRAT or GRUT for maximum growth. If the election is made to apply part or all of the GST exemption to a GRAT or GRUT, that application takes place at the end of the grantor's retained interest.[24] The entire value of the trust fund, valued at that time, is subject to GST or, at least, "uses up" the grantor's GST exemption. GST design of a GRAT or GRUT makes only slightly more sense if the grantor needs or wishes to retain a substantial percentage payment, simply because the opportunity for growth of principal during the grantor's retained interest term is diminished.

GRATs and GRUTs are grantor trusts under the substantial ownership rules for federal income tax purposes because the trust income is or may be distributed or held for future distribution to the grantor.[25] This does not necessarily present a disadvantage, as explained in the following paragraphs that describe the "intentional" grantor trust.

.063 Grantor retained use trust

Central to the concept of GRATs and GRUTs is the planning advantage of the unified transfer tax "discount" available through retention of a temporary income-like interest in property, coupled with the fixing of the unified transfer tax valuation as of the original date of transfer of assets to the trust. Through exceptions contained in Code Sec. 2702,[26] the very specific retained interest payments to the grantor, required for GRATs and GRUTs, are *not*

---

[22] Rev. Rul. 82-105.
[23] Rev. Rul. 76-273.
[24] Code Sec. 2642(f)(3).
[25] Code Sec. 677(a).
[26] Code Sec. 2702(a)(3)(A)(ii) and (c)(4).

required if the assets placed in trust are the grantor's residence or unimproved land or nondepreciable tangible property. These statutory exceptions make the tax planning advantages of the GRAT and GRUT available for transfers in trust of certain non-income-producing property.

These trusts are sometimes generally called grantor retained income trusts (GRITs), even though they produce little, if any, income. This is based on a planning technique that was available prior to RRA '90.

In some cases, the grantor may wish to ensure retention by family members of a residence or tangible property such as works of art, jewelry, rare automobiles, or other collectibles. A GRAT or GRUT does not serve this purpose because the asset to be transferred produces no income. The trust can make GRAT or GRUT payments to the grantor only if the asset placed in trust is sold, which is exactly what the grantor is trying to avoid. Instead, retention of the *use* of the property supports the allocation of a portion of the value to the grantor's retained interest. The balance of the value (representing the present value of the remainder) is a gift of a future interest. By fixing the valuation components as of the date of transfer, residence and tangible property trusts can avoid the transfer tax on any appreciation in the value of the assets that may occur during the retained use term.

Like GRATs and GRUTs, retained use trusts may provide that a qualified interest be retained by the grantor or held by certain other family members.[27] Reference here is made only to retention of qualified interests by the grantor for convenience and because it is likely that most planning opportunities will involve retention of qualified interests.

There are several rules that apply specifically to trusts designed to hold tangible property:

(1) Decisions by the grantor not to exercise reserved rights during the retained interest term must not have a substantial effect on the valuation of the remainder.[28] This rule could be detrimental to planning in a few cases involving assets that, by their nature, deteriorate or otherwise change value with use or lack of use. It should leave numerous opportunities available, however, for most types of tangible property.

(2) Valuation of the retained interest must be based on the facts and circumstances of each case rather than on the mechanical application of the current-interest-rate-based formula prescribed by Code Sec. 7520.[29] This places a more cumbersome burden on the taxpayer-grantor or his advisers to find evidence of sales or rentals of comparable property.

(3) According to the regulations,[30] the nature of the property must be such that no depreciation deduction would be available if the property were used in a trade or business. Typically, this requirement is satisfied by virtue of the fact that the property does not have an ascertainable useful life, usually the case for tangible property with artistic or intrinsic value.

Tangibles trusts may permit commutation, whereby the grantor's interest is terminated before the end of the retained interest term. An additional gift tax event at the time of the termination may be avoided if the grantor receives a payment from the trust or from the remaindermen of the discounted present value of the remaining term interest.

---

27 Code Sec. 2701(e)(2).

28 Code Sec. 2702(c)(4).

29 Code Sec. 2702(c)(4)(B) and Reg. § 25.2702-2(c)(3).

30 Reg. § 25.2702-2(c)(2)(A).

The rule that places a value of zero on non-qualified retained interests does not apply to the transfer of a personal residence in trust where the right of use and occupancy is retained by the grantor.[31] Favorable transfer tax treatment includes valuation "discount" equal to the discounted present value of the grantor's retained interest and avoidance of tax on any appreciation that may occur during the retained interest term. These are the same advantages attributed to GRATs, GRUTs, and tangible property trusts. In order to qualify, the regulations prescribe two alternative methods. They are distinguished as the personal residence trust (PRT) and the qualified personal residence trust (QPRT).

PRTs and QPRTs share a number of common requirements: [32]

(1) Number of retained use trusts and properties. The trust may hold only one personal residence or a fractional interest in one residence. This must be either the grantor's primary residence or one other. If there are multiple trusts holding fractional interests in the same residence, the trusts are treated as one. The grantor may hold retained interests in no more than two PRTs or QPRTs.

(2) Adjacent structures and land. The property may include additional structures, if used for residential purposes, and adjacent land provided that it is "reasonably appropriate" considering the residence's size and location. Presumably, this covers such structures as detached garages, storage sheds, cabanas, and, in appropriate circumstances, separate guest houses and non-commercial stables. In a "hunt country" area, perhaps even extensive amounts of property may pass the "reasonably appropriate adjacent land" test.

(3) Mortgages and personal property. The fact that the property is subject to a mortgage does not disqualify the trust, but no personal property, such as household furniture, may be held by the trust.

(4) Primary residential use. It must be clear that the principal use of the property by the grantor, spouse, and dependents is as a personal residence. Partial use of the premises for some business activities is allowed. For instance, areas of the structure used to meet with clients or patients or for day care of children do not result in disqualification if these uses are clearly secondary. However, a residence that also functions as a bed and breakfast or hotel cannot qualify.

(5) Use and occupancy. If there is concurrent ownership of a residence by husband and wife, they may transfer their shares of ownership to a single retained interest trust provided that, during the retained interest term, the residence is occupied only by the spouses and their dependents. The regulations seem to allow for the possibility that the grantor might be in a nursing home or otherwise unable or not inclined to use the residence during the retained interest term. The implication is that lack of actual occupancy does not disturb the tax consequences. Pertinent phrases are "available at all times for use by the term holder,"[33] and "when occupied by the term holder."[34]

In addition to these common requirements, the PRT is subject to more restrictions than those placed on the QPRT. In particular, a PRT may not hold any asset other than an interest in a qualified residence. That precludes funding the trust with additional financial assets that could be used to pay for

---

[31] Code Sec. 2702(a)(3)(A)(ii).

[32] Reg. § 25.2702-5.

[33] Reg. § 25.2702-5(b)(1).

[34] Reg. § 25.2702-5(b)(2)(iii) and (c)(2)(iii).

upkeep, taxes, utilities, and other costs of maintaining the residence. The grantor must plan on paying these costs with personal funds.

A PRT may not sell the qualified residence that it holds. If the residence is damaged or destroyed by fire or other disaster or is taken for public use through court proceeding, the insurance or condemnation proceeds are termed "qualified proceeds." The trust document must require reinvestment of qualified proceeds, including any interest earned, in a replacement residence within two years.

Commutation is the only possible escape hatch for the grantor of a PRT. Through commutation, the trust fund or the remaindermen pay the grantor the value of the balance of the retained interest prior to the expiration of its term. This could take place either at the time qualified proceeds are received or while the qualified residence is still owned by the PRT. It might even be used by a grantor who becomes ill or otherwise finds it unlikely that he will live beyond the expiration of the retained interest. In this way, inclusion of the total value of the residence in the grantor's estate might be avoided. The regulations neither permit nor prohibit commutation and it is, therefore, probably unwise to authorize it specifically in the PRT document. Instead, it may be regarded as a potential means of terminating the PRT if situations warrant, pending future developments.

The additional flexibility of the QPRT lies in its ability to hold certain amounts of cash, sell a qualified residence, and be converted into a GRAT. In addition to those requirements that are common with PRTs, requirements for qualification of a QPRT, imposed by regulation,[35] are:

(1) Income of the trust must be distributed to the grantor annually or more frequently.

(2) No distributions from trust principal may be made to any beneficiary, other than the grantor, during the retained interest term.

(3) While certain amounts of cash may be held, the QPRT may not hold any assets other than a qualified residence for the entire term of the trust. Cash may be deposited for the purchase of the initial qualified residence or to replace a qualified residence, for improvements, and for payment of expenses, including mortgage payments, for up to a six-month period. The trust document must require the trustee to (1) compare the amount of cash held by the trust with the amount permitted at least quarterly; and (2) distribute any excess immediately to the grantor.

(4) Sales, insurance, or condemnation proceeds must be reinvested in a replacement residence within two years. Otherwise, the trust loses its qualification as a QPRT.

(5) Within 30 days after a trust ceases to be a QPRT, the trustee must have the discretion either to distribute the remaining assets to the grantor or to convert the trust into a GRAT. The GRAT payments must begin from the time the sale, destruction, or condemnation occurs (or, at least, interest must be paid to the grantor from that time), and the rate of payments from the GRAT to the grantor must be based on the rate used in valuing the original retained interest.

(6) The QPRT trust document must prohibit commutation.

Unlike GRATs and GRUTs, there is little doubt about the consequence of death of the grantor during the retained use term of a tangibles trust or of a PRT or QPRT. The nature of the interest retained is that of "income" or

[35] Reg. § 25.2702-5(c)(3) et seq.

"possession or enjoyment," which causes inclusion of the entire date-of-death value of the trust in the grantor's estate.[36] If the grantor dies during the retained interest term, the entire date of death value is included in the grantor's taxable estate for federal estate tax purposes. However, in that case, the amount reported at the inception of the transfer as a taxable gift is not treated as an adjusted taxable gift for purposes of the estate tax calculation. Also, the grantor's estate is entitled to a gift tax credit if the original transfer caused the payment of any gift tax. Therefore, it may be said that the tax consequences at the grantor's death during the retained interest term are no worse than if the transaction had not been undertaken.

.064 Intentional grantor trust

Traditionally, the application of the grantor trust rules was regarded as a disadvantage. Even if the trust income is actually accumulated or distributed to a beneficiary other than the grantor, under the substantial ownership rules, the grantor may be required to include the trust income on his personal income tax return. This represents a kind of "phantom income" to the grantor who is treated as the substantial owner. The presumption that this results in an overall income tax disadvantage follows from the income tax rate structure that existed prior to 1987. The grantor's total taxable income, particularly if it included the income of the trust, might have been subjected to tax rates of up to 50 percent, while the trust or the beneficiary might have been subject to a tax rate of as little as 11 percent.

The current income tax rate structure presents quite a different picture. In particular, there is much less advantage in causing trust income to be taxable at the trust level, even apart from considerations of the trust income accumulation rules. While the percentage rates of income tax imposed on trusts are the same as those for individual taxpayers, trusts now reach higher brackets with much lower amounts of taxable income. For instance, in 1995, married taxpayers filing separately (the least favorable individual income tax rate structure) pay income tax at the lowest rate of 15 percent on the first $19,500 of taxable income, while trusts remain in the 15 percent bracket only on the first $1,550 of taxable income. Also, trusts reach the highest income tax rate of 39.6 percent when taxable income exceeds just $7,650, compared with married individuals filing separately who are subject to the top rate only on taxable income in excess of $128,250. The rate structure now subjects the accumulation of significant amounts of income within the trust to higher income tax rates. As a result, strategies that cause the grantor to be treated as the substantial owner may be considered more favorable, or at least less disadvantageous.

There are limitations on the maximum amount that can be placed in a living trust free of gift tax. The $10,000 annual gift tax exclusion is only available to the extent that a transfer to the trust can qualify as a present interest in property according to actuarial principles. The $600,000 credit-sheltered equivalent, while a substantial amount in absolute terms, represents a small percentage of the total value that some potential grantors can afford to set aside. Married couples can contribute up to $1,200,000 to an irrevocable living trust with no current gift tax payable through the use of gift splitting. At that point, however, they would have fully utilized the benefits of the gift and estate unified credit available to both husband and wife. If the couple has substantial additional wealth, they may make additional transfers in amounts exceeding the annual exclusion only with significant gift tax cost.

---

[36] Code Sec. 2036(a)(1).

It is possible to design an irrevocable living trust so that the grantor is treated as the substantial owner for income tax purposes, but the trust is not subject to the string section rules for estate tax purposes. In fact, the grantor retained interest trusts, discussed at .061 through .063, above, are all examples. There are several advantages to this arrangement:

(1) While the value of money or property transferred to the trust is added back to the transferor's taxable estate as a post-1976 taxable gift, it is added back at the date of transfer value. Any appreciation that occurs after the date of the gift is free of both gift and estate taxes.

(2) By paying the income tax, the grantor reduces the amount that he might otherwise have accumulated and added to his taxable estate. While the payment of income tax is not usually looked upon as a desirable means of estate reduction, so long as someone in the family has to pay tax on the income produced by the trust, it makes better sense for a senior family member with a large potential estate to do so.

(3) Because the grantor pays the income tax, the trust may accumulate income free of tax and free of the trust accumulation distribution rules. Alternatively, distributions may be made to a beneficiary other than the grantor free of income tax. The result is a shifting of more wealth from the grantor to the natural objects of his bounty. In this regard, the grantor's payment of the income tax may be viewed as a good alternative to making additional gift transfers.

While gifts in excess of the available exclusions and exemptions are subject to significant rates of transfer tax, the grantor's payment of tax on income accumulated within a grantor trust or paid to trust beneficiaries has never been counted as a taxable gift. This may be attributable to the essential nature of the gift tax, a tax imposed on *voluntary* gift transfers. Under the substantial ownership rules, since the income tax law forces the grantor to pay the income tax if the substantial ownership rules apply, the grantor can hardly be treated as making a voluntary imputed gift to the trust beneficiaries who benefit thereby. Nevertheless, the IRS has ruled privately[37] that the grantor will be treated as making a separate, additional gift to a trust in the amount of income tax paid by the grantor because of the substantial ownership rules. There is an exception where the trust is required to reimburse the grantor for income tax imposed on the grantor that would otherwise be borne by the principal of the trust. If the IRS presses this theory and ultimately prevails, the effectiveness of using the intentional grantor trust as a means of transferring additional wealth will be limited.

.065 *Lifetime creation of bypass trust*

Inflation poses a threat to personal financial well-being, particularly in retirement. There are those who would like to take advantage of gift-giving programs, through trusts or otherwise, with the dual motivation of seeing their descendants benefit from their wealth during their own lifetimes and taking advantage of tax planning strategies. Some are discouraged by the thought that they might be giving away funds that will be needed later in life to keep up with the cost of living. This fear may result in the accumulation of wealth beyond the actual needs of the individual or of the married couple, exacerbating estate and generation-skipping transfer tax problems. In fact, the same inflation that drives up the cost of living, resulting in the need for more

[37] IRS Letter Ruling 9444033, CCH IRS LETTER RULINGS REPORTS.

resources, may also increase the value of the family assets, causing higher potential taxes in the end.

It has already been pointed out that transfers in trust by which economic benefits are retained by the grantor result in inclusion of the date-of-death fair market value of the trust in the grantor's taxable estate. For this reason, there is no tax planning advantage in establishing a trust for one's own benefit for life. For married couples, however, a trust fund may be used to remove the post-transfer appreciation of the trust property from the estates of both husband and wife while effectively keeping the income produced by the trust fund available for the couple's use so long as either of them lives. The basic design of this trust fund, and its estate and gift tax consequences, are as follows:

> (1) One spouse, referred to as the "transferor spouse," establishes an irrevocable living trust for the benefit of the other spouse, referred to as the "beneficiary spouse," for life. All income is payable to or for the benefit of the beneficiary spouse, and there may also be provisions to distribute principal to the beneficiary spouse if needed. The creation of a trust fund for the benefit of the grantor's spouse for life is not equivalent to establishing a trust for the grantor's own benefit and does not result in application of the estate tax string section rules.
>
> (2) The remaindermen of the trust fund are the couple's children or others intended by the couple to receive the balance of their resources after both spouses are deceased.
>
> (3) In addition to any other nongeneral powers of appointment, including limited withdrawal powers, which the transferor spouse may wish to include, the trust document gives to the beneficiary spouse the power, exercisable by a provision in his or her will, to postpone distribution of the remainder by directing that the trust continue after his or her death, in order to distribute the income and possibly even some of the principal to any person other than the beneficiary spouse, his or her estate, or creditors. The intention is to have the beneficiary spouse exercise this nongeneral power of appointment in order to cause the trust to continue for the benefit of the transferor spouse for life in the event that the transferor spouse survives the beneficiary spouse. However, no binding obligation may actually be placed on the beneficiary spouse to exercise this limited power of appointment in this manner.

If the beneficiary spouse actually dies first, resulting in continuation of the trust for the benefit of the transferor spouse because of the provision in the beneficiary spouse's will to that effect, there is little or no practical difference between it and a trust fund that the transferor spouse might have established for his or her own benefit for life. There is an important distinction for estate tax purposes, however, between interests in trust that are retained by the transferor and interests in trust that are returned to the transferor by the independent act of another party, in this case, by the beneficiary spouse. The result is that, even if the transferor spouse survives and the trust continues for his or her benefit, at the subsequent death of the transferor spouse, the value of the trust fund is not included in the taxable estate of the transferor spouse under the string section rules.

A trust that may distribute income to the grantor or to the grantor's spouse is subject to the substantial ownership rules so that the transferor spouse must include all trust income on his or her individual income tax return.

.066 *Lifetime bypass trust—Gift and estate tax considerations*

The gift and estate tax consequences of transfers to a lifetime bypass trust are fairly complex. The actuarial value of the life income interest passing to the beneficiary spouse, computed under the rules of Code Sec. 7520, is a taxable gift of a present interest in property. As a result, the first $10,000 of this value may be excluded from the total taxable gifts made by the transferor spouse. Since this is a gift between husband and wife, gift splitting is not available with respect to this portion of the gift.

The actuarial value of the remainder is treated as a gift by the transferor spouse to the children or other remaindermen. Since it cannot be predicted whether or not the beneficiary spouse will exercise the non-general testamentary power of appointment, its existence is ignored for purposes of allocating the elements of the gift. The remainder is a future interest for which no gift tax annual exclusion is available; however, it is a gift by a married person to third parties. Therefore, if the beneficiary spouse consents, 50 percent of the value of the remainder is treated as a gift made by the beneficiary spouse to the remaindermen.

Upon the death of the transferor spouse, assuming full availability of the gift tax unified credit, the excess value of the life income interest over $10,000 plus 50 percent of the value of the remainder, valued as of the date of the transfer, is added as a post-1976 taxable gift to the computation of the transferor spouse's federal estate tax liability. Any appreciation of the trust principal that occurs during the term of the trust is free of estate tax.

Finally, at the death of the beneficiary spouse, 50 percent of the value of the remainder is added as a post-1976 taxable gift to the computation of the beneficiary spouse's federal estate tax liability. Neither the survival of the transferor spouse nor the beneficiary spouse's exercise of the limited power of appointment has an effect on the estate tax consequences.

It is an oversimplification to assume that, as a result of the single gift tax annual exclusion of $10,000 plus the unified credit exemption equivalent of $600,000 available to the transferor spouse, the maximum amount that can be placed in a lifetime bypass trust is $610,000. The maximum is actually greater than that sum because of the gift-splitting element with respect to the remainder portion of the gift. The actual amount depends on the allocation of values, based on the actuarial calculation, between the life estate and the remainder. This actuarial calculation, in turn, depends on the age of the beneficiary spouse. However, assuming that neither the transferor spouse nor the beneficiary spouse has made taxable gifts in the past, the following formula may be used to determine the maximum funding of a lifetime bypass trust:

$$G - \left[\frac{(k \times G)}{2} \right] = \$610{,}000$$

G, in this formula, represents the maximum value that the transferor spouse can place into the trust fund resulting in no gift tax payable; k is the factor for valuation of the remainder, under Code Sec. 7520. If the beneficiary spouse is age 60, for example, the actuarial factors are:

Life Estate:	.71621
Remainder:	.28379

The steps to solve the problem and find the maximum funding of a lifetime bypass trust are as follows:

$$(1) \quad G - \left[\frac{.28379 \times G}{2} \right] = \$\ 610{,}000.00$$

$$(2) \quad 2G - [\ .28379 \times G\ ] = \$\ 610{,}000.00$$

$$(3) \quad 1.71621 \times G = \$1{,}220{,}000.00$$

$$(4) \quad G = \$\ 710{,}868.72$$

The solution to the problem—that the transferor spouse, under these circumstances, may transfer $710,868.72 into a lifetime bypass trust with no gift tax currently payable—may be proved by separating the elements of the gift:

(1) Gift by transferor spouse to beneficiary spouse:	$710,868.72 × .71621 =	$509,131.29
Less annual exclusion:		– 10,000.00
(2) Gift by transferor spouse to remaindermen:	$710,868.72 × .28379 =	$201,737.43
Less 50 percent treated as gift by beneficiary spouse due to gift splitting:		– 100,868.72
(3) Total taxable gifts of transferor spouse:		$600,000.00

The gift tax on the total of the transferor's taxable gifts is offset by the gift tax unified credit.

In analyzing the potential estate tax saving that may result from this technique, it is important to remember that the only part of the value transferred to the trust that is removed from the couple's taxable estates is the amount that qualifies for the gift tax annual exclusion. In the preceding example, that is only $10,000 out of the total amount of $710,868.72 transferred to the trust. Upon the death of the transferor spouse, $600,000 is added to his or her taxable estate as a post-1976 taxable gift and, for the same reason, $100,868.72 is added to the taxable estate of the beneficiary spouse due to the gift splitting. However, any appreciation of the principal value of the trust fund that occurs after the trust has come into existence is excluded from both taxable estates. While successful investment results can never be guaranteed, where principal growth is achieved, it typically takes place over a considerable period of years. For this reason, if any estimate of potential tax saving based on lifetime creation of a bypass trust is to be presented to a potential grantor, the disadvantages, as well as the possible advantages, must be explained.

.067 Lifetime bypass trust—Possible disadvantages

The possible disadvantages of the lifetime bypass trust to be considered are:

(1) Principal growth is not certain to occur; growth estimates are only estimates.

(2) If the principal declines in value, the amount added back to the taxable estate as a post-1976 taxable gift is not reduced. If that happens, the result of using the lifetime bypass trust might actually be a higher estate tax than if the client simply continued to hold his savings and investments outright until death.

(3) There are some ongoing administrative costs that must be paid whether or not any tax saving is ever realized.

(4) In the event of divorce, the transferor spouse may not receive any financial offset on account of the irrevocable gift to the trust, and the beneficiary spouse must be expected not to exercise the power of appointment in favor of the transferor spouse.

.068 *Lifetime bypass trust—Possible advantages*

The possible advantages of the lifetime bypass trust to be considered are:

(1) Potential estate tax saving if appreciation of trust principal occurs. No estate tax is payable if the taxable estate plus post-1976 taxable gifts does not exceed $600,000. The estate tax rates above $600,000 begin at 37 percent and go as high as 55 percent under current law. In view of this, it is possible to predict the minimum and maximum potential tax saving on any trust principal appreciation.

(2) Removal of savings and investments from the probate estate of both husband and wife that may result in lower estate settlement costs.

(3) Immediate availability to the beneficiary spouse of the income from the savings and investments transferred to the trust and the ability to return this source of income to the transferor spouse if the beneficiary spouse predeceases the transferor spouse. In other words, the economic value is, in effect, retained for the joint lives of the husband and wife.

In order to present the possible estate tax saving potential, it is necessary to make assumptions concerning the length of the joint lives of the couple after the trust fund is established, the average annual growth of the trust principal, and the value of the couple's non-trust assets included in their taxable estates. The following presentation model is based on the death of the second spouse 20 years after the trust creation. It illustrates the consequences of various average annual principal growth rates. In order to achieve the minimum possible estate tax saving, the sum of each spouse's taxable estate, plus the adjustments for the post-1976 taxable gift to the trust, must total exactly $600,000. The maximum possible estate tax saving, at a tax rate of 55 percent, requires that the second taxable estate, plus the gift add-back, exceed $3,000,000, the value above which the top estate tax bracket of 55 percent is imposed.

ANALYSIS OF POTENTIAL ESTATE TAX SAVINGS
THROUGH LIFETIME BYPASS TRUST
INITIAL PRINCIPAL VALUE: $710,868.72
(All amounts rounded to nearest $100)

Average Annual Principal Growth	*Value in 20 Years*	*Cumulative Increase in Principal*	*Potential Estate Tax Saving*	
			Minimum	*Maximum*
2%	$1,056,300	$ 345,400	$131,700	$ 190,000
4%	1,557,600	846,700	340,100	465,700
6%	2,279,800	1,568,900	670,800	862,900
8%	3,313,300	2,602,400	1,209,300	1,431,300

.069 *Trusts that may hold S corporation stock*

The S corporation. The S corporation, a creature of federal tax law, derives its name from Subchapter S of the Internal Revenue Code. The most basic distinction of the S corporation is that there is no income tax imposed at the corporate level. Instead, the shareholders include a ratable share of each item of income, deduction, and credit on their individual income tax returns. Since enactment of the Internal Revenue Code of 1986, which was a major revision of the federal income tax system, there has been an increasing use of the S corporation in family businesses and other closely held businesses.

Subchapter C of the Internal Revenue Code provides the tax rules for corporations that are separate taxable entities. These are sometimes referred to as C corporations. For shareholders of C corporations, double taxation is a fact of life. Assuming the business is successful, the net earnings and profits are taxed at the corporate level at an annual rate of up to 35 percent. Distributions of profits by a C corporation to its shareholders are designated as dividends that are not deductible from the corporation's taxable income but that do represent taxable income to the shareholder-recipients. Those shareholders who are also employees may receive corporate payments in the nature of compensation that is deductible by the corporation and taxable as earnings to the recipient, so that not all corporate earnings are subjected to income tax twice. There are, however, limitations on the maximum amount that a corporation may pay out in the form of compensation to shareholder-employees.

The elimination of one entire layer of income tax is the principal advantage of the S corporation. There is also a significant advantage in the event of the liquidation of an S corporation. Any gain realized on the sale of corporate assets upon liquidation and any unrealized gain on such assets that are distributed to the shareholders as part of the liquidation process is not subject to tax at the corporate level. Since 1987, C corporations have been forced to pay income tax on these gains at the time of liquidation, even though C corporation shareholders pay tax on the excess of the value of all liquidation proceeds over the shareholders' adjusted cost bases for their C corporation stock.

There are some tax disadvantages to the S corporation as well. In particular, the shareholders are required to pay income tax each year on their ratable shares of the corporation's profits, even if the corporation needs to retain those profits for the capital needs of its business. In other words, S corporation shareholders frequently pay income tax on amounts that they do not actually receive.

Restrictions on organization as an S corporation. Not all businesses are permitted to operate as an S corporation. An S corporation's special benefits are limited to closely held businesses. In order to qualify, the following requirements must be met:

(1) The corporation must not have more than 35 shareholders.

(2) There must be only one class of stock. More complex capitalization, such as the use of both common and preferred classes of stock, precludes the election of S corporation status.

(3) The shareholders must all be U.S. citizens or resident alien individuals, decedent's estates, or certain types of trusts.

(4) The shareholders must unanimously elect, on a written form submitted to the IRS, to have the business entity treated as an S corporation.

(5) Corporations that are banks, insurance companies, or domestic international sales corporations (DISCs) and corporations that elect the Puerto Rico and possession tax credit are not permitted to elect S corporation status.

Trusts that may hold S corporation stock in general. The types of trust funds that are permitted to hold S corporation shares are voting trusts and trusts that fall under the substantial ownership rules for fiduciary income tax purposes, where a person who is a U.S. citizen or a resident alien is treated as the substantial owner of the trust. This qualification may be met even if the person treated as the substantial owner is someone other than the grantor.

Two additional types of trusts are permitted to hold S corporation shares without causing the loss of S corporation status, but only on the condition that the shares be transferred to an individual or to another trust that meets the requirements, within a brief time period:

(1) Trust funds that receive S corporation shares as distributions from a deceased shareholder's estate. These trusts may hold S corporation shares for up to 60 days after the death of the testator.

(2) Trusts that had been subject to the substantial ownership rules but where the person treated as the substantial owner has died and the trust continues in existence as a separate entity for income tax purposes. These trusts may hold S corporation shares for up to 60 days after the death of the person who had been treated as the substantial owner. However, if the entire corpus of the trust fund is included in the substantial owner's taxable estate, this trust fund may continue to hold the S corporation shares for up to two years. This rule illustrates the fact that not all trusts that fall under the substantial ownership rules for income tax purposes are includible in the taxable estate of the substantial owner at death.

Foreign trusts are not permissible S corporation shareholders. Presumably, the policy reason for permitting trust funds that are not separate income tax entities to own stock of S corporations is that, since some individual is directly taxed on the income which flows through the S corporation, there is no opportunity for avoidance of income tax by transferring S corporation stock into this type of trust fund. Since the Tax Reform Act of 1986 (TRA '86) (P.L. 99-514), however, any incentive to use living trusts as a means of reducing the effective income tax rate is dramatically reduced because a trust reaches the highest income tax bracket with a comparatively small amount of taxable income.

Specially qualified trust to hold S corporation stock—The QSST. Since 1986, taxpayers have been given the privilege of creating trusts that may own S corporation stock on the condition that some individual is directly taxed on the trust's share of the S corporation income, even though the very fact of this direct taxation represents an income tax planning advantage to the taxpayer.

Certain trusts, designated as qualified subchapter S trusts (QSSTs), which would not otherwise be subject to the substantial ownership rules, are permitted to be treated as subject to those rules so that the trust may own S corporation shares. The current trust beneficiary must elect, in a written instrument filed with the IRS, to be treated as the substantial owner of the trust, and the terms of the trust must meet the following conditions:

(1) There must be only one income beneficiary at a time, and the beneficiary must be either a U.S. citizen or a resident alien.

(2) The beneficiary's income rights must end upon the beneficiary's death or upon termination of the trust, whichever occurs first.

(3) If trust principal distributions are permitted, the only allowable recipient must be the current income beneficiary.

(4) Upon termination of the trust, the beneficiary who had been receiving the income must receive the entire balance of the trust fund.

None of the requirements for QSST status create the equivalent of a general power of appointment for federal estate tax purposes. Therefore, the value of a QSST is not necessarily included in the taxable estate of the beneficiary.

Example: A, a U.S. citizen, established a trust fund for the benefit of his wife, B, in the nature of a credit-sheltered equivalent bypass trust funded during her lifetime. Since the income beneficiary is the spouse of the grantor, A is treated as the substantial owner, and the trust is therefore permitted to own shares of an S corporation. After the death of A, if B survives and if B is not permitted to make principal withdrawals, the trust loses its substantial ownership status and is treated as a separately taxable entity. However, if the terms of the trust meet the QSST requirements, B may elect to be treated as the substantial owner after A's death.

During A's lifetime, no special election is needed in order for the trust to hold S corporation shares. The fact that A's spouse is the income beneficiary automatically causes grantor trust status. The fact that A is treated as the substantial owner does not cause inclusion of the trust in A's taxable estate at its date-of-death value. However, the trust may be included in A's taxable estate under one of the string sections. For instance, if under all of the facts and circumstances, A is the direct or indirect owner of 20 percent or more of the voting control of the S corporation, the value of the trust is included in A's taxable estate.[38] Therefore, special care must be taken in planning this type of a QSST for the owner of a substantial percentage of an S corporation's total outstanding stock.

After A's death, the trust would ordinarily lose its substantial ownership status for income tax purposes. If all of the QSST requirements are met, however, B may elect to be treated as the substantial owner in order to permit the trust to continue holding the S corporation shares. This election is significant for income tax purposes only. Upon the subsequent death of B and so long as there is no general power of appointment, the value of the trust fund is not included in B's taxable estate.

.07 Other Trust Ownership Roles in the Family Business

The intended revision of the string section rules[39] for federal estate tax purposes under the Revenue Act of 1987 (P.L. 100-203) was replaced by the creation of new Chapter 14. These laws placed severe restrictions on the ability to freeze the value of business interests held by senior family members. Transactions including the creation of multi-class family partnerships and corporations with common and preferred classes of stock had been used prior to 1988 in attempts to keep much of the growth in value of family businesses out of the taxable estates of older members of the family.

Irrevocable living trusts may provide a suitable substitute for such transfers, in some cases for the purpose of controlling the growth of business value for estate tax purposes. However, the transfer of ownership of stock to an irrevocable living trust after which the transferor continues to control at least 20 percent of the voting power of the corporation results in inclusion, under Code Sec. 2036(b)(2), of the transferred shares in the grantor's estate at date-of-death value, as explained at ¶ 402. The 20 percent requirement is met either by personal control of the voting power or by votes held by members of the grantor's family. This precludes some planning for the transfer of closely held corporation stock in order to achieve the objective of estate tax reduction.

---

[38] Code Sec. 2036(b).

[39] Code Sec. 2036(c), retroactively repealed by the Revenue Reconciliation Act of 1990 (P.L. 101-508).

Planning opportunities still exist for those who are willing to divide the business into segments and give away one or more segments, either to younger members of the family or to irrevocable living trusts.

Many businesses can be separated into component parts. A few examples are:

(1) Manufacturing businesses ordinarily include their own marketing and distribution functions. In start-up situations, all of these activities may be handled, or at least supervised, by a single person. However, with growth of the business, separate departments or divisions may emerge.

(2) Sales businesses may be divisible into wholesale and retail operations and frequently offer service to their customers.

(3) Restaurants may offer outside catering services.

(4) Construction firms sometimes acquire the ownership of properties for development and future rental or sale.

Instead of keeping the business intact and causing it to undergo some form of recapitalization as a means of passing growth in value to younger generation family members, successful planning strategies in the wake of the Revenue Act of 1987 may involve creatively splitting up the business and allowing younger family members or trusts to acquire ownership of whatever component part offers the greatest opportunity for growth of value.

Example: Thirty years ago, brothers A and B started a business incorporated under the name of A & B, Inc., which manufactures and distributes automobile parts. Within the past five years, A's child, C, and B's child, D, have come to work for their fathers. The business has experienced significant growth, to a point at which it is difficult to meet the current level of orders promptly. In addition, A & B, Inc. has the opportunity to expand its markets throughout much of the U.S. as well as overseas.

It is possible for A & B, Inc., or for A and B as individuals, to assist C and D in the acquisition or construction of additional manufacturing facilities. Either the corporation or the shareholders can guarantee loans undertaken by C and D after which A & B, Inc. may lease the facilities from the junior family members. It may be necessary for the parents to make gifts to the children in order to provide some initial equity for the acquisition or construction as well. Even if this results in gifts that exceed the available gift tax annual exclusions, the resulting elimination of property interests, together with their potential for appreciation, from the taxable estates of A and B may prove to be a worthwhile trade-off.

In addition, the expansion of markets might make outside distributorships and related marketing services desirable. Just as growing businesses often engage the services of independent firms to provide these functions, A & B, Inc. may hire a separate, newly created entity owned by C and D for this purpose.

It may be appropriate to handle the segmentation of A & B, Inc.'s developing business by allowing C and D personally to acquire facilities or to establish outside enterprises which, by providing services to A & B, Inc., wind up drawing off a fair share of the growth in value of the original business. Under some circumstances, though, A and B might prefer to cause one or more irrevocable living trusts to acquire ownership of the new facilities or new businesses. Some of the reasons for A and B to use trusts as an alternative to direct ownership are:

(1) A and B might decide that C and D need more experience and maturity before the responsibilities of property ownership and business management can be placed in their hands.

(2) If C and D acquire the ownership directly and either or both of them become divorced, their estranged spouses might be entitled to have the property and business values included in any divorce settlement. In some states, using a trust fund as an alternative to direct ownership by C and D may avoid such claims.

(3) A or B might have additional children who are not involved in the business but with whom the parents may wish to share some of the potential financial benefits of the growth potential. Giving these non-employee children shares of the direct ownership could lead to problems because the "outside" owners might place their own financial interests above the needs of the business. Through a trust, management control may be more easily maintained.

(4) The spouses of A and B may also be beneficiaries of the trust, thus preserving the economic benefits of growth to the generation level of A and B during most or all of their lifetimes without retaining the growing value in their taxable estates. An example of this is transferring ownership of new facilities or newly created service enterprises to credit-sheltered equivalent bypass trusts established by A and by B during their lifetimes.

(5) The ultimate estate planning goal may include generation skipping. The living trust could be designed to provide benefits to the spouses of A and B and then to continue during the lifetimes of C and D, finally distributing the remainder to their descendants. Since the initial value placed in the trust comprises minimal equity and maximum growth potential, it should be possible in many such cases to qualify the trust funds under the available GST exemptions of A and B.

¶ 504 TRUST PLANS ARISING AT DEATH

There are several trust plans available to the client that arise at the death of the grantor. Some of these plans are discussed below.

.01 Contingent Trust for Minor Children

For married couples with young children who have a total combined estate of up to $600,000 in value, the only motivation to plan for estate tax saving is the potential for growth of estate value or accumulation of additional wealth. In these cases, the decision is often to postpone estate tax planning in favor of a simpler approach.

The possibility of death of both parents while their children are young, however statistically remote, is a powerful inducement to provide for trusts in an estate plan. Ordinarily, a couple regards a trust as an unnecessary complication if either spouse is alive. For this reason, each spouse's will leaves the entire estate to the survivor. In the event that both parents are deceased, their wills might also provide for an outright distribution of the estate among the children, if the youngest child has attained a specified age. The only contingency in which a trust is provided for is the death of both parents while there is still a young child.

The wills of married couples with young children should also provide for the appointment of a guardian in case both parents are deceased. The guardian may or may not also be the trustee. Some couples prefer to divide the responsibilities of guardian and trustee among different relatives or close friends either to avoid any possible conflict of interest or simply to reduce the total time demands and responsibilities placed on either the trustee or the guardian. Consideration should always be given to authorizing the trustee to make payments from the trust fund directly to the guardian in order to defray any additional expenses incurred by the guardian in providing care to the children. A specific provision in the will or trust document granting such authorization may avoid the necessity of the trustee seeking special court permission to make these payments. Besides reimbursement of the obvious expenses of food and clothing, it may be appropriate to authorize reimbursement for child care, educational expenses, vacations, hobbies, and the costs of any other activities that the parents would have wanted to provide if living. Some couples elect to go beyond the basics in order to authorize payments to the guardians to assist with the cost of a home addition or the purchase of a larger residence, if needed, because of additional children brought into the guardian's family.

In the absence of a contingent trust for minor children, it may be difficult to make funds available even for the children's legitimate needs. In the event of both parents' death, state laws place various restrictions on the expenditure of a minor's inheritance, whether the inheritance is received by the child under a state intestacy law or outright under the terms of the parents' wills. Even if a guardian is appointed, it is ordinarily necessary to seek court permission for payments from the minor child's funds, which turns into a costly, time-consuming process. In order to preserve as much of the inheritance as possible for distribution to the child at a specified age according to state law, the court may take a very conservative attitude toward requests for payments. When this fact of estate settlement law is explained to them, most couples seem to prefer the flexibility that a contingent trust offers.

A common oversight in estate planning for contingent trusts is failure to coordinate nonprobate assets that pass at death via beneficiary designation with the contingent trust plan. This may result in the court-mandated control of such assets outside the trust, even though a valid testamentary trust is established.

Example: H and W are married with three minor children. H's will leaves his entire estate to W, or if W predeceases H, to a contingent, sprinkle trust for the benefit of the children until the youngest child reaches age 25, at which time the trust is to be distributed equally among the children. W's will leaves her entire estate to H, or if he predeceases her, to the trust fund created under H's will. The assets of H and W are as follows:

Estate Plan of H and W
Value and Ownership of Assets

Description	*Ownership:* *H*	*W*	*Joint*	*Contractual*
Home			$125,000	
Savings	$5,000	$ 5,000	10,000	
Stocks & Bonds		10,000	15,000	
Life Insurance Death Benefits:				
(1) on H's life				$150,000
(2) on W's life				100,000
Retirement Plan Benefits:				
(1) H's plan				35,000
(2) W's plan				15,000
Totals	$5,000	$15,000	$150,000	$300,000

The individual probate estates of H and W are only $5,000 and $15,000, respectively. However, if both husband and wife die before their children reach age 25, the value of their jointly held assets passes into the contingent trust under the terms of the survivor's will. The only potential problem relates to the contractual assets. For instance, H and W may have designated each other beneficiary of their life insurance policies and retirement plans, and they may have designated their children as equal contingent beneficiaries. If this is not modified to name the trust as contingent beneficiary after the wills are executed, the estate plan of H and W will largely fail in the sense that the benefits payable upon the surviving spouse's death are not controlled by the will but pass to the children directly and must be subjected to court supervision outside the trust. If H and W should die simultaneously, none of the death benefits, which total $300,000 and comprise more than 60 percent of the combined estate wealth, will be included in the trust fund.

While the contingent trust for minor children is not used as a strategy to avoid or reduce gift, estate, or generation-skipping transfer tax, it has great personal importance during the parents' lifetimes. It provides them peace of mind through the assurance that the financial resources which they leave can be used for the benefit of their children in a flexible manner, as nearly as possible approximating the financial benefits that the parents would have provided if living.

.02 Credit-Shelter Equivalent Bypass Trust

The bypass principle described at ¶ 502 and further explored at ¶ 503 of this chapter may be employed through a trust fund that arises at the death of the first spouse. This may be accomplished through a revocable living trust established initially for the benefit of the transferor spouse, which functions as a will substitute and continues after the death of the transferor for the benefit of the surviving spouse. As an alternative, the bypass trust may be established as a testamentary trust under the will of the first deceased spouse.

Many estate planners are of the opinion that, after the bypass trust is set aside, the next objective should be to obtain the marital deduction for the entire excess value of the first deceased spouse's estate over the credit-shelter equivalent amount. In this manner, the amount of estate tax imposed on the first estate is always zero. The goal of this approach is to postpone payment of any estate tax until the death of the surviving spouse. The principal advantage that this produces is the continued earnings power, during the survivorship period of the second spouse, of any amount of estate tax which might have been imposed on the first estate.

.03 Passing Up the Advantages of the Marital Deduction and Estate Equalization

Establishing the credit-shelter equivalent bypass trust and then using marital deduction transfers to cause a zero estate tax liability in the first estate has its appeal. However, there is a possible disadvantage in any case in which the second taxable estate, including any value passed via marital deduction transfers from the first estate, exceeds $1 million. The significance of the $1 million value is as follows:

(1) If the second taxable estate does not exceed the $600,000 unified credit exemption equivalent, there is no federal estate tax payable at the death of the second spouse; but

(2) If the value of the second taxable estate is more than $600,000 and not more than $1 million, the estate tax rate is 37 percent. This is the

lowest effective rate of federal estate tax, so that the "bunching" of assets in the second taxable estate resulting from marital deduction transfers causes no disadvantage; therefore

(3) Any excess in value of the second taxable estate over $1 million caused by marital deduction transfers from the first estate results in a higher than minimum rate of estate tax.

Where the combined wealth of the couple results in a second taxable estate only moderately in excess of the $1 million level, the client may not wish to take any special steps. Estate planning is subject to constant change resulting from acquisition and expenditure of resources as well as fluctuations in value. Also, after the death of the first spouse, the survivor may find it necessary to consume some of the principal of the family wealth. For these reasons, the use of the bypass trust in the first estate, coupled with marital deduction transfers of all assets in excess of the credit-shelter equivalent amount, may be the best approach.

In larger estates, however, the benefits of the credit-shelter equivalent trust plus marital deduction transfers can cause a significant increase in the total estate tax imposed on the combined wealth of husband and wife.

Example: H and W, a married couple, have no jointly held assets. The total value of H's estate is $1,500,000 and the separate value of W's estate is $3,000,000. H and W are considering the use of trusts in their estate plan for the potential benefits of financial management as well as estate tax savings.

If H dies first, the combination bypass trust and marital deduction transfers of the balance of H's estate to W causes the following result:

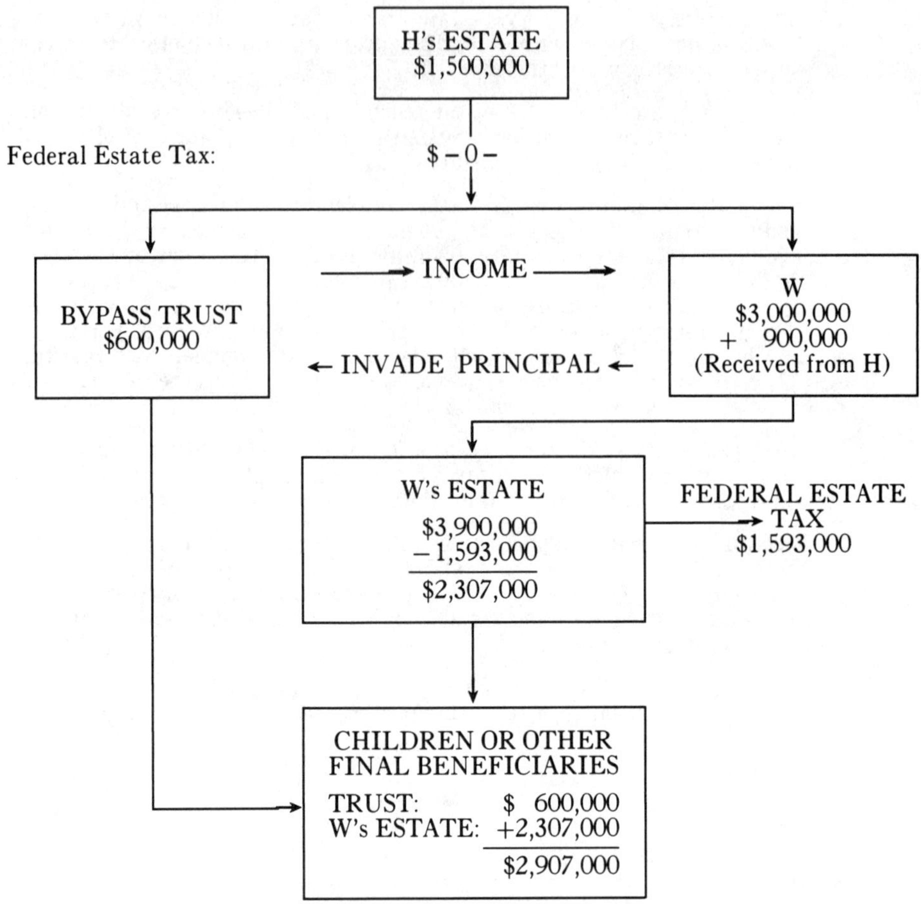

The result is that the entire amount passed from H to W becomes subject to the maximum federal estate tax rate of 55 percent in W's estate. Instead, H may decide to transfer nothing directly to W but to place his entire estate in the bypass trust. This results in a trade-off: H's estate gives up the benefit of the marital deduction and pays some estate tax, but the combined amount of estate taxes paid by both estates is lower. The following diagram depicts the consequences:

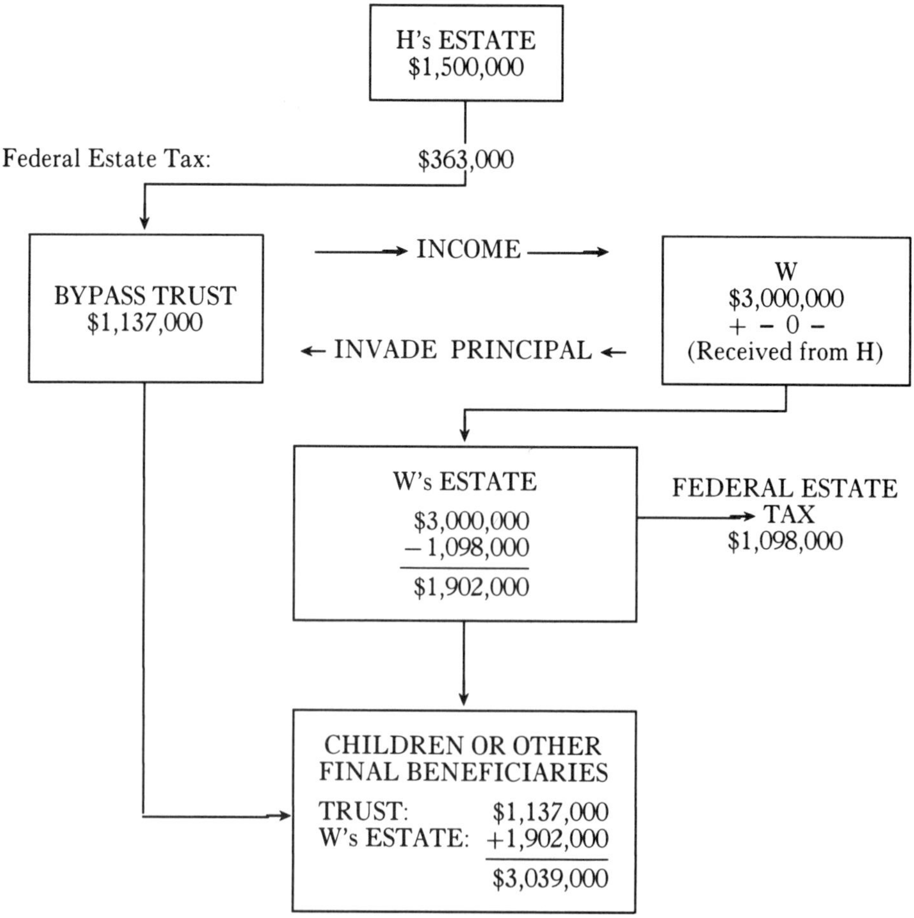

Faced with a substantial estate tax at the death of the first spouse in return for an overall estate tax saving, the client may be well advised to elect the use of marital deduction transfers in order to reduce the first estate's tax liability to zero, even though this results in a larger combined estate tax result. In the preceding example, the total overall tax saving was $132,000 ($3,039,000 – $2,907,000), which is not an inconsequential sum. To obtain the tax saving, however, it was necessary to incur a federal estate tax in the first estate in the amount of $363,000. The economic loss of earning power on $363,000 at a six percent annual compounded rate of return equals the full potential estate tax saving of $132,000 in a little more than five years. The conclusion to be drawn is that foregoing the marital deduction only results in an economic benefit if the second spouse dies shortly after the first spouse, which is ordinarily difficult to predict and to plan for in advance.

In planning for the contingency of the spouse whose separate estate is larger dying first, estate equalization is sometimes recommended. This technique places the responsibility on the executor or trustee, under the terms of the will or will-substitute trust, to divide the estate into the bypass trust part and marital part in such proportions that, after the division, the taxable estates are equal as of the date of death of the first spouse. This makes it necessary for the executor or trustee not only to compute the taxable estate of the deceased spouse but also to make a hypothetical calculation of the value of the surviving spouse's estate as if the survivor had also died. For instance, in the preceding example, if W's will provided for estate equalization and if W predeceased H, the result would be as follows:

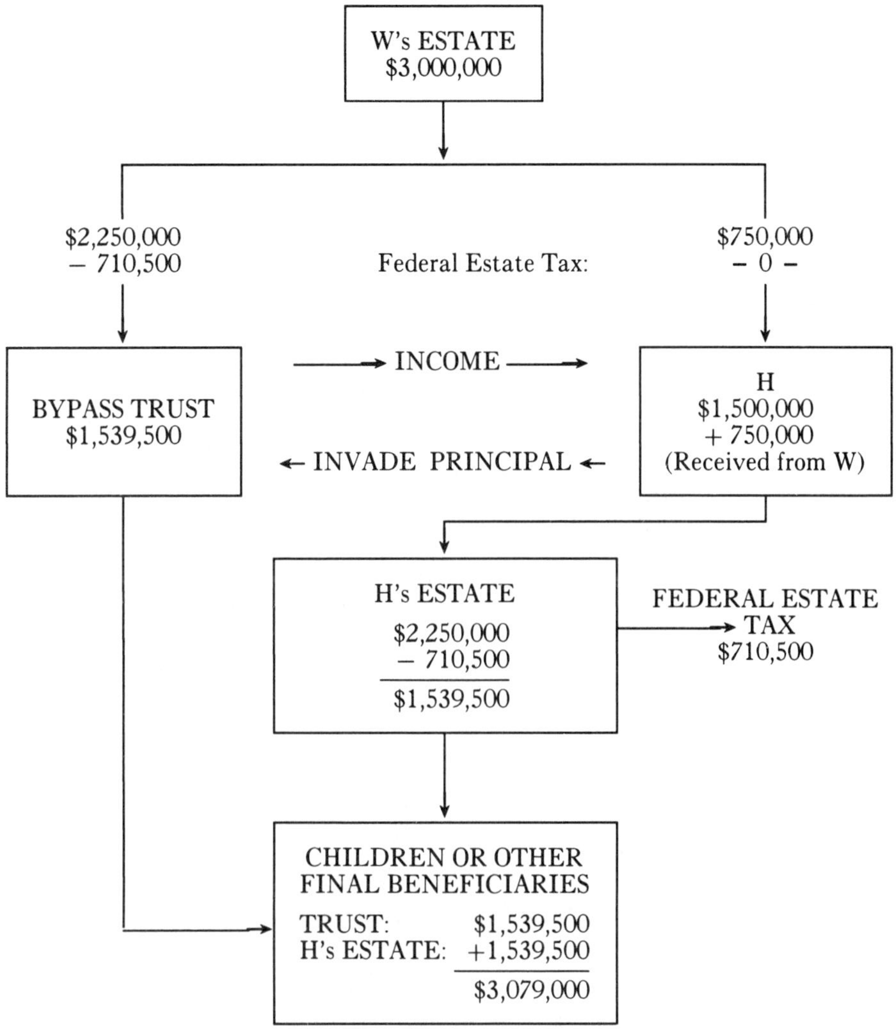

The overall estate tax result is improved, in this case in the amount of $40,000 ($3,079,000 – $3,039,000) by comparison with the example in which H dies first leaving his entire estate to the bypass trust. The reason for the additional saving is precise equalization of the amounts subjected to tax in each estate, which avoids differences in tax brackets. Also, actual equalization is impossible because there is certain to be some change in the value of the estate of the surviving spouse during the period of survivorship. More importantly, however, estate equalization suffers the economic disadvantage of loss of earning power on the estate tax paid at the death of the first spouse. The advantage of postponement of all tax payment until the second death is a strong argument in favor of using the credit-shelter equivalent bypass trust in combination with marital deduction transfers for the balance of the first estate.

.04 Marital Deduction Trusts

In the preceding discussions of the combination of a credit-shelter equivalent bypass trust with marital deduction transfers of the balance of the first spouse's estate to the surviving spouse, the examples have been based on outright transfer of the marital deduction portion to the survivor. As an alternative, however, many couples prefer to place the marital deduction portion of the first estate into a trust for the benefit of the surviving spouse. The term "A and B trust" in estate planning refers to the use of a marital deduction trust, designated as the "A trust," and a credit-shelter equivalent bypass trust, designated as the "B trust." Some attorneys prefer to use the terms "marital trust" and "family trust" in wills and trust agreements.

The motivation to use a trust for the marital deduction portion may result if the surviving spouse prefers to avoid the responsibilities of financial management or the transferor spouse wants to give less than complete and outright control to the recipient spouse and still hopes to avoid or postpone gift and estate tax on the transfer. The latter motive is often encountered in cases of a second marriage where each spouse has children by his or her respective first marriage. Depending on the needs of the surviving spouse, as well as other personal factors affecting the transferor spouse's planning decisions, the credit-shelter equivalent share may be distributed directly to the children of a prior marriage or held in trust for their benefit, with no intervening interest passing to the surviving spouse.

A trust fund to last during the lifetime of the surviving spouse with the remainder distributable to children or other final beneficiaries is an example of a terminable interest. The discussion of the estate tax marital deduction at ¶ 401.03 points out that, as a general rule, the transfer of a terminable interest in property to the surviving spouse may not qualify for the marital deduction. There are two types of trust funds to which property may be transferred for the lifetime benefit of the surviving spouse with respect to which the marital deduction is permitted.

.041 Life income and power of appointment trust

Estate planning specialists sometimes refer to this type of marital deduction trust as the "section 2056(b)(5) trust," a reference to the specific provision of the Internal Revenue Code on which it is based.

Where assets included in the taxable estate of the first deceased spouse are transferred to a trust fund for the benefit of the surviving spouse and the following two requirements are met, the federal estate tax marital deduction is available to the estate of the first spouse.

(1) All of the income must be payable to the surviving spouse for life. The time interval of periodic income distributions must be yearly (or more frequently) beginning from the date the principal assets are received into the trust and begin to produce income. In case of a testamentary trust, the estate tax regulations do not require that the income generated on estate assets that are later placed into the marital deduction trust must be accounted for and distributed to the surviving spouse. However, if it appears from the terms of the will or other relevant circumstances that the executor could unreasonably delay funding of the trust and thereby delay income payments to the surviving spouse, the marital deduction could be disallowed.

The transfer to a marital deduction trust of assets that do not produce income does not automatically result in loss of the marital deduction if the trustee is required by the terms of the trust or by local law to sell and reinvest unproductive assets or if the surviving spouse has the right to require the trustee to take such action. For instance, if the deceased spouse's estate includes a vacation home that contains an object of art, both of these assets might be transferred to the marital deduction trust so that the surviving spouse can have the use and enjoyment of the property. So long as the surviving spouse has the right to require a sale of these items by the trustee (but simply chooses not to do so), the marital deduction is permitted.

Most types of accounting adjustments that reduce the income payable to the surviving spouse are also permissible without loss of the marital deduction. For instance, the trust terms may permit amortization of bond premiums and depletion allowances to be deducted from income and added to trust corpus. Trustee discretion to determine whether items of receipt or disbursement constitute income or principal is also allowed unless it is determined that the overall purpose and effect is to deprive the spouse of the normal right to income or other enjoyment of the property, which is typical of a trust life beneficial interest.

(2) By the terms of the trust, the surviving spouse must possess a general power of appointment exercisable by the surviving spouse alone and in all events. This requirement is not met, for instance, if the surviving spouse must obtain the consent of any other person to exercise the power or if the right to exercise the power terminates upon remarriage by the surviving spouse.

The power of appointment may be one that is exercisable during the lifetime of the surviving spouse or it may be only a testamentary power of appointment, exercisable in favor of the surviving spouse's estate. Since a right to make withdrawals from principal is an example of a power of appointment in favor of the holder of the power, the surviving spouse's unlimited right for life to withdraw from trust principal is sufficient. There is an important distinction in the fiduciary income tax treatment that depends on the nature of the surviving spouse's power of appointment:

(1) If the power of appointment is exercisable only upon the death of the surviving spouse, the trust is treated as a separate taxable entity for fiduciary income tax purposes. Income tax caused by corpus transactions, such as capital gains, is paid from trust principal.

(2) If the surviving spouse has the unlimited power to withdraw trust principal during life, the surviving spouse is treated as the substantial owner of the principal under the grantor trust rules.[40] Therefore, the surviving spouse must include all items of income, as well as any deductions or credits resulting from trust principal transactions, on the spouse's individual income tax return even if no principal withdrawals are actually made.[41]

(3) No person may have the right to appoint any part of the trust fund that qualifies for the marital deduction to anyone other than the surviving spouse during the surviving spouse's lifetime. This makes it necessary to review all trust provisions in order to determine whether the

---

[40] Code Sec. 678(a).

[41] Code Sec. 671.

combination of powers and rights is within specification. These are some examples:[42]

Example (1): The surviving spouse is entitled to all income for life, payable annually, and has the power to appoint the entire principal value to his or her estate by will. The surviving spouse also has the power to make distributions from trust principal to the children, so long as this power is not used to discharge a support obligation of the surviving spouse. Although it is possible for the principal of the marital trust to be distributed to someone other than the surviving spouse during his or her life, marital deduction qualification is preserved because it is only the surviving spouse who can cause the principal distribution. It is worth noting that any such principal distributions to the children constitute a gift by the surviving spouse of a present interest in property. To the extent that the distributions do not exceed $10,000 per year per recipient, the gift tax annual exclusion applies and, therefore, the total eventually included in the taxable estate of the surviving spouse is reduced. In this case, since the surviving spouse does not have the right to withdraw from principal for his or her own use, the substantial ownership rules do not apply. The income tax liability on trust corpus transactions is borne by the trust fund rather than by the surviving spouse.

Example (2): The surviving spouse is entitled to all income for life, payable annually, and has the power to appoint the entire principal value to his or her estate by will. The trustee has the power to make unlimited principal distributions from trust principal to the surviving spouse during life.

Here, all requirements for the marital deduction are met, but the first deceased spouse made somewhat more liberal benefits available to the survivor than the required minimum. If the surviving spouse is also the trustee, the trustee's power to distribute principal to the surviving spouse is treated in the same manner as if the surviving spouse held that right personally, so that the survivor is treated as the substantial owner of the principal for fiduciary income tax purposes. However, if the trustee is someone other than the surviving spouse, the trust, as a separate income tax entity, is liable for the income tax on any corpus transactions.

Example (3): The surviving spouse is entitled to all income for life, payable annually, and has the power to appoint the entire principal value to his or her estate by will. The trustee, which is not the surviving spouse, has the discretion to make principal distributions to the surviving spouse for any purpose or to the children, if necessary, to provide for educational expenses.

The marital deduction may be disallowed with respect to transfers from the estate of the first deceased spouse to this trust. The fact that a person other than the surviving spouse (in this case, the trustee) has the power to make distributions to any person other than the survivor makes the marital deduction unavailable. Even though the power to distribute is severely restricted both as to permissible recipients and as to the use of the funds, the marital deduction is lost.

---

[42] Code Sec. 2056(b)(5); Reg. § 20.2056(b)-5.

Although the surviving spouse must possess a general power of appointment over the Code Sec. 2056(b)(5) trust, it is permissible for the transferor spouse to specify how the property is to be distributed after the death of the surviving spouse in case the survivor fails to exercise the power of appointment. This is known as "a gift in default of appointment." Typically, the transferor spouse includes a provision in his or her will granting a general power of appointment to the surviving spouse and directing that any part of the trust fund not effectively appointed by the survivor is to be distributed to children or other intended remaindermen.

The taxable estate of the surviving spouse includes the value of any trust fund that qualified for the marital deduction in the first deceased spouse's estate as a life income and power of appointment trust. Possession by the survivor of the general power of appointment causes this result, which is in line with the underlying intention of the estate and gift tax system—to make it possible to eliminate all tax upon interspousal transfers so long as any assets received by the surviving spouse are taxed when the survivor dies.

The principal disadvantage of the life income and power of appointment marital deduction trust is the requirement that the surviving spouse possess a general power of appointment over the trust principal. To some married couples who are considering estate planning alternatives, concern exists that their spouse will: (1) survive, (2) later become remarried, and (3) predecease the new spouse. If the power of appointment is exercised, the new spouse may then retain the wealth that, it was hoped, would eventually have passed to children or others. In limited form, the marital deduction has been part of federal tax law since 1948, and Code Sec. 2056(b)(5) has been included in the Internal Revenue Code in its present form since 1954. Throughout the history of marital deduction planning, specialists in this field have noted the frequent negative reaction of clients to the general power of appointment requirement.

.042 Qualified terminable interest property

The Economic Recovery Tax Act of 1981 (ERTA) (P.L. 97-34) introduced a permissible alternative to the life income plus power of appointment marital deduction trust, better known as qualified terminable interest property (QTIP). This makes it possible to create a terminable interest in property for the lifetime benefit of the surviving spouse that may or may not be held in trust and that qualifies for the marital deduction. Clearly, one aim of QTIP was the elimination of the power of appointment problem, which so many people found objectionable.

In order to obtain the marital deduction for a QTIP transfer, the following requirements must be met:[43]

(1) The surviving spouse must be entitled to the income of the subject property according to the same rules as those explained with respect to the Code Sec. 2056(b)(5) trust.

(2) No person may have any power to make distributions to anyone other than the surviving spouse during the survivor's lifetime.

(3) The executor of the transferor spouse's estate must make an election on the federal estate tax return to treat the transfer as QTIP.

---

[43] Code Sec. 2056(b)(7).

It is also possible to make a QTIP election in connection with any lifetime transfer that meets the above requirements.[44] The election is then made by the transferor spouse on the gift tax return. There is an additional tax consequence that follows a QTIP election besides permitting the marital deduction to the transferor spouse. Specifically, the value of any property with respect to which a QTIP election has been made is included in the taxable estate of the beneficiary spouse even though the beneficiary spouse holds no power of appointment over the subject property.[45] This is another illustration of the basic thrust of the gift and estate tax system that permits tax-free interspousal transfers but imposes a tax at the death of the second spouse. To prevent any inequity caused by this rule, the extra estate tax imposed on the estate of the surviving spouse because of the inclusion of a QTIP amount is paid from the QTIP trust or from property held outside of the trust that qualifies for the QTIP. The surviving spouse may waive this special tax allocation rule if he or she so desires.

Alternative designs for QTIP use. Where the QTIP is used, questions as to the disposition of the bypass share may arise.

> **Example:** H and W were each previously married. Each have children by their respective first marriages, and it is a principal goal of each spouse to insure that his or her separate estate eventually passes to his or her own children. However, both H and W wish to provide for the financial needs of the surviving spouse during the survivor's lifetime. Each spouse's estate exceeds the credit-sheltered equivalent value for estate tax purposes.

Under these circumstances, two examples of estate plans using QTIP trusts for the benefit of the surviving spouse that might be appropriate for H and W are:

(1) If H and W agree that the surviving spouse will be adequately provided for through the survivor's separate estate, along with the income on the portion of the first deceased spouse's estate that exceeds the credit-sheltered equivalent value, each of their wills may be designed as follows:

(a) The credit-shelter equivalent portion may be divided among the deceased spouse's children or may be held in trust for their benefit, with no intervening benefits distributable to the surviving spouse.

(b) The balance of the deceased spouse's estate may be placed in a QTIP trust, under the terms of which the surviving spouse receives income for life, but does not have access to principal. At the death of the surviving spouse, the balance of the QTIP trust is either distributed to the children of the first deceased spouse or is held in continuing trust for their benefit.

(2) If H and W prefer to keep all of the income of their combined estates available for the needs of the surviving spouse for life, both the credit-shelter equivalent portion and the excess, or marital portion, may be placed in separate trust shares. The income from both the bypass trust and the QTIP trust are payable to the surviving spouse for life. Upon the death of the surviving spouse, both of the trusts are distributed to the children of the first deceased spouse. The estate of the surviving spouse is distributed directly to the surviving spouse's children.

---

[44] Code Sec. 2523(f).

[45] Code Sec. 2044.

It is not necessary, for any tax planning purpose, to restrict the rights of the surviving spouse to the income of the QTIP trust. Any right to withdraw principal, as well as any trustee power to make principal distributions to the surviving spouse, even if it amounts to a general power of appointment held by the surviving spouse, makes no difference in the tax consequences when the survivor later dies. This is so because, by virtue of the QTIP election, the trust is fully taxable in the survivor's estate. It seems, however, that the inclination is to make QTIP trusts somewhat more restrictive because the entire QTIP concept came about as a means of gaining the marital deduction in the first estate without giving the surviving spouse control over the principal. Of course, there is also a middle ground. The transferor spouse may provide that, in addition to income, the survivor have access to principal of the QTIP share limited by an ascertainable standard, or the transferor spouse may delegate the power to make principal distributions for the surviving spouse's needs to a trustee who is someone other than the survivor.

.043 Qualified domestic trust (QDOT)

As explained at ¶ 402.053, the marital deduction is generally not available if the surviving spouse is not a U.S. citizen. An exception to the rule is permitted for assets transferred from the first spouse to a trust fund for the benefit of the survivor that meets specific requirements.[46] This trust is called a qualified domestic trust (QDOT). The underlying objective is to make sure that the unified transfer tax is imposed on the assets, if not at the death of the first spouse, then later. If the marital deduction were allowed for transfers to a noncitizen spouse without restriction, no tax might ever be imposed. The survivor could move outside the U.S., taking the untaxed inheritance left by the first spouse. If the survivor is neither a citizen nor a resident of the U.S. at his or her subsequent death, the survivor's estate is not subject to estate tax.

The QDOT rules are intended to create a mechanism for postponing the imposition of tax when assets pass from the first spouse to the QDOT. Tax is imposed either when principal distributions are made from the QDOT to the noncitizen spouse or upon the death of that spouse.[47]

The rules for qualification of a QDOT are summarized as follows:

(1) At least one trustee must be a U.S. citizen, either an individual or a domestic corporation. Appointment of corporations in a trustee capacity is restricted by state and federal law primarily to banks with trust powers or trust companies. The U.S. trustee must have the power to withhold tax on distributions from the QDOT.[48] Each trustee is personally liable for the tax imposed on distributions.[49]

(2) The executor of the first spouse's estate must make an election under Code Sec. 2056A to qualify the trust as a QDOT.[50]

(3) The trust must meet any other requirements established by regulation.[51]

The calculation of tax on a distribution from a QDOT, and on the balance remaining at the death of the noncitizen spouse, generally follows the gift tax calculation. The tax on principal distributions during the noncitizen spouse's lifetime is calculated by treating the deceased spouse's taxable estate and any

[46] Code Secs. 2056(d)(2) and 2056A.
[47] Code Sec. 2056A(b).
[48] Code Sec. 2056A(a)(1).
[49] Code Sec. 2056A(b)(6).
[50] Code Sec. 2056A(a)(3).
[51] Code Sec. 2056A(a)(2).

previous principal distributions as if they were taxable gifts. Likewise, at the death of the noncitizen spouse, the tax is calculated on the balance remaining in the QDOT, by treating the first deceased spouse's taxable estate and any principal distributions made during the life of the noncitizen spouse as if they were taxable gifts.[52] In case of any principal distributions made before the estate tax on the first deceased spouse's estate is finally determined, the tax is imposed at the highest gift and estate tax rate in effect. After the estate tax on the first deceased spouse's estate is finally determined, it may be that the tax calculated at the highest rate is greater than that based on the general gift tax calculation. If so, a claim for credit or refund of the excess must be made within one year after the date of the final estate tax determination.

Distributions of income from a QDOT to a noncitizen spouse, though subject to income tax, are exempt from the "postponed" estate tax. An exemption is also allowed for hardship distributions.[53] Proposed regulations specify that a hardship for this purpose means "an immediate and substantial financial need relating to the spouse's health, maintenance, or support" but states that even if a hardship condition is present, the principal distribution from the QDOT is not exempt if the noncitizen spouse has other available financial resources such as marketable securities or certificates of deposit.[54]

.05 Coordination of Bypass Trust and Marital Shares

Where the estate plan is to set aside a credit-shelter equivalent bypass trust with marital deduction transfers of the balance of the first taxable estate, certain adjustment provisions are necessary. In order to accomplish the zero estate tax objective in the first spouse's estate, it is necessary that the entire value of the first taxable estate in excess of the credit-shelter amount be transferred to the surviving spouse. However, there may be expenses and charges incurred in estate administration that are ordinarily paid from the residuary estate. To the extent that these charges reduce the amount passing to the surviving spouse, the marital deduction is diminished, resulting in some amount of estate tax payable by the first spouse's estate. The estate tax itself might be payable from the residuary estate, which further reduces the marital deduction and further increases the estate tax payable. If the amounts paid from the residue are proper estate tax deductions in their own right, such as debts, funeral costs, and estate administration expenses, the problem may be eliminated. Although the payment of these charges reduces the amount that qualifies for the estate tax marital deduction, these items are nevertheless deductible from the taxable estate. In case of administration expenses, it is up to the executor to elect either to claim an estate tax deduction or an income tax deduction for the amounts paid; deductions from both estate and income taxes are not allowed.[55] If the executor pays administration expenses from the residue and elects the income tax deduction, the marital deduction is reduced without any corresponding estate tax administration deduction. Payment of state death tax from the residuary estate causes further complications because this expenditure reduces the marital deduction, thereby increasing the estate tax, but results in a credit against the tax payable.

Example: W's will provides that the credit-sheltered amount be set aside in a bypass trust and that W's residuary estate be distributed outright to W's surviving spouse, H. Under the law of W's domicile

---

[52] Code Sec. 2056A(b)(2)(A).

[53] Code Sec. 2056A(b)(2) and (3).

[54] Prop. Reg. § 20.2056A-5(c)(1).

[55] Code Sec. 642(g).

state, administration expenses and debts, as well as any state death taxes, are paid from the residue. W's total estate is valued at $1,000,000, consisting entirely of probate assets subject to loans outstanding in the amount of $50,000, and the estate is required to pay funeral expenses of $10,000, administration expenses of $25,000, and state death tax of $40,000.

The executor might well elect to claim the administration expenses on the fiduciary income tax return of the estate under the mistaken assumption that the combination credit-shelter and marital deduction would completely eliminate the estate tax. While making the federal estate tax calculation and completing the federal estate tax return, it might not become apparent that the payment of the federal estate tax itself, as well as the payment of the state death tax, reduces the amount passing to the surviving spouse, thereby lowering the marital deduction allowed.

An initial summary of W's estate is as follows:

Gross Estate		$1,000,000
Debts	$ 50,000	
Funeral Expense	10,000	
Administration Expenses (Claimed for income tax)	-0-	
State Death Tax (Results in credit, not deduction)	-0-	
Amounts Paid from Residue and Deducted		– 60,000
Subtotal		$ 940,000
Marital Deduction		
Net Probate Estate	940,000	
Less Credit-Shelter Amount to Be Set Aside in Bypass Trust	–600,000	
Less Amounts Paid from Residue but Not Deducted		
Administration Expenses	– 25,000	
State Death Tax	– 40,000	
Tentative Marital Deduction		–275,000
Tentative Taxable Estate		$ 665,000
Tentative Federal Estate Tax Before Credits		$ 216,850
Credits Against the Tax		
Unified Credit	$ 192,800	
State Death Tax Credit (Smaller of amount paid or amount found in Internal Revenue Code Sec. 2011(b) table)	16,600	
Total Credits		– 209,400
Tentative Federal Estate Tax		$ 7,450

The payment of items from the residuary estate that are not deductible for federal estate tax purposes results in a net tax payable. The amount of $7,450 is described as "tentative" because the payment of this tax itself further reduces the marital deduction which, in turn, increases not only the taxable estate and the gross estate tax but also increases the credit for state death tax. The actual estate tax payable is \$11,119.40. This result is obtained through the following formula:

$$\text{Correct Estate Tax} = \frac{\text{Tentative Estate Tax}}{\text{1 minus [F.E.T. Bracket \% minus S.D.T. Bracket \%]}}$$

The federal estate tax (F.E.T.) and state death tax (S.D.T.) bracket percentages are 37 percent and four percent, respectively, as obtained from the tables in Code Secs. 2001(c) and 2011(b) (see ¶ 1001).

Excerpt from Code Sec. 2001(c)

(c) RATE SCHEDULE.—
(1) IN GENERAL

If the amount with respect to which the tentative tax to be computed is:	The tentative tax is:
. . .	. . .
Over \$ 500,000 but not over \$750,000	\$155,800, plus 37% of the excess of such amount over \$500,000

Excerpt from Code Sec. 2011(b)

(b) AMOUNT OF CREDIT.—The credit allowed by this section shall not exceed the appropriate amount stated in the following table:

If the adjusted taxable estate is	The maximum tax credit shall be:
. . .	. . .
Over \$440,000 but not over \$640,000	\$10,000 plus 4% of the excess over \$440,000

In the preceding example, the formula results as follows:

$$\text{Correct Estate Tax} = \frac{\$7,450}{\text{1 minus [37\% minus 4\%]}}$$

$$\text{Correct Estate Tax} = \frac{\$7,450}{\text{1 minus 33\%}}$$

$$\text{Correct Estate Tax} = \frac{\$7,450}{67\%}$$

$$\text{Correct Estate Tax} = \$11,119.40$$

If the taxable estate, gross estate tax and state death tax credits are recomputed based on a reduction of the marital deduction by this same amount, the net federal estate tax payable would be correctly computed by using the following formula:

Corrected Summary of W's Federal Estate Tax Computation

Gross Estate		$1,000,000.00
Debts	$ 50,000.00	
Funeral Expense	10,000.00	
Administration Expenses (Claimed for income tax)	-0-	
State Death Tax Credit (Results in credit, not deduction)	-0-	
Amounts Paid from Residue and Deducted		– 60,000.00
Subtotal		$ 940,000.00
Marital Deduction		
Net Probate Estate	940,000.00	
Less Credit Shelter Amount to Be Set Aside in Bypass Trust	– 600,000.00	
Less Amounts Paid from Residue but Not Deducted:		
Administration Expenses	– 25,000.00	
State Death Tax	– 40,000.00	
Federal Estate Tax	– 11,119.40	
Marital Deduction		– 263,880.60
Taxable Estate		$ 676,119.40
Federal Estate Tax Before Credits		$ 220,964.18
Credits Against the Tax		
Unified Credit	$ 192,800.00	
State Death Tax Credit (Smaller of amount paid or amount found in Internal Revenue Code Sec. 2011(b) table)	17,044.78	
Total Credits		– 209,844.78
Correct Federal Estate Tax		$ 11,119.40

The formula for computing the correct federal estate tax was comparatively simple in this example because the amount of federal estate tax paid did not cause a change in either the federal estate tax or state death tax bracket percentages. Where a bracket change is encountered, the computation is somewhat more involved.

.06 Reducing Complexity

Convoluted computations, such as those above, should be unnecessary because the usual objective of the combination credit-shelter and marital deduction estate plan is to avoid altogether the payment of any tax in the first deceased spouse's estate. There are actually two methods of accomplishing this objective and avoiding the problem just described:

(1) The will or the trust document, if controlling, may specify that any amounts that are ordinarily payable from the residuary estate, and

that are not deductible for federal estate tax purposes, must not be paid from the residuary estate. Such amounts must be paid from the credit-shelter pre-residuary portion thus reducing that portion.

(2) The division of the credit-shelter and marital portions might be redesigned so that the marital share is the pre-residuary part and the credit-shelter portion becomes the residuary estate. The pre-residuary marital portion is then described as the *smallest* amount that will result in no federal estate tax being payable by the estate because of the marital deduction, taking into account the effects of the unified and state death tax credits.

The calculation of the pre-residuary marital share begins with the entire value of the taxable estate, but it is then reduced by whatever amount can pass free of tax because of the availability of the unified and state death tax credits. In this manner, any amounts paid from the residue that are deducted for estate tax purposes automatically reduce the pre-residuary marital share. On the other hand, any amounts paid from residue that are not deducted for estate tax purposes do not reduce the marital share.

The separation of the marital part is caused by a clause in the first deceased spouse's will or trust document. However, this testamentary document does not control the deceased spouse's so-called non-probate assets. Any jointly held assets that pass to the surviving spouse or contractual assets with respect to which the surviving spouse is the beneficiary can automatically qualify for the marital deduction. Since the formula clause describing the marital share begins with the entire value of the deceased spouse's taxable estate, including non-probate assets, it is necessary for this clause to direct that the value of any non-probate assets passing to the surviving spouse is to be subtracted from the marital share. Otherwise, the marital share may be so large as to leave less than the optimum amount in the residue that passes into the bypass trust.

Traditionally, marital deduction planning for estates has been described in terms of maximizing the tax saving in the estate of the first deceased spouse. However, it is advantageous from the point of view of overall tax planning for both spouses' estates to reduce the marital share by placing as much into a bypass trust as possible without paying any tax in the first estate. Therefore, the objective is to utilize the marital deduction only to the extent necessary to accomplish the zero tax goal. Perhaps it is for these reasons that the pre-residuary marital share technique has come to be known as the "maximum/minimum" marital deduction method.

Example: The estate plan of H and W is to use a credit-sheltered bypass trust through the maximum/minimum marital deduction method. H dies first, and the assets of H and W (assuming there are no liabilities) are as follows:

Summary of Value and Ownership of Assets

Description	*Ownership:* *H*	*W*	*Joint*	*Contractual*
Home			$200,000	
Savings, C.D.s	$175,000	$50,000	10,000	
Stocks & Bonds	460,000	25,000	100,000	
Life Insurance Death Benefit (on H's life)				$50,000
Totals	$635,000	$75,000	$310,000	$50,000

Based on the values used in this example, it is easy to see the difference in result caused by including the direction for an adjustment in the marital share to take into account amounts that pass directly to W, the surviving spouse, outside of the will. The total value included in H's taxable estate is:

H's separate assets	$635,000	
One-half of jointly held assets	155,000	
Life insurance proceeds	50,000	
H's total taxable estate		$840,000

The optimum result is achieved if $240,000 in value of assets included in H's taxable estate passes to W in a manner that qualifies for the marital deduction and the balance of $600,000 can be placed in the bypass trust. However, if the will gives this amount to W without referring to the non-probate assets, the result is as follows:

H's total taxable estate		$840,000
Amounts passing to W:		
Jointly held assets to the extent included in H's estate (50 percent of value)	$155,000	
Life insurance	50,000	
Maximum/minimum marital amount under H's will	240,000	
		−445,000
Balance available to fund bypass trust		$395,000

Only $395,000 out of an ideal total value of $600,000 passes into the bypass trust in this case. However, if the will had provided for an adjustment for the non-probate assets passing to W that qualify for the marital deduction, the result would change as follows:

H's total taxable estate			$840,000
Amounts passing to W:			
Jointly held assets to the extent included in H's estate (50 percent of value)		$155,000	
Life insurance		50,000	
Maximum/minimum marital amount under H's will	$240,000		
less			
Value of assets passing to W outside the will qualifying for marital deduction	205,000		
Transferred to W under H's will		35,000	
Total transferred to W			−240,000
Balance available to fund bypass trust			$600,000

.07 Using QTIP in a Generation-Skipping Plan

The following sections explore planning opportunities to reduce generation-skipping transfer tax (referred to throughout this section as GST) in coordination with the credit-shelter and marital deduction estate plan.

.071 Conflict between zero first estate tax and the utilization of GST exemptions

Through the use of one or more QTIP trusts, it is possible for a married couple to coordinate the marital deduction and credit-sheltered portions of the estate of the first deceased spouse and also to take maximum advantage of the GST exemptions available to husband and wife.

The discussions and examples above emphasize the planning concept of setting aside the maximum amount sheltered from estate tax by the unified credit first and obtaining the marital deduction for the balance of the estate. The GST exemption may be claimed for the credit-sheltered trust. However, the maximum credit-sheltered amount is only $600,000 while the GST exemption is $1,000,000. This results in what may appear to be a "no-win" situation:

(1) If the transferor spouse places the full $1,000,000 GST exemption amount into the bypass trust (for which the estate tax marital deduction is not available), there will be an estate tax payable at the death of the first spouse. As previously explained, this is usually regarded as a disadvantage.

(2) If the transferor spouse places only the $600,000 estate tax unified credit-sheltered equivalent into the bypass trust, the transferor may "waste" 40 percent of the available GST exemption.

The strategy used to solve this dilemma is to place not only the $600,000 credit-sheltered equivalent into the bypass trust and to use QTIP trusts for the balance of the estate, but also to find a way to cause some of the marital deduction share of the estate to qualify for the GST exemption of the first deceased spouse.

The GST exemption of the transferor spouse is not ordinarily available to offset value placed in a QTIP trust because, under the Internal Revenue Code, QTIP trust value is included in the taxable estate of the beneficiary spouse who is, therefore, treated as the transferor of the QTIP for GST purposes. In other words, in the ordinary case, the transferor spouse's GST exemption cannot be used to shelter QTIP amounts from GST, but the beneficiary spouse's GST exemption can be so used. The Internal Revenue Code does permit a special election,[56] however, by which the transferor spouse can be treated as the transferor with respect to amounts that qualify for the marital deduction as QTIP.

.072 Making full use of both GST exemptions

In order to use the GST exemptions of both husband and wife and also to coordinate the credit-sheltered bypass and marital deduction portions of the estate of the first deceased spouse, the following general strategy may be used:

[56] Code Sec. 2652(a)(3).

(1) The estate plan of the first deceased spouse includes a credit-sheltered equivalent bypass trust to which the transferor spouse's GST exemption is applied. The results of this are:

(a) The trust receives up to $600,000 of value that is sheltered from estate tax through the unified credit.

(b) This trust is not included in the taxable estate of the beneficiary spouse, who possesses no general power of appointment.

(c) The trust continues beyond the lifetimes of the children of the transferor spouse but is free of GST because of the allocation of the transferor spouse's GST exemption.

(2) The first deceased spouse also creates a QTIP trust equal in value to the excess of the GST exemption available over that part of the GST exemption applied to the credit-sheltered bypass trust. The special election is made to cause the first deceased spouse to be treated as transferor of this trust for GST purposes so that it is possible to allocate the balance of the first deceased spouse's available GST exemption to this trust. If the credit-sheltered bypass trust were equal in value to $600,000, the separate QTIP-GST exempt trust would receive a total of $400,000 in value. As previously discussed, however, certain expenses are usually paid out of the credit-sheltered portion so that its value is frequently less than the full $600,000 credit-sheltered amount. For this reason, the QTIP-GST exempt trust may be larger in value than $400,000.

The QTIP-GST exempt trust continues beyond the lifetime of the surviving spouse and also beyond the lifetimes of the children. The tax consequences of this trust are:

(a) In the estate of the first deceased spouse, the value of the trust qualifies for the marital deduction.

(b) The full value of this trust is included in the estate of the surviving beneficiary spouse, at its value as of the date of his or her death, due to the QTIP election.

(c) For GST purposes, the inclusion ratio of this trust is zero, causing even appreciation of the principal value of the trust that may occur after the death of the first deceased spouse and before the death of the second deceased spouse to be free of GST.

(d) Since the first spouse is treated as transferor of this trust for GST purposes, the GST exemption of the second spouse is not diminished.

(3) There is yet a third trust established by the first spouse to contain the entire remaining balance of the first estate. The QTIP election is made with respect to this trust, but no special GST transferor election is made. The disposition of the trust after the death of the second spouse may parallel the QTIP-GST exempt trust. The tax consequences are:

(a) In the estate of the first deceased spouse, the value of the trust qualifies for the marital deduction.

(b) The full value of this trust is included in the estate of the surviving beneficiary spouse, valued as of the date of his or her death, due to the QTIP election.

(c) The beneficiary spouse is treated as the transferor of this trust for GST purposes. If the beneficiary spouse's GST exemption has not been allocated to other transfers, it may be allocated to this second QTIP trust. However, the beneficiary spouse's GST exemption must be applied against the full value of the second QTIP trust. That is to say, appreciation that may occur after the death of the first spouse uses up the second spouse's GST exemption. Assuming that the second spouse makes no other GST transfers, if the second QTIP (non-GST exempt) trust exceeds $1,000,000 in value at the death of the second spouse, the inclusion ratio of this trust exceeds zero.

The estate plan of the first spouse is depicted in the following diagram.

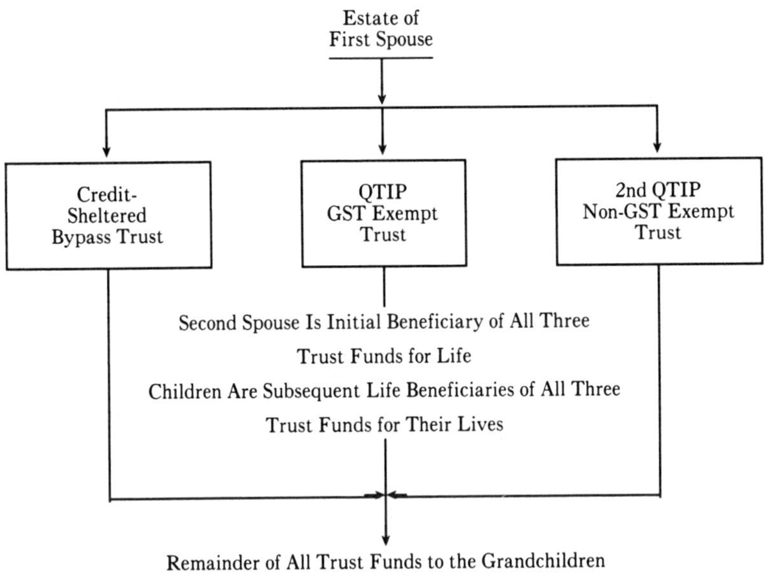

It is worth noting that if the first spouse wishes to make the special election to be treated as transferor of a QTIP, that election must pertain to the entire QTIP transfer. This makes it necessary to establish a separate QTIP trust in order to utilize fully both GST exemptions.

.08 Types of Formula Clauses

Whether the pre-residuary credit-sheltered bypass trust method or the maximum/minimum marital deduction method is used to set aside a bypass trust and also to cause a tax liability of zero in the estate of the first deceased spouse, it is necessary to use a written formula describing the computation of either the credit-shelter or the marital portion. There are two different approaches to the creation of these formula clauses that cause distinctly different consequences.

.081 Pecuniary formula clause

As the name suggests, the pecuniary formula clause describes either the credit-sheltered equivalent part or the maximum/minimum marital part in terms of a dollar amount. A simplified version of each follows:

(1) *Credit-sheltered pre-residuary part:* ". . . the largest amount that can pass free of federal estate tax in my estate because of the availability of the unified and state death tax credits. . . ."

(2) *Maximum/minimum marital part:* ". . . the smallest amount that, if transferred to my surviving spouse, will result in elimination of all federal estate tax otherwise payable by my estate, taking into account the unified and state death tax credits available to my estate for federal estate tax purposes. The amount hereby given to my surviving spouse shall be reduced by the value of all assets that pass to my surviving spouse other than under the terms of this document to the extent that such assets are included in my taxable estate for federal estate tax

purposes but only if the value of such assets qualifies for the federal estate tax marital deduction in my estate."

The pecuniary formula clause places an obligation on the executor or trustee to set the specified amount aside as if this amount were a debt. If the value of the estate changes during the course of administration and before the pecuniary amount can be set aside, the amount nevertheless remains unchanged. However, if assets are transferred in kind to satisfy the pecuniary obligation, a taxable exchange occurs for income tax purposes.

Example: D's estate is required to set aside the sum of $600,000 in a credit-sheltered bypass trust by the terms of D's will. The executor of D's estate transfers 1,000 shares of the common stock of XYZ corporation, with a value of $600 per share, to the bypass trust. XYZ had a value of $500 per share on the date of D's death.

As a result of this transfer, D's estate must report a capital gain[57] in the amount of $100,000 on the estate's fiduciary income tax return for the year in which the in-kind transfer to the trust is made. The election available to the fiduciary in the case of transfers of assets in kind, as described at ¶ 303, does not apply in this type of taxable exchange. It must be recognized, however, that this poses an income tax disadvantage only in the case of in-kind distributions of appreciated property. Where the value of assets has decreased between the date of death and the date of distribution, the estate is entitled to a capital loss even though no assets are actually sold. The distributing fiduciary also has the ability to pick and choose from the assets available to fund the pecuniary amount and may base the choice, in whole or in part, on the relative income tax consequences.

There is another, much more problematic, complication flowing from fluctuation in the value of assets that occurs before the pecuniary amount is set aside when the pecuniary pre-residuary credit-shelter formula is used. Either partial loss of the marital deduction or forced transfer of a disproportionately large amount to the surviving spouse (which is later subject to estate tax in the second taxable estate) can result. Suppose, for example, that the first deceased spouse's estate is valued at exactly $1,200,000 and consists entirely of probate assets and that the surviving spouse has no separate assets. Given this situation, if the credit-sheltered amount were placed in a bypass trust and the balance transferred to the surviving spouse, there should be no estate tax liability. The following table compares the zero tax scenario with the consequences of either a 20 percent increase or a 20 percent decrease in the value of the first spouse's estate after death but before funding of the credit-sheltered bypass trust.

Type of Value Fluctuation	*Date of Death Value*	*Date of Distribution Value*	*Amount Placed in Bypass Trust*	*Residue, i.e., Marital Share*
No Change in Value	$1,200,000	$1,200,000	$ 600,000	$ 600,000
20% Increase in Value ...	1,200,000	1,440,000	600,000	840,000
20% Decrease in Value ...	1,200,000	960,000	600,000	360,000

The effect of the value increase is to force the fiduciary to distribute a larger amount to the surviving spouse. At the death of the surviving spouse, this may result in a larger estate tax liability.

[57] Rev. Rul. 60-87, 1960-1 CB 286.

Where the value of the estate assets decreases after the date of death but before the estate is distributed, there is no reduction in the amount that must be transferred to the surviving spouse if the full marital deduction needed to bring about the zero estate tax result is to be available. As the preceding table shows, however, after setting aside the credit-sheltered bypass amount, the fiduciary is left with less than the amount that must be transferred to the surviving spouse in order to qualify for the marital deduction. Unless the testamentary document contains a special provision requiring a rollback of the credit-sheltered pecuniary amount in case of a drop in value, some estate tax will be payable by the first estate. This result may be viewed as potentially more serious merely because it causes an estate tax problem now rather than at some time in the future.

.082 *Fractional share of the residue formula clause*

Rather than create an obligation to set aside a specific amount based on the first spouse's estate tax valuation date, the fractional share of the residue formula divides the credit-sheltered bypass and marital shares based on the relative percentages of the estate value which each share would have represented if the division had taken place on the estate tax valuation date. This is accomplished by including an actual fraction in the testamentary document. The following are simplified examples:

> (1) *Credit-sheltered fractional part:* ". . . that fractional part of my estate of which the numerator is the largest amount that can pass free of federal estate tax in my estate because of the availability of the unified and state death tax credits and the denominator is the entire value of my taxable estate as determined for federal estate tax purposes. . . ."
>
> (2) *Maximum/minimum marital fractional part:* ". . . the fractional part of my estate of which the numerator is the smallest amount that, if transferred to my surviving spouse, will result in elimination of all federal estate tax otherwise payable by my estate, taking into account the unified and state death tax credits available to my estate for federal estate tax purposes and the denominator is the entire value of my taxable estate as determined for federal estate tax purposes, provided, however, that both the numerator and the denominator of this fraction shall be reduced by the value of any asset, to the extent included in my taxable estate, that passes to my surviving spouse other than under the terms of this document and for which the marital deduction is allowed to be applied to my estate for federal estate tax purposes. . . ."

The effect of the fractional share of the residue formula clause is to cause the theoretical division of each individual asset of the estate into percentage shares immediately as of the date of death—for example, where in case the credit-sheltered equivalent-fractional formula (the percent) computed by reference to the fraction of each asset of the estate belongs to the bypass trust and the remaining percentage of each asset belongs to the surviving spouse.

The distribution of assets to the respective recipients does not automatically result in a taxable exchange for fiduciary income tax purposes because the distributing fiduciary is not satisfying a dollar amount obligation through the in-kind transfer of assets that have an increased or decreased value. Therefore, the regular election concerning recognition or nonrecognition of gain or loss upon in-kind distributions applies. Also, since the division theoretically occurs as of the estate valuation date, increases or decreases in the value of assets that occur before the actual division and distribution cannot cause any loss of the estate tax marital deduction, such as that which can occur in the case of a decrease in asset value where a pecuniary pre-residuary credit-sheltered clause is used.

There are practical disadvantages to fractional clauses, however, that must be considered. While the division theoretically occurs as of the estate valuation date, in reality, many months or even several years must pass before it is ordinarily possible to make the final distribution. In the meantime, every time any amount of corpus expense is paid from the estate, it reduces either the marital share (in case of payments that are otherwise deductible for estate tax purposes) or the credit-sheltered share (in case of payments not otherwise deductible). This means that the fraction is constantly changing during the period of estate settlement. It is, therefore, impossible to make interim, partial distribution of either or both shares without some form of adjustment mechanism. While cash adjustments are possible, the adjustments needed in case of distribution of share of stock of a particular corporation or mutual fund, parts of the principal value of individual bonds or fractional undivided interests in real estate pose greater challenges.

Typically, the administration of a decedent's estate involves various payments of expenses and taxes over a period of more than one year. It may also require the sale of some assets to pay those expenses and taxes, which, in turn, results in capital gain issues, all of which cause adjustments to the fraction. Words cannot describe the anguish experienced by the accountant, attorney, or paralegal assistant who is faced with the task of computing the fraction, first based on the estate valuation, then taking into account all of the adjustments caused by various payments, sales, and distributions, and finally creating a schedule of final distribution based on the fraction as adjusted. This procedure has been known to reduce grown men and women to tears! In fact, after going through such a nightmare, more than one firm has resolved never to use the fractional share of residue method in planning again, despite the fact that it has at least some theoretical advantages over pecuniary formulas.

.09 Special Considerations for Residents of Community Property States

As noted at ¶ 104.013, nine states have community property systems. Despite variations among the community property laws of these states, as a general rule all property acquired by a husband and wife during the marriage is automatically community property. This means that each spouse is considered to own 50 percent of the value of the property.

.091 General advantages

There are actually several estate planning advantages resulting from community property. These are listed below.

(1) In the event of the death of either spouse, the cost basis for determining gain or loss upon future sale of property is stepped up based on the estate tax valuation. The basis step-up affects the surviving spouse's part of the community property even though only the deceased spouse's part is included in the first taxable estate.[58] This is in contrast,

[58] Code Sec. 1014(b)(6).

for instance, to the basis treatment of property held as joint tenants by a married couple in a noncommunity property state, where only one-half of the value of the property is included in the taxable estate of the first to die, but the cost basis is adjusted with respect to only one-half as well.

(2) Community property has the natural consequence of estate tax equalization which, as discussed at .04, above, avoids so-called over-qualification of the marital deduction and makes it more likely that each spouse's estate will own a sufficient amount of wealth to make establishment of a bypass trust possible.

(3) There is no automatic survivorship feature of community property. While this may prove to be a financial disadvantage to the surviving spouse, from an estate tax planning viewpoint, it helps to prevent the disruption of bypass planning that can result from holding too much value in assets held jointly with right of survivorship or in contractual assets of which the surviving spouse is the recipient of any death benefits.

(4) Any part of the transferor spouse's share of community property that is given to the recipient spouse, either during lifetime or at death, qualifies for the marital deduction.

In view of this, the use of a credit-sheltered bypass trust is facilitated. The first deceased spouse may provide, through any of the formula clauses, for the transfer of the most desirable amount out of the community property to the bypass trust and for the transfer of the balance to the surviving spouse or to a marital deduction trust.

However, in a noncommunity property state, emphasis may be placed on maximizing the bypass trust on the theory that this causes the best overall estate tax result, it postpones payment of any estate tax until the death of the second spouse, and, during the surviving spouse's lifetime, the economic benefits of the bypass trust are available to the survivor. Where the total value of the first estate is less than the $600,000 credit-sheltered amount or only moderately exceeds that amount, an additional consequence may be that the survivor ends up owning very little wealth personally. Some people regard that as a disadvantage. The result differs in the community property state because it is clear that the surviving spouse will be the owner of at least 50 percent of the community property.

.092 *Trading principal for income*

There might be a variety of motives for the transferor or first deceased spouse to seek a certain concession from the recipient or surviving spouse concerning the disposition of part or all of the community property after both husband and wife are deceased. In case of a second marriage, the motivation might be to limit the total share of the community property that ultimately passes to the children of the surviving spouse's first marriage. Even if this is not a consideration, the first deceased spouse might want assurance that his or her children or other intended final beneficiaries will eventually receive as much of the total value of the community property as possible.

The concession that the first deceased spouse may seek from the survivor is that, at the survivor's death, all or whatever is left of the total amount of community property will pass to the first spouse's intended recipients. In return for this assurance, the first spouse may be willing to give to the survivor the income interest from the first spouse's share of the community property.

This is accomplished by a provision, in the will or living trust of the first deceased spouse, that places all of the community property in a trust designed to pay income to the surviving spouse for life but not designed to qualify as a marital deduction trust. Since the first deceased spouse is thereby transferring more than his or her share of the community property, the surviving spouse can elect to retain the survivor's share separate and apart from the trust. In the event that the survivor so elects, however, the will or trust agreement of the first deceased spouse provides that the survivor does not receive an income interest in the trust, which then holds only the first deceased spouse's share of the community property. The effect of this arrangement is to force the surviving spouse to make an election, and the arrangement is called a "forced share" or "forced election trust."

The first spouse is not obligated to give any interest in his or her share of the community property to the survivor. Therefore, the surviving spouse receives something of value if no election to keep the survivor's share outside the trust is made. The value received by the survivor is the life income interest in the first spouse's share of the community property.

If the surviving spouse does not elect to keep his or her share outside the trust, the survivor is treated as making a transfer of the survivor's share with a retained life income interest in that share. Ordinarily, the full value of the trust, to the extent attributable to the transfer by the surviving spouse, would be included in the survivor's taxable estate.[59] In this arrangement, however, the surviving spouse has received consideration for the transfer of the survivor's share. Therefore, at the surviving spouse's subsequent death, there is included in the survivor's taxable estate the value of the trust to the extent attributable to the survivor's share of the community property, less the value of the income interest in the first deceased spouse's share, calculated as of the time the survivor was forced to decide whether to accept the value trade.

> **Example:** H and W are both age 65 and are residents of a community property state. The couple owns only community property that has an aggregate value of $1,200,000. H's will directs that all of the community property is to be held in trust with the income payable to W for life and, thereafter, for the benefit of the children of H and W until the youngest child reaches age 30. The will directs that, if W elects against the will to retain her one-half of the community property outside the trust, the trust fund is to be held only for the benefit of the children, with no intervening income interest for W's benefit. At H's death, W does not elect to retain her share of the community property outside the trust and receives an income interest in the entire trust fund. W dies five years after H, at which time the trust fund has a total value of $1,500,000.

In this example, the total value of H's estate, which is one-half of the value of the community property, or $600,000, is sheltered from the estate tax by the unified credit available. No marital deduction is needed to achieve a zero estate tax result.

At W's subsequent death, one-half of the value of the trust is included in W's taxable estate, valued at W's date of death. The inclusion results because half of the original value is attributable to W's share of the community property, treated as transferred by W to the trust. The value included in W's

[59] Code Sec. 2036(a)(1).

taxable estate is reduced, however, by the value of the income interest in H's share of the community property. This value is determined as of the last date by which W could have elected against the will under state law. If the applicable federal rate as of the election date was eight percent, the value to be included in W's taxable estate is calculated as follows:

One-half of the value of the trust at W's date of death		$750,000
Less		
Value of H's share of community property	$600,000	
Factor for W's life estate[60]	390,528	
Difference		209,472
Value included in W's taxable estate		$540,528

Had W elected against H's will in order to keep W's share of the community property outside the trust fund, that share would have been subject to estate tax at W's death. Assuming equal appreciation of trust and non-trust assets, W's estate would have included $750,000 of value rather than $540,528.

¶ 505 DISCLAIMERS IN ESTATE PLANNING

The following sections discuss the use by a beneficiary of disclaimers and their advantages and disadvantages to estate planning.

.01 Gift Tax Advantage and Post-death Planning

As described at ¶ 401.07, the intended recipient of a lifetime gift or inheritance may choose to reject the gratuitous transfer which, in turn, can result in the passing of ownership to an alternate recipient. If this rejection constitutes a qualified disclaimer, the intended recipient is not treated as making a taxable gift to the person who actually receives the subject property. In the context of post-death planning, the disclaimer is an effective tool which can enable the shifting of wealth in ways that achieve both tax and nontax advantages. In appropriate circumstances, it can be used to redirect transfers to the surviving spouse, thereby preserving the marital deduction that might otherwise have been lost.

Example (1): S is about to receive 80 percent of the stock of F&S Corp. as an inheritance from the estate of his deceased father, F. S already owns the other 20 percent of the F&S stock. The total value of estate F is $2,500,000, including the F&S stock, valued at $1,500,000. F's will leaves all of the estate, with the exception of the F&S stock, to F's surviving spouse, M.

If the F&S stock passes from the estate of F to S, ignoring any available deductions for debts and expenses in order to illustrate a simple calculation example, the basic estate calculation is as follows:

Value of F's estate	$2,500,000
Marital deduction (entire estate except for value of F&S stock)	1,000,000
Taxable estate	$1,500,000

[60] Valued under Code Sec. 7520, assuming an applicable federal rate of eight percent.

Gross estate tax	$ 555,800
Unified credit	–192,800
Estate tax payable subject to any available credit for state death tax	$ 363,000

Although the estate tax can be paid in installments over a period of up to 15 years, the family might wish to postpone the tax altogether until M's death. This may be accomplished if S is willing to disclaim 40 percent of his inheritance. Assuming that the disclaimed portion becomes part of the residuary estate under the applicable state law, the disclaimed shares pass to M as a result of the disclaimer and thereby qualify for the marital deduction. In the particular facts of this example, even after the disclaimer, S winds up with control of the corporation. The revised estate tax calculation following the disclaimer is as follows:

Value of F's estate	$2,500,000
Marital deduction (includes 40 percent of the F&S stock which F had owned)	1,900,000
Taxable estate	$ 600,000
Gross estate tax	$ 192,800
Unified credit	–192,800
Federal estate tax payable	$ –0–

Naturally, the ultimate result of this disclaimer will be the inclusion of an additional $900,000 of value in M's estate. The additional tax payable at the time of M's death can be expected to exceed the estate tax payable by F's estate if no disclaimer had been made, as shown by this comparison:

Potential Estate Tax Payable by the Estate of M
(assuming M's entire estate is received from F)

	If S makes Disclaimer	*No Disclaimer*
Taxable estate	$1,900,000	$1,000,000
Gross estate tax	735,800	345,800
Unified credit	–192,800	–192,800
Estate tax payable subject to any state death tax credit	$ 543,000	$ 153,000
Additional estate tax payable by M's estate due to disclaimer	$ 390,000	
Estate tax paid by F's estate if no disclaimer made	–363,000	
Net additional estate tax	$ 27,000	

However, this example does not take into account the potential growth in the value of M's assets, which include a significant percentage of the F&S stock if the disclaimer is made. However, if M survives F by a sufficient period of years, the value of the use of the money that would otherwise have been paid out in the form of F's estate tax, coupled with additional estate planning measures that may be taken during this period, may well make up the difference. For instance, the annual earnings on F's potential estate tax (assuming S makes no disclaimer) may be estimated as follows:

$363,000	×	8%	=	$29,040
F's Estate Tax		Assumed Earnings Rate		Annual Earning Potential

Unless M is in poor health or at an advanced age, it is likely that these earnings, which would have been lost altogether if the disclaimer had not been made, could purchase enough life insurance on M's life to pay at least the increase in M's potential estate tax and possibly even the entire amount of M's potential estate tax liability.

On the other hand, if the result of an inheritance by the surviving spouse would be to cause a bunching of wealth in the survivor's estate and wasting of the credit shelter available to the first estate, a disclaimer by the surviving spouse may be used to deflect assets.

Example (2): Spouse 1 and Spouse 2 each have separate property valued at $1,000,000. Spouse 1's will leaves the entire estate to Spouse 2, who is the survivor.

Spouse 2 may disclaim up to 60 percent of the inheritance without causing the payment of any estate tax by the estate of Spouse 1, as the following simplified calculation model illustrates:

	If Spouse 2 Disclaims 60%	*No Disclaimer*
Gross estate of Spouse 1	$ 1,000,000	$ 1,000,000
Marital deduction	–400,000	–1,000,000
Taxable estate of Spouse 1	$ 600,000	$ –0–
Gross estate tax	$ 192,800	$ –0–
Unified credit	–192,800	–192,800
Estate tax payable	$ –0–	$ –0–

At the subsequent death of Spouse 2, the removal of additional assets from the second taxable estate that the disclaimer caused has the effect of reducing the estate tax payable:

	Spouse 2 having made 60% disclaimer	*No Disclaimer*
Separate estate of Spouse 2	$ 1,000,000	$ 1,000,000
Amount received from estate of Spouse 1	+ 400,000	+ 1,000,000
Gross estate of Spouse 2	$ 1,400,000	$ 2,000,000
Gross estate tax	$ 512,800	$ 780,000
Unified credit	– 192,800	– 192,800
Estate tax payable subject to any state death tax credit	$ 320,000	$ 587,200
Estate tax saved by estate of Spouse 2 due to disclaimer	$ 267,200	

If growth of the second estate occurs after the death of Spouse 1, although the amount of estate tax will increase, the savings resulting from the disclaimer is proportionately increased as the total value of the estate is pushed into higher marginal estate tax brackets.

There is the practical question to face: Can Spouse 2 economically afford to give up the income potential of 60 percent of the estate of Spouse 1?

.02 Disclaimer Trust—Planning in Advance for the Use of the Disclaimer

Some clients have misgivings about the use of any kind of trust in their estate plan. At the time of planning, the total value of the family assets may be near the credit-sheltered equivalent amount of $600,000, so that it cannot be predicted with certainty whether or not any estate tax saving will actually result from the use of trusts. The client's attitude might be that a trust should only be used if estate tax saving will result. Some dislike the idea of forcing the surviving spouse to give up a measure of financial freedom by placing part or all of the first deceased spouse's estate in a bypass trust.

Advanced planning for the use of a disclaimer may provide a solution in some of these situations. The technique involves a two-part disposition of the bulk of the first spouse's estate created under the terms of the will or will-substitute living trust. The first aspect of the disposition is to direct the transfer of the estate to the surviving spouse. This is a direct testamentary transfer with no strings attached. The second aspect of the disposition is a provision concerning what is to happen to any part of the transfer that the surviving spouse decides to disclaim. The second aspect of the disposition requires that, in the event of a disclaimer, the disclaimed portion of the first deceased spouse's estate is to be held in a bypass type trust for the benefit of the surviving spouse. In this manner, it becomes possible for the surviving spouse to give away part or all of the inheritance, including its unwanted tax consequences in the second taxable estate, without giving away the economic benefits of the income of the property during the survivor's lifetime. Schematically, the concept may be presented as follows:

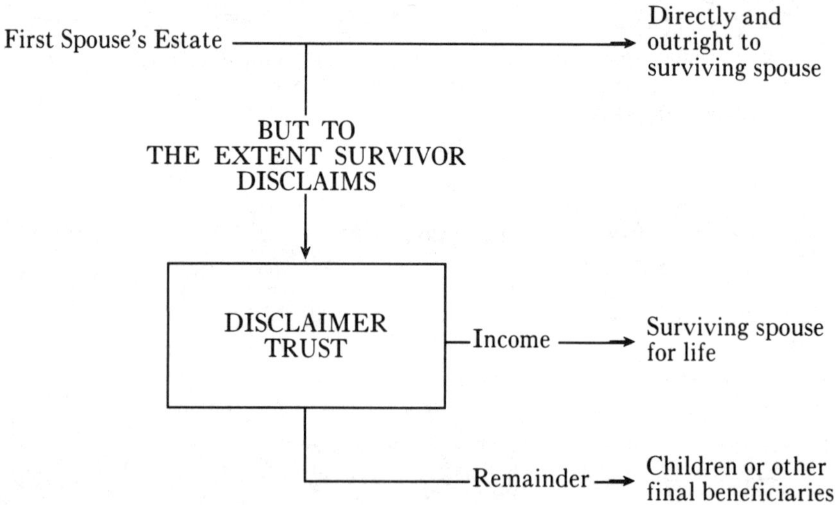

In order to optimize estate tax avoidance through the full use of the unified credit available to each spouse's estate and to postpone payment of any estate tax liability until the death of the surviving spouse, the survivor should consider disclaiming whatever percentage of the value of the first deceased spouse's estate turns out to be equal in value to the $600,000 credit-sheltered amount. If, at the death of the first spouse, the financial condition of the family has not progressed well, so that the total value of the survivor's estate, including that inherited from the deceased spouse does not significantly exceed the credit-sheltered amount, the survivor may dispense with the bypass trust by simply not exercising the right to disclaim. As a result, the entire estate of the first spouse passes to the survivor. The bypass trust is available if the survivor wants it, but the survivor is not forced to have a trust fund.

Planning in advance for the use of the disclaimer bypass trust is not appropriate in all cases. In second marriage situations, where each spouse has children by his or her first marriage, the tendency is to force creation of a bypass trust. In fact, very often a second QTIP trust is used to hold the marital deduction share of the first estate, unless the decision is made to forgo the marital deduction altogether.

Disclaimer trust planning is most appropriate for couples who have had long-term marriages, whose children are the offspring of both the husband and the wife, and whose intention is to place a high degree of control in the hands of the survivor.

The principal disadvantages of the disclaimer trust are:

(1) The technique may be used to establish an "elective" trust fund only for the benefit of a surviving spouse. It may not be used to make an outright transfer to a child, for instance, with an alternative trust for the benefit of the same child in the event of a disclaimer. The distinction follows from one of the basic requirements of the qualified disclaimer for gift tax purposes: As a result of the disclaimer, the disclaimed property must pass either to someone other than the disclaimant or to the surviving spouse of the transferor (that is, whether or not the disclaimant is that surviving spouse).

(2) If the surviving spouse disclaims, the trust that receives the disclaimed transfer may not permit the surviving spouse to have any power of disposition over the principal. Not even a limited power of appointment can be given to the survivor. This results from another of the basic gift tax qualified disclaimer requirements: As a result of the disclaimer, the property must pass without any direction on the part of the disclaimant as to its subsequent disposition.

In the case of a regular bypass trust, it is possible to give the surviving spouse fairly free access to the principal of the trust fund through the creation of ascertainable standard and five-and-five withdrawal powers. The survivor may even be permitted to dispose of the remainder through a testamentary non-general power of appointment. None of these special privileges may be given to the surviving spouse under the terms of a disclaimer trust. Therefore, it is fair to say that the survivor must be very certain of his or her willingness to give up access to the principal and its ultimate disposition before making the decision to disclaim. It is possible to permit a trustee, other than the surviving spouse, to make principal distributions to the disclaiming beneficiary. Where the value of the disclaimer trust does not represent the largest segment of the overall wealth available to the beneficiary, the decision can be made more easily and based primarily on the ultimate estate tax consequences.

¶ 506 SURVIVING SPOUSE'S ACCESS TO TRUST PRINCIPAL

Whenever a trust is held for the benefit of a surviving spouse, a basic issue in trust design is the degree of freedom that the beneficiary spouse is to have in obtaining distributions of trust principal. Too much freedom might be contrary to the grantor spouse's wishes and might cause inclusion of the trust in the taxable estate of the beneficiary spouse. On the other hand, too little freedom could cause the beneficiary financial hardship.

.01 Understanding the Client's Motive

Clients frequently raise the question of how much control is to be placed in the hands of the surviving spouse to obtain principal of a trust fund established by a transferor spouse after the transferor's death. This question can be prompted by any of several opposing motives:

(1) The couple who has had a long and happy marriage may be trying to give the greatest possible measure of financial control to the survivor consistent with estate tax saving.

(2) Second marriage partners may want to impose significant restrictions on availability of principal to the survivor in order to preserve principal for the children of their previous marriages.

(3) The client may not believe that his or her spouse is capable of handling the responsibility of financial management of a substantial amount of principal value.

In view of this dichotomy, it is important for the financial consultant to probe carefully into the backgrounds and feelings of husband and wife before discussing this subject. It would be inappropriate, perhaps even embarrassing, to answer this question for one couple with the comment "you can design your trust so that the surviving spouse has no right to obtain principal whatsoever." For another couple, the answer that "your surviving spouse can have access to the trust fund almost as freely as if he were the outright owner" might be the direct opposite of what the client is expecting. Nevertheless, both answers can be correct and each is appropriate in the proper setting.

A primary distinction must be made in the degree of freedom of access to principal that can be given to the surviving spouse in marital deduction trusts as contrasted with bypass trusts.

.02 Access to Principal of the Marital Deduction Trust

From an estate tax viewpoint, there are no restrictions that must be placed on the survivor's ability to obtain trust principal from a marital deduction trust. Whether the trust is a life income plus power of appointment type or a QTIP, the full value is included in the taxable estate when the second spouse dies. Even an unrestricted power to withdraw principal cannot change this estate tax result. Of course, if the estate plan includes both a marital deduction trust and a bypass trust, it is important to place a required priority on principal withdrawals. This makes it necessary for the surviving spouse to withdraw from the marital trust exclusively before any withdrawals are made from the bypass trust. The result is depletion of the trust fund that is taxed in the estate of the surviving spouse before any assets are taken from the trust that is tax free at the survivor's death.

If the purpose of the grantor-spouse is to restrict the survivor's access to principal, however, distinctions must be made between the life income plus power of appointment trust and the QTIP. Both types of marital deduction trust may provide only income to the beneficiary spouse for life with no lifetime right to principal. However, with respect to the life income plus power of appointment type, if the survivor has no right to trust principal during life, he must possess a general power of appointment exercisable at death. Since the QTIP rules contain no requirement of access to trust principal by the beneficiary-spouse, the QTIP is the natural choice for those who wish to prevent the surviving spouse from controlling the ultimate disposition of the trust fund.

.03 Access to Principal of the Bypass Trust

Bypass trusts, unlike those that qualify for the marital deduction, are intended to be excluded from the taxable estate of the surviving spouse. In order to accomplish this, it must be clear that the surviving spouse does not hold a general power of appointment.

For the couple motivated to restrict or prevent principal access by the surviving spouse, the simple solution is to give the survivor no right to obtain trust principal at all under the terms of the trust document.

If the client's purpose is to place maximum principal access in the hands of the beneficiary-spouse, however, careful design of the rights given to the spouse is needed. The provisions of the trust granting access to principal, however generous, must not amount to a general power of appointment. Below is a listing of the ways in which it is possible to make principal available to the spouse. It is permissible to include only one of these powers; however, even if all of the powers are combined, the cumulative effect is not considered to be a general power of appointment.

(1) The right to withdraw the greater of $5,000 or five percent of trust principal in any year on a noncumulative basis.

(2) The right to withdraw principal to the extent necessary to provide for the needs of the surviving spouse. These withdrawals must be limited by an ascertainable standard relating to health, support, maintenance according to accustomed standard of living, or education.

(3) The trustee has the power to make principal distributions to the surviving spouse. Note that this may be included even if both five-and-five and ascertainable-withdrawal rights are held directly by the spouse. There is no need for limitations on the power of an independent trustee to make principal distributions to the spouse. However, if the surviving spouse is the trustee or a cotrustee, any powers held in the capacity of trustee are treated as if held by the spouse-beneficiary directly. An unrestricted trustee power to distribute would then be treated as a general power of appointment in the hands of the spouse.

Some advisers suggest that it is necessary to make a choice between naming the surviving spouse as a cotrustee and excluding the unlimited trustee power to make principal distributions to the spouse or including the unlimited distribution power but choosing trustees other than the spouse. There is an alternative, however, for those couples who want maximum flexibility over principal and still want to name the spouse as a trustee. This involves designing the unlimited principal distribution power so that, although the surviving spouse is a cotrustee, he or she is not permitted to participate in any decisions concerning principal distributions.

(4) A power given to a surviving spouse, either personally or in the capacity of trustee, to make principal distributions from the trust so long as qualifying restrictions are placed on this power. These qualifiers prohibit exercise of the power in favor of the spouse, the spouse's estate, and creditors. This makes it possible for the survivor to direct principal distributions to children or other relatives. For instance, trust principal may be made available to help with the cost of a child's education, wedding, home acquisition, etc., or to assist in the support of an elderly dependent relative.

If the beneficiary spouse has the power to remove the trustee and appoint a successor, the view of the IRS is that any powers held by the trustee must be treated as if they were held by the beneficiary spouse. As a result, some attorneys include much more restrictive trustee discretionary powers of distribution where the client requests that the spouse-beneficiary be given the right to "fire" the trustee.

It is not necessary to choose between extremes concerning the surviving spouse's access to trust principal. Even in the case of a second marriage, it is often advisable to include at least a discretionary right held by the trustee or by some other party to make some principal available in order to prevent unforeseen hardship.

Throughout this chapter, the diagrams used to illustrate trust design concepts suggest that the surviving spouse can "invade" principal. This assumes that the transferor spouse wishes to give at least a minimum degree of principal access to the survivor. These invasion powers are not required, however, and where they are used, the principles explained in the preceding discussion apply in all cases.

The rules that govern expanding or restricting principal access over the bypass trust apply equally to the irrevocable life insurance trust, discussed in Chapter 6, where there is a surviving spouse as beneficiary.

Chapter 6

Life Insurance Trusts

¶ 601 OVERVIEW

Naming a trust fund as the beneficiary of a life insurance policy is a planning technique used to impose control over the insurance proceeds after the death of the insured person. Although it is possible to designate a testamentary trust as beneficiary, neither the will nor the testamentary trust will have legal force or effect until after the testator's death. For this reason, the ownership of the insurance policy may not be transferred to the trust during the lifetime of the insured. If a living trust is used, the trust may be the designated beneficiary and ownership of the policy may also be transferred to the trust.

Sometimes, living trusts are established for the sole purpose of acting as a receptacle for life insurance proceeds. Such a life insurance trust may contain only nominal assets besides the beneficiary designation of the insurance policy. Alternatively, the same trust may hold substantial assets and may be used for financial control or "caretaker" or other living trust functions, with life insurance management as a secondary purpose.

The insurance trust agreement may be revocable or irrevocable. However, only the irrevocable life insurance trust yields estate tax savings.

There is the question of payment of life insurance premiums once the trust is established. In cases of testamentary trusts and revocable living trusts designated as the life insurance beneficiaries, the creator of the trust, who is ordinarily the insured person, typically continues to make the premium payments. Due to the revocable quality of these trusts, such payments constitute incomplete gifts for gift tax purposes. On the other hand, where the ownership of a life insurance contract is transferred to an irrevocable living trust, any cash surrender value of the policy on the date of its transfer, as well as the amount of subsequent policy premiums paid by the grantor, is a taxable gift.

"Unfunded" life insurance trusts are either revocable or irrevocable living trusts that do not hold investments producing income with which to pay the policy premiums. "Funded" life insurance trusts, usually irrevocable living trusts, pay the premiums from investments held in the trust fund.

The life insurance trust is designed to be coordinated with the family's overall estate plan in the following ways:

(1) The life insurance death benefits paid into the trust may be needed to pay debts, funeral expenses, estate settlement costs, and death taxes. If so, the trust must authorize use of its funds for these purposes. In contrast to this free and flexible payment approach, if the trust is designed to keep the insurance proceeds free of federal estate tax, payments of this kind must be prohibited.

(2) Where the estate plan calls for division of assets between credit-sheltered bypass and marital deduction shares, the life insurance trust

must be fitted into the overall picture. It may be combined with either share or split between the shares, depending primarily on whether the life insurance proceeds are subject to federal estate tax.

(3) The insurance trust may fulfill a special purpose, making it appropriate to be segregated from the other assets of the estate. Even so, the total estate expenses and taxes must be considered so that the separation of trust assets does not cause the balance of the estate to be subject to added costs and taxes and to be unintentionally diminished in this manner.

¶ 602 REVOCABLE LIFE INSURANCE TRUSTS

A revocable life insurance trust permits the grantor to cancel the insurance policy in the trust at any time. The following sections discuss the characteristics, purposes, and tax consequences of this type of trust.

.01 Common Characteristics

In the most common case, a revocable life insurance trust is established by a person who is insured under one or more life insurance policies. A nominal amount of money is transferred to the trust, and the trust is designated as beneficiary of the life insurance policies. However, the grantor-insured retains the incidents of ownership of the policies and continues to pay the premiums.

The trust may provide for a "pour-back" to the estate. This is a provision that permits or requires the trustee to make payments from trust income or principal to the estate of the grantor if funds are needed for debts, funeral and estate settlement expenses, or taxes. The pour-back is extremely useful where there is a lack of estate liquidity. Examples include cases in which the decedent's single largest asset is an interest in a closely held business or in real estate holdings. Death can occur at a time that is not optimal for the sale of these kinds of special assets. The life insurance proceeds paid to the trust represent a source of ready cash. There is, however, a potential disadvantage to the pour-back. A provision requiring the trustee to make payments to the grantor's estate can expose the life insurance proceeds to the claims of estate creditors. Ordinarily, life insurance is free of this liability. In an attempt to avoid this problem, some attorneys recommend including only a discretionary power, in the hands of the life insurance trustee, to make pour-back distributions.

Instead of direct pour-backs, insurance trusts are sometimes designed to permit direct payments of certain categories of estate expenses from the trust fund. These may include funeral expenses, taxes, and estate administration costs. This is sensible, because the insurance trust fund is so often the main source of liquid assets. There are those who go a step further and require the trustee to perform duties that are ordinarily the responsibility of the executor, such as preparation of the federal estate tax and state death tax returns. The rationale lies in the fact that trust funds will be needed to pay death taxes, as well as the costs of professional services, in connection with the preparation and audit of the tax returns. This justifies giving the trustee the power to help bring about the most favorable result.

A common situation that might be looked upon as the opposite of a pour-back is a direction in the grantor's will that most or all of the grantor's residuary estate is to be added to the life insurance trust fund. This is the "pour-over." Pour-backs and pour-overs are not mutually exclusive. During the period of administration of an estate that holds substantial illiquid assets, the availability of funds from a life insurance trust through a pour-back may be a desirable alternative to the sale of estate assets in order to raise needed cash. After settlement of the same estate, the illiquid assets may be transferred in kind to the life insurance trust, which then functions as the primary mechanism to accomplish the estate planning goals. This scheme of things may be visualized as follows:

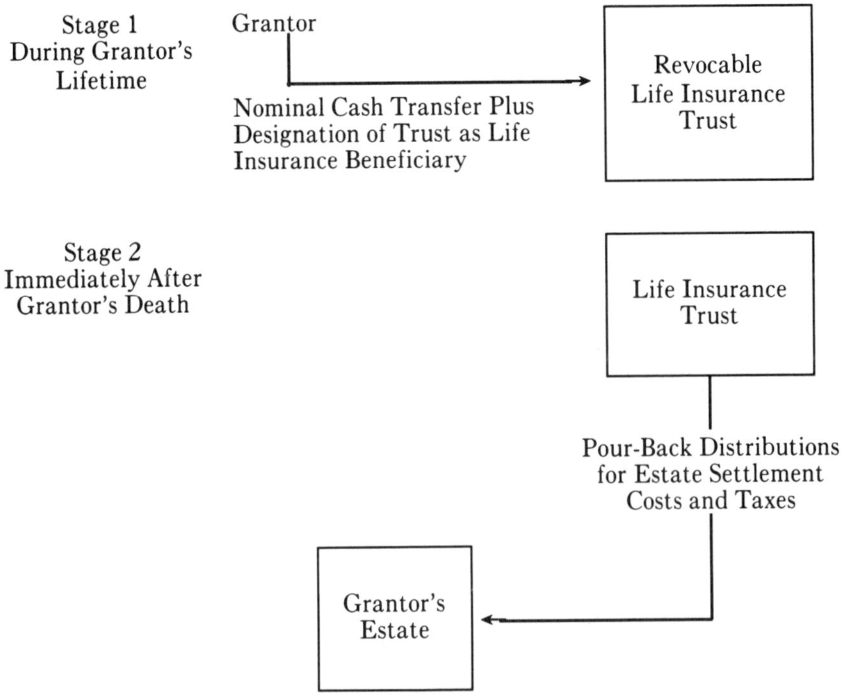

Stage 3
At Estate
Settlement

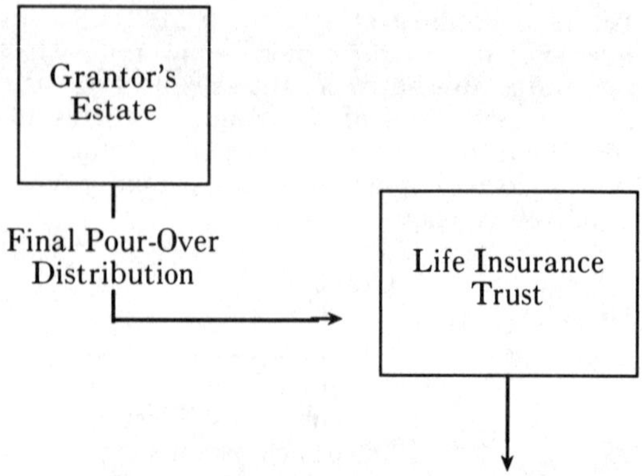

Stage 4
Ongoing Trust
Administration

A. Trust holds balance of life insurance proceeds plus grantor's residuary estate.
B. Trust continues for the benefit of the grantor's family.

If the estate plan includes bypass, marital deduction, and generation-skipping strategies, these provisions are included in the terms of the insurance trust agreement. A schematic diagram of the estate plan might then proceed as follows:

Stage 4
Ongoing Trust
Administration

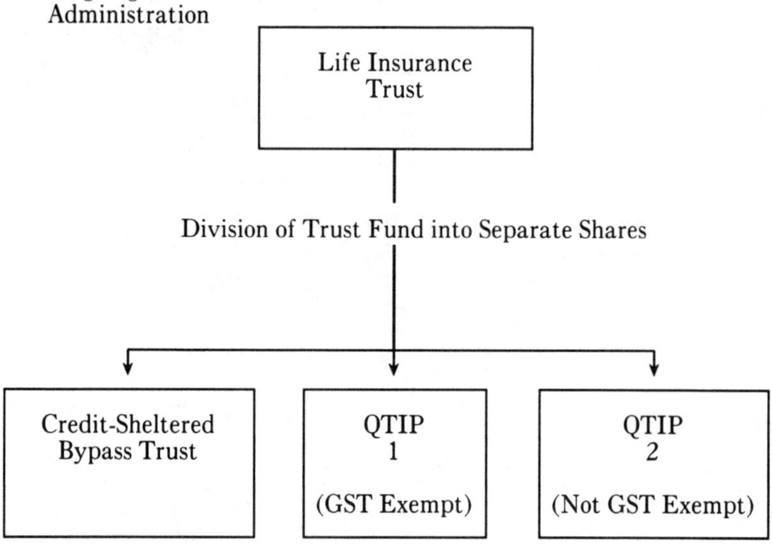

.02 Purposes

The revocable life insurance trust is used for one or more of the following purposes:

(1) To provide a receptacle for life insurance proceeds that is beyond the reach of estate creditors.

(2) To provide privacy. The main framework of the estate plan is spelled out within the terms of the insurance trust agreement, which is not a public document. The will, which is available for public inspection, reveals little, if anything, about the grantor's plans for the management and distribution of wealth.

(3) To make liquid assets available for the expenses of estate settlement and for the payment of taxes by the estate through pour-backs or through direct payment of these expenses from the insurance trust funds.

(4) To act as the central mechanism for ongoing management of the grantor's wealth.

.03 Tax Consequences

This type of trust is not designed or intended to reduce gift tax, estate tax, generation-skipping transfer tax (referred to throughout this section as GST), or income tax prior to the grantor's death. It may serve tax planning purposes afterwards, however. Below is a summary of the tax consequences.

Gift tax. Due to the trust's revocable quality, any amounts of money transferred to the trust fund, as well as the designation of the trust as beneficiary of the life insurance, is an incomplete gift. This makes it possible to place large sums in the trust fund if circumstances make it appropriate to use the life insurance trust for caretaker functions or for other living trust purposes. Trust distributions during the grantor's lifetime to persons other than the grantor are taxable gifts, but distributions to the grantor's spouse can qualify for the marital deduction.

Income tax. The grantor is treated as the substantial owner of a revocable life insurance trust during his lifetime due to the existence of the power to revoke. After the grantor's death, the trust is treated as a separate taxpayer, unless a beneficiary possesses a right to make withdrawals sufficiently extensive to cause the beneficiary to be treated as the substantial owner.

Estate tax. The full value of the insurance trust is includible in the taxable estate of the grantor. The power of revocation is enough to cause this result under the estate tax string sections. As to the life insurance proceeds, however, the fact that the grantor typically retains the incidents of ownership of the insurance policies up to the date of death would also cause inclusion of the policy proceeds in the grantor's taxable estate. At the grantor's death, the marital deduction is available for amounts distributed to the surviving spouse, as well as for the value of any trust share that meets the life income plus power of appointment or QTIP marital deduction requirements.

Generation-skipping transfer tax. There is no GST taxable event during the lifetime of the grantor. The preceding discussion and illustration mentions the fact that the trust may continue after the grantor's death and thereafter function as a generation-skipping trust. If so, the GST exemption must be allocated among the trust shares, including the life insurance proceeds, based on their value as of the grantor's death. Therefore, this trust plan removes neither appreciation of trust assets, which may occur before the grantor's death, nor life insurance proceeds from the GST taxable base.

¶ 603 UNFUNDED IRREVOCABLE LIFE INSURANCE TRUSTS

Besides sharing most of the planning advantages available through revocable trusts, irrevocable life insurance trusts offer potential estate tax savings by placing the proceeds of the grantor's life insurance completely outside of his taxable estate. These trusts may provide lifetime benefits to the grantor's surviving spouse and be excluded from the taxable estate of the survivor so long as no power held by the surviving spouse is the equivalent of a general power of appointment. In this light, the irrevocable life insurance trust may be viewed as being parallel in function to the bypass trust in that it provides benefits to the surviving spouse without being included in the survivor's taxable estate. In fact, it is a common practice to design the overall estate plan so that the life insurance trust, which is a living trust, is combined with the credit-sheltered bypass trust after the death of the first spouse.

.01 Visual Presentation of an Unfunded Irrevocable Life Insurance Trust

The life insurance trust, if properly designed and maintained, is outside the scope of the GST. A schematic diagram of an estate plan incorporating an unfunded irrevocable life insurance trust follows.

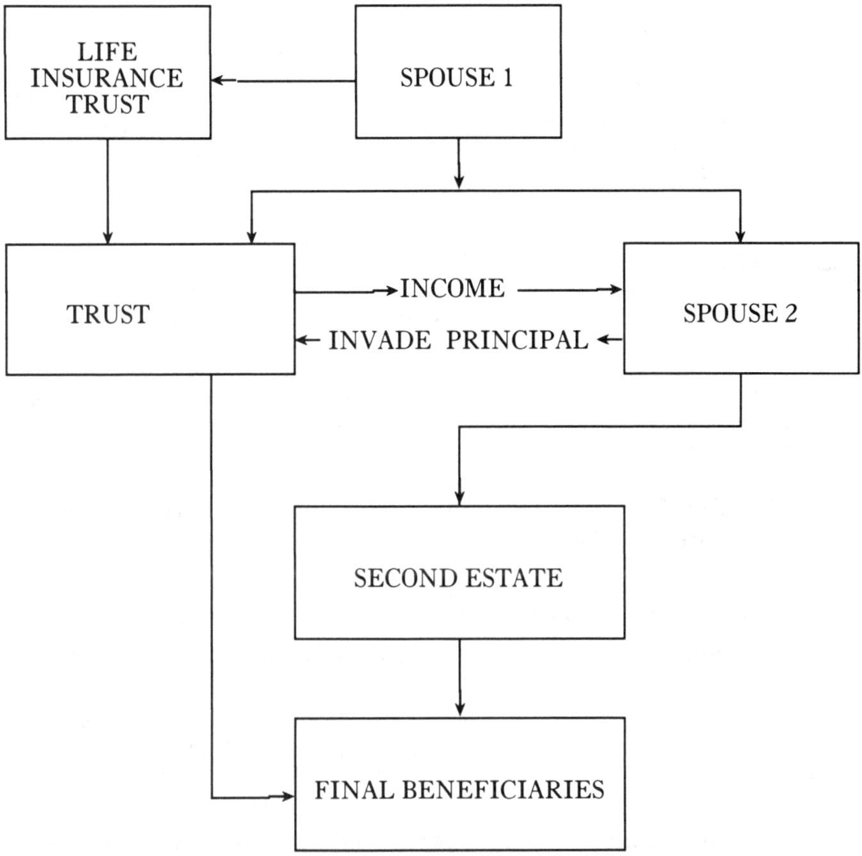

The design of the trust document and the steps to establish and maintain this trust must be followed with precision if the estate tax and GST planning advantages are to be obtained. Some of the key points to be observed are explained in the following sections.

.02 Restrictions and Other Considerations in Trust Design

For estate tax purposes, a number of restrictions must be placed in the trust in order to avoid application of the string sections, that is, to make certain that the life insurance proceeds are not included in the grantor's taxable estate. These restrictions include the following:

(1) The trust must be irrevocable, and the grantor must have no right to amend or alter the trust terms.

(2) It must not be permissible to make any income distributions to the grantor or for the grantor's purposes or needs, and trust property must not be available for the grantor's use.

(3) There must be no power, such as a sprinkle power, by which the grantor can control the benefits flowing from the trust among beneficiaries. Any prohibited power held by the grantor, either individually or

in the capacity of trustee, would subject the date-of-death value of the trust, including life insurance proceeds, to estate tax.

(4) Potential reversions must also be avoided. For instance, if the trust provides life income to one beneficiary and the remainder to another, with no direction as to the disposition of the trust in the event that both beneficiaries predecease the grantor, the possibility of a reversion exists.

In order for the trust to provide benefits to the surviving spouse without being included in the survivor's taxable estate, there must also be some restrictions placed on the beneficiary-spouse's access to the trust principal. The objective is to avoid any right possessed by the surviving spouse that can be treated as a general power of appointment. Although this includes unrestricted withdrawal rights, a right to withdraw that qualifies for either the ascertainable standard or the five-and-five test can be given to the grantor's spouse without resulting in inclusion of the trust fund in the beneficiary-spouse's taxable estate.

.03 Specific Tax Considerations in Planning for an Irrevocable Life Insurance Trust

As discussed at ¶ 402, two requirements must be met in order to avoid inclusion of life insurance proceeds in the grantor's taxable estate.

Requirement (1). The life insurance proceeds must not be receivable by the executor of the insured's estate.

Requirement (2). The grantor must not possess any of the incidents of ownership of the life insurance policies on his date of death and must not have made a gift transfer of the ownership within the three-year period preceding death.

These two requirements, together with the estate tax string section rules and the possible gift tax consequences of lifetime transfers to the trust, must all be planned for in advance. The basic guidelines that emerge are as follows:

(1) The life insurance trust must be established more than three years before the death of the grantor-insured. The trust must be irrevocable; otherwise, the grantor will have sufficient control over policy ownership so that the second requirement will not be met.

(2) All incidents of ownership of the life insurance policies must be transferred to the trust more than three years prior to death.

Creative planners have attempted to avoid the problem caused by death of the grantor during the three-year period after the irrevocable life insurance trust is established. By designating the trust as the original applicant and owner of the policy, in theory the grantor will never have been the owner of the policy. Therefore, no issue of a transfer of policy ownership within three years of death should ever arise.

(3) At the death of the grantor, amounts paid from the trust to the grantor's estate are subject to estate tax because of requirement (1). Where the estate is not liquid, this may pose a serious problem. It is possible, however, to use cash paid into the life insurance trust indirectly by permitting the trustee to purchase assets from the grantor's estate at fair market value. This strategy offers the advantages of solving the

liquidity problem while avoiding the need to sell estate assets that the family wishes to retain.

(4) The gift tax implications of all transfers made by the grantor to the trust must be considered. Such transfers include the original transfer of life insurance policies to the trust, as well as any subsequent transfers of cash that the trust uses to pay insurance premiums. Only transfers of life insurance policies that have existing cash value present the potential for a reportable gift tax event. Term life insurance should have little or no gift tax value, and the gift value of newly issued traditional whole life policies is likely to be small in most cases. Gift tax considerations in connection with the original policy transfers to the trust become significant only where (a) traditional whole life policies have been outstanding for a sufficient period of time (before being transferred to the trust) so that there is more than a minimal cash value; and (b) an attempt is being made to transfer so-called single-premium whole life insurance into an irrevocable trust.

Single-premium whole life insurance has grown in popularity in recent years. It is a life insurance contract designed to take advantage of the income-tax-free accumulation of earnings still permitted within life insurance contracts. Therefore, unlike most policies that seek to keep the cash outlay low, the single-premium contract intentionally carries a premium, or "investment," that is as high a percentage of the policy death benefit as possible while still meeting the Internal Revenue Code's definition of life insurance. The cash value, including interest or other investment accumulations, may be drawn on during the insured's lifetime. While withdrawals can constitute taxable income to the extent of accumulated earnings, the income tax benefit of deferred taxation will have been realized. At death, the full policy proceeds are free of income tax when paid to the beneficiary.

Despite these potential advantages, single-premium life is not necessarily well suited to the irrevocable life insurance trust. From an estate tax point of view, the planning objective of this trust is removal of the life insurance death benefit from the grantor-insured's estate. If the policy has a significant cash value when transferred to the trust, however, that value must be added back to the grantor's estate at death as a post-1976 taxable gift. Since the ratio between lifetime value and death benefit is intentionally kept to a minimum in single-premium life contracts, the estate tax planning advantage is greatly diminished.

After ownership of most life insurance policies has been placed in the trust, ongoing premiums must be paid. Either the transfer of cash to the trust for use in paying premiums or direct premium payment by the grantor constitutes a taxable gift. Since the unfunded life insurance trust does not ordinarily contain assets other than the insurance policies, the payment of premiums cannot be considered the gift of a present interest in property for which the gift tax annual exclusion is available. Each premium payment could therefore be treated as a post-1976 taxable gift which, as a future interest, is added back to the grantor's taxable estate undiminished by the annual exclusion. Depending on how long the grantor lives and how many premiums he pays, the cumulative effect of these add-backs might significantly offset the benefit of eliminating the policy death benefit from the grantor's taxable estate.

.04 Creating a Present Interest Through the *Crummey* Withdrawal Power

The planning solution to this dilemma lies in arranging to have the grantor transfer cash to the trust for use in paying premiums but causing the cash transfers to be treated as present interest gifts to the trust beneficiaries. This is accomplished by including a provision in the terms of the trust that grants to one or more beneficiaries the right to make trust withdrawals in the maximum amount of $5,000 per year. The beneficiaries are informed of each cash transfer by the grantor to the trust and are given an opportunity to exercise their withdrawal privileges. Although there may be a nonbinding understanding that no such withdrawals will ever be made, the right to withdraw transforms the cash transfers into present interest gifts by the grantor to the trust beneficiaries. Once the beneficiaries have passed up the opportunity to make their limited trust withdrawals, the trustee is permitted to use the cash to pay insurance premiums.

The annual limitation on withdrawals may be set at $5,000 per beneficiary, even though the gift tax annual exclusion is $10,000 per year, per recipient. This is to avoid a "reverse" taxable gift by the beneficiary to the trust. Each beneficiary's failure to make a withdrawal is treated as the release or lapse of a general power of appointment by that beneficiary. For gift tax purposes, a taxable gift by the beneficiary may occur to the extent that the value which could have been withdrawn exceeds the greater of $5,000 or five percent of the value of the trust. As discussed at ¶ 401.022, however, it is possible to design a "hanging" power so that the limitation of annual withdrawals can be increased to $10,000 per year, per recipient.

These limited withdrawal rights are called "*Crummey*" powers, named for a court decision[1] establishing the validity of the planning technique. The IRS recognizes the principle that cash transfers to irrevocable life insurance trusts, subject to *Crummey* powers, constitute present interest gifts providing that the following conditions exist:

(1) Each beneficiary who holds a *Crummey* power must be notified when cash transfers to the trust are made and must be given a reasonable period of time during which withdrawal rights can be exercised.

(2) The beneficiary must be capable of making the withdrawal. That is, there must be no legally binding restriction. The requirement can be met on behalf of minor or incompetent beneficiaries so long as a guardian might be appointed who could make the withdrawal on the beneficiary's behalf. It is not necessary that a guardian actually be appointed for this purpose.

(3) If there are multiple *Crummey* power holders, one gift tax annual exclusion may be obtained with respect to each if the trust terms provide that each withdrawal right is reduced proportionately in the event that the total available in the trust fund is insufficient to satisfy all of the withdrawal rights.

(4) Ideally, each holder of a *Crummey* power should possess an actual beneficial interest in the trust other than the *Crummey* power itself. For example, if the trust provides for life income to the grantor's spouse, with the remainder in equal shares to their three children, it

---

[1] *Crummey v. Comm'r*, 397 F2d 82 (9th Cir. 1968).

should be possible to create four valid *Crummey* powers, one held by the spouse and one held by each child. This would make it possible for the grantor to make cash transfers of up to $20,000 to the trust each year without making any gifts that exceed the available gift tax annual exclusions, as illustrated below:

4	×	$5,000	=	$20,000
Total number of *Crummey* power holders		Maximum yearly withdrawal allowed to each power holder		Maximum yearly cash transfer to trust excluded from gift tax base by annual exclusions

Notice that the total withdrawals might be increased to $40,000 with four withdrawal powers controlling $10,000 each if the withdrawal rights are designed as "hanging" powers. If the yearly life insurance premiums exceed this sum, the grantor might wish to create additional *Crummey* powers without giving any real trust benefits to persons other than his spouse and children. The IRS will disallow an annual exclusion based on a *Crummey* power held by any person who does not possess either a present interest (other than the *Crummey* power) or a vested remainder interest. If relatives such as sons-in-law or daughters-in-law are designated as trust beneficiaries whose only beneficial interest is a *Crummey* power, the IRS will not agree that gift tax annual exclusions are allowable with respect to these additional power holders. It is difficult to find support for the IRS's position, however, and the Tax Court has not followed it.[2]

.05 GST Considerations Involving an Irrevocable Life Insurance Trust

The following sections provide planning techniques that consider the generation-skipping transfer tax (GST) and a funded and unfunded irrevocable life insurance policy.

.051 Keeping the life insurance free of GST as well as estate tax

The irrevocable life insurance trust may continue beyond the lifetime of the grantor's spouse and children so that, at some point, distributions can occur that may be in the nature of taxable distributions or taxable terminations for GST purposes. If the initial beneficiaries of the trust are skip persons, the original transfer might be a direct skip.

It is possible, however, to achieve total avoidance of GST through the use of the irrevocable life insurance trust. The key to achieving this goal is to qualify each transfer by the grantor to the trust for the $10,000 annual exclusion for gift tax purposes and to allocate as much of the grantor's GST exemption to each transfer as necessary so that the trust maintains an inclusion ratio of zero for GST purposes. The reasoning behind this is:

(1) The $10,000 maximum annual exclusion, based on one or more *Crummey* powers (including hanging powers), applies for gift tax purposes but, in the case of many irrevocable life insurance trusts, it does not apply for GST.[3] If all transfers to the trust can be covered through the availability of one or more annual exclusions, no taxable gift may occur, but it is necessary to allocate a portion of the grantor's GST exemption to

---

[2] *M. Cristofani Est. v. Comm'r*, 97 TC 74 (1991), acq. in result only, 1992-1 CB 1.

[3] Code Sec. 2642(c)(2).

each transfer in order to maintain the inclusion ratio of the trust at zero for GST purposes.

(2) If a GST zero inclusion ratio is achieved, no future trust distributions are subject to GST.

(3) Provided that the irrevocable life insurance trust is properly designed, the receipt of life insurance proceeds at the death of the insured has no effect on the GST inclusion ratio.

The secret to the success of this technique stems from the inherent quality of traditional whole life insurance: Relatively small amounts are paid during the premium payment period of the policy in return for a relatively large sum received by the beneficiary in the future. The relatively small premium amounts can qualify for the annual exclusion, usually through the use of *Crummey* powers. As long as the total amount of premium payments is predictable (as in the case of a vanishing premium policy), it is possible to plan in advance for the portion of the total GST exemption of the grantor that will have to be allocated in order to maintain the GST zero inclusion ratio. Later, the receipt of the life insurance death benefit is a "nonevent" for GST purposes. As a result, all distributions are free of GST regardless of the generation assignment.

As previously mentioned, efficient organization of the estate plan requires that the insurance trust be coordinated with other testamentary plans. If it is appropriate to use the classic bypass and marital deduction arrangement, care must be exercised in authorizing any combinations of trust shares. The guiding principle is that the irrevocable life insurance trust should only be combined with other trusts if the GST exemption has been allocated to such other trusts so that the inclusion ratio of the combined trust fund is always zero. After the death of the grantor, it may be appropriate to combine the irrevocable life insurance trust with the bypass share, if the bypass trust has a GST zero inclusion ratio, which should ordinarily be the case. After the subsequent death of the surviving spouse, any separate QTIP or other marital deduction share with an inclusion ratio of zero may also be combined with what had originally been the separate irrevocable life insurance trust.

All of this combining of trust shares presupposes that the trust design is such that, at some point in the future, distributions will be made to skip persons. If the grantor's plan is to cause all of the trust funds ultimately to be distributed to his children, the issue of combining only those trust shares that have GST inclusion ratios of zero is irrelevant.

.052 Visual presentation of an unfunded irrevocable life insurance trust with GST planning implications

A typical estate planning diagram aimed at taking maximum advantage of an unfunded irrevocable life insurance trust with GST implications follows:

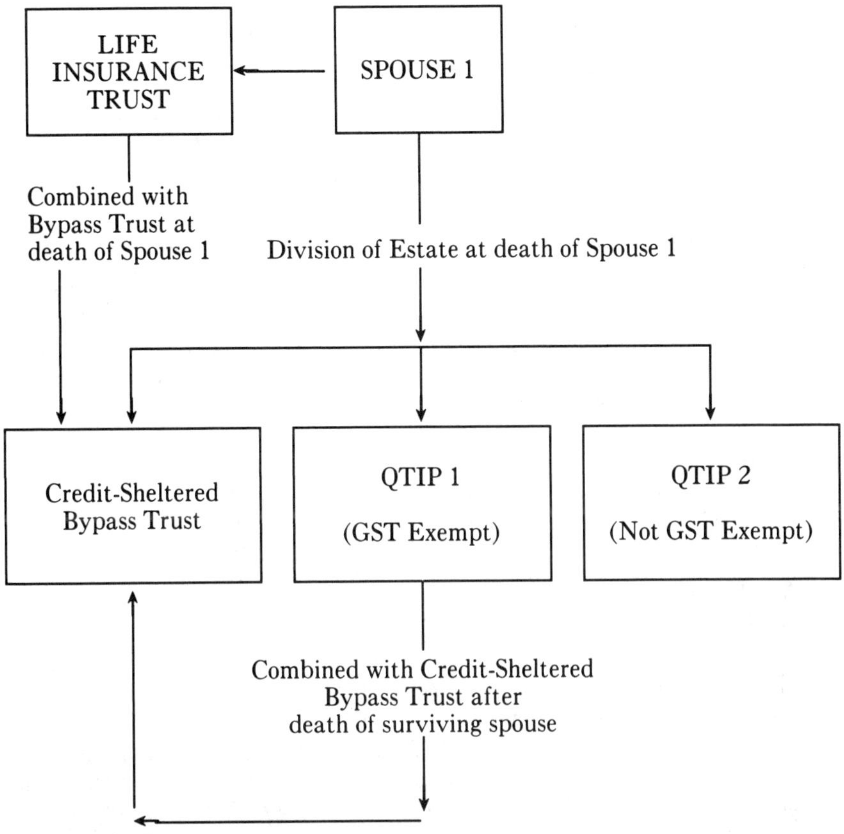

Upon the death of the surviving spouse, the separate GST exemption available to the survivor may be utilized to further advantage. Depending on the total value of QTIP 2, which is not GST exempt, and the value of the estate of the surviving spouse, two alternatives need to be considered.

Alternative (1). Assuming that the full $1,000,000 GST exemption is available to the surviving spouse and that the total value of QTIP 2 does not exceed that amount, the executor of the surviving spouse's estate may allocate enough of the available GST exemption to QTIP 2 in order to cause this trust share to have an inclusion ratio of zero. This is possible because the beneficiary spouse is treated as the transferor of QTIP 2 for GST purposes. QTIP 2 may then be combined with what had originally been the irrevocable life insurance trust. In addition, any balance of the GST exemption available to the estate of the surviving spouse may be allocated to separate assets of the surviving spouse which, under the terms of the survivor's will, can also be combined with the same trust share. At this point, the combined GST exempt trust will contain shares from five separate sources:

(1) The assets of what had originally been a separate, irrevocable life insurance trust;

(2) The credit-sheltered bypass share under the will of Spouse 1;

(3) QTIP 1, as established under the will of Spouse 1;

(4) QTIP 2, which is added in at the death of Spouse 2, and against which part of the GST exemption of Spouse 2 has been allocated; and

(5) The maximum portion of the balance of the estate of Spouse 2 for which the survivor's remaining GST exemption is available.

Alternative (2). If QTIP 2 is large enough that it exceeds the GST exemption of the surviving spouse, it may be desirable to design the trust so as to permit the surviving spouse to cause the transfer of only a part of QTIP 2 with the other combined, GST-exempt trust shares. The part of QTIP 2 to be transferred in this manner would be equal to the surviving spouse's available GST exemption. In this manner, the inclusion ratio of the entire combined trust would remain at zero.

Example: H and W are married with three adult children and six grandchildren. Their separate estates are valued at $1,100,000 and $750,000, respectively. H purchases a life insurance policy on his life with a face value of $800,000 and transfers the policy to a newly established irrevocable living trust. The trust is to pay income to W for life, then income in equal shares to the children for life and, after the children are deceased, the remainder to the grandchildren in equal shares. H's will establishes three trust shares:

(1) Share 1, the credit-sheltered equivalent amount, is to be combined with the life insurance trust upon the death of H. H's GST exemption is allocated to Share 1.

(2) Share 2, a QTIP trust, is to be equal to the excess of the GST exemption available to H's estate over that part of H's GST exemption allocated to Share 1. H's executor makes the special GST election so that H is treated as the transferor of Share 2 for GST purposes. After W's death, Share 2 is added to Share 1 and the life insurance trust.

(3) Share 3 is also a QTIP trust, but H's executor does not make the special GST election with respect to this share. Therefore, W is treated as the transferor of this share for GST purposes.

W's will directs that her GST exemption is to be allocated to Share 3 established under H's will and, as his will permits, directs that upon her death, Share 3 is to be added to Share 1, and thus combined with the life insurance trust as well. W's will also provides that, after payment of taxes and expenses from her residuary estate, an additional amount is to be added to Share 1, equal in value to any GST exemption remaining after the allocation to Share 3. Thereafter, if any balance of W's residuary estate remains, it is to be distributed to the children in equal shares.

In the following diagram, which illustrates the flow of assets, several points should be noted. First, the amount shown within the life insurance trust is the face value, which is not paid into the trust until the death of H.

Second, for simplicity, the maximum credit-sheltered amount is shown as passing into the bypass trust, Share 1. Actually, that share would ordinarily be diminished by estate settlement costs as explained at ¶ 504.

Third, the diagram makes no allowance for appreciation of any trust shares between the time of the death of H and the death of W. Appreciation of Shares 2 and 3 would have the effect of increasing W's taxable estate, and appreciation of Share 3 would have the additional effect of using up a greater part of W's available GST exemption.

Finally, the assumption is that W survives H and that the plan does not take advantage of other available strategies to provide for the possibility of the reverse order of death.

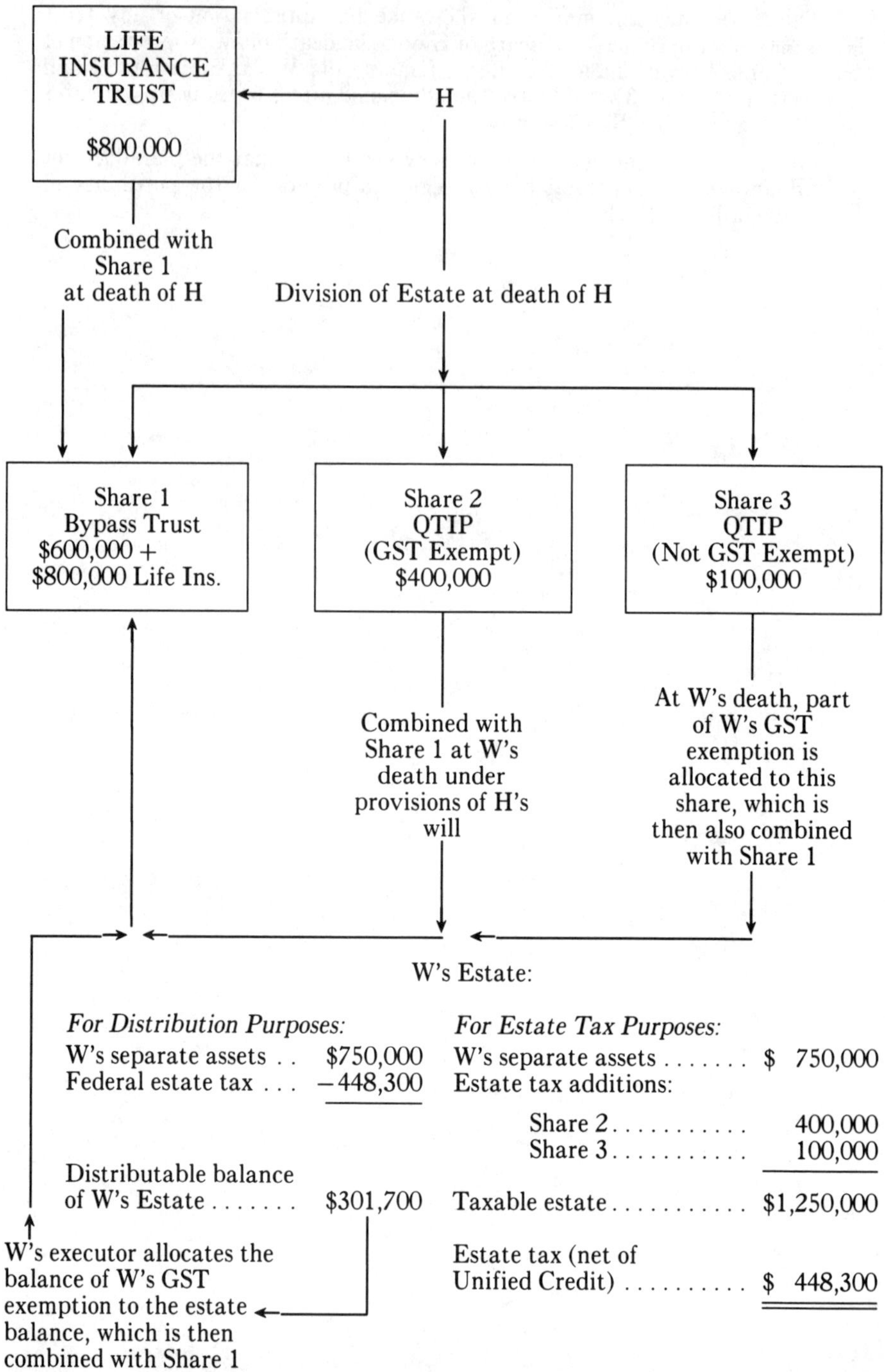
LIFE INSURANCE TRUST
$800,000
H
Combined with Share 1 at death of H
Division of Estate at death of H
Share 1
Bypass Trust
$600,000 +
$800,000 Life Ins.
Share 2
QTIP
(GST Exempt)
$400,000
Share 3
QTIP
(Not GST Exempt)
$100,000
Combined with Share 1 at W's death under provisions of H's will
At W's death, part of W's GST exemption is allocated to this share, which is then also combined with Share 1
W's Estate:
For Distribution Purposes:
W's separate assets . . $750,000
Federal estate tax . . . –448,300
Distributable balance of W's Estate $301,700
For Estate Tax Purposes:
W's separate assets . . . . $ 750,000
Estate tax additions:
Share 2 400,000
Share 3 100,000
Taxable estate $1,250,000
Estate tax (net of Unified Credit) . . . . $ 448,300
W's executor allocates the balance of W's GST exemption to the estate balance, which is then combined with Share 1

The final result of the estate plan presented in this example is that all of the assets of the separate estates of H and W are kept free of GST. This is made possible by judicious allocation of the GST exemptions that are available to H and to W and by the fact that the life insurance proceeds are completely outside of the GST system. The life insurance exemption is accomplished because all transfers to the irrevocable life insurance trust are exempt from gift tax, as well as GST, through the gift tax annual exclusions. The total of the amounts ultimately combined in Share 1, which has a GST inclusion ratio of zero throughout, is $2,201,700, computed as follows:

The life insurance proceeds paid directly into the irrevocable life insurance trust at the death of H	$ 800,000
The amount that is sheltered from estate tax in H's estate because of availability of the unified credit (credit-sheltered bypass portion). This is Share 1, and the irrevocable life insurance trust is combined with it at H's death. This part is shielded from GST by allocation of part of H's GST exemption	600,000
Trust Share 2, a QTIP that utilizes the balance of H's GST exemption and that is combined with Share 1 at the death of W	400,000
Trust Share 3, also a QTIP, to which part of W's GST exemption is allocated	100,000
The balance of W's residuary estate, after payment of the federal estate tax. In this case, the balance of W's GST exemption was sufficient to cover this full balance	301,700
Total	$2,201,700

There are several planning advantages to be noted from this example. The final combined value of the trust exceeds the sum of the two GST exemptions available to H and to W because no part of either of their exemptions was needed to offset the life insurance proceeds. The only "erosion" of the family's financial capital resulted from the federal estate tax imposed on W's estate. This erosion was more than recovered through the life insurance proceeds.

If H's estate were greater in value, the excess would have been placed in Share 3. This, in turn, would have resulted in a need to use up a larger part of W's GST exemption. Alternatively, the second GST exemption could have been exceeded if the total value of W's separate estate had been larger. The result in either event would cause the need to modify the final flow of assets by transferring from W's residuary estate to Share 1 only so much of W's estate balance as could be covered by W's GST exemption. In this manner, the inclusion ratio of Share 1 is kept at zero. As described in this example, the final provision of W's will takes care of this aspect by providing that, if the GST exemption is exceeded, the balance of W's estate is to be distributed outright to the children. Since this outright distribution would not pass to any skip person, GST would not apply.

H's will should also include careful directions as to any permissible principal distributions that might be authorized prior to final distribution of the remainder to the grandchildren. By setting the priorities correctly, it is possible to make sure that principal that would be subject to tax is dispersed before any distributions are made from trust shares that are shielded from estate tax or GST. The priorities are:

(1) Any principal to be withdrawn by W or distributed to W by the trustee must be taken first from Share 3, which is included in W's taxable estate as a marital deduction trust and which is also subject to GST upon its termination.

(2) If Share 3 is completely distributed to W and, during her lifetime, additional principal is to be withdrawn or distributed, the next source is Share 2. Although this share is exempt from GST, since it is a marital deduction trust, it is included in W's taxable estate.

(3) Only in the event that both Shares 3 and 2 are fully distributed during W's lifetime should any principal distributions be made from the combination of the life insurance trust and Share 1. This trust is designed to bypass W's taxable estate and is exempt from GST as well.

¶ 604 CHOOSING THE TYPE OF LIFE INSURANCE FOR IRREVOCABLE LIVING TRUSTS

The traditional purpose of life insurance is to make up for the loss of family income that occurs at the death of a parent or other person who had been providing support. It should be clear from the preceding discussions that this traditional use of insurance may complement the planning for a revocable living trust, which is designed to coordinate the estate plan of the grantor rather than to save estate tax and GST.

The central goal of the irrevocable life insurance trust, however, is a different matter. The very reason for the irrevocable nature of this trust is to place the life insurance proceeds outside of the grantor's taxable estate. In most cases, this is indicated where the potential estate tax is already significant. The insurance exists for the specific purpose of replenishing the wealth that will be consumed by tax. This is a specialized use of life insurance, quite distinct from the traditional purpose with which this financial tool is most often associated. The parent of young children with limited present financial resources might be identified as having a proportionately higher need for life insurance coverage than the retired individual who is financially independent and whose children are self-sufficient. Ironically, only those whose wealth is sufficiently extensive so as to lead to a considerable potential estate tax need to consider the specialized use of life insurance within an irrevocable trust. Ordinarily, these people have sufficient resources so that their deaths would not result in financial hardship for their families.

Thus, the ideal candidate for this type of planning is typically older and wealthier than those who most commonly buy life insurance. This can present a problem to the financial consultant who introduces the concept of life insurance in connection with irrevocable living trusts. The client may see himself as having little or no need to protect his dependents from economic loss and suspect the financial consultant of just trying to make an insurance sale. In order to overcome this problem, it is necessary to explain the basic concepts of tax-oriented estate planning, to convince the client that this specialized use of life insurance really has nothing to do with the traditional replacement of earning capacity and to point out that this is appropriate in situations that are almost the economic opposite of those with which most people associate life insurance.

.01 Basic Policy Types

The very fact that the holding of life insurance within the irrevocable living trust is a specialized use has a significant impact on the type of life insurance policy that is appropriate. In order to understand the choices involved and to judge the types of insurance policies that make sense and why, it is necessary to review basic aspects of some of the more common forms of life insurance contracts generally available.

.011 Annual renewal term (ART)

As the name suggests, this type of insurance contract pays a benefit only if death actually occurs during the time period for which the coverage is in effect. The "renewable" feature means that the insured has the right to maintain the coverage by paying continuing premiums without being required to take continuing physical examinations. Each year, the premium cost increases to reflect the fact that the insured is a year older and, therefore, that the actuarial probability of death is increased. Term insurance premiums pay purely and exclusively for the insurance protection for a limited period of time. If the insured does not die, no payment is made by the insurance company to anyone. The premium cost structure may be visualized as follows:

PREMIUM COST ILLUSTRATION

ANNUAL RENEWABLE TERM LIFE INSURANCE

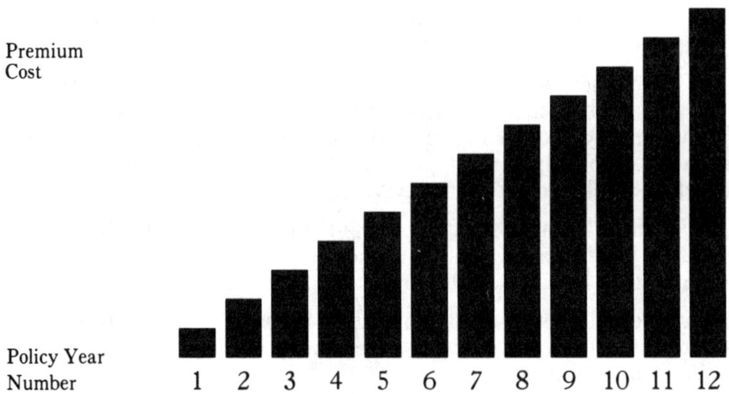

The main distinguishing feature of term insurance is low premium cost relative to that of whole life insurance during the early years of the policy. Due to the increasing cost that comes with increasing age, however, this annual cash premium difference eventually reverses itself.

Crossover of ART cost. An individual who is investigating different types of life insurance coverage and who studies the initial annual cost, as well as future years' cost comparisons, soon discovers a certain pattern developing as follows:

(1) In the early years, the cash outlay for term insurance is much lower.

(2) At some point in the future, the yearly outlay of the term insurance equals and then exceeds that of the whole life policy.

(3) Further in the future, the annual premiums on the term insurance are so great that it becomes economically inadvisable to retain the policy.

The reversing cost pattern should not lead to the conclusion that term insurance is bad and that whole life insurance is better. The choice of the best type of insurance contract varies depending upon the circumstances of the proposed insured and the motivation for obtaining the insurance contract.

Most financial advisers favor term insurance for young married couples with children because premium costs are an important factor in such cases. Assuming that the family has a limited budget, the decision of policy types may result in choosing between struggling to pay the premiums on a whole life policy with an inadequate death benefit and purchasing a sufficient amount of term insurance with no financial strain. If the family is reasonably successful in savings and investment programs, by the time the term insurance premiums become too expensive, the children are self-sufficient and the parents are financially independent. In the ideal setting, the insurance coverage is no longer needed by the time the cost becomes prohibitive. This ideal term insurance scenario is often encountered and might even represent the majority of existing and potential family life insurance situations. However, the factors that would prompt a financial counselor to recommend term insurance in the young family situation do not apply in cases where the use of an irrevocable life insurance trust is advisable.

Analyzing ART vis-à-vis an irrevocable life insurance trust. In choosing the type of life insurance policy to be placed in an irrevocable life insurance trust, the following factors must be recognized:

(1) The reason for considering an estate planning alternative as complex and sophisticated as the irrevocable living trust is that the family has already acquired such a level of wealth that estate tax, GST, or both are potentially serious problems. The ability to pay premiums should not be an obstacle in such cases.

(2) Because the purpose of insurance is to replace wealth that will be consumed by death taxes, this insurance need will not diminish in the future. In fact, as family wealth grows, this need can increase.

Any insurance policy whose cost has the potential to increase to prohibitive levels during the insured's lifetime is self-defeating in the context of the irrevocable life insurance trust.

The types of policies that should be considered are those in which the annual premium cost remains constant, decreases, or ceases in the future. This favors the use of various types of whole life insurance for irrevocable trust plans. Before examining the basic characteristics of the major types of whole life insurance, some of the variations of the annual renewable term policy will be discussed.

.012 Level premium term insurance

As an alternative to annual increases in the premium cost, a term policy may be designed to keep the yearly cost constant for a specified number of years with scheduled premium increases at future intervals. For example, the annual premium might increase once every five years. The first year's premium payment will be higher than that of an ART policy, but the ART premium for the fifth policy year will exceed the level term premium cost. This diagram illustrates the cost progression of level term:

PREMIUM COST ILLUSTRATION

FIVE-YEAR LEVEL TERM LIFE INSURANCE

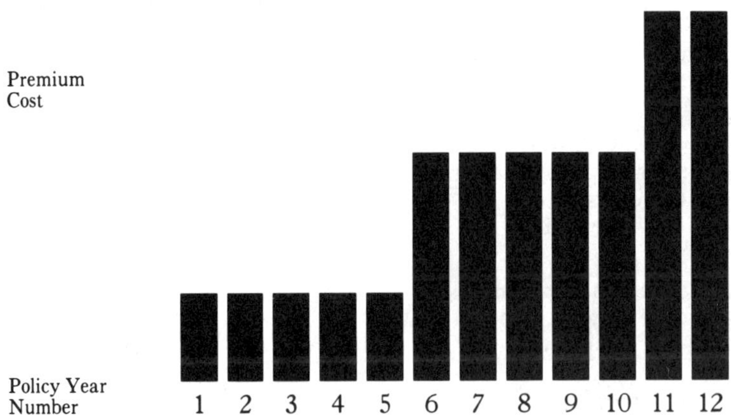

.013 Group term insurance

Life insurance is often provided by employers as a fringe benefit to employees. The employer pays the premiums, but the employee names the beneficiary. An organization may also make insurance available to its members. Examples include state teachers' unions, bar associations, CPA societies and other groups of professionals. In case of employer-provided group term insurance, if specific plan requirements are met, the employer is entitled to an income tax deduction for the premiums paid, even though the employee is not required to include the value of the life insurance coverage in taxable income. If an employee's death benefit exceeds $50,000, the part of the employer's cost allocable to such excess is taxable as compensation to the employee.

Providing life insurance through the medium of an employer or through other groups results in reduced costs of marketing and sales to the insurance company. A single insurance salesperson can sell several hundred or even thousands of policies through one sale closing. The premium cost of group term insurance may be much lower than comparable ART or level term insurance purchased individually. This reflects both savings at the insurance company level and competition in the insurance industry for the highly desirable group business. The premium structure may be either ART or level term. In some cases, whole life insurance is purchased in employer-provided group term life insurance programs.

.014 Decreasing term

The need for life insurance coverage may decrease in some cases. An example is the young married couple who requires significant amounts of coverage while the children are living at home and are financially dependent. As the children become capable of supporting themselves and the parents gradually accumulate financial resources, which will protect the welfare of the surviving spouse, the potential economic loss upon death of either parent diminishes. The transition between a large life insurance need and a small need is usually gradual.

The decreasing term policy is designed to have an annual premium cost that remains constant during the existence of the coverage. The death benefit decreases, however, on a year-by-year basis. As is the case in any variation of ART, the cost of providing the insurance increases each year. In case of decreasing term, the approach is to buy as much death benefit as a non-increasing annual premium outlay affords. The trade-off is gradually diminishing coverage.

Decreasing term is a popular insurance product for use in connection with home mortgage loans. At the outset, the death benefit is equal to the original amount of the mortgage loan. As the outstanding principal payoff amount of the mortgage decreases, so does the life insurance death benefit. The goal is to make sure that if the parent dies, the family will have an unencumbered home.

The use of decreasing term within an irrevocable life insurance trust is the exact opposite of what is needed. If the insured gradually acquires more wealth during his lifetime, the potential death taxes constantly increase.

.015 Deposit term

This is a form of level term, typically offered for 10-year periods, in which the purchaser pays a substantial initial deposit in addition to the periodic premiums. In effect, the interest earned on the deposit keeps the premiums lower than otherwise possible. However, the policyholder is not entitled to receive the interest that is not treated as taxable income. The deposit is returned when the term ends if there is no renewal.

.016 Whole life insurance

It is fair to state that within every whole life insurance policy there is a term policy. The first year's premium for the whole life policy is substantially greater than that for the term policy. However, the premium cost of a traditional whole life policy never increases. Part of each premium pays for the actual insurance death benefit coverage in exactly the same manner as term insurance. The balance of the premium is held by the insurance company as if in a savings account within the policy. As long as premiums are paid up to date, the savings element, referred to as the policy "cash value," eventually increases to a level at which it can be used to pay the premiums for the remainder of the insured's lifetime. After that point, the policy owner no longer needs to make payments, and the policy is said to be "paid up."

It is fair to compare whole life insurance with decreasing term coupled with a savings program. As the cash value grows, the true life insurance is diminished. At death, the beneficiary receives a payment that really consists of the accumulated cash value plus whatever is left of the decreasing insurance death benefit. These two combined elements are always equal to the total stated death benefit of the policy, known as its "face value." The whole life policy is dynamic in the sense that the proportions between the elements are always changing; each year the cash value increases and the true life insurance decreases. Except in unusually structured policies, the beneficiary does not receive the face value in addition to the cash value. If the insured lives long enough, the cash value may grow to a point at which it is equal to the policy face value. At that point, the policy ends and the face value is paid even though the insured is still living. The relationship between the gradually increasing cash value element and the gradually decreasing true life insurance element of whole life insurance may be expressed as follows:

WHOLE LIFE INSURANCE
RELATIONSHIP BETWEEN CASH VALUE
AND TRUE INSURANCE DEATH BENEFIT

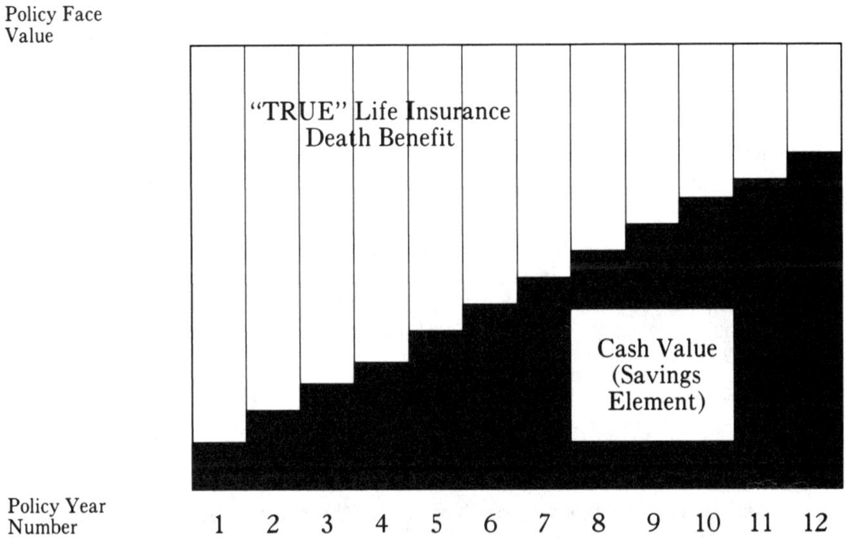

The owner of the whole life insurance policy is permitted to borrow from the cash value. In the past, the rate of interest charged on policy loans was much lower than rates charged on bank loans. When interest rates in the general economy rose to record levels in the late 1970s and early 1980s, borrowing on policy cash values increased sharply, negatively affecting the issuing insurance companies, many of which were forced to sell investments at losses in order to honor policyholder loan requests. As a result, the more recent trend is toward higher interest charges on policy loans.

From the borrower's point of view, this type of interest expense falls into the category of personal interest under the Tax Reform Act of 1986 (TRA '86) (P.L. 99-514). The itemized deduction for personal interest was phased out between 1987 and 1990 and eliminated thereafter. These factors have caused a drastic reduction in the use of preplanned borrowing programs, which had been popular just a few years ago. The technique involved paying four of the first seven years' premiums and borrowing cash value in order to pay most or all of the other premiums. The policy owner also paid the interest on the loan which was then a permissible income tax deduction. The objective was to pay to the insurance company the smallest amount necessary to keep the policy in effect. This was known in the insurance industry as the "minimum deposit" method. The net cost to the policyholder, considering potential income tax savings resulting from interest deductions, might actually have been less than term insurance. The loan balance might have been repaid only from the policy proceeds upon death of the insured. Higher interest rate charges and loss of the interest deduction reduce the advantage of minimum deposit plans.

.017 Stock whole life and mutual whole life

A basic distinction among companies that offer whole life insurance policies lies in the form of ownership and plan of profit distribution of the company. Some are established as corporations organized for the purpose of generating profits for their stockholders. These are the so-called stock insurance companies. The opposite are the mutual insurance companies, which return any profits they make to the policy owners in the form of policy dividends. We should not conclude that mutual companies are by nature preferable to stock companies.

The objective in the stock company is to keep the premium outlay lower than that of the mutual company. Lower out-of-pocket cost or a shorter premium period before the policy becomes "paid up" may turn out to be a better bargain than the potential to share in the mutual company's profits as a policyholder.

The mutual company's premium costs may be greater, but each year there is the possibility that policy "dividends" will be declared that can put the mutual policy on an even or better footing compared to the product offered by the stock company. The policy owner has several choices as to how the dividends may be credited.

Dividends may be:

Paid in cash. This is not treated as taxable income, but rather as an adjustment in the overall cost of the policy.

Used to reduce premiums. This helps the mutual policy catch up with the stock company policy, which may have offered a lower initial premium rate. Mutual company policy dividends usually increase over the years the policy is kept in effect. At some point, it is possible for the annual dividend to exceed the premium charge if the mutual company is able to sustain its dividend declarations.

Accumulated. Any dividend accumulations are accounted for separately from the policy cash value and are credited with interest. These accumulations may be withdrawn by the policy owner without cancelling the policy coverage. Unlike the policy cash value, at the death of the insured, dividend accumulations are paid to the beneficiary in addition to the policy's face value.

Used to purchased paid-up additions. This means that each dividend buys a small amount of additional death benefit for which no future-year premiums are payable. If this option is chosen, it is possible to reduce the basic policy death benefit on a year-by-year basis in amounts equal to the paid-up additions that are being added. This results in a constant death benefit, and it may rapidly reduce the premium outlay. Alternatively, the basic policy face value may be retained. Considering the combination of the basic face value and the incremental increases through paid-up additions, an annual increase in the total death benefit occurs. This can be an ideal choice for the irrevocable life insurance trust in situations where the grantor's wealth, as well as the grantor's potential estate tax, is also increasing.

Used to purchase one-year term insurance. If dividends are spent in this manner, the amount of total death benefit tends to be greater in the early policy dividend years. For the same dividend dollar, a much greater death benefit can be obtained if that benefit expires at the end of one year. If the death benefit is permanent and requires no future premiums, the amount of coverage must be reduced. However, if the paid-up-additions option remains in effect long enough, the cumulative amount of the permanent death benefit might overtake the total coverage available through the one-year term arrangement.

The prospective purchaser of a whole life insurance policy must make careful comparisons between the relative advantages of stock company and mutual company products. If the insurance is being obtained as part of an estate plan involving an irrevocable life insurance trust, a central concern should be for permanence of the insurance coverage in consideration of the permanence and certainty of the future estate tax liability.

.02 Metamorphosis of the Whole Life Policy

Growth of the cash value within any whole life insurance policy is what makes it possible to achieve paid-up status. If the cash value accumulates at a higher rate, it is possible either for the policyholder to pay a smaller premium or for paid-up status to be achieved sooner, or both. In recent years, new insurance products have been introduced that permit the policyholder some choice as to how the cash value is to be invested.

The oldest existing whole life insurance policies credited interest on the cash value at rates as low as 1½ percent per year. Various forms of competition have brought about higher rates, but the interest rates paid by a traditional whole life policy cannot really compete with such financial products as savings certificates or bonds. For one thing, the insurance company must be in a position to guarantee the rate for the lifetime of the insured. In order to credit interest on cash values, the insurance company must be able to obtain a sufficient return on investments in the general economy. Given the nature of its commitments, it is incumbent on the insurance company to make investments in a very conservative manner. If the rate promised on policy cash values is too high, a prolonged downtrend in interest rates could jeopardize the ability of the insurance company to meet its obligations and thereby undermine the security of those who depend on policy benefits. Although competition in the industry drove rates somewhat higher, at a time when savings certificates were offering rates in excess of 10 percent per year, a four percent annual rate on the cash value of a traditional whole life policy was considered good.

Over the years, vendors of financial products who are in competition with the whole life insurance industry have argued that it makes better sense to buy the least expensive term life insurance and then to set aside the difference between the premium cost of the term and the amount that would have been paid for the whole life policy and put it into some form of savings or investment program. According to this "buy term and invest the difference" argument, the accumulations of the outside investment fund will always be greater than the buildup of the cash value in the whole life policy. However, comparisons between whole life and term with a "side fund" are tricky. Earnings accumulated on the cash value are not currently subject to income tax, are guaranteed by the insurance company, and are not subject to fluctuation. Therefore, any valid comparison must take into account the income tax impact on the side fund and the nature of the guarantees, if any, of the savings or investment program. Nevertheless, if four percent per year is considered a good return on whole life cash value, it is not difficult to conceive of a combination of term insurance with a safe savings program that delivers a superior long-term result. The proponents of these alternatives to whole life insurance, who sometimes refer to themselves as "term-ites," may have been responsible for further innovations developed by life insurance companies.

.021 Introduction of universal life and its progeny

Perhaps the most dramatic of these innovations was the introduction of a variation of whole life that has come to be known as "universal" life insurance. The original universal life insurance products were comparable to a term life insurance policy combined with a money market fund. Upon issuance of the policy, a relatively large sum is deposited with the insurance company. The interest credited is equal or nearly equal to the rate credited on money market funds, which, at the time universal life was introduced, was more than twice the rate of interest then being credited on most traditional whole life policies. The cost of the life insurance, computed in virtually the same manner as ART, is simply deducted from the interest earnings within the policy. The insurance charge is fixed and increases in the same manner as ART, but the rate earned on the policy cash value is not guaranteed to remain the same and changes frequently to reflect short-term interest trends. When rates are high, the accumulations within the cash value far exceed the amounts needed to pay for the ongoing cost of the death benefit. When rates fall, however, it is possible that "principal" of the savings element might be needed, in addition to the income, in order to continuing paying for the coverage. The universal policy is flexible in this regard; the policy owner has the choice of either permitting cash value to be diminished or electing a reduction in the death benefit.

This is a major departure from the traditional concept of whole life insurance in which guarantees are a central element. One of the benefits long associated with the whole life policy has been that the owner always knows that the cost of maintaining the policy will not change. However, it is only the fact that the insurance company is relieved of the investment risk created by changing interest rates that enables the company to credit current rates to universal policy cash values.

In some of the original universal life policies, the amount initially required to be transferred into cash value was so great that, even if rates were to fall dramatically, the interest earnings would be enough to maintain coverage and still cause a significant buildup of ever-increasing cash value. There was an ulterior motive in designing universal life policies in this manner. Since the accumulations within the cash value are not subject to income tax, a form of tax-deferred investment was created. If the policy owner wanted to use the accumulated cash, withdrawals or policy loans could be taken. As a general rule, cash withdrawn from a life insurance policy is not subject to income tax unless the cumulative amount withdrawn exceeds the cumulative amount of premiums paid. Under present law, funds obtained through policy loans are not treated as withdrawals and do not constitute taxable income. Upon the death of the insured, in almost all cases, the death benefit is free of income tax regardless of how much cash value had been accumulated within the policy. All of this gave universal life insurance the appearance of a financial product that seemed too good to be true. The potential for income tax avoidance has led Congress to place limitations on the advantages offered by this product in two ways.

First, strict requirements must be met in order for a policy to qualify as life insurance. These requirements relate to the difference between the total cash value and the face value of the policy. For example, if a universal life insurance policy were to have a cash value of $10,000 and a face value or death benefit of $11,000, there would be absolute certainty not only that the cash value earnings would cover the insurance cost but also that substantial additional accumulations would occur. By requiring a minimum "spread" between cash value and death benefit, the disguised use of universal life as a tax-deferred piggy bank is prevented.

When earnings on the cash value increase so that the minimum spread is not met, the universal life policy's death benefit increases which, in turn, increases the ongoing insurance cost. This tends to keep the value accumulations under control. It also makes it necessary for the insurance company to provide much more sophisticated reports to universal policyholders. Unlike the traditional whole life policy where the face value never changes and the accumulation of cash value may follow a scheduled progression that can be predicted with accuracy for 20 years or more into the future, the universal policy can have monthly fluctuation in both the death benefit and the savings element.

Second, the Technical and Miscellaneous Revenue Act of 1988 (TAMRA) (P.L. 100-647) placed new restrictions on tax-free borrowing from life insurance policies. The law now identifies a new class of life insurance designated as the "modified endowment contract." Amounts received from modified endowment contracts during the life of the insured, including policy loans, are treated as taxable income first (to the extent of earnings within the policy) and then as tax-free recovery of basis.

Money market interest rates dropped considerably in the years shortly after the original introduction of universal life. This may have caused some disappointment among policyholders who had purchased the product with expectations built upon interest rate assumptions in the 10 to 12 percent range. As the earnings on cash values fell, so did policy death benefits, accumulations, and the enthusiasm of the owners of universal life. Despite its difficulties, however, universal life has made it acceptable for insurance companies to offer products in which the advantage of competitive rates of interest in return for acceptance of some fluctuation in traditional guarantees is presented.

.022 Emergence of interest-rate-sensitive whole life

A variation of the whole life policy, based on the universal life concept, next surfaced and came to be known as "interest-rate-sensitive" whole life. In this type of policy, the rate of interest credited to cash value is guaranteed by the insurance company for a specific period of time, such as one to five years. The resulting decrease in volatility of face value and cash accumulation makes this variation more appealing than universal life to many policy owners. The insurance company is not merely passing along a money market rate in this case, but has the potential to make a profit if it can earn more on its funds than it credits on the cash value or to suffer a loss if its investments produce less. The guarantee period is relatively short, however, which reduces the degree of risk in making the rate guarantee. As a result, it is possible for the insurance company to offer rates that are, at least initially, higher than the rates for money market funds. Consequently, the initial rate is considerably greater than that of the traditional whole life competitor. At the end of a guarantee period, if interest rates in the general economy are higher, the rate that the insurance company is able to offer may increase, causing a decrease in the premium for the next succeeding period of years. On the other hand, if outside interest rates have fallen, the policy owner may be given the choice between paying a higher premium or accepting a reduction in the policy death benefit.

Rather than the large initial payment associated with the universal life products first offered, the premium structure of the interest-rate-sensitive contract is annual or otherwise periodic and more nearly resembles that of traditional whole life. As a result, the accumulation of cash value does not tend to approach the minimum spread specified in Treasury regulations. It should not, therefore, be regarded as a disguised form of tax-deferred savings plan.

Does this make interest-rate-sensitive life insurance better than traditional whole life? The answer lies in a factor that can never be predicted: future interest rate trends. At the outset, the purchaser of the interest-rate-sensitive policy should pay less for the same amount of death benefit because the rate guaranteed for the initial period is greater than it is for the traditional whole life policy. If, after the policy is purchased, interest rates fall and remain relatively low for an extended period of time, the owner of a traditional, guaranteed whole life policy should wind up making a lower total cash outlay and maintaining a constant policy death benefit. In this situation, the owner of the interest-rate-sensitive contract should either pay more or accept a reduced death benefit or both. On the other hand, if rates of interest in the general economy rise and remain higher than rates prevailing at the inception of the policies, the cumulative amount paid by the purchaser of the interest-rate-sensitive contract should be considerably lower. If we believe that interest rates will never go in one direction and stay there, but will continuously fluctuate, we must accept the proposition that neither product is inherently superior.

Once a traditional whole life policy reaches paid-up status, the death benefit remains constant, and no future premiums are ever payable. Although the interest-rate-sensitive contract can reach a tentatively paid-up status, if interest rates fall, the insurance company may require the owner to make a choice between paying additional premiums or reducing the policy death benefit.

Either traditional whole life or the interest-rate-sensitive variety can be used in connection with an irrevocable life insurance trust. Ideally, the choice should be based on the grantor's preference either for the guarantees and stability associated with the traditional contract or for the possibility of lower total cost or higher death benefit for the same cost that may be had through the interest-rate-sensitive variety.

.023 Considerations respecting the Crummey *power*

There are, however, some special issues concerning the use of a life insurance trust that involves *Crummey* withdrawal powers.

First, since a limited amount of cash can be transferred to the trust without exceeding the total excluded from taxable gift status by the *Crummey* powers, selecting an interest-rate-sensitive product may result in a larger death benefit at the outset.

Also, if interest rates drop and the policy premium increases, the trust may be forced to accept a reduction in the death benefit. The alternative would be for the grantor to pay a larger amount to the trust in order to sustain the full policy. If this larger payment exceeds the amount covered by the *Crummey* powers, the grantor will have made a post-1976 taxable gift in the amount of the excess, which is then required to be added to the grantor's taxable estate upon death. Of greater concern is the potential GST result. Where the design of the irrevocable life insurance trust is such that distributions can constitute GST taxable distributions, a GST taxable termination or a direct skip, the result of a larger gift by the grantor is the necessity of allocated a greater amount of the grantor's GST exemption or a GST inclusion ratio in excess of zero. The latter would defeat one of the principal goals of the trust—complete avoidance of the GST system.

.024 Disappearing premiums

Universal life and interest-rate-sensitive policies, as well as traditional whole life contracts, have the potential to reach "paid-up" status. The number of premiums paid before this occurs depends on the age and health of the insured, the rate of interest credited on the policy cash value, and the amount by which the premium payment exceeds the pure cost of the life insurance coverage.

In recent years, a variation has been offered in which the amount of the premium is increased sufficiently to cause the policy to become paid up much more quickly. Some purchasers of life insurance find appealing the idea of paying premiums for a limited number of years in return for permanent coverage, even if it means that the amount of each year's premium is considerably higher than that charged for policies on which premium payments must be continued for life or for a long period of time. These are referred to by such terms as "disappearing premium" policies.

Suppose that a prospective life insurance applicant found out that the premium for a whole life policy would be $6,000 per year beginning at age 45 and continuing until death or until age 65, at which point paid-up status would be reached, and the applicant decided that the insurance protection was worth the outlay. If that applicant is told that he can pay $9,500 for the same amount of death benefit on a policy that becomes paid up after the eighth or ninth yearly premium is paid, which policy should he choose? The answer depends on the actual differences in premiums, the financial situation of the applicant, and the insurance coverage needed. Interest-rate-sensitive whole life can also be arranged to offer a kind of disappearing premium. However, if rates of interest fall, the premiums may have to be paid for a longer period of time than anticipated at the time of issuance.

A disappearing premium policy can be ideal within an irrevocable life insurance trust. If the amount of coverage required by the grantor to offset the potential estate tax can be purchased for a premium cost that can be transferred to the trust without exceeding the gift tax annual exclusions available through *Crummey* withdrawal powers, the grantor can cause the trust to become self-sufficient within a relatively short period of time. There is, however, one additional advantage. When the policy premiums disappear, if the value of the grantor's estate has increased so that it may be possible for the estate tax to exceed the death benefit of the policy owned by the trust fund, the grantor might consider purchase of an additional disappearing-premium policy.

.025 *Adding an insured in order to subtract premium cost*

The existence of the marital deduction makes it possible for married couples to eliminate any potential federal estate tax in the estate of the first deceased spouse. With careful planning, the estate tax imposed on the survivor's estate can be reduced through the use of bypass trusts, and the estate tax payable can be offset through life insurance held in an irrevocable life insurance trust.

If the estate plan can be designed to postpone payment of any estate tax until the death of the second spouse, it stands to reason that the life insurance trust that is designed to offset the estate tax can afford to postpone collection of policy proceeds until the surviving spouse dies.

The life insurance industry's product response to this fact is the second-to-die policy. This is a form of whole life policy on which there are two insureds, who are usually husband and wife. No death benefit is paid when the first spouse dies, regardless of the order of death. Instead, the death benefit is payable only after both insureds are deceased. Premium payments ordinarily continue after the death of the first spouse. There may be a disappearing-premium design, but the schedule of termination of premium payments is not affected by the first death.

The principal advantage of the second-to-die policy is that the premium cost is substantially reduced. The insurance company pays nothing until both insureds have died and the actuarial joint life expectancy of two people is always greater than that of one person, even if the two are the same age.

At the death of the first spouse, there may be a bypass trust and a marital share that can be distributed outright to the survivor or held in a marital deduction trust. Since premium payments must continue to be made on the second-to-die policy held in the irrevocable life insurance trust, the greatest advantage can be obtained if the second spouse voluntarily makes cash transfers to the trust rather than using funds from the bypass trust for this purpose. In this manner, the ongoing cost of maintaining the policy is taken from sources that are subject to tax at the death of the surviving spouse instead of from funds that bypass the second estate for estate tax purposes.

Given the informed choice between a regular whole life or interest-rate-sensitive whole life policy and a second-to-die policy, a significant number of grantors elect the regular policy. Despite the lower cost and other practical considerations, their rationale is:

(1) The life insurance proceeds collected upon the death of the first spouse may serve as a source of support, if needed, for the survivor.

(2) If support is not an issue, earnings on the insurance proceeds may be accumulated or the trust may be invested for growth. In this way, if the taxable estate of the surviving spouse grows after the death of the first spouse, there will be a larger, nontaxable pool of capital in the life insurance trust upon the death of the surviving spouse, which will offset the increased estate tax payable.

.026 Variable life

Universal life and interest-rate-sensitive whole life policies represent the introduction of an element of risk and reward to life insurance, an arena previously regarded as virtually risk free. The cash accumulation within these policies earns interest at rates that fluctuate with financial markets. The risk is that the interest rate earned over time may be less than originally expected. If so, the death benefit may be reduced, the premium amount may increase, more premiums may be payable, or the policy may even lapse. If the interest rate earned is greater than expected, rewards are realized in the form of higher cash value accumulation, resulting in reduced premiums or increased death benefit. In a sense, variable life goes one step further by permitting the policy owner to choose additional investment options for the cash accumulation portion of the policy. These investment options include the equivalent of longer maturity bond mutual funds and stock mutual funds. The result is greater potential for fluctuation in value, that is, increased risk and reward.

Variable life is comparable in some respects to universal life insurance. The premium paid exceeds the cost of the pure ART-type insurance coverage. The accumulating cash value, however, is placed in one or more of a series of investment funds that may be chosen by the policy owner. These funds are virtually identical to mutual funds, except that investments may only be placed in them through the purchase of a life insurance contract. As in the case of "families" of mutual funds offered through most fund management companies, many investment choices are available, including conservative or aggressive growth stock portfolios, U.S. government or corporate bond portfolios, money markets, and fixed accounts. The policy owner has the right to exchange part or all of the policy cash value between portfolios.

The insurance cost is deducted from the accumulating value of the variable life contract. Because of the nature of the investments involved, there is the potential for values to increase far more quickly than in any other form of life insurance policy. Investment gains and earnings are not subject to income tax as long as they are accumulated. If the investment performance is good, the policy owner may benefit through decreased or discontinued premiums or the policy's death benefit may be increased automatically. Poor investment results, however, may necessitate additional premium payments, a decreased death benefit, or a combination of both. It is possible to suffer a loss of investment principal within the cash value of a variable life insurance policy.

Opinions as to the advisability of variable life are divided. There are those who feel that life insurance, by its very nature and in view of its primary purpose, should be subject to little or no risk. For the prospective purchaser of life insurance whose financial resources are adequate, and who has a fair understanding of the potential risks and rewards, variable life may be perfectly appropriate.

In the context of the irrevocable life insurance trust, variable life has its place. This type of trust is only indicated in estate plans where the level of wealth is significant to begin with, so that there is some level of risk tolerance. The following attributes would tend to support the decision to place a variable life policy within an insurance trust:

(1) The grantor's assets, outside of the trust fund, include a significant amount of growth-oriented investments, making it likely that the

ultimate potential estate tax will increase. Since successful investment results within the variable life policy can result in an increasing death benefit, the grantor may believe that this potential justifies the fluctuations in the policy cash value and the death benefit that are certain to occur.

(2) The grantor's total financial resources are sufficiently extensive so that the investment income generated exceeds living expense requirements by a margin that is likely to result in a constant, gradual increase in estate value and, therefore, in potential estate tax.

¶ 605 FUNDED IRREVOCABLE LIFE INSURANCE TRUSTS

Some clients wish to place other assets, in addition to insurance policies, in an irrevocable life insurance trust so that the fund itself is capable of paying the insurance premiums as they come due. This section explores methods of "funding" the insurance trust and various tax consequences.

.01 Making the Trust Self-Supporting—Single Premium Whole Life as a Funding Choice

The purpose of "funding" a life insurance trust, that is, placing cash or other financial assets in the trust fund during the lifetime of the grantor, is to make the trust self-sufficient in the sense that it can pay the ongoing life insurance premiums from the income and principal of the trust itself. This eliminates the need for annual gifts of cash to the trust and the cumbersome procedures of the *Crummey* withdrawal power.

The amount needed to assure that the life insurance premiums will continue to be paid varies according to the age of the grantor-insured, the type of life insurance purchased, and the plan regarding maintenance of principal. If the intention is to pay the premiums from the trust income and keep trust principal intact, a larger amount of principal is required. Instead, the grantor may wish to direct the trustee to use principal as necessary if it is clear from the terms of the policy that it will become paid up before the entire trust fund is depleted.

Another alternative is the use of single premium whole life insurance. In the discussion of unfunded life insurance trusts at ¶ 604, it was pointed out that single premium whole life is not necessarily appropriate because the difference or "spread" between the single premium payment and the death benefit is intentionally kept to a minimum. Since a primary advantage of the insurance trust is causing that spread to escape estate tax and GST, single premium whole life does not seem to be the best choice. Some might want to use this alternative, however, in view of the following advantages:

(1) Avoidance of the need to transfer cash or investments to the trust fund with ongoing concern about the ability of the trust investments to produce enough income to maintain the life insurance. In the case of single premium life, it is as if income is being earned on the large portion of the single premium not immediately used for the true insurance cost. This income continues to pay for the coverage. In the case of a fixed single premium policy, the insurance company guarantees that the income will always be sufficient to keep the stated death benefit of the policy in force. With a variable single premium life policy, if the invest-

ment performance is good, the death benefit, as well as the cash value, may increase. Poor investment performance can result in a drop in value, but the policy holder can elect to maintain the death benefit by permitting greater consumption of the remaining cash value base or reducing the death benefit in order to prevent cash value deterioration.

(2) Freedom from income tax reporting requirements. The internal cash buildup that occurs within a single premium whole life insurance policy is not subject to income tax during the period of accumulation. If the only asset within a funded irrevocable life insurance trust is a single premium whole life policy, the trust has no reportable taxable income.

.02 Income Tax Considerations and Their Impact on Investment Alternatives

Almost any form of savings or other investment can be placed in a funded irrevocable life insurance trust. Income tax considerations during the grantor's lifetime cannot be ignored, although the overall estate planning objective of the grantor should be the principal motivating factor.

The fact that the trust income can be used to pay premiums on any life insurance policy in which the grantor or grantor's spouse is the insured causes the trust to fall under the "grantor" trust rules discussed in Chapter 3. Where the grantor is the named insured, as is the case in an irrevocable life insurance trust, all items of income, credit, and deduction resulting from trust transactions are reportable on the grantor's personal income tax return. Considerations that may affect trust investment decisions are discussed below.

(1) Municipal bonds may be a logical choice for some of these trusts. The tax-exempt character of the interest that these bonds produce remains tax exempt in the grantor's hands so that there is no federal income tax consequence. Unless the bonds are called prior to maturity, the annual income which they produce is constant and predictable in amount. If the trust holds a traditional whole life insurance policy, it is possible to transfer a specific principal amount of municipal bonds to the trust, which will produce just enough income to pay the insurance premiums.

(2) The trust may hold a form of disappearing-premium whole life. In that case, one investment choice is a series of zero coupon bonds. These investment instruments are purchased at a discount from face value based on a combination of the length of time to maturity and the bond's rate of interest. The bonds pay no periodic interest but accumulate until the stated maturity date, at which time the full face amount is paid.

Where the trust holds a disappearing-premium policy, it is a simple matter to purchase one zero coupon bond corresponding with each future policy premium to be paid. There are zero coupon bonds available with maturities ranging from just a few months to more than 21 years.

Transfers to irrevocable life insurance trusts constitute taxable gifts, and, in the case of a funded life insurance trust, the amount transferred is likely to exceed any available gift tax annual exclusion. If a series of zero coupon bonds is used as the investment base, the deep discount feature results in a lower total beginning principal amount.

Example: A trust purchases a disappearing-premium whole life policy on a grantor's life with a face value of $750,000. The policy requires eight premium payments of $9,000 each, for a total of $72,000. The grantor transfers $9,000 to the trust in order to pay the first premium and transfers an additional sum of $58,361 to enable the trustee to pay the seven remaining premiums, which total $63,000. Seven zero coupon bonds each with a maturity value of $9,000 are purchased, with one maturing each year for the next seven years, carrying an average yield to maturity of 6.5 percent. The total present cost of these bonds is $58,361.

As a result of this transaction, the grantor has completed funding of an irrevocable life insurance trust that will make available $750,000 to provide income to his family during the lifetime of his surviving spouse and to offset the estate tax that will be imposed upon the death of the survivor. Although the total cost of the insurance is $72,000, the total taxable gifts made by the grantor (assuming that no part of the value transferred is covered by the gift tax annual exclusion) is $67,361.

If the zero coupon bonds purchased are issued by the U.S. government or by corporations, the interest on all of the bonds is subject to income tax each year, even though only one of the bonds makes a maturity payment in any single year. The income tax is imposed on the grantor. The trust could purchase tax-exempt municipal zero coupon bonds instead; however, the yield to maturity would be smaller, making a larger initial taxable gift transfer to the trust necessary. From an estate tax viewpoint, the grantor's payment of the income tax on trust investments has the beneficial effect of preventing the grantor from accumulating additional wealth only to pay even more estate tax in the future.

(3) A totally different strategy focuses on causing the assets of a funded irrevocable life insurance trust to perform double duty—pay the life insurance premiums and also generate principal growth outside the taxable estate of the grantor.

Consider the above example involving a life insurance policy with a face value of $750,000 and a disappearing premium of $9,000. Instead of trying to determine the minimum amount needed for the trust to pay the insurance premiums, the grantor might try to figure out the maximum amount that he can afford to transfer to the trust fund without hampering his own financial security. If that happens to be $300,000, for instance, the rate of investment return needed to pay the insurance premium is only three percent of the available principal.

With these proportions to work with, the trustee can structure an investment program with a primary emphasis on growth of principal and a secondary emphasis on income. If the grantor lives for 20 years and the trust averages a rate of growth of five percent in addition to the income produced during that time, the trust principal, excluding the life insurance proceeds, will be approximately $796,000. Upon the death of the grantor, the only estate tax impact is the add-back to the grantor's taxable estate of the post-1976 taxable gift in the amount of $300,000, even though the trust value including the life insurance proceeds should exceed $1,500,000.

.03 Funded Irrevocable Life Insurance Trusts and GST Planning

If the plan of distribution of an irrevocable life insurance trust is to make all distributions, including the remainder, to the spouse and children of the grantor, GST does not apply.

Where the design of the trust is such that it is possible for future distributions to constitute GST taxable events, care must be taken at the time assets are transferred to the trust fund. Because comparatively large amounts are needed in order to make the trust self-sufficient in paying insurance premiums, it is not uncommon for transfers to the trust to exceed the available gift tax annual exclusions. Since the GST annual exclusion is not available based on transfers subject to the *Crummey* withdrawal power, the entire amount transferred affects the future GST calculation. It is possible for the grantor to allocate some or all of the $1,000,000 GST exemption in order to cover the funding of the life insurance trust. If this step is not taken or if the value placed in the trust exceeds the sum of available annual exclusions plus the GST exemption, then in addition to a present gift tax liability, future trust distributions to skip persons will be subject to GST.

> **Example:** A establishes an irrevocable life insurance trust, designated as the owner and beneficiary of a whole life insurance policy on A's life with a face value of $2,000,000 and an annual premium of $40,000. A also transfers $600,000 in cash to the trust in order to enable the trust fund to pay the ongoing life insurance premiums. The trust provides that, after A's death, the income is to be paid to A's spouse for life, then life income to A's children in equal shares for their lives, with the remainder in equal shares to A's grandchildren.

In this situation, A might have elected not to include *Crummey* withdrawal powers because it would have been clear that the value transferred to the trust far exceeds the available gift tax annual exclusions. In view of the large sum placed in the trust, it might have been A's purpose to prevent any actual withdrawals from the trust fund until after his death. With no *Crummey* powers, considering the fact that no beneficiary is actually entitled to receive any distributions until after A's death, no part of the value transferred to the trust by A can qualify as a present interest in property. A could have made the decision to utilize the unified credit in order to prevent the payment of any gift tax at the time of the transfer and in consideration of the substantial estate tax savings that might result from keeping the life insurance proceeds free of estate tax in both his own estate and that of his spouse.

If A does not allocate a sufficient amount of his GST exemption to this transfer in order to cause the trust to have an inclusion ratio of zero, there is no present tax liability. The gift tax is eliminated by the unified credit. Assuming that A lives for at least three years after establishing the trust fund, the death benefit should also be excluded from A's taxable estate. However, the future GST liability will severely diminish the distribution of the remainder among the grandchildren.

For the sake of this example, assume that at distribution of the remainder, the principal of the trust has neither appreciated nor diminished in value so that it is equal to the amount of the original cash transferred by A plus the life insurance proceeds collected at A's death, for a total of $2,600,000.

In order to calculate the GST payable, it is first necessary to compute the inclusion ratio:

$$\frac{\text{GST exemption allocated to original transfer in trust by A}}{\text{Value of subject transfer}} \times \frac{0}{\$600{,}000} = 0.0 \text{ Applicable Fraction}$$

When the applicable fraction is subtracted from the number 1, the result is an inclusion ratio of 1 or 100 percent. At the distribution of the remainder, GST is calculated as follows:

$2,600,000	×	(55%	×	1.0)	=	$1,430,000
Value of remainder which is a taxable termination for GST purposes		GST Rate		Inclusion Ratio		GST Payable

It is noteworthy that the GST payable is more than 200 percent of the original amount of cash transferred by A, which was the only cash transfer to the trust. This result occurred even though there was no appreciation of trust principal because:

(1) The GST inclusion ratio is calculated at the time of the original transfer, in this case, at the funding of the irrevocable life insurance trust.

(2) If no part of the grantor's GST exemption is allocated to the transfer, while there is no present gift tax payable due to the unified credit, the future and severe GST consequences are fixed. The creation of an unfavorable GST inclusion ratio cannot be changed.

(3) The GST amount payable is exacerbated by the fact that the life insurance proceeds are included in the taxable base upon which the GST is calculated.

Life insurance proceeds that have successfully avoided the federal estate tax may be caught by the GST in either of two ways. Besides the failure to allocate the grantor's available GST exemption to the initial funding transfer, the total value transferred to the irrevocable life insurance trust may exceed the exemption. However, unless the excess is substantial, the part of the trust fund eventually consumed by GST cannot begin to approach the proportion illustrated in the example above.

Chapter 7

Charitable Trusts

¶701 OVERVIEW

It is possible to establish a trust fund for the direct and exclusive benefit of charities. Such trusts are governed by the same rules that apply to private foundations. Unlike trust funds created to benefit family members or other noncharitable beneficiaries, charitable trusts are not limited by the rule against perpetuities.

The definition of a charitable gift under the tax law is surprisingly broad in scope. It includes gifts to the United States and its possessions, to any state or political subdivision of a state or the District of Columbia, and to organizations usually regarded as charitable in nature. If it is to be recognized as a charity, an organization's existence must be for religious, scientific, literary, and educational purposes or for the prevention of cruelty to children or animals. This listing is not exclusive, and there are some limitations as well. Qualification for charitable status cannot be achieved if private individuals can receive or share in an organization's profits or if the organization engages in political activities.

Gifts by individuals to charity are generally allowed as itemized deductions for income tax purposes up to a maximum of 50 percent of the donor's adjusted gross income.[1] In the case of gifts of appreciated property, where capital gain would have been recognized had the asset been sold, the donor may deduct the full fair market value and is not required to pay tax on the appreciation. However, the income tax deduction is limited to 30 percent of the donor's adjusted gross income for these in-kind donations.[2] The donor can elect a trade-off, however. If the income tax deduction for appreciated property is based on the cost basis, the maximum deduction goes back to the 50 percent of adjusted gross income level.[3] Not all appreciated property yields a charitable deduction equal to its fair market value. Any difference between cost basis and fair market value that would not have resulted in capital gain upon sale of the property is not deductible.[4] This limits the income tax deduction for inventory (that is, for items held for sale to customers in the ordinary course of business) to its cost basis, and it reduces the available deduction for many types of business property for which depreciation is allowed.

If the amount or value of the donor's charitable contributions exceeds the 50 or 30 percent limit, the excess is carried forward and treated as a charitable contribution in the succeeding year. Subject to the same percentage limitations, excess charitable contributions may be carried forward for up to a maximum of five years.

Gifts to charity are fully deductible for gift tax purposes, and there are no percentage limitations.[5] A full estate tax deduction is allowed for bequests and

---

[1] Code Sec. 170(b)(1)(A).
[2] Code Sec. 170(b)(1)(B).
[3] Code Sec. 170(b)(1)(C)(iii).
[4] Code Sec. 170(e)(1)(A).
[5] Code Sec. 2522.

nonprobate transfers to charity, such as the designation of a charity as the beneficiary under a life insurance policy or IRA.[6]

Charitable trusts may also be designed to provide some benefits to family members or other individuals separately from the trust's charitable distributions. Under specific rules of the Internal Revenue Code, income, estate, and gift tax benefits are available even though the trust is not held exclusively for charitable purposes. In general, these trusts must provide for a charitable interest that arises either before or after that of the noncharitable beneficiaries. Because of this temporal division or splitting of beneficial interests, these trusts are described as "split-interest" trusts. Where trust distributions are made first to the noncharitable beneficiaries followed by the distribution of the remainder to a charity, the trust is described as a "charitable remainder trust" (CRT).[7] Where the order of benefits is reversed, so that trust benefits are payable to a charity for some period of time followed by the remainder distribution to the family member, the trust is called a "front-end charitable trust" or a "charitable lead trust."[8] Since these forms of charitable trust have the most direct application in family trust and estate planning, this chapter is devoted exclusively to the split-interest charitable trusts.

Charitable split-interest trusts presented a significant problem prior to 1969. Before then, the Internal Revenue Code permitted income, gift, and estate tax advantages even if these trusts allowed discretionary distributions to the noncharitable beneficiary.

> **Example:** A transfers $100,000 to a charitable remainder trust established to pay the income to A's daughter, D, for life, with the remainder to A's favorite charity. The trustee is also directed to make principal distributions from the trust fund for D's education, health, and support.

The design of this trust is straightforward. It appears to be motivated by the desire to give a substantial benefit to the charity after providing a lifetime source of financial support to D. The problem is that, at the inception of the trust, it is very difficult to determine what, if anything, the charity will ever receive. If D goes on to higher education, including a graduate or professional program, or if D falls victim to a prolonged illness or is incapacitated so that she cannot work, the trustee might find it necessary to distribute most or all of the principal of the trust fund to D or to spend it for her needs. If A receives a charitable income tax, gift, or estate tax benefit on the presumption that part of the value transferred to the trust would eventually pass to charity, it would be impractical to require A or A's estate to recapture the tax benefit. Prior to 1969, there were many instances of serious disagreement between the IRS and taxpayers as to what part, if any, of the value transferred to a split-interest trust should be deductible as a charitable transfer. Precise valuation was impossible because of the inherent uncertainty as to whether or not discretionary principal distributions would be made. For this reason, the Tax Reform Act of 1969 created very specific requirements for split-interest charitable trusts to qualify for tax deductions. This results in the need for extraordinary caution in the preparation of charitable split-interest trust documents. Unless an entire checklist of detailed provisions appears in the will or trust agreement, the expected tax saving is lost. This makes work in the charitable split-interest trust area a demanding subspecialty within the estate planning field.

---

[6] Code Sec. 2055(a) and (d).

[7] Code Sec. 664.

[8] Code Sec. 170(f)(2)(B).

The term of a split-interest charitable trust can vary considerably. For the charitable remainder types, distributions must be made to a noncharitable beneficiary for life, for the joint lives of two or more persons, or for a specified period of time. The time period for those trusts that are not based on one or more lifetimes may not exceed 20 years. At the conclusion of the noncharitable interest, the trust may continue to make income distributions to one or more qualified charities, even in perpetuity. Charitable lead trusts are not subject to a limitation on the number of years during which trust distributions are paid to charity.

Split-interest trusts can be inter vivos or testamentary. The tax benefits for transfers to these trusts vary according to when and how the trust is established and the length and nature of the charitable and noncharitable beneficial interests.

¶ 702 CHARITABLE REMAINDER TRUSTS

The Internal Revenue Code[9] defines two categories of charitable remainder trust (CRT): the charitable remainder annuity trust and the charitable remainder unitrust. The difference between the two types of trusts involves the amount payable to the noncharitable beneficiary. Certain requirements for qualification are common to both types of CRT. There are a number of highly technical clauses that must be included in the trust document in order to meet the standards established in the tax law. Highlights of the common requirements are listed below.

(1) All charitable remainder trusts must make a distribution to a noncharitable beneficiary during each year prior to the remainder distribution to charity.

(2) The amount of this annual distribution must be specific and may not be related to the income that the trust produces.

(3) During the term of the trust, no amounts may be paid other than the specified annual amount. This means that it is not possible to permit discretionary distributions from a CRT according to an ascertainable standard relating to health or support needs of a beneficiary or in case of extraordinary financial emergency.

(4) At the conclusion of the noncharitable trust term, there must be either an outright distribution of the remainder to a qualified charity or the trust must continue exclusively for charitable purposes.

If the only noncharitable beneficiaries are the grantor and the grantor's spouse, the unified transfer tax consequences are quite favorable.

(1) The value attributable to the grantor's interest is not subject to tax.

(2) The value attributable to the spouse's interest qualifies for the marital deduction.[10]

(3) The value of the trust is not included in the taxable estate of the non-grantor spouse.[11]

It is permissible to provide that two or more consecutive noncharitable beneficiaries, other than the grantor and spouse, are to receive annual pay-

[9] Code Sec. 664.

[10] Code Secs. 2056(b)(8) and 2523(g).

[11] Code Sec. 2044.

ments prior to the charitable distribution. In that case, more complex actuarial calculations are used to obtain the factors for valuing the remainder and the interim interests.[12]

When a charitable remainder trust is created, there must be a realistic likelihood that something will pass to or for the benefit of charity at some point in the future. A trust cannot qualify if the mathematical probability that any remainder amount will pass to charity does not exceed five percent.[13]

Charitable remainder trusts are subject to certain penalty taxes, which are also imposed on private foundations, for acts of self-dealing[14] and for certain expenditures, such as expenditures to influence legislation.[15]

.01 Charitable Remainder Annuity Trust

In the annuity version of the qualified CRT, the annual sum paid to the noncharitable beneficiary is a constant dollar amount calculated as a percentage of the initial value placed in the trust fund.[16] The grantor determines the percentage, which is stated in the terms of the trust document. It must be no less than five percent. The amount determined by multiplying the specified percentage by the initial value of the trust remains the same each year. The noncharitable payout amount does not change if the principal value of the trust increases or decreases.

If the grantor chooses a relatively small percentage and the total interest or other investment earnings of the trust exceed the noncharitable payout, the excess is accumulated within the principal of the trust fund and ultimately inures to the benefit of the charity. If the trust earns less than the amount needed to make the required noncharitable distributions, the deficit is paid out of trust principal.

After a charitable remainder annuity trust has been established and cash or investments have been placed in the trust fund, the controlling document must prohibit any subsequent additional transfers into the trust fund. Apparently this requirement exists because it is not permissible to modify the annual annuity payout amount. Therefore, subsequent additions to the fund would have a distorting effect.

.02 Charitable Remainder Unitrust

The main difference between the charitable remainder annuity trust and the unitrust is that the amount paid from the unitrust to the noncharitable beneficiary can change each year, whereas that amount remains constant in the charitable remainder annuity trust.

The noncharitable annual payment from a unitrust is a fixed percentage of the principal value of the trust fund.[17] The percentage is set by the grantor under the terms of the trust document. As with the charitable remainder annuity trust, the unitrust annual payout must be five percent or more. However, this percentage is applied to the total value of the trust fund as

---

[12] IRS Publication No. 1457, "Actuarial Values Alpha Volume" (1989); IRS Publication No. 1458, "Actuarial Values Beta Volume" (1989); and IRS Publication No. 1459, "Actuarial Values Gamma Volume" (1989).

[13] Reg. § 20.2055-2(b). See also Rev. Ruls. 70-452, 1970-2 CB 199, and 77-374, 1977-2 CB 329.

[14] Code Sec. 4941.

[15] Code Sec. 4945.

[16] Code Sec. 664(d)(1).

[17] Code Sec. 664(d)(2).

recomputed in each year of the unitrust. If the fund increases in value, the amount payable to the noncharitable beneficiary increases; if the value of the trust fund falls, the payment to the beneficiary is reduced. In the ordinary unitrust, the annual payout amount is not tied in to the trust income. The unitrust must accumulate any income earned in excess of the payout amount. These accumulations result in an increase in the total value of the unitrust, which causes a higher unitrust payout amount in future years. The opposite may also occur. If the payout amount exceeds the income earned, the trustee is required to make up the difference from the principal of the trust fund. This diminishes the total value of the trust, causing a lower payout amount in future years. In a sense, the inherent nature of the charitable remainder unitrust permits greater flexibility in planning. The potential grantor can choose a payout percentage that is small enough to result in excess income being generated by the unitrust. As a result, the value of the trust fund is likely to increase gradually, from year to year. Unlike the annuity trust in which increases in the total value benefit the charitable remainder exclusively, this gives the noncharitable beneficiary a constantly increasing unitrust payout amount. In this manner, the grantor can plan on helping the beneficiary cope with the potential consequences of inflation.

Unlike the charitable remainder annuity trust, it is permissible to make additional contributions to a charitable remainder unitrust after the initial funding. Such additions increase the total value that affects the amount of the annual payment to the noncharitable beneficiary.

There is an alternative type of unitrust as well. This may be referred to as the "income maximum" type.[18] In this variation, the trust document directs the yearly distribution of a specified percentage of the annually recomputed value of the trust fund to the noncharitable beneficiary. As in the case of the other CRTs, the annual payout percentage equals or exceeds five percent. However, this type of CRT provides that, if the actual accounting net income of the trust is less than the amount of the unitrust payout, the trustee is to distribute only the net income. The trustee keeps a record of the unitrust deficit (that is, the difference between the unitrust percentage payout amount and the income actually distributed to the noncharitable beneficiary) for each year in which a unitrust deficit occurs. If, in any future year of the trust, the accounting net income exceeds the unitrust percentage payout amount, then in addition to that year's unitrust payout amount, the trustee distributes to the noncharitable beneficiary the lesser of:

(1) the excess of the current year's accounting net income over the current year's unitrust percentage payout amount; or

(2) the cumulative amount of unitrust deficits, not previously distributed, from the preceding trust years.

The income maximum type of charitable remainder unitrust offers more planning advantages and more flexibility than any other type of CRT. This trust allows for some assurance that the principal will remain intact, which can be an important objective of the grantor. If the property placed in trust does not produce enough income to support the required unitrust payout, principal assets do not have to be sold in order to make up the shortage. The characteristics of this CRT also make it possible to structure a trust investment program that offers more flexibility in coping with inflation. If the

[18] Code Sec. 664(d)(3).

trustee initially invests for growth, choosing, for instance, low dividend paying quality growth stocks, it is likely that unitrust deficits will build up in the early years of the program. In fact, the more successful the investment program, the greater the unitrust deficits are likely to be. Subsequently, after the value of the CRT fund has increased and perhaps when the noncharitable beneficiary's needs are greater due to inflation, the trustee can change the investment mix in order to generate a higher income flow. Growth of trust fund value will have brought about an increase in the unitrust percentage payout amount. However, even if the trust income exceeds the current year's unitrust payout requirement, the accumulated unitrust deficits will make it possible for the trustee to pay the excess income to the noncharitable beneficiary.

> **Example:** G, who is now age 55, plans to retire in 10 years, at age 65. One of G's intentions is to leave a substantial portion of his estate to his alma mater. G establishes a charitable remainder trust to which he contributes $100,000 in cash. The trust directs unitrust payments to G of five percent each year, with the remainder to be distributed at G's death outright to his alma mater. If the accounting net income (ANI) of the trust is insufficient to pay the unitrust amount in any year, only the amount of ANI is distributed. In any year in which ANI exceeds the unitrust payout, the excess ANI is distributed to the extent of any prior year's built-up deficits.

If the applicable federal rate in effect at the time the trust is funded is eight percent, G receives a present charitable deduction of $39,678 as explained at .03, below. The trust fund can be invested for growth or accumulation so that no ANI is produced during the 10-year period prior to G's retirement. As a result, no distributions are made to G during that time, but the trust builds up a large reserve amount of unitrust payout deficits. At G's retirement, the trust fund can be reinvested so that it begins to produce ANI.

Suppose the trustee invests the entire fund in U.S. government zero coupon bonds with a 6.5 percent yield and a maturity date near the time G plans to retire. By then, the trust fund will have accumulated $162,887. Because no ANI is produced by the zero coupon bonds, the trust will have a reserve of unitrust payout deficits of about $62,000. At G's retirement, the fund can be invested to produce ANI. If the level of income is seven percent, the entire amount, about $11,400, is distributed to G because of the lack of payments in previous years. In fact, it should take almost 20 years for the trust to make up all of the built-up deficits it "owes" G. Meanwhile, G will be receiving annual distributions in excess of 11 percent of his original contribution, and that does not take into account the effects of the income tax saving that G realizes from his initial charitable deduction.

.03 Tax Consequences upon Funding the CRT

For inter vivos CRTs, there are two tax benefits: (1) an income tax deduction for the actuarial present value of the remainder interest; and (2) a gift tax deduction of the same amount.

The relationship between the amount of the tax deductions and the fair market value of the assets placed in the CRT depends upon a combination of the annual percentage payout to the noncharitable beneficiary and the length of time for which the trust is likely to exist prior to its remainder distribution to charity. As determined by the grantor, the length of time may be a specific period of up to 20 years. If the trust lasts for one or more lifetime periods, life expectancy assumptions enter into the computation. The higher the annual noncharitable payout and the longer the length of time before the charitable remainder distribution, the smaller the percent of charitable deduction. Conversely, a lower noncharitable payout percentage and shorter term of existence of the trust result in larger charitable tax deductions. The actual amount of the charitable deduction is calculated, under the rules of Code Sec. 7520, with reference to the terms of the trust, the percentage payout to the noncharitable beneficiary, and the applicable federal rate. Where the term of the trust is based on one or more lives, life expectancy is used as the term. In addition to the government publications referred to at note 12, above, there are PC-based software programs available to assist in this regard, and the National Office of the Internal Revenue Service provides calculation assistance under some circumstances.

These are a few examples of income tax deductions involving the transfer of $100,000 to a charitable remainder unitrust with quarterly distributions based on an annual payout rate of five percent, where the applicable federal rate is eight percent:

Age of Noncharitable Beneficiary	*or*	*Specific Term of Trust*	*Deduction Factor*	*Amount of Charitable Deduction*
55		N/A	.35960	$35,960
70		N/A	.55851	55,851
N/A		10	.61367	61,367
N/A		20	.37661	37,661

Transfers in kind to an inter vivos CRT result in a special income tax benefit to the grantor. The factor for the present value of the charitable remainder is applied to the full fair market value of the property transferred in order to determine the grantor's tax deductions, even if that value exceeds the grantor's cost basis. The grantor is not required to report the excess of the asset's fair market value over its cost basis as taxable gain. An exception to this favorable result is certain property that is subject to mortgages. Where the outstanding mortgage loan balance exceeds the grantor's cost basis in the property and where the grantor is relieved of liability on the loan at the time of the transfer to the trust, the grantor must report taxable income resulting from the elimination of the indebtedness. Also, the transfer of appreciated property to a CRT must be completed before the process of selling the asset begins, and it must be the trustee who makes the decision to sell and who initiates the sale process. Otherwise, the grantor is subject to personal income tax on the gain. In the case of property transferred in kind to a CRT where the fair market value is less than the grantor's cost basis, the charitable deduction is limited to the product of multiplying the appropriate actuarial factor by the asset's fair market value. Therefore, the grantor should derive a greater overall tax benefit by selling the asset, recognizing a tax loss, and using the cash proceeds of sale to fund the CRT.

The use of the CRT as a means of avoiding capital gain on the sale of appreciated assets has gained popularity in recent years, to the extent that some advisers recommend it as a planning technique even for clients who have little or no charitable motivation. The combination of an up-front charitable income tax deduction plus elimination of tax on a large potential capital gain act as a strong inducement. The disadvantages are:

(1) loss of access to the principal of the trust fund; and

(2) removal of the money or property transferred to the trust from the estate of the grantor that is ultimately available for distribution to children or other noncharitable beneficiaries.

As a trade-off for the grantor's loss of access to the principal, it is possible to choose a comparatively high percentage payout, subject to the requirement that the probability of a charitable remainder must exceed five percent, as explained at .05, below.

In addition, life insurance, owned either directly by noncharitable beneficiaries or by an irrevocable trust, can be used to replace part or all of the inheritance that might otherwise have passed to children or others were it not for the use of the CRT. The use of life insurance in tandem with the CRT has come to be known as the "wealth replacement" strategy.

The funding of a testamentary CRT occurs after the death of the testator, whose will provides for the split-interest bequest and establishes the trust terms. The decedent's estate receives a federal estate tax deduction for a portion of the value given to the CRT, calculated in the same manner as the gift tax charitable deduction for inter vivos CRTs. However, the estate is not entitled to an income tax deduction for the actuarial value of the remainder. Cost basis issues and potential taxable gain are not generally as prevalent because of the basis step-up of assets within a decedent's estate which occurs upon death.

.04 CRT as a Separate Taxable Entity and Income Taxation of the Noncharitable Beneficiary

The CRT is a separate taxpayer under the fiduciary income tax system, as opposed to a grantor trust subject to the substantial ownership rules.

The CRT virtually never pays income tax. An ordinary trust fund is entitled to a deduction for distributions to beneficiaries but pays income tax on any income that is accumulated and also on capital gains in most cases. The CRT simply is not subject to income tax except to the extent that it generates unrelated business taxable income and income from debt-laden property in certain cases. The CRT does not need to claim a deduction for distributions to beneficiaries because the trust is not subject to income tax. However, the CRT is required to report the amount and nature of all distributions to noncharitable beneficiaries. There is a special tier system with respect to the flow of income through the CRT. Specifically, the trust must treat amounts distributed to the beneficiary as described below.

First Category: The distribution must consist of ordinary taxable income produced by the trust to the extent of the trust's current-year taxable income plus taxable income produced by the trust in prior years, to the extent that these amounts of accumulated income were not previously treated as distributed.

Second Category: If the distribution exceeds the amounts specified in the first category, the excess is treated as capital gain produced by the trust for the current trust year plus any capital gain of the trust for prior years that was not previously treated as distributed.

Third Category: If the distribution exceeds the sum of the amounts specified in the first and second categories, the excess is treated as other income of the trust for the current year plus undistributed amounts of other income from prior years. This would include any tax-exempt municipal bond interest. If so, the tax-exempt quality is retained in the hands of the noncharitable beneficiary.

Fourth Category: If the distribution exceeds the sum of the amounts specified in all of the previous categories, the excess is treated as a principal distribution that is not taxable income to the recipient.

To some, tax-exempt municipal bonds are a natural choice of investment for CRTs. If the interest produced by these bonds is the only income generated by the trust and if this interest income equals or exceeds the required CRT annual distribution, all annual payouts to the noncharitable beneficiary are free of income tax. The comparative safety of the principal of municipal bonds provides good security of the remainder for the benefit of the charity. This scenario conflicts with another popular technique—funding the trust with appreciated property. The capital gain generated within the CRT upon the sale of these assets would create a large pool of second-category taxable income that would postpone the effects of the tax-exempt quality of annual distributions to the beneficiary.

> **Example:** A creates a charitable remainder annuity trust which is required to distribute six percent of the initial fair market value of the trust to A's nephew, N, for life. Upon N's death, the trust remainder is to be distributed to Alma Mater University, a qualified charity. A transfers common stocks to the trust with a cost basis of $50,000 and a fair market value of $200,000. The trustee sells the stocks and reinvests the proceeds in municipal bonds yielding six percent annual interest.

The trust generates $150,000 of capital gain through its first investment transactions, but no income tax is payable because the gain is recognized within the CRT. Since the fair market value of the assets transferred to the trust is $200,000, and the annuity payout is six percent per year, the trustee is required to distribute $12,000 to N. The annual payout can be made from the interest produced by the municipal bonds. However, all annual payouts to N are treated as taxable capital gain for approximately the first 12 years of the trust, until the total second-category income created by the initial stock sale is exhausted.

.05 Combination QTIP and CRT

It is possible to eliminate all gift and estate tax on a transfer to a CRT where the only noncharitable beneficiary is the grantor's spouse or where the grantor and spouse are joint and survivor noncharitable beneficiaries. The yearly CRT payout amounts are treated as the equivalent of the spouse's lifetime income interest in qualified terminable interest property by special provision of the Internal Revenue Code. Therefore, the excess of the total value transferred over the portion of the value for which a charitable deduction is allowed, qualifies for the marital deduction. The sum of the QTIP marital deduction plus the charitable gift deduction is equal to 100 percent of the value transferred.

¶703 CHARITABLE LEAD TRUSTS

A trust may be established to make annual distributions to charity, followed by the distribution of the remainder to a noncharitable beneficiary. In other words, the beneficial interests of the charity and the noncharitable beneficiaries are reversed by comparison to the CRT. There are actually two different designs of charitable lead trust possible. In the first, there is an immediate income tax deduction for the actuarial present value of the present charitable interest, but the grantor is treated as the substantial owner of the trust during the charitable term. In the second, the grantor receives no immediate charitable income tax deduction, but the trust is treated as a separate taxable entity and the grantor does not include the trust income on his personal income tax return.

.01 Immediate Income Tax Deduction Charitable Lead Trust

The Internal Revenue Code[19] permits the grantor to take an income tax deduction for the actuarial present value of the present interest passing to charity. The deduction is based on the amount of money or value of property placed in trust, valued as of the date of transfer. The deduction takes into account the term of the trust, the amount that is distributed to charity, and the applicable federal rate as required by Code Sec. 7520.

In order to qualify for this deduction, two specific requirements must be met:

(1) The charitable beneficiary and the noncharitable beneficiary of a CRT must receive the same type of payout. In other words, the charity must receive an annual payout that is either an annuity payout or a unitrust payout.

(2) The grantor must be treated as the substantial owner of the trust under the fiduciary income tax rules.

The overall effect of these requirements is to give the grantor an income tax deduction with one hand and take it away with the other. The grantor receives what may be a substantial income tax deduction when the money or property is placed in the charitable lead trust. However, during the years in which the trust is being held for charity, prior to the distribution of its remainder to noncharitable beneficiaries, the grantor must include all items of income and deduction flowing from the trust in his personal income. As a general rule, this means that, if the grantor's income tax bracket remains constant in the year of transfer to the trust and subsequent years, the amount of income tax saved through the initial deduction should approximate the amount of income tax "paid back" because of the inclusion of the income tax on the grantor's personal return during the years of the trust's charitable distributions. The grantor could establish a charitable lead trust in a year for which he is subject to the highest income tax bracket and could include the trust income in his taxable income in years for which he is subject to the lowest tax rate. Receiving a substantial payout of deferred compensation or redemption of a business ownership interest are examples of situations that present this kind of planning opportunity.

The grantor trust or substantial ownership rules of fiduciary income taxation (Code Secs. 671–678) are applied on a year-by-year basis. It is

[19] Code Sec. 170(f)(2).

possible that the trust could cease being treated as a grantor trust during the charitable term. If so, the grantor is required to recapture part of his initial charitable income tax deduction. The recapture amount is computed by subtracting the remaining actuarial value of the charity's income interest, calculated as of the date on which the trust is no longer a grantor trust, from the amount of the charitable deduction previously allowed.

One trust design that causes the grantor to be treated as the substantial owner is a reversion to the grantor at the conclusion of the charitable term, so long as the actuarial value of the reversion exceeds five percent of the initial value transferred into the trust. This type of trust could be used by the grantor who:

(1) wishes to give an immediate benefit to charity; and

(2) needs to have the corpus returned for his own support at some point in the future.

As long as the term of the trust is not so long that the reversion has a value of less than five percent and the inclusion of the taxable income during the years of the trust causes no distortion of the grantor's income tax bracket, the use of a charitable lead trust is indicated.

.02 Income Exclusion Charitable Lead Trust

If the design of the trust is such that the grantor is not treated as the substantial owner for income tax purposes, no immediate income tax charitable contribution deduction is allowed.[20] However, a gift tax charitable deduction is permitted for transfers to inter vivos charitable lead trusts, and an estate tax charitable deduction is permitted for transfers to testamentary charitable lead trusts so long as the initial charitable trust benefit is either in the form of a guaranteed annuity payment or is an annual payment equal to a specific percentage of the annual value of the trust.[21] These annual payout requirements parallel those of the noncharitable payments from a CRT but are not as specific. There is no minimum percentage annual payout requirement and no maximum length of years for the charitable payment period. Also, a longer charitable payout term and a higher annual payout amount result in a greater gift or estate charitable deduction.

The income exclusion charitable lead trust is taxable as a separate taxpayer for fiduciary income tax purposes. However, it is entitled to an income tax deduction, not limited by a maximum annual percentage, for amounts paid or permanently set aside for charity. If the charitable payout amount is equal to or greater than the trust's taxable income for any year, the trust's income tax liability is zero. If the trust has taxable income, including any capital gains, in excess of the charitable payout amount, the trust must pay income tax, and any excess ordinary income is subject to the fiduciary income tax accumulation distribution rules at the time the remainder is distributed.

The charitable gift or estate tax deduction allowed for an initial interest passing to charity results in the ability ultimately to transfer much higher sums to the noncharitable remaindermen. Where the trust qualifies for the income exclusion rather than the initial charitable deduction, the grantor's income tax consequences can actually be enhanced.

---

[20] Code Sec. 170(f)(2).

[21] Code Sec. 2522(c)(2)(B).

Example: C, who is widowed, has total assets of $3,000,000. Out of a total taxable income of $200,000 per year, C has been contributing approximately 60 percent or $120,000 to qualified charities. C wishes to continue to favor the same charitable organizations during his lifetime while leaving the bulk of his estate to his children.

C establishes a charitable lead trust to which he contributes $1,500,000. The trust is directed to pay an annuity of eight percent of the initial value of the trust, which is $120,000 per year, to qualified charities for a period of 15 years. Thereafter, the remainder is distributed to C's children.

Assuming that C does not have a reversionary interest equal in value to more than five percent at any time and that no aspects of the trust design are such that C would be treated as the substantial owner for income tax purposes, this will be an income exclusion type charitable lead trust. The annual amount paid to charity from the trust is equal to the yearly contributions that C had previously donated. The following table illustrates the comparative income tax result of this arrangement, with the continuation of C's current contributions in lieu of establishing the trust and also with the result had C used an immediate deduction charitable lead trust design. For the sake of simplicity, it is assumed that C's charitable contributions are his only source of itemized deduction. C's available personal exemption is ignored, and the amount of income tax is based on the rates in effect for 1995 for a married taxpayer filing jointly.

	Immediate-Deduction Lead Trust	*Income Exclusion Lead Trust*	*No Trust—Continue Yearly Gifts*
C's income before current year charitable contribution	$ 80,000	$ 80,000	$ 200,000
Plus amount of trust income included under grantor trust rules	+120,000	-0-	-0-
C's adjusted gross income	$ 200,000	$ 80,000	$ 200,000
Current year charitable contribution	-0-	-0-	120,000
Reduction of charitable deduction due to exceeding the 50% limitation	n/a	n/a	−20,000
Maximum carryforward charitable deduction in case of immediate-deduction type charitable lead trust for up to the first five years	100,000	n/a	n/a
Reduction of charitable deduction due to phaseout of itemized deductions	−2,579	n/a	−2,579
C's allowable charitable contribution deduction	−97,421	-0-	−97,421
C's taxable income	$ 102,579	$ 80,000	$ 102,579
C's income tax	$ 27,067	$ 20,068	$ 27,067

In the case of the immediate deduction charitable lead trust, the income tax burden becomes much worse after the first five years. After that, C is no longer able to carry forward the previously unusable portion of the initial charitable deduction to which he is entitled as a result of the transfer to the trust. He must continue to include the income produced by the trust in his taxable income, but he obtains no corresponding income tax deduction even though the trust is making distributions to charity. As a result, C receives only $80,000 of income on his own but must pay income tax on $200,000, resulting in an annual federal income tax liability of $61,370 (1995 income tax rate structure). This undesirable burden may be alleviated if the trustee invests in municipal bonds, since the trust's income would then retain its tax-exempt quality in the grantor's hands.

The establishment of an income exclusion charitable lead trust by C appears to offer the best overall advantages. Through this trust design, C is able to cause a constant level of benefit to be distributed to the charity, although he is no longer making direct, personal donations. C's personal income tax is reduced and, even though his children will receive the full value of the trust when the remainder is distributed, C obtains a substantial charitable deduction for gift tax purposes. The present actuarial value of the charitable lead interest and the noncharitable remainder interest as of the trust's inception are calculated under the rules of Code Sec. 7520. In C's case, if the applicable federal rate is eight percent and the annuity payments to charity are made at the beginning of each year, these calculations are as follows:

Total Value	*Actuarial Factors*		*Present Values*	
Placed in Trust	*Charitable Lead*	*Remainder*	*Charitable Lead*	*Remainder*
$1,500,000				
	.739541		$1,109,312	
		.260459		$390,689

After subtracting the present value of the charitable deduction, the total of C's taxable gift is only $390,689. If C has made no previous taxable gifts, the full gift tax will be offset by the unified credit available. The full benefit of the transfer will be seen at the time of C's death. The amount placed in the charitable lead trust, including any appreciation of principal that may have occurred, is excluded from C's taxable estate. The only adjustment is the add-back of C's post-1976 taxable gift. In order to create a dramatic illustration of the potential estate tax benefit, the following comparison chart assumes that C dies 15 years after establishing the charitable lead trust, near the time the trust was scheduled to terminate, and then the remainder is distributed to C's children.

	No Trust	*Charitable Lead Trust*
(1) C's total assets prior to creating the charitable lead trust	$ 3,000,000	$ 3,000,000
(2) Less full amount transferred to trust	n/a	−1,500,000
(3) C's total assets after establishing charitable lead trust	$ 3,000,000	$ 1,500,000
(4) Growth of C's assets @2% per year for 15 years	+1,037,605	+518,802
(5) Plus add-back of post-1976 taxable gift	n/a	+390,689
(6) Amount effectively subject to estate tax upon C's death	$ 4,037,605	$ 2,409,491
(7) Federal estate tax after unified credit	$ 1,668,683	$ 788,651

(8) Federal estate tax saved		$ 880,032
Total value passing from C's estate to C's children after federal estate tax [(3) plus (4) minus (7)]	$ 2,368,922	$ 1,230,151
Plus trust remainder (includes 2% annual appreciation of trust principal)	n/a	+2,018,803
Total value passing to C's children	$ 2,368,922	$ 3,248,954

The increase in the total value that the children receive is equal to the estate tax saved. Creation of the charitable lead trust results in a significant reduction in the amount of C's taxable gift while also causing complete exemption of any appreciation of trust principal from gift and estate taxes. The comparison does not take into account the value of the use of the principal during the 15-year period. Had C transferred an equivalent amount of after-tax investment earnings to his children during the 15-year period, especially considering the availability of the gift tax annual exclusion, the overall results would have been much closer. This means that a true economic "profit" on a charitable lead trust is unlikely. Where a grantor, such as C, is inclined to make significant charitable gifts not solely motivated by tax savings, the results of the charitable lead trust can prove superior to other forms of charitable giving.

¶704 CHARITABLE "CROSS"

For individuals and families who support charities during life and also intend to leave part of their estates for charitable purposes, the use of both a charitable lead trust and a charitable remainder trust is worth consideration. The charitable lead trust replaces what had been the grantor's annual charitable giving program, and the charitable remainder trust takes the place of what would have been a charitable bequest through a will or living trust. At the grantor's death, the two trusts are said to "cross," that is, change their respective charitable and noncharitable beneficiaries. The charitable lead trust, used to make annual distributions to charity during the grantor's lifetime, crosses over to distribute the remainder to the grantor's children or other noncharitable beneficiaries. Also at the grantor's death, the charitable remainder trust, from which annual distributions to the grantor or other noncharitable beneficiary had been made, crosses over to distribute the remainder to charity.

The potential advantages of the charitable cross are:

(1) The immediate income tax deduction for the transfer to the charitable remainder trust.

(2) A reduction in the unified transfer tax, relating particularly to the charitable lead trust, because the value of the taxable gift is "discounted" by the present value of the initial charitable interest.

(3) The removal of the post-transfer appreciation of assets placed in the charitable lead trust from the grantor's taxable estate.

The client who would be interested in this strategy is one who has an established, ongoing charitable giving program. Reduction of disposable income through the charitable lead trust distributions is not a disadvantage. There is a loss of access to principal of both charitable trusts, however, that must be taken into consideration in the planning process.

Example: G is age 62 and unmarried with total assets of $1,500,000. G's will leaves one-fourth of her estate to a national health research foundation that meets the requirements of Code Secs. 170(c), 2055(a), and 2522(a). The balance of G's estate is to be distributed to a brother and other family members. Each year, G makes contributions to the foundation and various other charities that total $15,000 to $20,000.

G might reproduce her plan in a modified manner by creating two irrevocable living trusts. A charitable lead annuity trust of $300,000 directing the payment of six percent to charities at the beginning of each year can replace G's current charitable giving program. The remainder of the charitable lead trust is distributed to G's brother upon her death. A separate charitable remainder trust, designed to pay G quarterly unitrust amounts that total six percent each year and to distribute the remainder to the health research foundation, can substitute for G's charitable bequest.

This is a summary of the consequences of G's modified plan.

(1) Assuming that G is not treated as the substantial owner of the charitable lead trust under Code Sec. 671, G receives no income tax deduction for the value of the charitable interest in that trust. The income produced by the trust, however, is excluded from G's taxable income and is reported as taxable income of the trust, which is entitled to a deduction for amounts distributed from the trust to charity.

(2) The value of the charitable lead interest, computed under the rules of Code Sec. 7520 using an eight percent applicable federal rate, is $173,448. That amount reduces the value of G's taxable gift to her brother of the remainder interest.

(3) G's gift to her brother of the remainder interest in the charitable lead trust is valued at $126,552. As a present taxable gift of a future interest, no part of the value qualifies for the gift tax annual exclusion. However, unless G has made substantial prior taxable gifts, the gift tax is offset by G's unified credit.

(4) The amount treated as a gift to G's brother is taken into account at G's death as a post-1976 taxable gift. The balance of the trust value, all of which passes to G's brother, escapes the unified transfer tax system. That results in elimination of gift or estate tax on the value attributed to the charitable lead interest as well as any appreciation or accumulations within the trust fund that take place during G's lifetime.

(5) G is entitled to an immediate charitable contribution deduction for the present value of the remainder interest that passes at her death to the foundation from the charitable remainder trust. Under the rules of Code Sec. 7520, using an eight percent applicable federal rate, the deduction is $116,949.

(6) The value of the charitable remainder trust is fully deductible for estate tax purposes, just as the outright charitable bequest under G's will would have been.

Because clients who make substantial annual charitable gifts are likely to include a charitable bequest in their estate plans, the charitable cross is a transaction that the financial consultant should discuss in appropriate cases.

Chapter 8

Professional Services for Trusts and Settlement of Accounts

¶ 801 PROFESSIONAL SERVICES REQUIRED BY TRUSTS

Trusts require a variety of professional services due to the complexity of property ownership rules, income and transfer taxes, financial management, and accounting requirements. Besides drafting the trust document, an attorney is needed during the administration of the trust, as questions arise, and at the time of the final settlement. Preparation of annual income tax returns and accounting settlement statements is often done by a certified public accountant. Unless the trustee is personally knowledgeable in the investment field, the services of a registered investment adviser who manages investment portfolios may be used.

The functions of the trustee, as well as those of each of these professionals, are examined in this chapter. Also examined is the issue of the propriety of paying for professional services from the trust fund in certain circumstances.

.01 Trustee

A wide array of duties is assumed by the trustee of a testamentary or inter vivos trust. Even if the services of related professionals are used, the ultimate responsibility for the proper administration of the trust rests with the trustee.

.011 Basic responsibilities

Simply stated, the trustee is obligated to follow the directions set out in the trust document concerning how the trust is to be handled and distributed. This function must be carried out exclusively in the interest of the beneficiaries and in a manner that is most efficient and cost effective. The following discussion focuses on some of the primary activities performed by the trustee.

Segregating and safeguarding trust assets. The trustee is accountable for all money, investments, and other property transferred into the trust fund. In order to fulfill this requirement, it is necessary for the trustee to keep adequate records, to take care of the physical custody of the trust assets, and to make those assets productive.

In some cases, this is as simple as depositing all of the trust funds in a bank account or investing in a mutual fund. The bank account or mutual fund periodic statements should provide an adequate source of records for income tax as well as account settlement needs, and either of those simple investment choices can provide safety of the funds and productivity of investment earnings. On the other hand, in cases where the value of the trust is greater, it may be appropriate to diversify the funds among bank deposits, securities, real estate, and direct participation types of investments. If so, recordkeeping and safeguarding take on more complexity.

There is a universal restriction against commingling of trust fund assets with the trustee's personal assets. Even a small amount of commingling for a brief time period can result in serious punitive action. A simple example of the violation of this principle is the deposit of trust funds into the trustee's individual bank account until such time as the funds are placed in other investments registered in the name of the trust. Commingling causes the appearance of impropriety as well as the potential exposure of trust assets to the claims of personal creditors of the trustee. This must be scrupulously avoided. The trustee is, technically, the legal owner of all trust assets. As such, it is the trustee who has the power to initiate purchases and sales of assets on behalf of the trust. However, it is necessary that, as any money or property comes into the trustee's hands, it is registered in a manner that makes it clearly identifiable as the property of the trust. This is accomplished through the proper description on the title of bank accounts, investment accounts, and individual registration of other investments. For instance, an acceptable registration form for the assets of a testamentary trust might be:

John Smith, Trustee U/W (under the will of) Robert Johnson, deceased.

Assets properly registered are not subject to personal claims against the trustee.

Keeping the trust fund productive. It is an obligation of the trustee to invest trust funds so that they are productive. Interest-bearing accounts and certificates of deposit are examples of productive investments, but so are corporate stocks. In fact, even if a stock pays no dividend but offers the potential for increasing in value, it may be an appropriate trust investment.

A small non-interest-bearing balance in an identified trust checking account may have been regarded as a necessary expedient in past years. More recently, with the availability of interest on checking accounts and check writing privileges on money market funds, this is becoming less justifiable. In any event, large uninvested sums are not proper for a trust.

Avoiding self-dealing. Trustees are generally forbidden to enter into transactions with the trust for the purpose of making a personal profit.

Instances of self-dealing may be encountered most frequently in the form of loans from the trust fund to the trustee. Interest-free loans, loans at less than prevailing interest rates, and loans with little or no collateral security are most suspect. However, even loans with adequate security and a fair rate of interest advanced by the trust to the trustee are, at best, inadvisable.

Another danger area is participation by the trustee in the same direct investments as those in which the trust invests. For example, if the trustee, as an individual, owns a 50 percent interest in an office building and the trust owns the other half, there is the potential for conflicts of interest. Ownership by the trustee of securities traded on public securities exchanges or in the over-the-counter market does not pose the same problem unless the trading volume of a particular security is unusually small.

Maintaining impartiality among beneficiaries. It is necessary for the trustee to balance the interests of the beneficiaries. That is, the trustee must consider whether an administrative decision will result in one beneficiary receiving more while another receives less, either presently or at any time in the future. Decisions that cause uneven results arise and must be resolved. Although the trustee cannot please all of the parties all of the time, he must avoid a pattern of decisions that favors one or more beneficiaries over others.

> **Example:** The trust document of Trust D requires that all income be distributed monthly to beneficiary B for life. In addition, trustee T is to make distributions from the principal of the trust fund to the extent necessary, in T's judgment, to enable B to maintain his accustomed standard of living. At B's death, the balance of the trust is to be distributed to remainderman R.
>
> The golf club of which B has been a member for 20 years has informed B that he must pay a special assessment of $25,000 for much needed, extensive capital improvements.

T might decide to make a discretionary distribution of $25,000 from the principal of the trust fund to B in order to enable him to pay his assessment. Being a member of the golf club appears to be an element of B's accustomed standard of living. If T makes the distribution, the final remainder amount ultimately distributed to R will certainly be smaller.

It might be necessary for T to consult an attorney for guidance on his decision. Although this is a discretionary payment, a legal opinion would be helpful. The attorney would advise T concerning the trust laws of the state having jurisdiction over the trust: Have that state's courts interpreted a beneficiary's standard of living in an expansive or restrictive manner in previous cases? Have trustees been criticized for being too liberal in similar situations? Is the trustee required or permitted to look into B's own financial resources before making his decision?

Maintaining adequate and accurate records and filing income tax returns. Recordkeeping in connection with a trust fund serves several important functions. The income tax reporting requirements alone are a sufficient reason to keep accounts of all income and expense items. However, it is also necessary for the trustee to be in a position to account for all transactions of the trust—both as to income and principal—to a court and to the beneficiaries. The records must be capable of reconstructing transactions from the inception of the trust up to the date of the final distribution and settlement.

Distributing trust income and principal. The terms of the trust should specify the time intervals of income distributions, which may be annually, quarterly, monthly, or even weekly. There may also be required principal distributions at various intervals. The trustee is required to comply with such requirements and also may be called upon to take additional steps.

If the beneficiary becomes mentally or physically incapacitated, the trustee could begin to use the trust funds to pay the beneficiary's expenses directly. It is best to grant specific permission, under the terms of the trust document, to the trustee to take this step, and a great many trust documents do so. For example, the trust instrument could provide that, if the beneficiary is declared incompetent, future trust distributions be made to a court-appointed guardian.

In some cases, the trustee and the beneficiary reach an understanding that the trustee will pay the beneficiary's bills directly from the trust, even if there is no disability involved, but simply for the beneficiary's convenience.

Arrangements can be made to have personal bills, payable by the beneficiary, submitted directly to the trustee for payment.

.012 Choice of trustee

Desirable qualities. The first step in choosing a trustee is to examine the legal requirements and restrictions under the laws of the state that will govern the trust. Some states require that a trustee be a resident of the state. Nonresidents may be permitted to serve in a trustee capacity only if there is some specific degree of family relationship between the testator or grantor and the trustee.

As a practical matter, consideration should be given to the ability of the trustee to carry out his responsibilities as such. This means examining the following issues, among others:

(1) The relationship between the age of the prospective trustee and the number of years before the trust will end or is likely to end. For testamentary trusts, the difference in age between the testator and the trustee should also be considered. Where age factors make it unlikely that the trustee will live to complete the job, alternate or successor trustees should be appointed. In fact, it is advisable to designate a successor in every case because of the possibility of unexpected death or incapacity of the primary trustee.

(2) The experience of the trustee in financial matters. While there can be no specific set of qualifications, previous trust or estate experience and investment experience are very helpful.

(3) The demonstrated business judgment of the prospective trustee.

(4) The ability of the trustee to get along personally with the intended beneficiaries and the degree of sympathy expressed by the trustee toward the beneficiaries' needs and aspirations.

(5) An understanding by the prospective trustee of the grantor's objectives in establishing an inter vivos trust or planning for a trust through his will and a willingness to work toward those goals.

(6) A willingness to undertake the responsibilities of administering the trust even if it interferes with other activities of the trustee.

Comparatively few individuals possess these desirable trustee qualities as well as the technical knowledge that is needed concerning accounting, tax, and investment matters. Therefore, the grantor should take into account the potential need for the trustee to pay for the services of one or more related professionals as a trust expenditure. State laws may not permit the trustee to charge the cost of all professional services to the trust fund. Instead, some of these costs may reduce the amount of the trustee's compensation. It is appropriate in some cases to specify in the trust document that a particular type of expense, not ordinarily chargeable to a trust, may be paid as an allowable expense.

Example (1): T has used the services of ABC investment advisors to manage his investment portfolio for many years. T has asked his attorney to prepare a will in which he will leave most of his estate in trust for his children and grandchildren. In T's will, the testator's oldest child, O, is designated as trustee. Since the law of the state of T's domicile does not authorize investment advisory fees as a trust expense, T's attorney has suggested the inclusion of a special provision in T's will that allows O to hire ABC in order to manage the trust's investments and to pay ABC's fees from the trust fund.

Choice of a corporate trustee. State law restricts the appointment of non-individual entities as trustees. For instance, at his client's request, attorney John Smith can appoint himself as trustee under his client's will. If the client believes that an alternate or successor trustee makes sense, John Smith might be appointed as trustee with his son and law partner, William Smith, as alternate. It would not be permissible, however, to appoint the law firm of Smith and Smith as trustee.

Generally, state laws permit banking corporations to be appointed as trustees; however, not all banks are qualified to offer trust services. Some states permit special qualification of trust companies that do not offer other banking services.

The advantages of using a corporate trustee are:

(1) Since the corporation is perpetual, the grantor does not have to be concerned about the possibility of the trustee's death before termination of the trust.

(2) Well-organized and well-staffed trust companies may have several trust customer representatives or trust officers involved with the administration of the trust fund. This eliminates problems that can arise if the trustee is on vacation or ill when there is urgent trust business.

(3) The corporate trustee can maintain a staff of qualified specialists in the areas of administration, accounting, and tax. Since the work of the trust department involves only trust services, the personnel are likely to become capable in this highly specialized field. Also, this may eliminate the need to pay for additional professional services from the trust.

(4) A bank or trust company is financially responsible. Occasionally, there is the report of a trustee absconding with trust funds. Where there is a corporate trustee, even if it were possible for an employee to gain access to trust funds, the bank would be required to make up any loss. In fact, state laws that require fidelity bonding of trustees exempt corporate trustees from the requirement because the bank's assets stand behind its fiduciary obligations.

The disadvantages of using a corporate trustee do not necessarily apply to all banks and trust companies; these generalizations are largely a matter of opinion and personal impression. Within the trust department of a single bank, there may be some trust beneficiaries who hold their trustee in high regard and others who wish that the bank had never been appointed. To some extent, this is a matter of the personal relationship between the trust beneficiary and the bank employee who serves him. The following is merely a listing of a few unfavorable impressions expressed by some who have had experience with corporate trustees.

(1) Since the bank employees are not relatives, a feeling of lack of personal involvement and understanding may exist. In the extreme, the corporate trustee is regarded as "cold and impersonal."

(2) Family members who are trust beneficiaries do not necessarily have any voice in the selection of a particular trust company representative to handle their trust fund. If a less-than-cordial relationship devel-

ops, there may be little or nothing that can be done about it. On the other hand, trust company personnel have their own lives to lead, and they may be reassigned within the bank or take another employment opportunity. This results in a change of face and the need to reestablish rapport.

(3) A bank or trust company usually manages the investments of trust funds in-house. Investment performance results vary widely. Some are very impressive, while others do not compare favorably. If the beneficiaries are not pleased with investment results, they may have little recourse until the final distribution of the trust fund. Even in the event of a court-supervised final settlement, no action is likely to be taken against a corporate trustee due to poor investment performance unless there is evidence of willful misconduct or other serious mismanagement, which is a remote possibility.

The financial consultant may be called upon for advice on the selection of a trustee, including the advisability of selecting a corporate trustee. Accordingly, the financial consultant must develop the ability to investigate the atmosphere of a prospective trust department.

The following examples describe two fictitious trust departments. Neither description is based on an actual company, and any similarities between real companies and these illustrations are only coincidental. The purpose of the examples is to focus on the elements that a financial consultant would find desirable and those he might identify as undesirable. Also, information concerning these elements is not publicly available. This must be discovered through references and contacts within the financial community.

Example (2): The First Ideal Trust Company

What is striking about this trust department is the longevity of employment of its personnel. Several of the senior trust officers remember working on family trust matters for the grandparents of the current trust beneficiaries whom they serve.

While the workload is heavy, care is taken that two or more representatives are personally acquainted with each trust file. This includes personal acquaintances with the beneficiaries of each trust as well as an understanding of the trust terms. The customers of First Ideal Trust each know their trust officers on a first-name basis. Within each trust administrative group there is an administrative specialist and an investment specialist assigned to each case. Reassignments of trust officers to a different group of cases is virtually unheard of except in instances of promotions and retirements.

Investments are monitored by an investment committee. All holdings of a particular security are cross-referenced so that any decision regarding purchase and sale can be carried out for all affected trust funds at the same time. Each position is reviewed weekly, or even more often. The individual portfolio of each trust fund is reviewed monthly. When a new trust account is opened, no investments are made until the committee has reviewed the personal history of the present beneficiaries as well as the remaindermen. The goal is to structure the portfolio to meet the needs of all beneficiaries. The issue of whether or not each trust portfolio continues to serve the entire family's needs in terms of present investment return and future potential is the subject of an annual review of each individual trust account.

The trust division is a profitable sector of First Ideal Trust Company. Referrals of new customers from the banking division are frequent, resulting in a continuous rate of growth of assets under management over the past 20 years.

Example (3): Mediocre Bank & Trust

Turnover at Mediocre B & T has been relatively high in recent years. Trust department personnel tend to hold their jobs for two or three years and then move on, either within the bank or to another company. Some trust beneficiaries have complained that each time they call to discuss their trust, they find that a new trust officer has been assigned to their file.

Typically, a Mediocre B & T trust officer or customer representative is responsible for over three hundred trusts. As a result, the tendency is to work only on emergencies most of the time. The motto "the squeaky wheel gets the oil" is often heard.

Mediocre B & T uses a consulting service to assist with investments. This service makes available to the trust officers a list of securities recommended for purchase and a list recommended for sale. It is the duty of the individual trust officer to review each of his accounts whenever a new "buy list" or "sell list" becomes available. If a trust is holding uninvested cash in principal, purchases are ordinarily made by reference to the buy list, and any items held by a trust that appear on a new sell list are sold on an account-by-account basis. Department policy does permit some discretion to trust officers in this regard. Some of the younger members of the staff, in particular, have made a reputation by purchasing investments for trusts that they themselves have researched and found to have good potential. Unfortunately, some embarrassing losses have resulted from non-list investment purchases on a few occasions. There is an annual investment review of each trust account in which the bank's investment committee, consisting of two senior trust officers and two other members of Mediocre's board of directors, interrogates each individual trust officer concerning the content of each trust's portfolio.

The trust division of Mediocre B & T has not shown a profit in more than five years. However, senior management has decided to continue offering trust services in order to be competitive as a full-service bank. Management has ordered the head of the trust division to come up with a cost-cutting plan in order to trim losses in an effort to put the division on at least a break-even basis.

In view of the differences in the quality of service resulting from the degree of excellence of a particular trust department, it is not sufficient for the financial consultant to adopt a blanket policy in responding to client questions concerning the advisability of choosing a corporate trustee. The professional adviser best serves his client if he explores the advantages and disadvantages of individual trustee appointment as well as the advantages and disadvantages in choosing a corporate trustee. If the decision to choose a corporate trustee is made, careful investigation of the trust department's organization and the quality of its personnel is essential.

Alternatives to the exclusive appointment of a corporate trustee. One viable alternative to choosing between an individual trustee and a corporate trustee is to choose both. Some families prefer to have the corporate trustee for the sake of its administrative capabilities and possibly also for its investment expertise, but they also insist on the appointment of an individual as co-trustee in order to insure the personal concern that, some believe, only a family member or close friend can provide.

Another possibility is to include a provision in the trust document that gives the beneficiary or a majority of the beneficiaries the right to change the trustee. There are those who believe that, if a corporate trustee knows it can lose an account, it may show a greater degree of attention. The power to remove a trustee and appoint a replacement may cause unwanted tax results in some cases. For instance, if an individual beneficiary has the right to appoint himself as the successor trustee, that individual is treated as possessing all powers actually held by the trustee, even if no replacement occurs. If the trustee's powers include the right to make discretionary distributions, it is possible that the beneficiary will be treated as the substantial owner of the trust principal for purposes of the fiduciary income tax rules. Some trust distribution powers, if held by a beneficiary, could constitute a general power of appointment, resulting in a taxable gift upon exercise, release, or lapse of the power, or in the inclusion of the trust fund in the beneficiary's taxable estate at death. The power held by a beneficiary to replace one corporate trustee only with the appointment of another corporate trustee should pose no tax problems.

Yet another approach has been described as the "unbundling" of trust services. This allows a family to appoint an individual trustee or individual co-trustees and authorize the trustee or trustees to retain a corporate trust company for specific services such as safeguarding of assets, maintaining records, preparing periodic reports and tax returns, or managing investments. In this manner, the individual trustee is able to obtain just the combination of services that would be inconvenient to perform personally.

.02 Attorney

Legal services come into play at various intervals during the design, administration, and settlement of the trust. No professional other than an attorney should ever be involved in the preparation of a trust document. Regardless of the degree of related experience that other professionals have, the nuances of meaning and legal implications of each phrase can only be analyzed by an attorney who has specialized training and experience. While a great many attorneys have the facility to prepare ordinary wills or even simple trust documents, those who possess the level of knowledge needed to deal with complex trust design are few. These tend to be attorneys whose practice is limited exclusively to this field. This requires a level of understanding of both the law of trusts and estates and of specialized tax issues far greater than the majority of attorneys would ever have the opportunity or inclination to achieve.

The problem is that the general practitioner, if asked about his willingness and ability to handle a complex trust matter, may honestly believe that he can always manage it, perhaps with a little extra time and effort. The client who is facing decisions that may affect the quality of life of his family, including his descendants for generations, may want more than a generally competent legal practitioner who can "muddle through" the matter. Some help is available from state or local bar association attorney referral services. These professional groups can identify the truly qualified specialists in the field. Also, trust officers are in a position to know which attorneys have the greatest knowledge and talent in their geographic area.

Besides the initial design of the estate plan, including preparation of the necessary will and trust document, a major part of the attorney's function has to do with the final settlement of the trust. The attorney may prepare or supervise the preparation of the final accounting statements. If the settlement is to be reviewed in court, the attorney must prepare the necessary papers that accompany the account statement and appear in court to answer any objections. If an out-of-court settlement of the account is appropriate, the attorney must identify all parties who possess a legal interest in the termination of the trust and prepare documents by which each party may consent to the settlement. The attorney for the trust is called on to recommend to the trustee whether a court settlement or an informal settlement should be pursued.

During the on-going administration of the trust, the attorney may be called upon for advice for a variety of reasons. The trustee, even if it is a corporate trustee, may need assistance in the interpretation of duties and obligations as set forth in the trust document or may seek the attorney's guidance concerning discretionary distributions. Questions may also be raised by beneficiaries. To the extent that these require explanation of trust procedures or even entitlement to trust benefits, the attorney may be able to respond. However, at times trust beneficiaries may express general discontent with, or even specific claims against, the trustee. This puts the attorney for the trust in a difficult position. The attorney's obligation is to represent and defend the trustee, not to take a bipartisan approach between trustee and beneficiary. If serious criticism against the trustee is expressed by a beneficiary, the attorney may respond in the trustee's defense. At some point, the attorney has the obligation to explain his role to the beneficiary, including the potential conflict of interest problem. The attorney for the trust must suggest that the beneficiary consult with his own counsel in appropriate cases.

.03 Certified Public Accountant

The CPA designation is a professional credential that indicates a high level of knowledge and experience in accounting or tax matters, or both. While some accountants who have not met the requirements to obtain the CPA designation are qualified to assist in trust work, as well as in other accounting procedures, the CPA is naturally regarded as the first professional choice in this area.

As in the case of the attorney, the choice of accounting services for trust work must be made with great care. In-depth study of fiduciary income tax, estate and gift tax, generation-skipping transfer tax (GST), and trust account settlement procedures is not a required element in the undergraduate education program of colleges and universities that prepare students for CPA qualification. A business education curriculum leading to an undergraduate degree in accounting or in business with a concentration in accounting is the usual course recommended for a student who wishes to take the CPA exam. Without including any subjects devoted to the specialized field of trusts, there are already enough required courses in this curriculum to approach or exceed the total number of credits needed for the degree. This is necessary because of the size of the body of knowledge relating to other accounting subjects traditionally required.

As a result, the CPA who has an in-depth understanding of trust accounting, fiduciary income taxation, gift and estate tax, and GST is a specialist. While one or more of these specialists are likely to be found in any of the larger accounting firms, it is too much to expect in a smaller organization. This means that the client, perhaps with the assistance of the financial consultant, must be sure that the individual accountant or firm selected has the requisite knowledge and experience.

Some of the work that would otherwise be performed by the accountant is handled by the trust company in-house if the trust has a corporate trustee. This includes preparation of monthly or other periodic statements of activity, as well as asset listings and valuations and income tax returns. At the time of an interim or final account settlement statement, some corporate trustees prepare the settlement schedules within the trust division, while others refer this work to outside accounting firms. Where there is an individual trustee, it is often necessary to retain the services of a professional accountant for all statements and tax returns as well as for the final accounting.

¶ 802 SETTLEMENT OF TRUST ACCOUNTS

There are several purposes for the presentation and review of trust accounts. Several of the most important functions of a trust settlement are discussed below.

.01 Satisfaction of Beneficiaries' Rights

The beneficiaries can only be sure that they have received all to which they are entitled if there is an opportunity to review all of the transactions of the trust. Unless a detailed account settlement is presented, the beneficiaries might assume that all is in order when, in fact, losses or misplacements of funds have occurred. If there are any legitimate complaints against the trustee, presenting an interim or final account statement should provide the opportunity to discover them and seek any appropriate remedy. Where such a remedy requires some form of reimbursement payment by the trustee, the procedure is referred to as a "surcharge."

.02 Prevention of Future Claims Against Trustee

The accounting settlement serves a kind of "speak now or forever hold your peace" function. The interested parties are given a reasonable period of time after an accounting has been presented during which they can raise objections to any transactions or valuations. After these parties have been given this opportunity, and assuming that no valid objections are found, the trustee is relieved of liability with respect to his handling of the trust.

.03 Mathematical Proof of Account

The trust accounting and settlement procedures also serve the purpose of mathematically proving that all amounts of money and all property placed in the trust fund have either been spent for legitimate purposes of the trust or distributed to the beneficiaries. Both principal and income must be accounted for in this manner.

.04 Content of a Trust Settlement Accounting

There is considerable variation in the exact format of presentation of a trust account. The format may not even be uniform within a single state. However, there are certain similarities in the subjects that are covered and the type of detail that each of the account settlement schedules contains.

Trust settlement accountings are divided first into principal and income schedules and then, within each of these major categories, into several further schedules.

.041 Principal schedules

Inventory. This is a listing of the amount of money first placed in the trust fund or a detailed, item-by-item listing of other assets that may have been transferred in kind into the trust principal.

In the case of assets other than cash, the value listed in the inventory is the value of each asset as of the date of transfer to the trust fund. The purpose is to make it possible to determine whether the overall value of the trust fund has remained constant, increased, or decreased during the period of administration. The inventory value may differ from the cost basis that is used to determine the amount of gain or loss for income tax purposes upon sale.

> **Example:** G transfers 100 shares of XYZ stock into an inter vivos trust for the benefit of his children. G's cost basis for the stock is $10,000, but its value on the date transferred is $50,000.
>
> The trust's inventory value of the XYZ stock is $50,000 and its cost basis for determining gain upon any future sale of the stock is $10,000, with a possible adjustment if G paid any gift tax on the transaction.

Additions to principal. Particularly in the case of testamentary trusts, principal may be added to the trust at several different times. If the terms of the will give a part of the residuary estate to the trust fund, the executor may find it necessary to make interim, partial residuary distributions from the estate to the trust before the estate's final settlement. Amounts contributed to the principal after the initial funding of the trust are listed on a schedule of principal additions. The inventory value of these items is the value on the date of transfer, not the value on the date of creation of the trust.

State laws generally permit testamentary additions to trusts. Therefore, someone other than the grantor may add to an existing trust by will. Where a married person dies leaving a trust for the benefit of the surviving spouse and the trust is to continue after the survivor's death for the benefit of children, it may prove more cost efficient for the survivor to name the existing trust as the beneficiary of his estate rather than to establish a new, separate trust fund. Additions to an existing trust in this manner, whether made in cash or by the in-kind transfer of securities or other property, appear on the schedule of additions to principal.

Principal changes. This schedule is used to report any changes that take place in the principal assets. Some changes are outside of the trustee's control. For instance, stock splits, stock dividends, corporate name changes resulting from mergers or otherwise, spin-offs, and split-ups are all examples of transactions that cause changes in the number of units or description of assets held within the trust but which do not result from purchases, sales, or distributions of trust principal assets.

Purchases and sales. This schedule is used to permit a proof calculation showing that the total proceeds of assets sold is equal to the sum of the amounts paid for the purchase of principal assets (reinvestment) with any excess of sale proceeds being reflected in the principal cash. It is not the function of this schedule to report gain or loss.

For assets purchased by the trustee during the term of the trust, the cost becomes the inventory value.

Gain or loss upon sales or redemptions of principal assets. In a trust settlement account, the amount of gain or loss is calculated by reference to the net sale or redemption proceeds and the inventory value of the asset disposed of. The resulting gain or loss may not be the same as that which is properly reportable for income tax purposes.

Gains may be reported on a separate schedule from losses. However, in the final proof of the account, the net gain or net loss is the pertinent figure.

Principal expenses. All amounts paid from principal other than principal distributions to beneficiaries are listed on this schedule. This includes trustee principal commissions, payments for other professional services, such as attorneys, accountants, investment counsel, and others. It also includes income taxes that are properly chargeable to principal, such as income taxes resulting from capital gains realized on the sale of principal assets.

Principal distributions. As explained throughout the preceding chapters, instances of interim distribution of trust principal to beneficiaries are frequently permitted, either on a scheduled or discretionary basis. Some trusts also permit limited principal withdrawals by beneficiaries.

Where assets of the trust are sold so that the proceeds can be distributed in cash, the sale proceeds are included on the purchase and sale schedule and the gain or loss is included on the gain or loss schedule. Payment of the sale proceeds to the beneficiary is then listed on the distribution schedule.

Where principal assets are distributed in kind, the value listed on this schedule may be the inventory value in order to avoid disturbing the account proof. However, in order to portray the investment performance results more accurately, the trustee may include a separate schedule showing increases or decreases between inventory and date of distribution values as if these interim principal distributions were sales.

Unrealized appreciation or loss. This schedule lists the difference between the inventory value of each asset and its value as of the date on which the account settlement is prepared. Its purpose is to make possible a mathematical proof between original inventory and final remaining principal.

Principal remaining. This schedule lists the amount of cash, including bank deposits, plus an item-by-item listing of other trust assets valued as of the date of preparation of the account settlement.

Proof of principal account. If the foregoing format is used, the proof of the principal account does not involve the schedules labeled "principal changes" or "purchases and sales," because the information included on these schedules does not affect the proof.

The procedure to prove the principal account is shown by reference to the balance of the principal schedules described.

First Step:	Begin with total inventory value.
Second Step:	Add the total of any additions to principal.
Third Step:	Add the net gain or subtract the net loss upon sales or redemptions of principal assets.
Fourth Step:	Subtract the total of principal expenses.
Fifth Step:	Subtract the inventory value of principal distributions.
Sixth Step:	Add the net unrealized appreciation or subtract the net unrealized loss on remaining principal assets.
Final Step:	The result of the foregoing should equal the total value of principal assets remaining as shown.

.042 Income schedules

Income received. This schedule is presented on an item-by-item basis. It may be arranged in a purely chronological sequence or may list the income collected with respect to each principal item. In that case, the principal items may be listed alphabetically with a separate income entry for each amount of income collected in chronological order.

Income expenses. Items of expense properly chargeable to income are listed, typically in chronological order. An example of an expense that might fall into this category is ordinary maintenance costs associated with residential property that is held in the trust for the use of the beneficiary, not for the production of income.

> **Example:** D left his entire residuary estate in trust for the benefit of his son, S, for life. D's will authorizes trustee T to retain D's vacation home for S's use during his lifetime. T pays the expenses in connection with maintaining the residence. Items of expense, such as capital repairs, are paid from principal, while real estate taxes and ordinary maintenance are charged to income.

Another common example of an income expense is the portion of the trustee's commission chargeable to income under state law.

Income tax is usually payable from the income account only if the trust makes income accumulations. Since the trust is entitled to an income tax deduction for distributions to beneficiaries who report a corresponding amount of income on their personal income tax returns, where all income of the trust is distributed currently, there is no income tax to be paid by the trust.

Income distributions. All of the income distributions made by the trust during the entire period of time covered by the account settlement statement are listed. If the trust makes monthly income distributions, that means 12 separate entries for each year of the trust.

If there is more than one income beneficiary, the trustee may list all distributions separately for each beneficiary.

Undistributed income. Frequently, some income is collected between the date of the most recently preceding trust income distribution and the trust account settlement date. This sum is indicated on a separate schedule.

Proof of income account. The income account proof may be more simple than that of the principal account.

If the sum of the income expenses and distributions is subtracted from the total income received, the difference should equal the balance of undistributed income.

.05 Informal Trust Account Settlement

The trustee and the beneficiaries may wish to avoid the potential expense and delays attendant to a court-supervised account settlement. However, one of the primary purposes of account settlement is to relieve the trustee of any liability arising from his handling of the trust administration. Therefore, the trustee must be certain that the informal account settlement will accomplish this purpose. The attorney for the trust must be consulted in this regard.

In order to relieve the trustee of liability, it is necessary that:

(1) Each of the beneficiaries is satisfied with the trustee's administration, and each beneficiary agrees to release the trustee from any claims.

(2) Each of the beneficiaries is legally capable of approving the account settlement and releasing the trustee. Any beneficiary who is a minor or a mental incompetent is not capable of giving such approval and release. Accordingly, an informal trust settlement may not preclude claims from being made against the trustee at some time in the future.

The degree of detail presented to the beneficiaries in case of an informal trust account settlement varies. While a beneficiary should insist on the same information summarized in the preceding section of this chapter for content of a trust accounting, some agree to approve the trustee's release of liability based on far less information.

The most common informal settlement procedure is presentation on behalf of the trustee of some form of account statement, review by each party having an interest in the trust, either individually or with the advice of their own professional advisers, and execution by each beneficiary of a document that approves the account settlement and releases the trustee.

.06 Court-Supervised Trust Account Settlement

The settlement of a trust account may take place in court for any one of a number of reasons. Due to the age or infirmity of those having beneficial interests, the trustee or the attorney may feel that release of the trustee from claims would not be reliable without a protective court order approving the account. On the other hand, a beneficiary has the right to insist that the account be settled in court and may seek judicial settlement if the beneficiary does not approve some aspect of the settlement accounting.

Although there are wide differences as to the precise procedure for court settlement, the following common characteristics can be identified.

(1) *Presentation of petition to court by trustee.* The process begins with the filing of a document in the state court that has jurisdiction over trust and estate matters. This petition or similar document seeks court approval of the account settlement and release of the trustee from all liability connected with the administration of the trust for the time period covered by the accounting.

Court requirements may include a factual summary stating the name of the testator or grantor and some historical review of the administration of the trust in addition to a complete statement of account. In addition, a brief summary of the detailed principal and income schedules may also be necessary.

(2) *Notice to interested parties.* According to the individual requirements of state courts, the notice to interested parties may have to be accompanied by a full copy of the settlement account or only a copy of the abbreviated summary may be required.

In any event, each interested party is given the right to inspect the full accounting, as well as backup documentation, upon request.

Before the account is settled, the court may require that evidence of receipt of notice by all interested parties be submitted for the court's review (e.g., post office return receipts may be required).

(3) *Opportunity to respond.* Each interested party has the right to submit objections to the settlement of the trust account and the release of the trustee. Such objections are most usually required to be in writing and must be submitted within a specified period of time before the settlement hearing is scheduled.

In case of serious objections to the account settlement, it may be necessary for the court to schedule a full hearing, permitting the introduction of evidence and the testimony of witnesses in order to enable the court to make a determination.

(4) *Appointment of guardians.* Whenever there is an interested party who is a minor or mental incompetent, the court is required to appoint a special guardian whose obligations relate exclusively to the account settlement. This guardian should be either an individual whom the court believes to have special knowledge and experience in trust matters or a bank or trust company, appointed by the court, to fulfill the guardian's duties.

It is the responsibility of the guardian to review the trust account settlement papers as well as any additional trust records that the guardian believes necessary. The guardian should neither take a harsh view of the settlement accounting nor make a cursory overview. Instead, the guardian is expected to consider the request for account approval and release of the trustee in the same manner as if the guardian had a personal interest in the trust.

If the special guardian finds the trust settlement accounting to be in order, such person reports that fact to the court and consents to the judgment settling the account. However, the guardian is obligated to make objections to the settlement on behalf of the minor if justification exists.

(5) *Judgment of formal settlement.* If no objections are made by interested parties, the account approval and settlement and release of the trustee are routine. However, where objections have been raised, the judgment must address each point and either dismiss the objection or take whatever action the court determines to be appropriate.

Where a trustee is found to have been at fault, the ordinary remedy is called a "surcharge." A surcharge can be limited to a reduction of any balance of commissions payable to the trustee, or it may result in the requirement that the trustee make compensatory payments to the trust fund.

.07 Review of a Trust Settlement Accounting

To most people, a proposed trust settlement accounting has the appearance of an overwhelming mass of data that is difficult to comprehend. Since it is financial in nature, the advice of a professional, such as a financial consultant, is often sought. This makes it necessary to be able to spot transactions within an account settlement that are questionable. Naturally, if serious doubt results, an attorney should be consulted.

Even in case of a court-supervised account settlement, it should not be assumed that everything appearing in the trust accounting is permissible. The court might take the attitude that, if each interest party has had adequate notice and an opportunity to object and no objections have been made, the court has no reason to doubt the fairness of the account approval. The trustee may be aware of such an attitude and feel that there is little risk in trying to obtain approval for some transactions that are not entirely properly allowable. Because of this, items plainly appearing in various account statements must be inspected. The reviewer must, at times, read between the lines and may find it necessary to research state law as to the propriety of some listed transactions.

The following is a brief discussion of a few of the items that might bear close inspection within a trust settlement account.

.071 Trustees' commissions

The rate of commissions payable to trustees is set under state law, typically as a separate percentage of income and principal. While income commissions are usually a fixed percentage, the rate of principal commissions is more commonly expressed as a maximum. A range of compensation is necessary in order to avoid charging the same percentage for a simple trust that lasts for three or four years as that charged by the trustee of a complicated trust that demands a great deal of the trustee's time and attention and lasts for 20 years or more.

First, a calculation should be made to make sure that any legal maximum rate has not been exceeded. Second, if the maximum amount of commissions has been requested, the reviewer should consider whether such request is warranted by the particular circumstances of the trust.

.072 Expenses for professional services paid from trust

Some state laws specifically disallow the payment of certain professional fees by a trust on the theory that the trustee must either provide the services personally or bear the cost out of the trustee's commission. Examples include the expenses of investment counseling services and even accounting services.

While the expenses of legal services are generally allowable, where the trustee is also an attorney, the law may not permit charging both a full trustee's commission and also legal fees for what may be overlapping services.

.073 *Questionable expenses charged to trust*

There may be lavish or otherwise impermissible expenses incurred by the trustee or others that have been charged to the trust. For instance, the trustee is entitled to be reimbursed for such items as travel on account of trust business. However, where the trust owns an interest in a commercial building on the East Coast and the trustee resides on the West Coast, a two-week trip with first-class transportation and accommodations could be the legitimate subject of an inquiry, particularly where the building's day-to-day operation is handled by a professional real estate management company.

.074 *Omitted items of receipt*

Completeness of an account review involves checking that the income items reported include all income that should actually have been collected. This is a simple matter for trust assets such as bank accounts and bonds. Cash dividends paid on stocks held by the trust may require somewhat more research.

Capital changes pose a more difficult review problem. Stock dividend or stock split shares that are not accounted for by the trustee can only be discovered by reference to the historical records of each stock held during the term of the administration of the trust.

.075 *Investment review*

Investments that do not turn out for the best do not automatically justify a claim against the trustee. This is a hard fact of life that seems to escape a great many trust beneficiaries and their advisers.

By the time the account settlement is presented for approval, the reviewer has the advantage of 20-20 hindsight. Before a claim of mismanagement will be entertained, however, there must be some evidence that the trustee had a reason to know of negative characteristics about the investment at a critical time. A few examples follow.

(1) The investment had poor prospects at the time it was undertaken, but the trustee placed the investment anyway for a reason that cannot be defended. For instance, the trustee had a personal interest in the investment and needed others to participate in order to improve the prospects for success.

(2) The investment was never appropriate, considering all of the facts and circumstances of the trust and its present and future beneficiaries.

> **Example:** A trust fund to provide income to an elderly widow for life, with the remainder going to her children who have only moderate financial means, is invested entirely in the common stock of a newly organized corporation, the offering statement for which points out that the company is embarking on speculative ventures, cannot be certain to achieve any success, and is not expecting to be able to make any dividend distributions for several years, if ever.

(3) The investment was sound and appropriate for the trust at one time, but it fell in value due to a change in circumstances that were publicly known and well reported so that the trustee would have been

aware of the change if he had been paying proper attention to financial developments.

There are any number of examples of publicly traded stocks of major corporations, which, after having long records of growth and profit, suffered misfortune. In some cases, the value of these investments does not fall overnight but experiences a gradual decline. While the trustee cannot reasonably be criticized for failing to foretell the future, there comes a time when it is not prudent to continue waiting for the miraculous recovery that never comes.

Investments that pay little income but have growth potential do have their place in a well-diversified trust portfolio. The key is consideration of the needs and overall best interests of the present beneficiaries as well as the remaindermen.

Chapter 9

Trust Investments

¶ 901 OVERVIEW

The use of trusts dates back to a time when wealth was associated with the ownership of land and the revenues that land produced. As opportunities for other forms of investment developed, the trustee's responsibility grew.

The potential for income return and growth in value of an investment varies directly with the degree of associated risk. Ideally, all trust funds should be placed in the very safest investments, with no danger of loss of value, offering a high rate of current income as well as good prospects for growth. It would not be fair to say that the characteristics of high income, safety of principal, and growth are always mutually exclusive, but they are rarely present in the same investment at the same time.

Some trustees might make safety the primary concern, with income secondary, and growth potential nonexistent or a distant third. This follows the philosophy that trust funds represent serious money and that the trustee has no business accepting any degree of risk. The problem with such an approach is that it does not address all of the kinds of risk, nor does it necessarily fulfill all of the trustee's obligations. Along with the risk of possible loss of investment value, there is also the financial risk of erosion of purchasing power that results from inflation. One of the most fundamental responsibilities of a trustee is that of balancing the needs of the present beneficiaries with those of the remaindermen. If the trustee places all funds in fixed investments that produce a certain rate of income and can never decrease in principal, that also means that the trustee has made sure that the remaindermen will receive a final trust distribution that has no chance of keeping pace with rising costs.

> **Example:** T is trustee of a trust fund under his brother's will. The testator was killed in World War II and left a surviving spouse and two young children. The trust specifies that all income is payable to the surviving spouse for life, with the remainder in equal shares to the children. The initial value of the trust fund was $25,000, a considerable sum in the mid-1940s.

If T had placed all of the trust funds in fixed investments, such as bank accounts or bonds, the total income might have provided the widow initially with at least a minimal standard of living, but this would not have kept pace with her needs if she lived to a normal life expectancy. When the children divided the remainder in the 1970s or 1980s, they could not have expected their shares to be sufficient to purchase a home, put their own children through college, or provide a retirement income supplement, although any one of these goals could have been accomplished with half of the initial value of the trust at the time of its inception.

Where a trust fund's design makes it likely that the trust will continue for a significant period of time, the investment strategy must address future possibilities as well as current circumstances.

The investment experience of trust funds that were in existence through the several bleak financial times during this century have colored the judgment of some trustees, both individual and corporate. In the wake of the stock market decline after 1929, some trust documents reportedly contained restrictions on investments, limiting the trustee's choice to "good quality railroad bonds." The fact that, within just a few years, there was virtually no such thing as a good quality railroad bond attests to the fallacy of trying to identify one specific investment in a trust document. Nevertheless, state laws were enacted that created specific lists of permissible investments.

The greatest problem with investments in general is their cyclical nature. Business and economic cycles result in good investment performance in fixed investments for a while, followed by a downturn in favor of equities. Real estate seems to profit from high inflation but loses its appeal when inflation diminishes. Investments in precious metals and other natural resources respond to a variety of stimuli unrelated to the movements of other investments. Meanwhile, the trustee is required to do his best to provide for the needs of both present and future beneficiaries in the midst of volatile interest rate trends, stock market crashes, and worldwide financial upheavals.

While there is no single solution to the trustee's dilemma, if certain principles are followed, the trustee can at least avoid criticism and claims resulting from bad investment decisions while offering beneficiaries a reasonable hope of realizing their aspirations.

This chapter discusses legal restrictions and guidelines for trust investments, the concepts of diversification and asset allocation, and sources of professional investment management that trustees might use.

¶ 902 LEGAL LIST, PRUDENT MAN RULE, AND SAFEGUARDING CONSIDERATIONS

In an effort to protect beneficiaries from losses resulting from speculative investments, many states enacted statutes that came to be known as "legal lists." Rather than actually listing specific securities or bank accounts that trusts were permitted to acquire, these laws described in very specific terms requirements that had to be met in order for an investment to be permissible.

.01 Legislating Investment Strategy

With respect to bonds, the legal list statute described standards that were parallel to those used by bond rating services in arriving at quality ratings. The criteria for stocks were based on capitalization, earnings, and profitability. In other words, these were attempts to legislate investment strategy. While legal lists could be regarded as somewhat conservative, most would agree that, if legal list standards were followed, the results were likely to be reasonable safety with good prospects both in terms of current return on investment and in terms of capital appreciation. In fact, there are still examples of mutual funds, available to the public and not restricted to trust funds, which, by their own charters, limit their investment selection to stocks that meet the criteria of a legal list. However, it must be recognized that investments in legal list securities are not infallible. They do not insure against loss in all investment climates, and they cannot insure any specific rate of income return or growth rate. In dramatically bad stock markets, such as those that occurred in 1973 through 1974 and late in 1987, legal list investments experienced considerable losses. Even strict adherence to a legal list does not give the trustee absolute protection from criticism for poor investments. The trustee's accountability for investment results cannot be avoided simply by adopting a specific guideline or method. Developments in the financial markets or in the circumstances of the beneficiaries may make it necessary either to change specific investments or to modify the general investment strategy. If so, the mere fact that the trustee has not deviated from a legal list is of little importance.

Where the trustee is not an investment professional, use of a legal list can prove to be cumbersome. Doubts can arise as to whether or not a particular investment meets the criteria, and this may force the trustee to seek the advice of a professional investment adviser. On the other hand, the trustee who is experienced in investment matters does not need a legal list and may find it a hindrance, particularly where specific investments that the trustee chooses come close to, but do not exactly fall within, the legal list criteria.

.02 Treating Trust Investments as You Would Your Own

The trend in more recent times has been away from legal lists and toward a general, overriding concept known as the "prudent man rule" or the "prudent investment rule." This rule sets no specific standards for individual investments, but it requires the trustee to exercise the care and judgment in making trust investment decisions that a person of average prudence would exercise in handling his own financial matters or those of another. High-risk trust investments cannot be justified under this rule by proof that the trustee takes great risks with his own investments. The standard is based on a theoretical prudent person who, presumably, would never take inordinate risks. The effect of the prudent investment rule is to eliminate specific restrictions while placing the trustee at personal risk if speculative investments are made with trust funds. In discussing account settlements and surcharges, it was mentioned that just because an investment does not work out, the trustee is not automatically to blame, particularly since claims of bad investment management arise only after the fact and with the benefit of hindsight. However, past investment decisions are judged with hindsight in the context of the prudent investment rule. If an investment that turns out badly can be shown to have been ill-advised when made because of too much risk, as judged by the standard of the prudent investment rule, the trustee may be liable to surcharge. The ultimate objective of laws following these rules, then, is to grant the trustee wide flexibility in investment matters but to hold out the spectre of surcharge if too much risk is taken.

Experience with the prudent man rule over time has led some states to modify the rule. Under more modern laws, investment performance is judged on the overall results of the portfolio rather than on each individual investment. Some investments may incur losses, and others may yield gains. If the overall results are good, considering the environment of the economy and the financial markets, the trustee's account should be approved. However, this does not warrant "taking a flyer" on some individual, high-risk investments.

Even successful results do not justify the trustee's failure to observe the prudent investment rule. In reviewing account settlements, some courts have criticized trustees for extraordinarily good investment results because it was evident that inordinate risk was taken. This should serve as a warning to the trustee—he is not supposed to even try to "hit a home run" with trust investments. Instead, he must "aim for that clean single." If the investment climate is right, home run performance may result anyway, but there is less danger of a strikeout if economic conditions go the wrong way.

The prudent investment rule varies over time from state to state, and even from court to court within a state, according to the capability of the trustee and the circumstances of the beneficiary. For this reason, it is not possible to list specific attributes of the rule. It is possible, however, for the attorney who writes the trust document to include guidelines for the trustee to follow. So long as these guidelines are not susceptible to becoming outdated through general changes in the financial markets, they can offer an advantage to the trustee as well as to the beneficiaries.

The prudent investment rule can also operate to protect the trustee where losses occur due to rapid developments in the financial markets. In the case of trusts that experience losses during a stock market break such as that of October 1987, it would be difficult to convince a court that the theoretical prudent person should have foreseen the events.

There is at least one exception to the prudent investment rule under the laws of many states. This is based on an investment retention statute that permits the trustee, in the exercise of reasonable discretion and judgment, to retain assets transferred in kind to the trust. The situation often exists in cases of testamentary trusts where the decedent had personally owned one or more investments while living that pass into the trust through the decedent's estate. Even if these investments are not of a quality that would meet the prudent investment standard, the trustee may be justified in his decision not to sell. This exception can permit the trustee to retain stock of a closely held corporation where a sale might result in loss of control of the business by the decedent's family. It also allows the trustee to wait for the circumstances of an investment that is currently out of favor to improve before selling. Rather than rely on a state law to authorize retention of trust assets that a trustee would ordinarily sell, it is preferable to include a specific provision in the trust document providing guidance to the trustee about such assets as closely owned business interests, real estate, investments in limited partnership interests, and family heirlooms. This affords some assurance to family members that special assets will not be sold arbitrarily as well as some protection to the trustee against criticism for retaining properties not usually held in trust.

.03 Handling the Physical Segregation and Protection of Investments

The trustee is required to segregate trust investments in a manner that permits the trust's property to be distinguished easily and clearly from that which belongs to the trustee personally and also from the assets of other trusts or estates that may be handled by the trustee. The mixing or "commingling" of trust assets is prohibited.

The segregation requirement can be met through registration of trust investments in the name of the specific trust. Securities registered in trust name can then be physically held in a safe deposit box or other secure location. As an alternative, the trustee may choose to deposit the trust's investments in a bank or brokerage firm account. So long as the account is held in the name of the trust, it is generally not a violation of the segregation requirement if the securities are registered in a "street" or "nominee" name. Securities deposited in a bank custodial account are usually registered in a fictitious or nominee name used by the bank. All of the bank's custodial and trust account assets may be registered in this manner. This enables the bank to hold just one or just a few certificates representing the common holdings of all of its trust and custodial accounts and, therefore, permits certain efficiencies, such as in the collection of cash and stock dividends. The bank then uses its own data processing system to credit the trust's account as income items or sales proceeds are collected. While an individual trust's investments are not represented by an individual securities certificate, there is financial protection in that trust and custodial account assets are held in a fiduciary capacity and are not available to satisfy the claims of bank creditors.

Trust assets may also be deposited in brokerage accounts and held by the brokerage firm in street name. Here, a source of protection of the investments is the Securities Investor Protection Corporation (SIPC), a nonprofit entity formed under an Act of Congress that would make funds available for the protection of brokerage customers in the event of the failure of a SIPC member firm. SIPC, like the Federal Deposit Insurance Corporation (FDIC), is not an agency of the federal government.

Trustees are also permitted to deposit trust investments in clearing corporations, which act as central depositories for many financial institutions in an attempt to eliminate, so far as possible, the existence of paper in the securities industry. The clearing corporation holds securities for many entities and, when sales occur between participants or between the customers of participant institutions, the transfer of ownership is nothing more than a book entry.

.04 Corporate Trustee and Common Trust Fund

The typical bank trust department or trust company manages the investments of thousands of accounts in a fiduciary capacity. While each account should be treated individually to some extent, many share common investment needs and objectives. In order to enable banks to manage their trust account investments efficiently, state and federal laws permit the organization and use by banks of common trust funds. These are large portfolios of investments handled as a single account by the trust department. Part or all of the assets of the bank's trust accounts are deposited into a common trust fund and, through the bank's data processing system, each trust's share of the total value of the fund is tracked. Also, each trust's share of the income produced by the fund is distributed periodically or, if it is permissible and appropriate for an individual trust to accumulate, the income may be reinvested within the common trust fund, resulting in the ownership of an increased share of the total common fund by the reinvesting trust.

In many respects, a common trust fund is comparable to a mutual fund, except that investment opportunities are only open to trust funds for which the bank is acting as trustee. Securities law registration and offering restrictions make this limitation necessary. Bank trust departments and trust companies often create several common trust funds, each with a somewhat different investment objective. There may be a high-income fund, a tax-exempt fund, a growth fund, and a fund that is invested in a balanced manner with the objective of a combination of current income and growth.

The trust department might not place all of the investments of each of its trust accounts into common trust funds. Some trust funds may be placed partly or fully in individually selected stocks and bonds, and others may be fully invested in a common fund. This could be a function of a general trust department policy, or the decision could be left to the discretion of an individual trust officer or an investment committee. Ordinarily, however, the trust beneficiary does not have the right to decide this issue. Frequently, there are policies requiring that all trust accounts with a total value equal to or below a specified amount must be placed in one or more common investment funds. Some beneficiaries object to the idea of having their family's trust placed in a common trust fund for a variety of reasons. They may feel that the common fund is too impersonal or that their trust investments do not receive the same level of attention that an individually selected portfolio would have. On the other hand, the trust department regards the common fund as the hallmark of its investment philosophy and the standard for judgment of its investment performance. Furthermore, common trust funds may receive more frequent attention from the investment committee than individual trust accounts, since the common funds represent the bank's largest investment responsibility and the performance of these funds affects the greatest number of trust accounts. For this reason, daily review of the common trust fund investment positions may be expected.

When called on to evaluate a common trust fund, the financial consultant should investigate the following:

(1) *The size of the fund.* As a general rule, it is more difficult to achieve or sustain good investment results as the size of the fund increases.

(2) *Investment performance.* Where prior results have been good, it is important to find out whether the fund manager has been changed.

(3) *Flexibility.* This relates to the bank's policies concerning changing the investment direction (usually through exchanges into a different common trust fund), either at the request of the beneficiaries or as their circumstances change.

(4) *Cost.* Since less individual account attention is needed for trusts placed in a common trust fund, a lower trustee's fee may be justified.

¶ 903 ADOPTING AN INVESTMENT STRATEGY

The words "investment strategy" conjure up widely different meanings. To some, it is simply a matter of diversifying among six-month, one-year, three-year, and five-year savings certificates, while others immediately begin to think in terms of risk arbitrage and hedging techniques. In the context of trust investments, just having an investment strategy is of critical importance.

.01 Making the Decision That Some Strategy Is Needed

A plan for the investment of a trust fund should begin with a review of the objectives of the trust. If the grantor established a trust fund for the specific purpose of making it possible for a child to buy a home or start a business, that goal should be reflected, not only in the specific investment choices but also in the decision-making processes followed by the trustee in making selections. A testamentary trust intended to last for the lifetime of the surviving spouse and then to continue during their children's lifetimes, making its final distribution to more remote descendants, presumably requires more than a single short-term investment choice.

.02 Reviewing Beliefs and Principles

Regardless of the approach to be taken, the trustee should start by making a written summary of background considerations that should be reviewed with the beneficiaries. This serves as the basis for adopting a general investment approach, and it may also provide justification for the trustee's investment decisions if they are ever challenged.

Some of the topics that should be covered in the initial summary are:

(1) The anticipated term of the trust.

(2) The non-trust financial resources of present and future beneficiaries, to the extent that this may be discoverable and reasonably anticipated by the trustee.

(3) The initial principal value of the trust fund and the ability of that value to accomplish the grantor's present and future objectives for the beneficiaries.

(4) The grantor's attitude toward investments, including the grantor's own history of risk tolerance or risk aversion.

(5) The beneficiaries' investment attitudes.

(6) Elements of the general economic outlook at the time the trustee undertakes his fiduciary obligations, including:

(a) interest rate trends;

(b) the present age of the general business and economic cycles;

(c) the outlook for the stock, bond, and other financial markets;

(d) current trends in real estate and other direct-participation investments; and

(e) inflation.

.03 Investment Management Strategy and Style

Since grantors' intentions and beneficiaries' needs vary widely from case to case, different approaches to investment management are appropriate for different trust funds. Ideally, the grantor participates in the selection of an investment manager or an investment management style and provides family members or others with the right in the future to change managers or management styles as circumstances develop.

There is abundant evidence that a two-stage approach to investment portfolio management enhances the likelihood of long-term performance success. The first step, under this approach, is to make an asset allocation decision. Only then is the second step taken—selection of individual investments within the various asset classes. While strategies can be developed for many differing asset classes, most trust funds limit the classes to fixed-income securities, equity securities, and cash equivalents.

It is possible to limit a trust fund to only fixed-income or only equity securities. To do so, however, increases risk of either loss of principal or loss of purchasing power, over time, due to inflation.

There are two principal reasons for including fixed-income securities in a portfolio: (1) they provide a comparatively predictable stream of income; and

(2) they tend to reduce the overall volatility compared with a pure equity portfolio.

Following is a brief summary of some of the primary fixed-income investment strategies:

(1) *Buy-and-hold.* This means purchasing fixed-income securities and holding them until maturity or redemption, allowing for the flexibility to sell an individual security if conditions specific to it warrant such a move. This produces a high, predictable cash flow with moderate fluctuation of principal value. It may be appropriate for trust funds that have a long time-horizon with which to plan.

(2) *Index.* The purpose is to duplicate the investment performance of a widely followed bond index. Representative purchase techniques make it possible, however, to avoid the necessity of buying every bond in the index. This approach offers the potential of producing a higher return than a buy-and-hold strategy. The investment performance, including cash flow and principal preservation, gain, or loss, closely follows that of the index. Of course, the potential for fluctuation of principal is increased as well.

(3) *Dedicated portfolios.* These are designed to enable the trust to make planned future distributions at specified future time intervals. Examples are (a) immunization, the process of creating a fixed-income portfolio with an assured return for a specified time period unaffected by market interest rate changes; and (b) cash flow matching, through which periodic interest, as well as redemption or sales proceeds, is plotted against the anticipated future trust distribution schedule. As part of the program, serial maturities may be selected in a so-called "laddered" fashion.

(4) *Active fixed-income management.* The objective is the highest possible total return, and an increased level of risk is accepted. Techniques used in the pursuit of this goal include interest rate anticipation and financial analysis of specific securities.

Equity investments are included in a portfolio with the objective of accepting the higher potential volatility and principal risks inherent in equities in exchange for (a) the potential for principal appreciation in addition to dividend income; and (b) the potential for a higher total investment rate of return. Many believe overall portfolio volatility is reduced by combining stocks with bonds and cash equivalents.

While equity investment management tends to be highly individual, representative examples of some styles follow:

(1) *Passive.* The index fund is a good example. The philosophical approach is that the equity market, represented by a particular index, will provide a very good total investment rate of return over time. Rather than attempt to do better than the general market, the objective is to mirror its results. While these funds are broadly diversified, they do not typically purchase every single stock or bond in the index. Instead, representative selections of individual stock or bond issues are held. In this way, it is predictable that the total return of the fund will mimic the results of the entire index.

(2) *Market timing.* Asset allocation is the centerpiece of this strategy, but it is "tactical" rather than "strategic" allocation. As a result, the

equity, cash equivalent, and fixed-income proportions are subject to dramatic revision in order to avoid weakness and to take advantage of anticipated strength in these sectors of the financial markets. The market timer may employ a passive approach to selection of the underlying investments within each allocation segment. Alternatively, active portfolio management may be combined with timing.

(3) *Nondiversified.* This involves concentration on a particular market segment. Emphasis may be placed on certain industries or, more generally, on stocks that meet specific parameters concerning yield, the ratio of price to earnings, a trend of growth in dividends or earnings, or a combination of these factors. The result may be significant concentration in similar stocks. Examples of this style include:

(a) Regular growth. This refers to the selection of stocks that are expected to show growth of the rate of earnings that exceeds the market as a whole.

(b) Aggressive growth. There is little difference between aggressive growth and regular growth, except that it is believed that the stocks selected offer significantly greater potential for earnings growth than the market. That typically means stocks of smaller companies and naturally involves proportionately higher volatility.

(c) Conservative. The philosophy of this approach may be stated as follows: If you limit selection to stocks selling at prices near book value or near the rate of earnings per share, or stocks that pay relatively high dividends, the risk of loss is reduced and, over time, the overall return should be competitive, even with that of the more aggressive styles.

(4) *Sector rotation.* The goal is to identify the sector or sectors of the equity market that are most likely to experience the highest growth or total return over the near term and then to purchase stocks concentrated in such sector or sectors. This necessitates making significant shifts in the holdings of the portfolio from time to time, as one sector has reached its potential and another is judged ready to make an important move. Decisions to change sector concentration are based entirely or primarily on general economic forecasts.

(5) *Value.* The objective is to buy stocks that have a depressed selling price for any of a number of reasons specific to the industry or to the individual company. In any case, it is believed that the future value of the stock is high when compared with its current market price. The technique is usually characterized by an intermediate holding period (typically, a few years) for individual holdings. When the price of the stock reaches a desired level, it is sold even if the company exhibits continuing growth potential. That level is not necessarily based on a dollar price of the stock but rather on the relationship of the price to what may be a very complex formula relating to book value, earnings, dividend rate, etc.

The trustee does not necessarily have to follow a particular investment management style, but it is most important for the trustee to have a plan. This could involve the trustee's assuming personal responsibility for the selection of individual investments. The plan might be based on asset allocation with investments placed in pooled investment vehicles such as mutual funds. If permitted under local law and the creating document, the trustee might retain the services of a professional investment management firm.

.04 Threshold Choice Between Personal Investment Management and Outside Professional Investment Assistance

Once the initial summary has been made, the trustee should have at least a general idea of the types of investments to be held in the trust. The next step is to decide whether he will seek some form of professional investment management.

The trustee who has training and experience in investment matters may well decide to make all trust investment decisions personally, based on his own research and outlook. If any form of outside assistance is to be used, a number of specific issues must be addressed:

(1) *The qualifications of the adviser.* This includes experience in the field of investments as well as educational credentials. In addition, if the adviser offers investment advice for a fee, the trustee must ascertain that he is registered as required by state investment and federal securities laws. If the advice is given in return for purchase of investments through an investment dealer, the trustee must be sure that the representative is duly authorized. Registration as an investment adviser does not guarantee any extra protection to the trustee, who remains ultimately responsible for the results in all events. The trustee is always under an obligation to monitor the investment performance.

(2) *Specialization.* Certain investment advisers, securities dealers, and their representatives specialize in one particular type of investment, such as individual stocks, bonds, mutual funds, or real estate. That may be perfectly appropriate if that is how the trustee has already determined to place the trust investments. Otherwise, the trustee may wish to consider assistance from additional sources for different segments of the trust fund.

(3) *Delegation of investment discretion.* Not all registered investment advisers offer the service of individual portfolio management. Of those who do offer this service, some require that the investment decisions be handled by the adviser on a discretionary basis. The trustee is not consulted before any individual purchase or sale of investments takes place. There are also periodic reviews and progress reports.

The trustee must make certain that neither the controlling state law nor the individual trust document forbids the trustee to delegate investment decision making in this manner. The trustee should also realize that if the services of a discretionary account manager are used, the trustee is not relieved of liability for mismanagement or inappropriate investments.

.05 Sources of Professional Investment Assistance

Not all trust funds require professional investment assistance. Depending on the length of the trust term and the needs of its beneficiaries, a single form of investment as uncomplicated as a savings account may be entirely sufficient.

Where the size and term of the trust are longer and the trustee reaches the decision that outside, professional help is in order, a wide variety of services is available.

.051 *Mutual fund*

General characteristics. The investment company or mutual fund is a form of professional investment management well suited to many trust funds. The elements of a mutual fund are:

(1) *The custodian bank.* This institution holds the assets of the mutual fund for protection and recordkeeping purposes. The custodian does not make the individual investment decisions.

(2) *The management company.* In addition to providing one or more portfolio managers who select investments for the portfolio, the management company performs marketing and other administrative functions.

(3) *The portfolio.* This is a pool of investments that may include stocks, bonds, options and futures contracts, and other marketable securities. In recent years, there has been a trend toward specialization of investment types within mutual funds. For example, there are now mutual fund portfolios limited by prospectus to investments in stocks of companies within one specific industry or sector. It is still possible to find funds that hold a balanced portfolio consisting of a variety of investments.

(4) *The fund family and exchange privileges.* A single management company may offer several different mutual fund portfolios from which to choose, some specialized and others balanced. Typically, an investor has the privilege of redeeming his investment from one portfolio within the same family of funds and simultaneously placing the proceeds in another portfolio in the same family at no charge except for a nominal administrative fee. This moving of investments from one portfolio to another is referred to as a "fund exchange." For income tax purposes, it is treated as the sale of one investment followed by the purchase of another so that any gain or loss represents a currently taxable event.

(5) *The closed-end fund.* Some mutual funds undertake a single offering during which a specific sum of money or a maximum amount is obtained from investors in return for newly issued fund shares. The portfolio manager invests all of the proceeds and continuously manages the investments, selling and purchasing as conditions develop. No new money is invested in the portfolio, and no new fund shares are issued. When fund shareholders wish to sell, they sell the fund shares on a securities exchange or on the over-the-counter market. The market price of the closed-end fund share does not necessarily reflect the underlying value of the fund's assets precisely calculated on a per-share basis.

(6) *The open-end fund.* Other mutual funds permit new and existing investors to add money in return for newly issued shares on any business day. Instead of selling shares through an exchange or over the counter, the investor has the right to present shares for redemption by the fund at any time. The redemption price is the exact per-share value of the fund, calculated at the close of business on the date of the redemption, and is based on the total value of the portfolio divided by the total number of shares outstanding. This is known as the "net asset value."

(7) *The load and no-load funds.* In order to pay for the costs of marketing, some mutual funds charge a selling commission. Those which charge upon initial investment into the fund are known as "front-end load funds," while those that impose the cost upon redemption are called "back-end load funds."

No-load mutual funds do not charge selling commissions, but pay for their marketing costs through general charges to the portfolio. The cost of this general charge reduces the total income or total investment performance of the portfolio.

It is necessary for all mutual funds to impose general charges for the administrative expenses of fund management and for the compensation of the custodian bank and the management company. These general charges are common to both load funds and no-load funds.

Mutual fund as a trust investment; timing services. Because of the built-in costs, the permissibility of trust investments in mutual funds was once subject to question. By incurring the general charges, in addition to the trustee's commission, the trust beneficiaries were thought to be paying twice. State laws now generally permit trust investments in mutual funds.

The ability of the trustee to change investments with nominal cost to the trust through fund exchanges adds a flexible dimension to the investment process. The assistance of the fund's professional portfolio manager, who pays daily attention to individual investment positions as well as to trends and developments, and the trustee's ability to change the general investment course through a fund exchange if general conditions warrant are an impressive combination.

Fund exchanges can be used to modify the investment objective as the trust progresses through the term of its existence.

> **Example:** T is the trustee of a testamentary trust for the benefit of W, the testator's surviving spouse, for life, with the income to be paid to the testator's four children in equal shares thereafter.
>
> Since W has a significant income tax liability even before considering any trust income, T invests a portion of the trust fund in a mutual fund that holds tax-exempt municipal bonds. At W's death, T finds that the total income of each of the children is moderate. T exchanges the investment, within the same mutual fund family, for shares of a fund that holds higher yielding corporate bonds.

Judging the right time to make a fund exchange can be difficult. No matter how skillful the fund's portfolio manager may be, there always seem to be times when it would have been better to step aside from any particular mutual fund portfolio. There are specialized investment advisory services that offer assistance in this regard, known as "timing services." These services either recommend moving from one mutual fund portfolio to another or undertake to make fund exchanges on behalf of their customers on a discretionary basis. The trustee may view timing services as an added measure of safety and may use one in hopes of "smoothing out" the ups and downs of the market. It is important for the trustee to understand, however, that the timer makes his decision based on general trends in the economy and financial markets and utilizes technical market analysis as opposed to fundamental investment research. The timer does not have access to the actual portfolio position holdings of a mutual fund because this specific information is not published on a daily basis. Also, mutual fund timing services must be purchased, sometimes at a cost that is a percentage of the value of the funds under management. The trustee must be certain that incurring this added expense is permissible under his state law.

.052 Limited partnership

This is a form of investment organization that has grown in popularity over the last 20 years. Unlike shares of publicly traded corporate stock, limited partnership interests do not always have a ready market. The investor may have to be willing to commit the amount invested for a period of 10 years or more.

The structure of the limited partnership is divided into general and limited partners. The general partner, who should be knowledgeable of the particular investment undertaken, is personally liable with respect to management and also with respect to all expenses and debts incurred. The limited partners, who are the investors, are not liable and are ordinarily only at risk with respect to the amount that they choose to invest in the partnership.

Partnerships in general, including the limited partnership, enjoy an income tax advantage over corporations in that, except for certain publicly traded partnerships, there is no income tax imposed on the organization itself as a separate taxable entity. Instead, the partners report all items of partnership income, expense, and credit on their personal income tax returns in proportions set by the terms of a partnership agreement. Prior to the Tax Reform Act of 1986 (TRA '86) (P.L. 99-514), limited partnerships were popular as a form of tax shelter because it was then permissible to cause income tax deductions in excess of partnership taxable income to be reportable by the investor limited partners. Since 1987, however, the ability to pass through income tax deductions from limited partnerships to investors has been virtually eliminated.

Limited partnerships represent an excellent opportunity for trusts to invest a comparatively small amount, with specifically limited risk, in a type of investment that might not otherwise be available. For instance, if the trustee believes that real estate is desirable as an investment for part of the trust fund, he might choose from among the many limited partnerships that invest in real estate.

It is possible to participate in some of these investments with amounts as small as a few thousand dollars. This offers two advantages to the trust. First, the minimum investment is a fraction of the amount that would be needed to make an individual investment in real estate and, second, exposure of the balance of the trust fund to the risks that can flow from property ownership and mortgage debt are avoided.

There are specialized limited partnership investments available that invest in areas other than real estate, such as research projects and industrial equipment.

.053 Professional portfolio manager

Registered investment advisers who offer the service of individual portfolio management are a common choice for the investment of trust funds. These advisers handle the investment, in the aggregate, of billions of dollars of wealth for individuals, retirement plans, corporations, and family trust funds.

In evaluating professional portfolio management, the trustee must consider not only the cost of the service and whether the expense is legally permitted to be charged to the trust but also the investment approach that the particular portfolio manager intends to pursue. Since the trustee remains responsible for the trust fund even if the services of a portfolio manager are used, the trustee should take care to understand how the manager works and must review the manager's progress frequently.

A variety of management styles are used by different investment advisory firms. Some rely primarily on fundamental investment research while others use technical market analysis. Certain advisers handle only stocks, others manage bond portfolios exclusively, and some are experienced at a balanced approach.

Stock and bond portfolio managers can be further divided based on their selection processes, emphasis on income as opposed to growth, and the degree of stability or volatility in value that they expect. Before selecting a portfolio manager, the trustee had better become acquainted with the jargon so that he does not hire a "stock picker" who is a "contrarian" instead of a "rotator," or a "junk bond" manager when he really wanted to place the bonds in an "intermediate sector" approach.

In selecting a portfolio manager, the trustee may wish to ask himself the following questions:

(1) Does the philosophy and style of this manager match that of the grantor? Would the grantor have chosen this manager for himself and his family?

(2) Are the manager's goals in line with the current and long-term needs of the present and future beneficiaries?

(3) Would I place my own family's financial future in this manager's hands?

.06 Importance of a Disciplined Plan

By adopting and following a disciplined approach to investment management, the trustee gains many advantages. Some income beneficiaries are not satisfied with the amount of trust income they receive. An investment plan that takes into account the need for protection of purchasing power against the effects of inflation justifies less than maximum income. Over the long term, investment results based on a careful plan are most likely to bring about realization of the goals for which the trust was created. Finally, substantial defenses against criticism or surcharge of the trustee are established by a formal investment plan.

The trustee's plan should be in writing and should address:

(1) Current and future beneficiaries' needs.

(2) Adequacy of the trust fund to achieve its purposes. If the trust fund is not adequate, that should be documented in writing and appropriate steps should be taken. In extreme cases, the trustee should seek court approval of a plan that sacrifices some goals of the trust in order to realize others.

(3) The trustee's decision concerning asset allocation. This is necessary in every case, regardless of whether the investments are to be

individually selected by the trustee, managed by a portfolio manager, or placed in mutual funds or other pooled investments.

(4) The trustee's reason for investing the trust fund in individual investments, through a portfolio manager, in mutual funds, in other pooled investments, or through a variety of these alternatives.

(5) The need for periodic review and periodic change of the plan as dictated by changes in the needs of beneficiaries, as well as developments in economic conditions and financial markets.

The grantor creates a trust at a moment in time, with no knowledge of what will develop, to provide for beneficiaries, some of whom may not yet be born and whose needs will likely change in unexpected ways before the trust fund is finally distributed to them. Naturally, the trustee can never be assured of success, but a well-developed plan that is periodically re-examined offers the best potential.

Appendix

¶ 1001 INCOME TAX RATES FOR ESTATES AND NONGRANTOR TRUSTS

For Tax Years Beginning in 1996

If taxable income is:		*The tax is:*			
Over—	*but not over—*				*of the amount over—*
$ 0	$1,600	$ 0	+	15 %	$ 0
1,600	3,800	240	+	28	1,600
3,800	5,800	856	+	31	3,800
5,800	7,900	1,476	+	36	5,800
7,900	—	2,232	+	39.6	7,900

[**NOTE:** The 1996 tax rates were prepared by CCH editors based on the inflation-adjustment provisions of Section 1(f) of the Internal Revenue Code and the average of the Consumer Price Indexes (all urban consumers), published by the Department of Labor for each month in the 12-month period ended August 31, 1995. Please note that the official rates have not been released by the Internal Revenue Service at the date of publication.]

For Tax Years Beginning in 1995

If taxable income is:		*The tax is:*			
Over—	*but not over—*				*of the amount over—*
$ 0	$1,550	$ 0	+	15 %	$ 0
1,550	3,700	232.50	+	28	1,550
3,700	5,600	834.50	+	31	3,700
5,600	7,650	1,423.50	+	36	5,600
7,650	—	2,161.50	+	39.6	7,650

Estimated taxes. In general, trusts and estates are required to make quarterly estimated tax payments (with Form 1041-ES). However, estates and grantor trusts that receive the residue of a probate estate under the grantor's will are only required to make estimated tax payments beginning with tax years ending two or more years after the decedent's death. If a decedent dies without a will, a grantor trust that is primarily responsible for paying taxes, debts, and expenses of administration is not required to pay estimated taxes for the tax years ending within two years of the decedent's death.

An estate's fiduciary may distribute excess estimated tax payments to the beneficiaries during the tax year that the fiduciary reasonably expects to be the estate's last tax year. If the payments of estimated tax made by a trust (not an estate) exceed the trust's tax liability as shown on Form 1041, the trustee may elect to treat any or all of the overpayment as a payment made by the beneficiary and credited toward the beneficiary's tax liability. The election is made on Form 1041-T and must be filed on or before the 65th day after the close of the trust's tax year (e.g., March 6, 1996, for a calendar-year trust in tax year 1995).

¶ 1002 UNIFIED TRANSFER TAX SYSTEM

The estate tax liability is determined by applying the unified rate schedule to the cumulated transfers and subtracting the gift taxes payable. The cumulated transfers to which the tentative tax applies is the sum of (1) the amount of the taxable estate; and (2) the amount of the taxable gifts made by the decedent after 1976, other than gifts includible in the gross estate. Gift taxes to be subtracted in computing the estate tax include the aggregate gift tax payable on gifts made after December 31, 1976. For this purpose, the amount of gift taxes paid by a decedent after 1976 is to be determined as if the rate schedule in effect in the year of death was in effect in the year of the gift. Gift taxes payable on pre-1977 gifts are not subtracted from the estate tax.

Gift tax liability for any calendar quarter (for gifts made after 1970 and before 1982) or year (for gifts made before 1971 and after 1981) is determined by applying the unified rate schedule to cumulative lifetime taxable transfers and by subtracting the taxes payable for prior taxable periods. Preceding calendar periods are: (1) calendar year 1932 (after June 6) and 1970 and all intervening calendar years, (2) the first calendar quarter of 1971 and all quarters between that quarter and the first quarter of 1982, and (3) all calendar years after 1981 and before the year for which the tax is being computed. In computing cumulative taxable gifts for prior taxable periods, the donor's pre-1977 taxable gifts are to be taken into account, with the reduction for taxes previously paid to be based upon the unified rate schedule.

The generation-skipping transfer tax (enacted by the Tax Reform Act of 1986) (TRA '86) (P.L. 99-514) is applied at a flat rate derived from the maximum estate tax rate to direct skips, taxable distributions, and taxable terminations. The method for computing the taxable amount depends on whether a taxable distribution, a taxable termination, or a direct skip is involved. For a taxable distribution as well as a direct skip, the amount received by the transferee is subject to the tax. In the case of a taxable termination, the tax is applied to the value of the property in which the interest terminates. Three exemptions from the tax have been provided: (1) a $1 million per transferor exemption that can be allocated among several generation-skipping transfers, (2) a special $2 million per grandchild exemption for direct skips, and (3) an exemption for transfers to grandchildren of a grantor when the grandchild's parent, who is a lineal descendant of the granter, is deceased.

.01 Unified Credit

A single unified credit is provided for each taxpayer which is subtracted after determining the taxpayer's estate or gift tax liability. In effect, the amount of the unified credit available at death will be reduced to the extent that any portion of the credit is used to offset gift taxes on lifetime transfers. For estates of decedents dying in 1981 and thereafter, the credit was phased in as follows:

Year	Amount of Credit	Amount of Exemption Equivalent
1981	$ 47,000	$175,625
1982	62,800	225,000
1983	79,300	275,000
1984	96,300	325,000
1985	121,800	400,000
1986	155,800	500,000
1987 and thereafter	192,800	600,000

.02 Unified Transfer Tax Rate Schedule

The unified transfer tax rate schedule applying to estates of decedents dying (and gifts made) after 1984 appears below.

Column A	Column B	Column C	Column D
Taxable amount over	*Taxable amount not over*	*Tax on amount in column A*	*Rate of tax on excess over amount in column A*
$ 0	$ 10,000	$ 0	18%
10,000	20,000	1,800	20
20,000	40,000	3,800	22
40,000	60,000	8,200	24
60,000	80,000	13,000	26
80,000	100,000	18,200	28
100,000	150,000	23,800	30
150,000	250,000	38,800	32
250,000	500,000	70,800	34
500,000	750,000	155,800	37
750,000	1,000,000	248,300	39
1,000,000	1,250,000	345,800	41
1,250,000	1,500,000	448,300	43
1,500,000	2,000,000	555,800	45
2,000,000	2,500,000	780,800	49
2,500,000	3,000,000	1,025,800	53
3,000,000	....	1,290,800	55

Benefits phased out for transfers exceeding $10,000,000. The benefits of the graduated rates and the unified credit under the unified transfer tax system are phased out beginning with cumulative transfers rising above $10,000,000. This is accomplished by adding five percent of the excess of any transfer over $10,000,000 to the tentative tax computed in determining the ultimate transfer tax liability. For estates of decedents dying, and gifts made, after 1987, the tax is levied on amounts transferred in excess of $10,000,000 but not exceeding $21,040,000, in order to recapture the benefit of any transfer tax rate below 55 percent as well as the unified credit.

.03 Credit for State Death Taxes

The table below is to be used in calculating the amount of the credit available for state death taxes paid with respect to property included in a decedent's gross estate.

Estates of Decedents Dying After 1976 [1]

Adjusted Taxable Estate [2] *At least*	*But less than*	*Credit =*	*+*	*%*	*Of Excess Over*
$ 0	$ 40,000	$ 0		0	$ 0
40,000	90,000	0		.8	40,000
90,000	140,000	400		1.6	90,000
140,000	240,000	1,200		2.4	140,000
240,000	440,000	3,600		3.2	240,000
440,000	640,000	10,000		4	440,000
640,000	840,000	18,000		4.8	640,000
840,000	1,040,000	27,600		5.6	840,000
1,040,000	1,540,000	38,800		6.4	1,040,000
1,540,000	2,040,000	70,800		7.2	1,540,000
2,040,000	2,540,000	106,800		8	2,040,000
2,540,000	3,040,000	146,800		8.8	2,540,000
3,040,000	3,540,000	190,800		9.6	3,040,000
3,540,000	4,040,000	238,800		10.4	3,540,000
4,040,000	5,040,000	290,800		11.2	4,040,000
5,040,000	6,040,000	402,800		12	5,040,000
6,040,000	7,040,000	522,800		12.8	6,040,000
7,040,000	8,040,000	650,800		13.6	7,040,000
8,040,000	9,040,000	786,800		14.4	8,040,000
9,040,000	10,040,000	930,800		15.2	9,040,000
10,040,000	....	1,082,800		16	10,040,000

[1] There is a limitation on the credit in estates of nonresident aliens dying after November 13, 1966. See Code Sec. 2102. The table may not be used in computing taxes on estates of certain members of the Armed Forces.

[2] The adjusted taxable estate is the taxable estate reduced by $60,000.

Topical Index

References are to paragraph (¶) numbers.